A. Philip Randolph, Pioneer of the Civil Rights Movement

A. Philip Randolph

Chicago Historical Society

ioneer of the Civil Rights Movement

Paula F. Pfeffer

LOUISIANA STATE UNIVERSITY PRESS
Baton Rouge and London

Louisiana Paperback Edition, 1996
05 04 03 02 01 00 99 98 97 96   5 4 3 2 1
Designer: Laura Roubique Gleason
Typeface: Sabon
Typesetter: G & S Typesetters, Inc.

Library of Congress Cataloging-in-Publication Data

Pfeffer, Paula F., 1931–
    A. Philip Randolph, pioneer of the civil rights movement /
    Paula F. Pfeffer.

    Includes bibliographical references.
    ISBN 0-8071-1554-1 (cloth)   ISBN 0-8071-2075-8 (pbk.)
    1. Randolph, A. Philip (Asa Philip), 1889–   .   2. Afro-Americans—
Civil rights.   3. Trade-unions, Black—United States—History—20th
century.   4. Afro-Americans—History—1877–1964.   5. Civil rights
movements—United States—History—20th century.   6. Afro-Americans—
Biography.   7. Civil rights workers—United States—Biography.
I. Title.
E185.97.R27P44   1990
323.1′196073′0092—dc20
[B]   89-38650
                                                                      CIP

To my husband, Sam,
and my daughters, Beth, Cara, and Diana

If a man does not keep pace with his companions, perhaps it is because he hears a different drummer.
        —*Henry David Thoreau*

Contents

Acknowledgments

I have incurred a great many debts during the pursuit of this project. I particularly wish to thank June Sochen, who introduced me to the study of history as well as to the subject of A. Philip Randolph. In addition to being a mentor, she has become a friend on whom I can always count. Her counsel has been invaluable in this, as in most of my other academic endeavors.

My sincere thanks go also to Josef Barton and Robert Wiebe at Northwestern University for their guidance, and a special thank-you is due George Frederickson (now at Stanford University), who extended himself in countless ways. The example of meticulous scholarship and graceful writing style, in addition to the insights and support, provided by all three helped shape this book in its beginning stages. I would also like to acknowledge Sterling Stuckey, at the University of California, Riverside, who was never too busy to talk and offer encouragement. I am indebted as well to the outside readers of Louisiana State University Press, whose suggestions greatly improved the manuscript. Whatever errors of fact or interpretation that remain are my responsibility alone.

To my colleagues at Mundelein College, especially Sister Ann Harrington, B.V.M., chair of the history department, Prudence Moylan, and Sister Joan Frances Crowley, B.V.M., I extend my deep appreciation for their unfailing cooperation and congeniality. I also wish to acknowledge the help of Bernice Wilds, A. Philip Randolph's secretary, who not only shared reminiscences with me but also prevailed upon Mr. Randolph to permit me access to his private files, without which this book could not have been written. I can only hope that if alive today she, as well as he, would be pleased with the result.

Perhaps the greatest debt an author incurs is to the manuscript curators of the various research libraries utilized along the way. In my case, grateful thanks go to Archie Motley of the Chicago Historical Society. His knowledge of the collections is unsurpassed, and his assistance is legendary. The promptness, courtesy, and knowledge of the curators of the various presidential libraries is also much appreciated, as is the efficiency of the manuscript personnel at the Library of Congress. To Jean Curry and Sister Frances Loretta Berger, B.V.M., of Mundelein Library, and the unsung reference librarians of the Wilmette Public Library, who were never too busy to call in sources on interlibrary loan, I owe a debt of gratitude. My sincere thanks go also to Rolf H. Erickson of the Northwestern University Library circulation services department for his many kindnesses, not the least of which was (and continues to be) providing a congenial atmosphere in which to work. My deep appreciation goes, as well, to the staff at Louisiana State University Press, especially to Margaret Fisher Dalrymple, for her faith in the project, and to Catherine Landry, whose careful editing greatly improved the quality of the book.

Last, but certainly not least, I wish to acknowledge the succor, patience, and good humor of my husband Sam and my daughters Beth, Cara, and Diana through the years it has taken to complete this project. My debt to them goes far beyond anything that can be repaid by a mere dedication.

Abbreviations and Short Titles

(used in notes)

ALH	Archives of Labor History and Urban Affairs, Wayne State University, Detroit
ANP Release	Associated Negro Press Release, Claude A. Barnett Papers, Chicago Historical Society
APR Files	A. Philip Randolph Personal Files, A. Philip Randolph Institute, New York City
BFM Papers	B. F. McLaurin Papers, Schomburg Collection, New York Public Library
BSCP Papers, CD	Brotherhood of Sleeping Car Porters Papers, Chicago Division, Chicago Historical Society
BSCP Papers, LC	Brotherhood of Sleeping Car Porters Papers, Library of Congress, Washington, D.C.
CORE Papers	Congress on Racial Equality Papers, State Historical Society of Wisconsin, Madison
EFM Papers	E. Frederic Morrow Papers, Mugar Memorial Library, Boston University
ER Papers	Eleanor Roosevelt Papers, Franklin D. Roosevelt Library, Hyde Park, New York
FDR Papers	Franklin D. Roosevelt Papers, Franklin D. Roosevelt Library, Hyde Park, New York
Hearings	*Hearings*, Committee on Armed Services, Senate, 80th Cong., 2nd Sess. "Universal Military Training," 1948
HST Papers	Harry S. Truman Papers, Harry S. Truman Library, Independence, Mo.

JHM Papers	J. Howard McGrath Papers, Harry S. Truman Library, Independence, Mo.
LBJ Papers	Lyndon Baines Johnson Papers, Lyndon Baines Johnson Library, Austin
MLK Papers	Martin Luther King, Jr., Papers, Mugar Memorial Library, Boston University
NAACP Papers	National Association for the Advancement of Colored People Papers, Library of Congress, Washington, D.C.
NNC Papers	National Negro Congress Papers, Schomburg Collection, New York Public Library
NUL Papers	National Urban League Papers, Library of Congress, Washington, D.C.
RP Papers	Richard Parrish Papers, Schomburg Collection, New York Public Library
ULP Records	Urban League of Philadelphia Records, Urban Archives Center, Temple University, Philadelphia

A. Philip Randolph, Pioneer of the Civil Rights Movement

Preface

In my first history class with June Sochen at Northeastern Illinois University, I chose "Franklin Roosevelt and A. Philip Randolph" as my research topic, not because I had ever heard of Randolph, but because I was interested in Roosevelt. In the course of my research, however, I became fascinated with the elegant black Socialist who had the audacity to challenge the White House. Randolph's strong minority-group identification appealed to my own emerging sense that, as a woman, I too belonged to an out-group. In an effort to learn more about him, I did further work on Randolph.

When I began teaching, I included Randolph in my courses. The students were also intrigued by the man, yet only in rare instances had they heard of him prior to taking my class. Gerda Lerner has pointed out that depriving women of their history is equivalent to the rape of the mind. Obviously, the same holds true for Afro-Americans. It is with the hope of helping to prevent such an assault in the future that this book is offered.

I had the good fortune of meeting A. Philip Randolph in 1973 and again in 1976 while he was living in a project erected by the International Ladies Garment Workers Union in New York City. To my amazement, everything I had read about him turned out to be true—he was tall and handsome, had courtly manners, and, most incredible of all, did indeed speak with an Oxford accent. One could not help but be struck by the incongruity of hearing Socialist doctrine being articulated in terms of "the claaases" and "the maaases." Yet I soon forgot the Shakespearean pronunciation as I was struck by the sincerity of the man who so passionately believed in the rightness of his cause.

The most frustrating aspect of writing about Randolph is trying to capture the human being behind the public persona. According to his secretary, Bernice Wilds, Randolph did not really have much of a private existence: His career was his life. What follows, then, is not an attempt at a full-scale biography, but rather an analysis of Randolph's civil rights leadership. Although others have examined the formation of the Brotherhood of Sleeping Car Porters, there has not been a comprehensive study of Randolph's activity on behalf of black equality.[1]

My goal is to demonstrate that Randolph's ideologies and strategies provided the blueprint for the civil rights movement that emerged in the late 1950s and early 1960s. By looking at events through his angle of vision, we can gain new insights into the sources of success and failure of that movement. A secondary aim is to analyze the special difficulties encountered by a leader of a powerless out-group. I therefore examine Randolph's various movements in order to explore the nature of the methods he employed, the types of coalitions he attempted to forge, and the constraints placed on his leadership by both his followers' poverty and the racism of the dominant white community.

A "different drummer," Randolph was a unique black leader on several counts: He came to prominence through the labor movement, a nontraditional path for Afro-American spokesmen; he adhered to Socialist economic doctrines rather than traditional American capitalist theory; he fused a labor orientation with militancy on racial issues; he popularized the use of mass, nonviolent civil disobedience; and he more nearly resembled a Shakespearean actor than a labor leader in diction and bearing. Because he represented a minority group, alliances were crucial to Randolph's ability to function as a leader. Of necessity, consequently, this study focuses on the challenges Randolph encountered in his search for allies.

My method is highly selective, exploring the consequences for the black community of the strategies and movements Randolph devised to

---

1. Brailsford Reese Brazeal, in *The Brotherhood of Sleeping Car Porters: Its Origin and Development* (New York, 1946), and William H. Harris, in *Keeping the Faith: A. Philip Randolph, Milton P. Webster, and the Brotherhood of Sleeping Car Porters, 1925–37* (Urbana, Ill., 1977), have written about the organization of the porters' union. Manning Marable has attempted an assessment of Randolph's impact on the civil rights movement, but his analyses are hampered by a lack of primary source material. See, for example, Manning Marable, *Race, Reform and Rebellion: The Second Reconstruction in Black America, 1945–1982* (Jackson, Miss., 1984); Marable, *Black American Politics: From the Washington Marches to Jesse Jackson* (London, 1985), Chap. 2; Marable, *From the Grassroots: Essays Toward Afro-American Liberation* (Boston, 1980).

help Afro-Americans attain equality. Randolph's early career as a radical, the period in which he organized the Brotherhood of Sleeping Car Porters, and his subsequent activities within the American labor movement are given rather short shrift and certainly different emphasis from that employed by other authors.[2] I take up these aspects of Randolph's early career to show the origins of his ideologies and civil rights tactics, of his anti-Communist stance, and of the conflict of interest that developed because of his dual allegiance to the labor movement and his black constituency.

Because this work concentrates on Randolph's civil rights career after the founding of the Brotherhood of Sleeping Car Porters, much attention is paid to some of Randolph's less well-known involvements, such as his efforts to integrate the armed services and to found a new political party in the 1940s, and his Prayer Pilgrimage and youth marches for integrated schools in the late 1950s. His better-known March on Washington Movement in the early 1940s has been ably analyzed by Herbert Garfinkel, but is treated at some length here to provide early evidence of the problems Randolph would repeatedly encounter in his subsequent civil rights organizations.[3]

Situational charisma is a term applicable to a leader of normally non-messianic tendency who invokes a strong response because he offers, in a time of acute adversity, leadership that is perceived as a means of salvation from distress. Situational charisma may bring a leader such as Randolph to power; it cannot keep him there. To remain in power a leader cannot operate in isolation, but must form coalitions to increase available resources. This is particularly important for a black leader operating in a community with little in the way of skills and financial capital. But where could Randolph turn for allies? An alliance with white groups presented the danger of co-optation of the movement by the more highly skilled and better-financed whites. But organizational jealousies and competition for the meager assets of the black community militated against a truly effective coalition with black groups—a proposition borne out by Randolph's alliance with the National Association for the Advancement of Colored

2. The radical period has been covered by Theodore Kornweibel, Jr., *No Crystal Stair: Black Life and the Messenger, 1917–1928* (Westport, Conn., 1975). Jervis Anderson has written a popular biography, *A. Philip Randolph: A Biographical Portrait* (New York, 1973), more than half of which is devoted to the period leading up to the recognition of the Brotherhood of Sleeping Car Porters.
3. Herbert Garfinkel, *When Negroes March* (Glencoe, Ill., 1959).

People, his most important black coalition partner. Sociologists explain that coalitions composed of leaders of organizations with different bases of strength are likely to diverge in their demands, expectations, and strategies, especially over time.[4] Through the years Randolph formed alliances with the established black organizations only to see them degenerate into wrangling as each party perceived its interests threatened.

Randolph's experiments with white coalitions also ran into difficulties, primarily because of the tendency of whites to assume control. Gary Marx and Michael Useem theorize that the inclusion of dominant-group members in a minority-group liberation movement gives rise to organizational conflicts, as the majority-group members disproportionately assume decision-making positions in the movement.[5] The history of Afro-American civil rights groups demonstrates the soundness of their observations.

In addition to alliances, movements require followers, and Randolph's organizations depended on a modernized, urbanized constituency. According to Martin Kilson, the urbanization experience was essential for black political development. As Afro-Americans first moved to urban areas in the pre–World War I period, a small group of blacks fashioned personalized links with influential whites, becoming their clients. Although the black bourgeoisie stressed that this clientage politics was "race politics," Kilson shows that in reality it was far more beneficial to the elites than to the black masses. Clientage politics thus failed to facilitate the political modernization of the black community. The failure, however, stimulated the institutionalization of cliques and interest groups as a type of black adaptation to urbanization. Kilson calls such institutionalization, exemplified by the National Association for the Advancement of Colored People and the National Urban League, interest-group articulation. Although it still required powerful white patrons, interest-group articulation wrought changes upon typical clientage politics, which was also rendered insufficient by the sheer growth of the urban black community beginning in 1915. It is more than a coincidence that Randolph emerged as a leader at a time when the old clientage politics was dying.

4. Robert C. Tucker, "The Theory of Charismatic Leadership," in Dankwart A. Rustow (ed.), *Philosophers and Kings: Studies in Leadership* (New York, 1970), 69–94; Nelson W. Polsby, "How to Study Community Power: The Pluralist Alternative," *Journal of Politics,* XXII (August, 1960), 474–84.

5. Gary T. Marx and Michael Useem, "Majority Involvement in Minority Movements: Civil Rights, Abolition, Untouchability," *Journal of Social Issues,* XXVII, No. 1 (1971), 81–104.

Since influential white patrons were a major political resource enabling the black community, or special interests within it, to derive benefits from the political process, ideological cleavages were downplayed. The deepest splits within the black community heretofore had involved the opposing ideologies of nationalism, or separatism, and integrationism. But the experience of clientage politics imprinted itself on the urban black leadership style, often irrespective of differences between radicals and conservatives or between nationalists and integrationists. Kilson deplores the "tendency among black leadership groups to depend excessively or uncreatively upon white allies or patrons"; Randolph, however, consciously designed all his undertakings to combat this overdependence.[6] The strategy he devised to help Afro-Americans rise above clientage politics and improve their condition—nonviolent, direct mass action—proved to have enduring influence, thus ensuring Randolph's position in American history.

6. Martin Kilson, "Political Change in the Negro Ghetto, 1900–1940s," in Nathan I. Huggins, Martin Kilson, and Daniel M. Fox (eds.), *Key Issues in the Afro-American Experience* (New York, 1971), II, 177.

I / A New-Style Leader Emerges

Why should a Negro worker be penalized for being black?
—A. Philip Randolph, 1935

The ambition to be a leader was an enduring theme in the life of A. Philip Randolph, the man who was to become one of the founding fathers of the modern civil rights movement. "Although I have never had a desire for wealth," he said late in his career, "I have had a passion to create a significant movement which would also benefit others."[1] The years between 1917 and 1925 served as preparation during which Randolph honed his public speaking technique and founded the highly respected radical journal the *Messenger*. Because he espoused socialism, labor unionism, and interracial class solidarity, doctrines foreign to most Afro-Americans, he attracted only a minute number of followers at this stage. Randolph nevertheless clung to these economic ideas and, as a result of experiences in the 1920s, added a virulent anticommunism to his theories. Consequently, much of the rhetoric and many of the strategies he would bring to his later civil rights activity were formulated when he began to organize the Pullman porters, in 1925. Thus before the end of the decade Randolph had acquired ideological convictions that would remain basically unchanged throughout his career. Not until 1937, however, when he succeeded in gaining recognition for the porters' union, would Randolph be able to overcome the handicap of his economic philosophy to achieve public recognition as a leader.

Born on April 15, 1889, into a religious family in Crescent City, Florida, Asa Philip Randolph was the second of two sons of an itinerant AME preacher who also operated a tailoring business to make ends meet. As an octogenarian, Randolph still remembered having to attend the prayer meetings his grandmother held every morning. He recalled "great pres-

1. A. Philip Randolph, "If I Were Young Today," *Ebony* (July, 1963), 82.

sure" brought to bear on him to become a preacher, but he remained "not greatly impressed." Still, Randolph said nothing affected him and his brother "as deeply as the church relationship. We grew up under it and in it, and our father was a part of it, and our mother was quite religious." Randolph nevertheless began to doubt Christianity at an early age and later became an atheist, although the teachings of Jesus combined with those of his father predisposed him to a belief in "the spiritual power of nonviolence."[2]

According to Randolph, his father was "coal black" and his mother, substantially younger, was "almost white," but they both "had an unusual sense of racial pride." As a youngster, Randolph listened to his father's parishioners complain about the problems of racial prejudice.[3] This exposure, combined with the experience of growing up in segregated Jacksonville, where the family had moved, raised his consciousness. Thus while the father's religious zeal left his sons unmoved, the elder Randolph's political and racial interests had a profound effect on them.

Although he sang and took part in church plays, Randolph was shy as a child. A serious youth, he thought of his brother James as being the gifted one. James, however, was to die a young man.[4] In adulthood, Randolph's tendency toward being a loner hampered his ambition to found a mass movement and made it difficult for him to share policy-making authority with other black leaders.

Randolph's parents, eager for their sons to have a good education and rise in the world, hired a tutor for them, and they both learned to read before they started school. The boys became intrigued by "words, their pronunciation, their meaning." The parents instilled self-confidence in their sons by constantly reiterating that they were as intellectually competent as any white and that they were "not supposed to bow and take a back seat for anybody," but rather stand up for their rights. Randolph read sermons aloud, imitating the tone of his father and other community preachers—a pastime that had a positive bearing on his later oratorical style.[5]

2. A. Philip Randolph to author, September 29, 1972; Randolph, "The Reminiscences of A. Philip Randolph," transcript of interview by Wendell Wray, 1972, pp. 5, 63, Oral History Research Office, Columbia University; Randolph, "If I Were Young Today," 82.

3. Randolph, "Reminiscences," 18, 66–67, 74.

4. *Ibid.*, 55, 63, 66–67, 74; *Messenger* (October, 1924), 314.

5. Randolph, "Reminiscences," 73–74.

In 1903 Randolph entered Cookman Institute in Jacksonville, which later became Bethune-Cookman College, and there enjoyed the advantages of a superior education. After giving the class oration on graduation day, Randolph began to experience despair because as a black he could find only manual labor jobs in the South. He had spent several summers in New York, traveling by ship because it was cheaper than the train, and even worked as a waiter on the Fall River Line. The experience provided him with his first opportunity for labor organization; he tried to organize the other black workers to protest the conditions in the "Glory Hole" where they slept.[6]

At age twenty-two Randolph decided to emigrate north, arriving in the city that became his permanent home, New York, in 1911. The fabled northern opportunities proving elusive, Randolph was again forced into taking a series of odd jobs to support himself and, in turn, became an elevator operator, a porter, and a waiter. In a more mature attempt at labor organization, he formed an Elevator and Switchboard Operators Union to fight against what he thought were oppressive working conditions, while at night he attended the City College of New York.[7] In addition, Randolph became involved with political radicalism through exposure to the soapbox oratory of the pioneer black Socialist Hubert Harrison, as well as that of white radicals like Elizabeth Gurley Flynn, "Big Bill" Haywood, and Eugene Debs. The pre–World War I era marked the height of the Industrial Workers of the World's public visibility, and the industrial unionism they advocated impressed Randolph as having great potential for unskilled black workers. He thus began to carve out an ideological niche that would separate him from other black leaders.

At this time Randolph also made a decision that influenced the style of his speech for the rest of his life: to learn, under the guidance of a tutor, to recite Shakespeare in Oxford-style English. After he began to play Shakespearean heroes for a Harlem theater group, Randolph met his future wife, Lucille Campbell Greene, a widow six years older than himself, whom he married in 1913. A beauty-shop operator with ties to Madame

6. *Ibid.*, 90–93; Edwin R. Embree, *Thirteen Against the Odds* (1944; rpr. Port Washington, N.Y., 1968), 214; Randolph, "If I Were Young Today," 82.

7. Randolph, "Reminiscences," 90–97, 216; William Dufty, "A Post Portrait: A. Philip Randolph," New York *Post*, December 29, 1959; "A. Philip Randolph," *American Labor*, I (August, 1968), 46–54.

Walker and her daughter, Lucille Randolph became a crucial source of financial support for her husband's subsequent undertakings.[8]

Through his wife Randolph met Chandler Owen, and the two budding intellectuals became partners of a sort. Owen acquainted Randolph with Lester Frank Ward's sociological theories regarding the importance of environment, and Randolph introduced Owen to the economic theories of Karl Marx. The pair worked out their own synthesis concluding that men could only be free if they were not subject to economic deprivation—a theory from which Randolph never deviated. They came to believe that since the Socialist party represented the interests of the worker, and since 99 percent of blacks were workers, their logical alignment should be with the Socialist party.[9] Attributing racial prejudice to capitalism, they gave a racial explanation for their acceptance of socialism. Concluding that only force, whether economic or physical, could secure full citizenship rights for Afro-Americans, they saw themselves as the vanguard of the "New Negro."

Randolph and Owen thus became catalysts for a small but influential black Socialist intellectual group that served as the center of their social life, as well as their work, and that looked toward a Marxian solution to the race problem. In November, 1917, they founded the *Messenger*, which, according to one authority, was "one of the most brilliantly edited magazines in the history of Negro journalism." Using the magazine to publicize their views, the editors attacked the established black leaders' lack of concern with the black masses and their financial dependence on white capitalists. Even W. E. B. Du Bois did not escape their barbs. Just as Booker T. Washington had seemed too conservative to the young Du Bois, Du Bois now seemed too conservative to the young Socialists. Randolph and Owen consequently demanded a new black leadership. They also supported the Socialist position that World War I was brought about to benefit the capitalist class and, therefore, was of little concern to the workers. Unwilling to fight abroad for a democracy that did not embrace blacks and resentful of the fact that Du Bois had accepted a cap-

8. Randolph, "Reminiscences," 104–105, 124–25, 129–30, 277; Dufty, "A Post Portrait," December 29, 1959; *Black Worker*, April, 1963, p. 1.

9. Randolph, "Reminiscences," 102, 144–49; "Randolph," *American Labor*, 47; "Some Reasons Why Negroes Should Vote the Socialist Ticket," *Messenger* (November, 1917), 34.

taincy in the army, Randolph and Owen were also not willing to stand by while blacks were subjected to physical abuse. For voicing such radical antiwar sentiments, they were briefly jailed in 1918.[10]

Idealistically, the editors believed in an alliance between black and white labor. Convinced that salvation for Afro-Americans lay in upgrading the race economically, Randolph felt improvement in the status of blacks could come only through labor organization. Unorganized workers, whether black or white, were potential scabs. While the old-line black leaders hoped gains made by blacks acting as strikebreakers could be maintained, Randolph and Owen realized that that was seldom the case. Scabbing might put bread on the table for a time, but it would not improve the economic status of blacks in the long run. The editors argued, rather, that capitalists ignored color in their exploitation of labor; hence black and white workers had the same interests and should work together to fight their common enemy. The capitalist system must go. The remedy for racial intolerance, they believed, lay in the socialization of industry, the nationalization of land, political enfranchisement, and revolutionary education for blacks. "When no profits are to be made from race friction," wrote Randolph in an adaptation of Marxian economic determinism to the race question, "no one will longer be interested in stirring up race prejudice."[11]

The "Great Migration" of southern blacks to northern industrial cities in search of wartime jobs and increased opportunities had resulted in overcrowding, with blacks spilling out of their narrowly defined ghetto areas. The subsequent competition with whites for jobs and the increased tensions led to antiblack riots, but few Afro-Americans saw socialism as an answer to their problems. To most blacks socialism represented a white man's movement, the party of the enemy, who denied them equality in employment and union membership. They were not incorrect. The Socialist and Socialist Labor parties avoided dealing with the "Negro problem" as such since they maintained that all classes of workers should be treated alike. Socialists equated racism with the general social problem and told blacks they would have to wait for the Socialist revolution to

10. Richard Bardolph, *The Negro Vanguard* (New York, 1959), 142; Chandler Owen, "The Failure of the Negro Leaders," *Messenger* (January, 1918), 23; Editorial, "New Leadership for the Negro," *Messenger* (May–June, 1919), 9; A. Philip Randolph, "The Negro and Economic Radicalism," *Opportunity* (February, 1926), 63; Dufty, "A Post Portrait," December 30, 1959; Randolph, "Reminiscences," 110–13, 220.

11. "The Cause and Remedy for Race Riots," *Messenger* (September, 1919), 21.

achieve complete social equality. "We have nothing special to offer the Negro," Eugene Debs admitted.[12]

To promote their goals Randolph and Owen became soapbox orators propagandizing on behalf of black unionism and socialism, an activity that brought them financial support from the *Jewish Daily Forward.* They even stood for office on the Socialist ticket. Randolph ran for state comptroller in 1920, while Owen and three other blacks, including Lucille Randolph, ran for the state legislature. None were elected, although Randolph polled 202,000 votes, running only a thousand behind Debs and well ahead of the rest of the ticket.[13] Their standing for office on third-party tickets, however, did little to change traditional Afro-American allegiance to the Republican party.

While participating in politics, Randolph and Owen began to take action to advance their ideas on economic welfare and to draw Afro-Americans into the labor movement. They began a job bureau, The Brotherhood, and from 1917 on they worked to organize blacks into unions and even tried to form a black labor federation. But their efforts encountered enormous obstacles: the racial prejudice of white workers, the opposition of the American Federation of Labor (AFL), the entrenched antiunionism in the Afro-American community based upon a long tradition of paternalistic relations with white employers, and the fact that scabbing often supplied the only opportunity for black employment. As a result, Randolph and Owen vacillated between organizing interracial labor groups, such as the National Association for the Promotion of Labor Unionism Among Negroes, and forming all-black groups, such as the United Negro Trades. When these early attempts to promote labor organization in the black community failed, Randolph claimed that white employers were relieved. He argued that they continued to promote racial antipathy as a means of forestalling mass unionization and denying both races better wages and working conditions.[14]

Believing that the black church was a reactionary institution because it

---

12. Eugene Debs, quoted in Theodore Draper, *American Communism and Soviet Russia* (New York, 1960), 315–16. See also Philip S. Foner, *American Socialism and Black Americans: From the Age of Jackson to World War II* (Westport, Conn., 1977), especially 258–64.

13. Randolph, "Reminiscences," 112, 114–15, 121, 123, 152–53, 158–59, 171–75; James Weinstein, *The Decline of Socialism in America, 1912–25* (New York, 1969), 73.

14. Sterling D. Spero and Abram L. Harris, *The Black Worker* (1931; rpr. New York, 1968), 387–89; Dufty, "A Post Portrait," December 29, 1959.

bowed to the money power in the community, Randolph and Owen also criticized black preachers for failing to educate the people and rouse them against the evils of disfranchisement and lynching. The editors of the *Messenger* thought the churches would be performing a higher function if they served as places to house cooperative stores.[15] Next to labor organization, Randolph thought cooperatives provided the best opportunity for blacks to raise themselves economically. He hoped the savings accrued by eliminating the middleman would benefit the entire race, and emphasized this theme from the earliest days of the *Messenger* to the last days of its successor, the *Black Worker*, in 1968.

Randolph and Owen's greatest difficulty lay in trying to sell the basically anti-ideological black masses on ideas that ran counter to their everyday experiences. As laborers knew from bitter contact, white workers would rather exclude than unite with their black brothers. In addition, the white American Socialist party, while professing proletarian aims, was composed, particularly in its leadership, predominantly of middle-class intellectuals—an irony that also applied to the black editors of the *Messenger*. Randolph and Owen might insist they wanted to reach the black urban proletariat, but their economic theories and "New Negro" appeal were in fact directed toward educated, middle-class blacks. The bulk of the *Messenger*'s support came from a small cadre of white and black intellectuals, and labor and Socialist circles.[16] This situation placed the editors in the ambiguous position of advocating black control of black ventures while accepting support from liberal whites, and of preaching a gospel of mass organization in terms that appealed to the middle class. Both contradictions would continue to plague Randolph throughout his career.

Already counseling the economic boycott as a strategy to obtain equality, in 1920 Randolph and Owen organized the Friends of Negro Freedom in an attempt to put together a national civil rights organization with local branches based upon their economic ideas. An important motivation for the new group was the fact that "at the present time there is not a national organization alleged to be fighting in the interest of Negroes which is controlled, in any considerable degree, by Negroes. On

15. Editorial, "The Failure of the Negro Church," *Messenger* (October, 1919), 6.

16. Randolph, "Reminiscences," 213; Abram L. Harris, "The Negro Problem as Viewed by Negro Leaders," *Current History Magazine of the New York Times* (June, 1923), 414; David A. Shannon, *The Socialist Party of America: A History* (New York, 1955), 53.

the contrary," complained the editors, "their leading organizations are controlled and officered by persons who are neither members of their class nor members of their race." While the Friends of Negro Freedom ultimately failed because it was subverted into a vehicle dedicated to bringing about the downfall of Marcus Garvey, the propaganda buildup for the group foreshadowed the rhetoric for the March on Washington Movement twenty years later.[17]

Randolph's early foray into public life ended when the editorial staff of the *Messenger* was split asunder by three major controversies in the early 1920s. All the disputes centered on differences in ideology. The first of these conflicts concerned the question of support for Marcus Garvey and his Back-to-Africa movement. The rift over Garvey brought into the open the second cause of discord, the simmering nationalistic rivalry between West Indian and American blacks. The third philosophical disagreement concerned the Socialist party division over the Bolshevik Revolution. Internal dissension, combined with government repression, led to the breakup of the radical *Messenger* group.

In 1916 Marcus Garvey arrived in a Harlem bursting from the mass migration of rural southern and West Indian blacks. Attracted by the promise of decent jobs and housing, the newcomers were soon frustrated by discrimination, second-class citizenship, and race riots. The National Association for the Advancement of Colored People (NAACP), the National Urban League (NUL), and the *Messenger* all directed their appeals to the middle class. Unlike the established integrationist betterment groups, Garvey addressed the disillusioned with a philosophy of mobility and racial separatism and argued that blacks would never receive justice in a white man's country. He stressed that blacks should not be over-concerned with political rights and social equality in the United States, but rather should strive to become as independent as possible. Touting a gospel of progress, Garvey attempted to enlist the masses behind black business enterprise.

Traditionally, Garvey has been portrayed as representing the national-ist side of the separatist-integrationist debate that has long occupied the Afro-American community. Historically, the nationalist philosophy has been based on escapism, and its adherents traditionally were drawn from

17. Editorial, "Friends of Negro Freedom," *Messenger* (April–May, 1920), 4; *Messenger* (February, 1923), 529. See also advertisement for Friends of Negro Freedom, *Messenger* (April, 1923), 681; Foner, *American Socialism and Black Americans*, 314–15, 324.

the lowest classes of blacks, who had little stake in American society and therefore nothing to lose. Of late, however, historians have begun to revise their explanations of the implications of Garveyism. Although they have somewhat different points of view, revisionists Judith Stein and Robert Hill both tie Garvey's influence to the period of economic expansion following World War I and the fact that the black community did not participate in the prosperity enjoyed by the dominant white society.

Stein argues that the pressures of an expanding capitalism affected Afro-Americans differently, depending upon their position in the social structure. Capitalism eroded old ways of life without creating a sufficient number of new careers for the displaced sons of peasants and artisans. Denied by racial discrimination the opportunity to compete for the inadequate number of professional positions for which their training and talent entitled them, members of the black elite were the most likely to be drawn to black nationalist solutions; separate black institutions seemed to offer the promise of opportunities withheld by the larger society. According to Stein, Garvey's uniqueness stemmed from his attempt to enlist the black masses behind the elite model of progress, and his failure resulted from his inability to keep the masses permanently mobilized behind the elite goals he had adopted.[18]

Hill, on the other hand, emphasizes that the ideal of success, central to Garvey's perspective, fit well with both the American cult of success and the Afro-American tradition of struggle to succeed despite white opposition. Although Garvey was impatient with the piety of traditional black religion, he managed to endow commercial undertakings with religious significance while at the same time combining the success creed with the doctrine of nationalism. Because blacks were kept from achievement by the dominant society, Garvey sought to give them the energizing philosophy of racial pride and promoted Africa "as the land of the black self-made man."[19]

Regardless of his attraction for the elite, Garvey soon attached the black masses to his United Negro Improvement Association (UNIA) through his stress on race power and pride in black skin, and his utilization of pageantry. Garvey's promotion of racial purity, black cultural and social separation, and his dramatic antics had enormous appeal for poor

18. Judith Stein, *The World of Marcus Garvey: Race and Class in Modern Society* (Baton Rouge, 1986), 3–6, 132.

19. Robert A. Hill (ed.), *The Marcus Garvey and Universal Negro Improvement Association Papers* (Berkeley, 1983), I, lxxxvi–lxxxvii.

blacks. True to his teachings, Garvey never solicited funds from whites or admitted them to membership in the UNIA. With the cry "Up, you mighty race!" he challenged blacks to improve their condition. Proud of his blackness, Garvey would not accept advertising in his journal, the *Negro World,* for products that claimed to whiten black skin or straighten black hair. These were the two most lucrative sources of revenue for the average black publication and, as such, were welcomed by the *Messenger.*

While his listeners appreciated Garvey's argument that blacks, as a minority, would never attain first-class citizenship in the United States, they were less enamored of his corollary: that the only workable solution to the Afro-American problem was the establishment of an independent black nation in Africa. But Garvey was also practical. He realized the impossibility of all blacks physically relocating in Africa and emphasized a return in the spiritual sense. Such a spiritual return, he reasoned, would help free blacks from the sense of inferiority that had been inculcated in them by white domination.

In the end, however, Garvey essentially misunderstood the conditions of the American black experience. His attempt to bargain with the Ku Klux Klan on the basis that he would remove blacks from America and make the country safe for white supremacy if the KKK would help make Africa safe for black supremacy provided the opportunity for his enemies to coalesce against him. In the past, historians have argued that Garvey split the Afro-American community because, in his native West Indies, English landlords used mulattoes as a middle-class buffer against the black majority. As a result, Garvey was prejudiced against mulattoes, it was argued, and the fact that most American black leaders were of mixed blood accounted for his antipathy toward them. Newer scholarship on Garvey claims that because he believed his opponents conspired to use the power of the state against him, Garvey tried to challenge their influence by provoking the issue of "social equality" while promoting commitment to the ideal of racial purity. Such a strategy increased competition within black American leadership. Regardless, aided by his spellbinding oratory and his denunciation of white paternalism and patronage, Garvey attracted a larger following and raised more money in a shorter period of time than any other black organization had ever done.[20]

20. Wilson Jeremiah Moses, *The Golden Age of Black Nationalism, 1850–1925* (Hamden, Conn., 1978), 265–66; Harold Cruse, *The Crisis of the Negro Intellectual* (New York, 1967), 257–58; Hill (ed.), *Garvey and UNIA Papers,* I, lxxxiv.

Garvey's popularity soon brought upon him the wrath of the integrationist-oriented established black leadership, especially that of the NAACP, as well as that of Randolph and Owen, despite the fact that Randolph had first introduced Garvey to a Harlem audience. The young black Socialists saw Garvey's separatism as antithetical to the black-white laboring-class alliance they advocated. Randolph became increasingly opposed to Garvey and utilized the editorial pages of the *Messenger* to mount a savage "Garvey Must Go!" campaign, labeling him "A Supreme Negro Jamaican Jackass." Garveyism "will not only not liberate Africa," argued Randolph, "but it will set back the clock of Negro progress by cutting the Negro workers away from the proletarian liberation movement expressed in the workers' efforts, political and economic, to effect solidarity, class consciousness, by setting them against, instead of joining them with, the white workers' struggle for freedom." [21]

Randolph's attitude toward Garvey revealed his ambivalence about a solution to the Afro-American problem. On the one hand, Randolph rejected Garvey's message that blacks should separate themselves from white society; on the other, he shared Garvey's strong sense of racial pride. But stress on race consciousness conflicted with Randolph's call for interracial working-class solidarity. Without solving his own dilemma, Randolph narrowed the broad aims of the Friends of Negro Freedom; it became primarily a Garvey-baiting organization. Ultimately, though, Garveyism failed, not because of Randolph and other black American leaders, but because it never identified a suitable alternative to the unsatisfactory conditions of American life. Instead of creating an economic power capable of demanding equal rights, Garvey initiated small business enterprises that could not compete with America's economic giants. [22]

The battle over Garvey brought the second theme of conflict among the *Messenger* editors to the fore—the ever-widening gulf between West Indian and American blacks. Coinciding with the migration of southern blacks to the North, the immigration of West Indian blacks to the United States resulted in much bitterness between the two groups. Because white Americans did not differentiate between blacks from the various Carib-

21. A. Philip Randolph, "The Only Way to Redeem Africa," *Messenger* (January, 1923), 569; Randolph, "Black Zionism," *Messenger* (January, 1922), 335.
22. Randolph, "Reminiscences," 131–33, 157; Hill (ed.), *Garvey and UNIA Papers*, I, lxxviii; Edmund David Cronon, *Black Moses* (Madison, Wis., 1962), 224; Foner, *American Socialism and Black Americans*, 324–33. In his "Reminiscences" (133) Randolph claimed that he had not been anti-Garvey, but that Owen had.

bean islands, regardless of their native language, an artificial unity was created among the newcomers, who, however, shared a background where class distinctions were more important than the color line. Coming mostly from the upper middle classes, the migrants to the United States were likely to be more skilled, more ambitious, and better educated than American blacks. They quickly proceeded to fill positions in the skilled trades and became proprietors of a large percentage of the black-owned businesses in Harlem.

Anti—West Indian feelings, consequently, were strongest among educated American blacks, who felt their position challenged by the newcomers. By the same token, West Indian blacks, who were in the majority at home, could not understand black-white relations in America. The fact that Garvey came from Jamaica intensified the bitter feelings between the two nationalities. It was not a coincidence that the old-line Afro-American leaders, particularly the officers of the NAACP, as well as Randolph and Owen, were in the forefront of the drive to have Garvey deported as an undesirable alien.[23]

With both groups represented on its staff, the *Messenger* was particularly susceptible to nationalistic rivalries. When the West Indian editor W. A. Domingo left the journal accusing Randolph and Owen of anti—West Indianism, the two denied that their stand against Garvey was motivated by nationalistic prejudice, maintaining that it was merely a *"coincidence"* that *"the large bulk of the Garvey followers are foreigners."*[24] Despite their protestations, the anti-Garvey campaign eventually degenerated into a West Indian versus black-American controversy.

The third ideological dispute to embroil *Messenger* staffers resulted from the Socialist party rift over the Russian revolution. Although he had originally hailed the Bolshevik Revolution, Randolph sided with the right-wing Socialists when the party split in 1919 and left-wing Socialists formed a new party affiliated with the Third International at Moscow. Randolph was unalterably opposed to taking direction from a source outside the United States. Most of the West Indian black radicals went

23. Randolph, "Reminiscences," 223; Alain Locke (ed.), *The New Negro* (New York, 1925), 343, 346; Gilbert Osofsky, *Harlem, The Making of a Ghetto: Negro New York, 1890–1930* (New York, 1968), 131–35; Cruse, *Crisis of the Negro Intellectual,* 124; Harold Cruse, *Plural but Equal: A Critical Study of Blacks and Minorities and America's Plural Society* (New York, 1987), 309–22.

24. "Open Forum—The Policy of the *Messenger* on West Indian and American Negroes: W. A. Domingo vs. Chandler Owen," *Messenger* (March, 1923), 639–45; "Garveyism and Anarchism," *Messenger* (October, 1922), 501–502.

over to the new Communist party, which, unlike the Socialist party, saw black workers as an important link in the world proletarian revolution and was prepared to give them special consideration. In contrast, most of the American black radicals remained with the Randolph and Owen Socialist faction—a situation that further aggravated the animosity between the two nationalities. "In subsequent years," according to historian Harold Cruse, "this split among the Negro Socialists was the root cause of more destructive rivalry in Harlem's Civil Rights and labor politics than the records reveal." [25]

These philosophical battles of the 1920s left their mark on Randolph, who blamed the "Communists' schism" for splitting the black Socialists "just as it did the white Socialists." As a result, Randolph became a militant anti-Communist. Perceiving the American wing of the party as part of an international conspiracy rather than an indigenous outlet for black grievances, Randolph rigidly adhered to a virulent form of anticommunism for the rest of his life, submerging his antipathy only briefly during the United Front era of the 1930s.[26]

Black as well as white Socialists suffered in the post–World War I period, when the country became fearful of radicalism. The resulting intolerance, as manifested in the Red Summer of 1919, the Palmer Raids, and ultimately immigration restriction, brought government repression of both black and white dissenters. Black radicals were even less tolerable to the dominant community than white radicals, claimed Randolph, because they preached a social equality that threatened the racial status quo. In this tense postwar atmosphere, the *Messenger* found its second-class mailing privileges revoked on occasion and was singled out by the Department of Justice as being "by long odds the most able and the most dangerous of all the Negro publications," and by the Lusk Committee in New York as being "distinctly revolutionary in tone." [27]

25. Cruse, *Crisis of the Negro Intellectual*, 40; Foner, *American Socialism and Black Americans*, 303–40.

26. Randolph, "Negro and Economic Radicalism," 63.

27. "A. Mitchell Palmer," *Messenger* (August, 1920), 75; U.S. Department of Justice, Investigation Activities, *Senate Documents*, 66th Cong., 1st Sess., No. 153, Exhibit No. 10, *Radicalism and Sedition Among the Negroes as Reflected in Their Publications* (1919), 172, 184; "Propaganda Among the Negroes," in State of New York, *Report of the Joint Legislative Committee Investigating Seditious Activities* (1920), Vol. 2, p. 1476. See also "Confidential. Memorandum for the Director of Military Intelligence," August 15, 1919, in Hill (ed.), *Garvey and UNIA Papers*, I, 491–93.

Thus the philosophical conflicts that splintered the *Messenger* editorial staff, combined with persecution by the government, fear of bolshevism, and prosperity in the dominant community, dissipated support for revolutionary socialism in the 1920s. The result was loss of Socialist financial support for the journal. After the division in its ranks, the *Messenger* began to compromise its political views and become more conservative on social questions. In 1923 the journal came out with a "Negro Business Achievement Number" stressing the mutual interest of black capital and labor, and by 1924 its masthead was changed from "The Only Radical Negro Magazine in America" to "The World's Greatest Negro Monthly." Langston Hughes noted that by 1926 the journal had become "a kind of Negro society magazine and a plugger for Negro business, with photographs of prominent colored ladies and their nice homes." The editors were accused "of being more interested in the financial support of their magazine than in building an economic organization." But when Socialist funding dried up, the black business community was the journal's only available source for backing, and Randolph admitted that the editors profiled black business leaders in exchange for their contributions.[28]

Tight for money and scarred by the ideological wars, Randolph began to tone down his radicalism. All of the organizations that he and Owen had founded disintegrated. While they could easily identify the problems in Afro-American life, the *Messenger* editors failed to advocate solutions and put together a mass movement to implement them. Randolph could rationally destroy the entire ideological basis upon which the Garvey movement was built, but the fact remained that Garvey had succeeded in putting together, in a remarkably short time, the type of mass organization that Randolph struggled all his life to achieve.[29]

The Garvey movement, the radical publications, and the Harlem Renaissance beginning to flower at this time were all products of the relative freedom of thought and expression available in the North. Black soldiers, having met with comparatively little discrimination in Europe, returned with a new perspective and greater self-assurance. But when the hopes of the war years were dashed by traditional American racism, and black veterans faced unemployment, segregation, and lynching, the rebuffs dealt

28. Langston Hughes, *The Big Sea* (New York, 1940), 233–34. See also George S. Schuyler, *Black and Conservative* (New Rochelle, 1966), 37–39; Spero and Harris, *The Black Worker,* 395; Randolph, "Reminiscences," 218, 222.
29. Kornweibel, *No Crystal Stair,* 170.

rising black expectations caused, in Randolph's view, a bitterness and anger that provided fertile ground for the rise of Garvey's type of black nationalism. Riots resulting from competition for jobs and housing demonstrated that the black masses had changed and were now prepared to meet violence with violence. Radicalism after the war, noted James Weldon Johnson, was "motivated by a fierce race consciousness."[30]

Although he both influenced and benefited from this intensified color sensitivity, Randolph could not be considered a leader in 1925. His organizational efforts having failed, he lacked a constituency. Furthermore, unresolved conflicts continued to plague him. Black control of black groups was important for black self-esteem, he argued, but how could Afro-Americans maintain control of their own movements when they were dependent upon white financial aid? How could unskilled blacks break their dependency on white patrons? How did one deal with the fact that after 1920 the one group of whites willing to grant a measure of equality to blacks were Communists and thus took their direction from a source basically unconcerned with furthering the interests of the United States? How could an intellectual leader espousing atheistic rationalism appeal to the masses traditionally accustomed to religious emotionalism? How could black laborers upgrade themselves economically through unionization if whites would not allow them into their unions? Above all, how could a leader unite all sections of the black community—integrationist and nationalist, West Indian and American, poor and middle-class—when he could not even hold his own small editorial staff together?

Randolph realized the necessity for blacks to maintain their group integrity while at the same time accommodating to the social structure of the dominant community. Ultimately an integrated society remained the ideal, if it was integrated upon a basis of complete equality and without assimilation of black ethnic identity. But how did one cope with the paradox presented by the fact that although an integrated work force was essential for black economic progress, the black middle class prospered largely from a segregated black economy? Aware of what historian Nancy Weiss has called the "anomaly of separatist efforts to secure integration," Randolph nevertheless judged separatism to be the better tactic in the

30. Randolph, quoted in Phyl Garland, "A. Philip Randolph: Labor's Grand Old Man," *Ebony* (May, 1969), 36; James Weldon Johnson, *Black Manhattan* (1930; rpr. New York, 1968), 246; Foner, *American Socialism and Black Americans*, 291–92.

short run—it appealed to the masses, it promoted black self-confidence, and it gave blacks necessary experience in decision making.[31]

Guiding the *Messenger* from economic radicalism to support for black business, Randolph displayed the vacillation between idealism and pragmatism that would distinguish his subsequent behavior. Yet he also displayed the dramatic flair and inspiring rhetoric, as well as the philosophy, that would characterize his later activities. He might play down his Socialistic beliefs and modify his views on pacifism to win a greater following, but the economic ideas Randolph developed during this early period never changed. America was the home of American blacks, and it was necessary for blacks to improve their position within American society. Blacks must raise themselves economically, Randolph believed, and social equality would follow. He perceived the existence of an upwardly mobile class of blacks who desired political and social recognition within America and would be willing to fight for it, but in 1925 Randolph had yet to identify and reach that class.

Having determined that no other personality "had dedicated his life to the organization of black workers," when Chandler Owen left permanently for Chicago in 1923, Randolph remained as the foremost articulator of the cause of black labor. After the Elevator and Switchboard Operators Union succumbed to white takeover, Randolph turned to the Pullman porters, whose job was the only one in which blacks predominated. Randolph's eloquence, interest in labor issues, and notoriety gained through editing the *Messenger* led to his working with sleeping-car porters Billy Bowes and Ashley Totten in organizing the Pullman porters in 1925. Admittedly, Randolph knew little of the actual work of the porters because he could not afford to ride on their cars. "I am not sure that I had ever seen a Pullman car then—much less ridden in one," he later recalled.[32]

The Pullman porters were considered the elite of black labor because they had steady jobs and traveled around the country. Randolph had felt

31. Nancy J. Weiss, "From Black Separatism to Interracial Cooperation," in Barton J. Bernstein and Allen J. Matusow (eds.), *Twentieth-Century America: Recent Interpretations* (New York, 1972), 67; Marable, *From the Grassroots*, 79–84.

32. Randolph, "Reminiscences," 215, 221, 226–29, 232–34, 237; "Randolph," *American Labor*, 48–49.

for some time, however, that the porters represented a large segment of exploited and underpaid black labor because they were not unionized. As far back as 1919, an editorial in the *Messenger* had dealt with the porters' problems and noted that they were dependent on tips to receive a living wage. The porters had legitimate complaints: Working long hours for little pay, they had no job security, being victimized or favored according to the whim of their supervisors. "Extra" porters were required to report regularly for work, but received no pay unless they were actually assigned. Porters had to spend their own money on shoe polish and other paraphernalia, buy their own meals, pay for their lodging at stopovers, and buy two uniforms a year—expenses that came to about thirty-three dollars a month, close to half their salary. They were not paid for the "preparatory time" in which they made the car ready and assisted passengers in the station, tasks that took from one to five hours. Furthermore, on long runs the porters were required to give the desires of the passengers precedence over their own need for sleep.[33]

For the average porter, however, joining a labor union meant choosing between steady, albeit low, pay and the near certainty of reprisals by the Pullman Company. Still, the porters offered opportunities that Randolph's previous targets for organization had not, primarily because they represented an occupation in which blacks had a near monopoly. The Pullman Company, incorporated in 1867, had relied on black porters from its inception.[34]

The Brotherhood of Sleeping Car Porters (BSCP) was formally organized on August 25, 1925, with Randolph at its head. Times were not fortuitous for the new union, however; even established white unions were losing members in the 1920s, Pullman's profits were down, and there were many unemployed blacks from whom the company could draw replacement porters. Pullman propaganda identified the company as a benefactor of the black race, leading many prominent blacks, as well as most of the black press, to oppose the BSCP.

Randolph's greatest advantage lay in the fact that he was not employed by Pullman and hence not dependent upon the company for his live-

33. Editorial, "The Negro in Public Utilities," *Messenger* (May–June, 1919), 6; Randolph, "Reminiscences," 232; Randolph, "Pullman Porters Win," *Opportunity* (October, 1937), 299; Randolph, "An Open Letter to Mr. J. P. Morgan," *American Federationist* (July, 1933), 704, 707, 708; Randolph, "Porters Fight Paternalism," *American Federationist* (June, 1930), 670–71; Randolph, "Reminiscences," 236.

34. Randolph, "Reminiscences," 231.

lihood. But identification as a radical made him extremely vulnerable to red-baiting, and Pullman did not hesitate to label him a Communist to frighten the porters. Randolph had personal liabilities as well; his "Harvard" accent, his courtly manners, and his impeccable dress made rapport between him and the average porter more difficult. Something in his presentation, nevertheless, reached out to his audience. "When I heard Randolph speak it was like a light," recalled E. D. Nixon, who became influential in the later civil rights struggle. "He done more to bring me in the fight for civil rights than anybody. Before that time, I figure that a Negro would be kicked around and accept whatever the white man did. I never knew the Negro had a right to enjoy freedom like everyone else." Nixon asserted: "When Randolph stood there and talked that day, it made a different man of me. From that day on, I was determined that I was gonna fight for freedom until I was able to get some of it myself."[35]

Randolph's atheism provided other grounds for personal attack. The inadequacy of the black church had long appalled him: Not only did emphasis upon the next world dilute pressure for change in this one, but black preachers failed to encourage their flocks to protest racial oppression because of the financial support they received from white capitalist philanthropists. As these benefactors were also opposed to labor organization, whether black or white, black churchmen were antagonistic toward the BSCP, giving Randolph no cause to change his opinion of the clergy. Furthermore, most black ministers, like most black laborers, did not understand the difference between a company union and a trade union. To Randolph's dismay, the preachers, like other members of the black bourgeoisie, thought Pullman paternalism beneficial and viewed the rise of the BSCP "with mingled suspicion, distrust and fear."[36]

Despite his opposition to the church, Randolph now realized, as he had not earlier, the dependence of his followers on the institution. He therefore submerged his own disbelief and appealed to the porters in biblical terms and with evangelistic zeal on behalf of the cause, never hesitating to remind his listeners that he was a preacher's son. He preferred to hold BSCP organizational meetings in churches when they could be obtained, and porters' meetings usually began with a prayer. Randolph's

35. E. D. Nixon, quoted in Studs Terkel, *Hard Times* (New York, 1970), 119.
36. Editorial, "The Failure of the Negro Church," *Messenger* (October, 1919), 6; A. Philip Randolph, "Negro Labor and the Church," in Jerome Davis (ed.), *Labor Speaks for Itself on Religion* (New York, 1929), 79–83.

willingness to adapt to the black church contrasted with the unwillingness of the Communist party to do the same, and perhaps accounted for
the fact that his espousal of mass action tactics ultimately prevailed while
the influence of the Communist party declined.[37]

But Randolph's gospel of labor solidarity was not readily accepted by
black workers, and he was regarded "by his own people as something of a
disturber of Negro peace." Randolph continued to maintain, however,
that only organization could change white labor's discrimination against
black workers in securing union cards and jobs, and make white workers
realize that the "salvation of the workers of both races are bound irre-
trievably together."[38]

Randolph believed race was the reason the Pullman Company refused
to negotiate with the porters' union, since Pullman had previously dealt
with labor unions. To sit down and bargain with blacks would imply
their equality—a concept Pullman was not ready to accept. Whites "cannot imagine that Negroes have grown up from children," wrote Randolph to colleague Milton Webster. "They can't believe that we are able
to handle our own affairs, that we are moving into the period of racial
self-reliance, nor can white people believe that there are any Negroes who
are not subject to corruption with money; hence the Brotherhood is a
marvel to them."[39]

Initially the BSCP seemed to be gaining support, and the Pullman
Company was sufficiently concerned to hire detectives to ferret out and
direct reprisals against union members. In 1928, when Pullman refused
to negotiate, Randolph was forced into calling for a strike. With justification, however, the BSCP was concerned the porters would not actually
walk out, and it did not have the organization or the finances to carry out
an extended strike. Therefore, on the advice of AFL head William Green,
who by now was befriending the BSCP, Randolph postponed the strike.[40]

After the aborted strike, morale fell, dues stopped coming in, and
membership dropped from its high of 11,684 in 1929. Publication of the

37. Randolph, "Reminiscences," 234, 221, 253; Victor Weybright, "Pullman Porters on
Parade," *Survey Graphic* (November, 1935), 574; Mark Naison, *Communists in Harlem
During the Depression* (Urbana, 1983), 281–82.
38. Stanley High, "Black Omens," *Saturday Evening Post*, June 4, 1938, pp. 14–15+;
Randolph, "Negro Labor and the Church," 79–83.
39. Randolph to Milton P. Webster, August 3, 1926, in BSCP Papers, CD.
40. Randolph, "Reminiscences," 263–67. New York *Times*, June 8, 1928, for the text
of a telegram from William Green to the BSCP.

Messenger ended, and the staff of organizers was decreased. The BSCP reached a low point in 1933 by which time membership had dwindled to 6,375, and to most observers it seemed that the union ceased to exist except in Randolph's imagination.[41]

But the political change in 1933, which brought in Franklin Roosevelt as president, had a profound effect on the fortunes of the BSCP, as it had upon all American labor. Roosevelt's New Deal sponsored the National Industrial Recovery Act, of which the most influential clause, Section 7A, gave specific guarantees to labor; workers were assured of the right to organize and select their own representatives free of interference from their employer. Without fear of reprisals for union activity, membership in the BSCP increased, as it did in other labor unions. The New Deal came just in time; without it the porters' union would most certainly have expired. But under the new, benevolent attitude toward labor, the BSCP finally won recognition from the Pullman Company. After twelve long, grueling years, on August 25, 1937, Pullman, one of the nation's most powerful corporations, signed a contract with the nation's first black union. A personal triumph for Randolph, the agreement brought some two million dollars in income to the porters and their families.[42]

Randolph did not obtain the victory unaided. He benefited from association with the AFL, as well as from the impetus to labor organization produced by Roosevelt's new labor laws. Once he became involved with organizing the porters, Randolph dropped his earlier radical stance of antipathy toward the AFL, arguing, "There is no hope for any group of workers without some power and history has shown that the labor movement is the source of power for workers." He now worked to forge an alliance with the Federation at the same time that he was striving to gain recognition from Pullman. He appealed to the AFL on the basis of self-interest: If blacks were not taken into the unions, he argued, no strike would be successful because an employer could always turn to the core of black strikebreakers.

When, because of a jurisdictional dispute, the Federation decided to issue separate federal charters to the various BSCP locals, Randolph was disturbed. Federal union status was one reason for black dissatisfaction with the AFL; federal unions were directly affiliated with the executive council, which could not negotiate wage agreements for any given craft.

41. Weybright, "Pullman Porters on Parade," 544; Kornweibel, *No Crystal Stair,* 272.
42. Randolph to Franklin D. Roosevelt, September 13, 1938, in FDR Papers.

A racist national union would thus become responsible for the economic protection of a black federal union, although the black union had no voice in the negotiations. Randolph agreed to the directly affiliated status for the BSCP with the understanding that the porters' union would receive an international charter as soon as the jurisdictional dispute was resolved.[43] Seven years were to pass, however, before the BSCP received its coveted international charter.

That the weak BSCP needed the AFL was obvious; the reasons for AFL interest in the black porters were more complex. William Green understood that masses of black laborers remaining outside the Federation constituted a body of potential strikebreakers that threatened the strength of the organization. In addition, he was concerned that the AFL exclusion of blacks gave the Communists ammunition with which to appeal to black labor. In his study of the BSCP, Brailsford Brazeal suggests that Green became kindly disposed toward Randolph's union because he believed it represented an acceptable alternative to communism. There is much merit to this view since Randolph was already on record as a confirmed anti-Communist with his public condemnations of the movement in the *Messenger.*[44]

While Randolph was still bitter over their role in splitting the *Messenger* group, the Communists tried to infiltrate the BSCP. They put on an intense campaign denouncing Randolph from press and platform on the basis that the porters' union was a form of segregation, and they tried to break up BSCP meetings in Harlem by sending "Negro Communists to them with chains on their hands and feet to demonstrate that Randolph was enslaving the Negroes again." According to writer Claude McKay, the Party was the "meanest enemy" of the porters' union. Convinced the Communists only used the American union movement for the "furtherance and advancement of the foreign policy of the Russian Communist State," Randolph remained constantly on guard to keep the Communists out of the BSCP. He utilized the porters to lead the fight among black workers against the Communist "menace" and the Communist goal of "rule or ruin" for trade unions. Randolph's success in preventing the Com-

43. Randolph, "Reminiscences," 223, 244; Randolph to James Weldon Johnson, n.d., in NAACP Papers; New York *Times,* March 30, 1928; Randolph to Webster, April 30, 1928, in BSCP Papers, CD.

44. Brazeal, *Brotherhood of Sleeping Car Porters,* 132; *Messenger* (August, 1923), 784, (July, 1925), 261; New York *Times,* January 5, 1926.

munists from penetrating the BSCP acted to reaffirm Green's "convictions that here was the man and the organization that could serve as an instrument for rallying Negro workers under the hegemony of the Federation."[45]

The importance of the AFL connection for the fledgling BSCP cannot be denied: The alliance brought the porters' union legitimacy, improved morale, expert advice, and a measure of financial aid. Yet, ideologically, its craft union structure and the racist policies of its member unions remained anathema to Randolph. Nevertheless, he did not switch allegiance when the Roosevelt administration's support for labor organization provided an alternative. Although the prevailing sentiment in the AFL held that unskilled workers were unorganizable, advocates of industrial organization, led by John L. Lewis of the United Mine Workers, set themselves up as a committee within the AFL and began organizing the mass-production industries in which the majority of blacks toiled. Rivalry between the AFL and the Committee on Industrial Organization (CIO) led to bitter conflict, and the CIO was formally expelled from the AFL at the 1937 convention, whereupon it became a rival federation.[46]

Because of the large numbers of blacks in the industries it represented, the CIO was forced to take a more egalitarian position toward black labor. Lewis, furthermore, had early befriended Randolph and the BSCP. Randolph later recalled being closer to Lewis than to any other man in the labor movement, including William Green.[47] Given Randolph's long history of advocating industrial unionism, the more liberal racial policies of the CIO, and his affection for Lewis, it might be expected that Randolph would have affiliated with the new federation.

Yet there is no record that Lewis ever invited Randolph's participation, nor that Randolph ever entertained the idea of changing affiliations.[48]

45. Claude McKay, *Harlem: Negro Metropolis* (New York, 1940), 220; A. Philip Randolph, "National Negro Labor Conference," *American Federationist* (September, 1930), 1054–55; *Black Worker*, February 15, 1930, p. 1, June 1, 1930, p. 1, August 1, 1930, p. 1; A. Philip Randolph, "One Union's Story," *American Federationist* (November, 1953), 20–23; Brazeal, *Brotherhood of Sleeping Car Porters*, 132.

46. Walter Galenson, *The CIO Challenge to the AFL* (Cambridge, Mass., 1960), 108. See also Thomas R. Brooks, *Toil and Trouble: A History of American Labor* (New York, 1971).

47. American Federation of Labor, *Report of Proceedings* (1932), 398–402; Randolph, "Pullman Porters Win," 299; Interview with A. Philip Randolph, September 4, 1973.

48. Melvin Dubofsky and Warren Van Tine do not even mention the issue in their biography of Lewis, nor is there any information on the subject in Randolph's, Lewis', or the CIO papers. See Dubofsky and Van Tine, *John L. Lewis: A Biography* (New York, 1977).

Perhaps Randolph felt he had bound the cause of the porters inextricably to Green and the AFL; although Green was not a crusader, he was supportive of Randolph and "sound on the racial question." Or perhaps, despite his profession of labor solidarity, Randolph believed that if he went over to the CIO, the BSCP would be swallowed up in a large racist, industrial railroad union. In the late 1930s the fight to obtain Pullman recognition of the BSCP was drawing to a head, and perhaps Randolph was too involved to consider a new alliance. When questioned on the subject, he maintained that he thought it wiser to remain inside the AFL and fight for greater equality than to leave and let the Federation continue its racist policies undisturbed. One must, said Randolph, break down discrimination "where it's at." There could be no emancipation for black people unless black workers had an emancipated labor organization, rather than merely a racial one, he argued.[49] Randolph may have sincerely believed his own rhetoric, or maybe his not taking advantage of the opportunity presented by the formation of the CIO was an early indication of his inner conflict between pragmatism and idealism.

Although he held the porters within the AFL, Randolph's goals quickly diverged from those of the Federation. Green was willing to use Randolph as a barrier to Communist penetration into black labor, but he was not prepared for Randolph's public exposure of racial discrimination within the AFL. Even before the BSCP had signed a contract with the Pullman Company, Randolph and the porters' union had become a force for racial justice in the American labor movement. After the Pullman victory, Randolph's civil rights activity within the AFL intensified; his newfound stature gave Randolph an operational power base from which to try to persuade the Federation to wipe out racial bias in all its unions. In what was to become his annual denunciation of racism within the AFL, Randolph argued, "Why should a Negro worker be penalized for being black; why should anybody be penalized for something over which he has no control?"[50] The AFL might continue its racially discriminatory policies, but Randolph intended to make certain these practices were widely publicized regardless of the tension it might cause between him and his most valuable ally.

The AFL, however, was forced to take a more tolerant position on civil rights in order to meet competition from the CIO. According to labor his-

49. Interview with Randolph, September 4, 1973.
50. American Federation of Labor, *Report of Proceedings* (1935), 810–811.

torian Walter Galenson, Randolph made an important contribution to
the liberalized posture of the Federation on black equality. Unfortunately,
the change in attitude among the top Federation officers was not mirrored
among the rank and file, who remained as antipathetic to blacks as ever.[51]

Randolph succeeded in cultivating his white supporters in the AFL
with a minimum of compromise of his principles. Although he downplayed his economic views and accepted the AFL craft basis of organization, he refused to sacrifice his racial beliefs; the BSCP remained black
led. Only when Randolph insisted he would rather withdraw the BSCP
from the AFL than submit to amalgamation with the racist Order of
Sleeping Car Conductors, which had decided to claim jurisdiction over
the porters, did the AFL executive council grant the BSCP's third application for a charter. The BSCP was finally granted sole jurisdiction over the
porters and awarded an international charter August 17, 1935—the first
charter awarded to an all-black union.[52]

One of the reasons for Randolph's success with the porters was his jour-
nalistic ability. After the aborted strike in November, 1929, when it
looked as though the BSCP would fail, Randolph succeeded in obtaining
money from the Garland Fund to begin publication of a new organ for
the union. Although historian Theodore Kornweibel maintains that the
strike experience convinced Randolph that the union would have to be
rebuilt by black hands alone, it was precisely at this time that he sought
help from the white Garland Fund.[53] Randolph called his new publication
the *Black Worker,* symbolic of the fact that it was devoted to the uplift of
all black labor, not just the porters. The *Black Worker* differed significantly from the *Messenger:* It was first and foremost a propaganda vehicle for the union and, therefore, far less ambitious in its aims. Using
newspaper rather than magazine format for lower overhead, it eliminated
all the frills of the *Messenger* and, unlike its predecessor, would never be
considered a model of black journalism.

From the beginning, Randolph used the *Black Worker* to indoctrinate
the porters with his views. According to his analysis in the first issue, "the

51. Ray Marshall, *The Negro and Organized Labor* (New York, 1965), 34–35; Galenson, *CIO Challenge to the AFL,* 626.
52. *Black Worker,* September 1, 1935, p. 1.
53. Kornweibel, *No Crystal Stair,* 272; Randolph, "Reminiscences," 101.

great, pressing and fundamental problem of the Negro is the awakening of the teeming millions of Black Workers" in order that "they may articulate and express their hopes, aspirations, yearnings and desires." The new vehicle aimed at increasing black self-esteem. In rhetoric reminiscent of Marcus Garvey, Randolph demanded, "UP WITH RACE PRIDE AND CLASS PRIDE. LONG LIVE THE SPIRIT OF THE 'NEW NEGRO'!"[54] During the Depression, when getting and keeping a job was the prime concern of most blacks, Randolph continually requested contributions for defense funds to prosecute cases against persons accused of lynching or to fight other antiblack abuses, and pressed the porters into attending protest meetings he called on behalf of one civil rights cause or another. The pages of the journal were liberally sprinkled with warnings of Communist tactics and methods, as well as exhortations to the porters to fight for their rights.

But the *Black Worker* was more than a political journal. Randolph also used it to influence the porters' moral values, counseling them to abide by such virtues as thrift, cleanliness, and abstinence from alcohol. Whether as a result of his prodding or of their own middle-class predilections, many porters owned their homes and sent their children to college, and pictures of offspring who were college graduates were proudly displayed in the *Black Worker*. Randolph's educational campaign led to BSCP members being better informed than most black workers; E. D. Nixon noted that when a porter talked, "Everybody listened because they knowed the porter been everywhere and they never been anywhere themselves."[55]

Randolph continuously stressed the theme that in founding the union, for the first time blacks had financed their cause with their own money. "Traditionally, Negroes have been expected, and generally have not failed to beg for what they need and want," he noted. The porters had broken this tradition, putting up a half million dollars of their own meager earnings in the twelve-year struggle preceding their victory. Randolph, Milton Webster, Ashley Totten, Bennie Smith, C. L. Dellums, and a few other veteran aides had borne the brunt of the sacrifice; none had received any pay for over half the life of the BSCP. Such sacrifices equipped the union

54. *Black Worker,* November 15, 1929, pp. 4, 1, 3.
55. Interview with Maida Springer Kemp, October 18, 1972; E. D. Nixon, quoted in Terkel, *Hard Times,* 118. See also Richard Thrulelsen, "Men at Work: Pullman Porter," *Saturday Evening Post,* May 21, 1949, p. 38+.

members to play a leadership role in black circles and to win respect, rather than pity, from their white friends. White respect for black achievement indeed constituted a new order.[56]

In the process of organizing and winning recognition for the BSCP, Randolph developed a loyal following that crowned him with names like "Mr. Black Labor" and "St. Philip of the Pullman Porters." *Opportunity,* the organ of the NUL, lauded him as "a great leader." Randolph's feat also received recognition in the white press. Obtaining a contract from Pullman was acknowledged by the *Saturday Evening Post* as the most important achievement that "the Negro on his own has accomplished in the field of labor organization." As the victory over the Pullman Company gave Randolph enormous prestige in both the black and white communities, the BSCP came to wield influence far greater than its limited membership warranted. The time when all Pullman porters were indiscriminately called "George" was nearing an end, for Randolph brought them the respect of the traveling public and confidence in themselves. The value of the union, in Randolph's opinion, lay in its demonstration that blacks indeed possessed a "spirit of self-help, self-initiative, and self-reliance." Almost from its inception Randolph proclaimed, "Never again will Negroes permit white people to select their leaders for them." The BSCP, he maintained, was a black movement that "stands for the self-expression and interest of Negroes by Negroes for Negroes."[57]

Now a prominent spokesman, in addition to leading the BSCP in negotiations, Randolph appeared in other forums new to black participation. He addressed conventions of the AFL, castigating his benefactors for their unfair racial policies, and he testified before agencies of the federal government interpreting the black position. When a black riot directed against white shopowners exploded in Harlem in 1935, Mayor Fiorello LaGuardia appointed Randolph a member of the New York City Commission on Race.[58]

In realizing his triumph, Randolph had the benefit of a group of powerful organizers and intermediary leaders within the BSCP, the most im-

56. *Black Worker,* October, 1937, p. 8.

57. Elmer Anderson Carter, "In the News Column: A. Philip Randolph," *Opportunity* (October, 1937), 294; High, "Black Omens," 38; Randolph to Webster, August 27, 1928, in BSCP Papers, CD.

58. Naison, *Communists in Harlem,* 140–50.

portant of whom was Milton Webster, head of the Chicago division. Despite the fact that Webster did not believe in socialism, a close working partnership, which historian William Harris has called a "symbiotic relationship," developed between Randolph and Webster.[59] Other secondary leaders such as B. F. McLaurin, Totten, Dellums, and Bennie Smith would prove of enormous value in Randolph's subsequent equality movements, enabling the union head to devote himself to public relations on a nationwide scale while they took care of the day-to-day operation of the BSCP. Only because he had such capable assistants would Randolph be able to spend so much time on civil rights activity.

Ironically, however, the BSCP was not run as a democratic organization. Although the union promoted better pay and working conditions, its leaders told the porters how to vote in order that they might keep their own positions—a practice also employed by the "sham" company union they overthrew. Indeed, Randolph and Webster ran the union as their own personal fiefdom. Even the selection of delegates for BSCP conventions was a hollow ritual.[60] Such autocratic leadership ill prepared Randolph for sharing decision-making power in his future civil rights organizations.

But any weaknesses in Randolph's leadership ability were not apparent in 1935; rather, his synthesis of labor solidarity and race militancy reached beyond the porters, appealing to a group of young black intellectuals. John P. Davis, Robert C. Weaver, Abram L. Harris, Ralph Bunche, and E. Franklin Frazier, among others, had become disenchanted by the failure of the established black rights organizations to cope with the economic distress of the Depression. Led by Davis, they proposed a National Negro Congress (NNC) and turned to Randolph as a prestigious name to head their new organization.[61]

59. Randolph, "Reminiscences," 275–76; Harris, *Keeping the Faith*.
60. See BSCP Papers, CD.
61. Although there has been no full-scale study of the NNC, several authors discuss the organization as part of their treatment of black life in the 1930s: Horace R. Cayton and George S. Mitchell, *Black Workers and the New Unions* (Chapel Hill, 1939); Wilson Record, *The Negro and the Communist Party* (Chapel Hill, 1951); and *Race and Radicalism* (Ithaca, N.Y., 1964); Cruse, *Crisis of the Negro Intellectual;* Irving Howe and Lewis Coser, *The American Communist Party: A Critical History* (1962; rpr. New York, 1974); Francis L. Broderick and August Meier (eds.), *Negro Protest Thought in the Twentieth Century* (Indianapolis, 1965); Gunnar Myrdal, *An American Dilemma* (New York, 1944); Raymond Wolters, *Negroes and the Great Depression: The Problem of Economic Recovery* (Westport, Conn., 1970). In 1970, in a "reassessment" of the NNC, Lawrence Wittner ar-

While all Americans were hard hit, the Depression proved catastrophic for black Americans. The majority of blacks had not shared in the prosperity of the 1920s; indeed, a common comment of the time was, "Negroes never knew the Depression started." As "last hired and first fired," they found themselves completely helpless in an economy that could not provide jobs for whites. A conference at Howard University in May, 1935, produced evidence that the Depression and New Deal "recovery" policies were forcing blacks into an even-lower economic and social position. Times were so bad that W. E. B. Du Bois felt compelled to emphasize economics, and began to counsel "voluntary self-segregation" and an "economic cooperative commonwealth" for the black community. The integrationist and noneconomically oriented NAACP could not tolerate this stance, which caused Du Bois's ouster as editor of the association's organ, the *Crisis*, in 1934.[62]

Although the Roosevelt administration was more attentive to the needs of minorities than any of its predecessors, it was not free from the misconception of Afro-American inferiority. With almost one-third of the black population on public assistance by 1935, the task of relief was monumental. Despite the sympathetic posture of Eleanor Roosevelt and the appointment of several blacks to advisory positions, lower minimum wage levels were designated for laboring-class blacks than for whites; the Tennessee Valley Authority recruited blacks only for unskilled jobs and would not train them in its apprenticeship programs; and the crop-reduction policy designed to help whites forced black sharecroppers and tenants from their farms since, with fewer crops to grow, their labor was not needed. Where minimum wage and maximum hours standards mandated by National Recovery Administration codes were enforced, blacks lost jobs because employers preferred hiring whites to paying blacks at

gued that it was not until the third NNC convention in 1940 that Communist and CIO influences became dominant. Based upon the NNC and NAACP papers, as well as sociological concepts such as "skills" and "resources," the interpretation represented here differs significantly from Wittner's (Wittner, "The National Negro Congress: A Reassessment," *American Quarterly*, XXII (Fall, 1970), 883–901). For documentation of Communist participation in the founding of the Detroit chapter of the NNC, see August Meier and Elliott Rudwick, *Black Detroit and the Rise of the UAW* (New York, 1979), 28–29, 45–50.

62. Robert L. Zangrando, *The NAACP Crusade Against Lynching, 1909–1950* (Philadelphia, 1980), 107–10; Lester B. Granger, "The National Negro Congress: An Interpretation," *Opportunity* (May, 1936), 151–53; Cruse, *Plural but Equal*, 383.

the higher rate. Even social security did not cover most blacks, because they worked in domestic and agricultural occupations. Restrictive covenants in housing were upheld by the Federal Housing Administration, and under the system of local administration of welfare, southern blacks seldom received the relief benefits earmarked for them by the federal government. Yet because of the strength of the southern bloc in Congress, the president refused to condemn social discrimination and segregation.

Under these circumstances a unified approach, such as that projected by the NNC, had great appeal for the young black intellectuals, who were convinced that the problems of Afro-Americans were attributable to essentially the same economic forces oppressing white workers and who criticized the older black leaders for placing too much emphasis on race.[63] Even blacks who were part of the Roosevelt administration were disillusioned by the New Deal's failure to cope with the special problems of Afro-Americans. These intellectuals, among whom Ralph Bunche was prominent, urged greater concentration on economics and interracial class solidarity to counter what they saw as the inability of New Deal programs to improve the lowly condition of blacks.[64] Thus Randolph was part of a growing trend of concern with economic issues among black leaders in the 1930s. He was, however, the only labor leader of the group.

Regardless of their ideology, urban blacks began to take to the streets in their distress. This situation provided fertile ground for the American Communist party, which, having changed its approach toward Afro-Americans, made inroads into the black community. At first envisioning a separate black state in the South, in response to the threat posed by Hitler the Party modified its strategy to a United Front Against Fascism in the 1930s. By denouncing segregation and discrimination in jobs, housing, public accommodations, and travel—all issues ignored by other whites—

63. See James O. Young, *Black Writers of the Thirties* (Baton Rouge, 1973), especially Chap. 2.

64. Ralph J. Bunche, "The Programs of Organizations Devoted to the Improvement of the Status of the American Negro," *Journal of Negro Education*, VIII (July, 1939), 543; Bunche, "A Critical Analysis of the Tactics and Programs of Minority Groups," *Journal of Negro Education*, IV (July, 1935), 308–20; Zangrando, *NAACP Crusade Against Lynching*, 107–10; Nancy J. Weiss, *Farewell to the Party of Lincoln: Black Politics in the Age of FDR* (Princeton, 1983), 39–79; 135–58. For an analysis of the interrelationship between liberal white and black thought and action vis-à-vis New Deal reform and black civil rights, see John B. Kirby, *Black Americans in the Roosevelt Era: Liberalism and Race* (Knoxville, 1980).

the Communists secured the allegiance of a number of prominent blacks during the United Front era, the time of greatest Communist gain in the United States. The Communists helped focus the militancy in some black movements, especially rent strikes, but other efforts, such as the "Don't Buy Where You Can't Work" campaigns, arose indigenously in the black communities. The growing success in labor organization and the greater display of mass-protest tactics made the established black organizations more receptive to an alliance with labor and the left, while the broad organizational base of the suggested NNC made it an ideal vehicle for the Communists' new program.[65]

Naïvely, its founders believed the NNC could unify the diverse groups and arouse the black masses to effective action.[66] They envisioned the NNC as an umbrella organization cutting across political alignments and philosophies to include all types of black groups and unite them on a fundamental program to deal with the economic, political, and social problems of Afro-Americans in the Depression. By tapping Randolph for the presidency, the founders hoped that black labor would become an integral component of the organization.

For his part, Randolph believed that it was important for black organizations to work together to improve the living conditions of the race, and the Communists' change to the United Front line facilitated his decision to work in cooperation with them. He therefore grasped at the NNC, thinking it would "give expression to collective judgements on the major problems confronting Black Americans." Its economic orientation appealed to him, as did the fact that it did not propose to absorb existing black organizations, but rather to "serve as a cementing force to bring them together and express the organized will" of the black community.[67]

Initiated in 1935, the NNC held three major conventions by 1940, the year in which Randolph's association with the organization ended. In addition, during this period local councils coordinated activities like the "Don't Buy" campaigns, the "Jobs for Negroes" movement, and rent strikes. All these efforts employed the boycott and picketing strategies, which, in the view of participant Ralph Bunche, gave blacks "some ink-

---

65. Naison, *Communists in Harlem*, Chap. 6; Harvard Sitkoff, *A New Deal for Blacks: The Emergence of Civil Rights as a National Issue, Volume I: The Depression Decade* (New York, 1978), Chap. 6.
66. Granger, "The National Negro Congress: An Interpretation," 151–53.
67. *Black Worker*, September 1, 1935, p. 3.

ling" of their "latent economic power and an acquaintance with the recognized weapons of labor." [68]

At first the NNC was backed by a broad spectrum of the Afro-American
community, including churchmen, teachers, social workers, and lawyers.
In an effort to attract the widest possible following, its founders, because
of the mixed makeup of the constituent groups, insisted that it remain
interracial. Secretary John P. Davis, a black lawyer and activist with close
ties to the Communist party, even reprimanded an NNC local for its attempt to exclude a group with an interracial membership because such
action would prevent affiliation with the NAACP and other "worthy
organizations." [69]

The low level of income and skills in the black community constituted
a formidable problem for the NNC. Its national office was continuously
short of money, and much of Davis' time and Randolph's contribution
went to fund-raising efforts. The laborious task of raising revenue from
folks who found five- and ten-cent stamps too "HIGH" made it most
difficult to carry out the organization's program and illuminated the obstacles to mounting a black self-help federation in the depths of the
Depression.[70]

To help staff local councils, Davis drew on contacts from his previous
black rights organization, the Joint Committee on National Recovery.
The NAACP proved a fruitful source for workers, even though it never
affiliated with the NNC, and the NUL supplied Lester Granger, among
others. Black Communists were also active members, as were Randolph's
BSCP lieutenants, who thereby gained experience in secondary-level leadership of a civil rights organization. McLaurin, Dellums, and Totten all
actively participated, but Webster proved obdurate because he was gener-

68. John Hope Franklin, *From Slavery to Freedom: A History of Negro Americans* (4th
ed.; New York, 1974), 408; August Meier and Elliott Rudwick, *Along the Color Line: Explorations in the Black Experience* (Urbana, 1976), Chap. 14; Bunche, "Programs of Organizations," 543.

69. Record, *Negro and Communist Party*, 155; Cayton and Mitchell, *Black Workers
and New Unions*, 416; John P. Davis to Frank Griffin, November 17, 1938, in NNC Papers.
Prominent sponsors were Elmer Carter of the NUL and M. O. Bousfield of the Rosenwald
Fund.

70. See, for example, Mattie L. Green to Davis, October 3, 1935, Robert Gunkel to
U. Simpson Tate, January 27, 1936, E. Ethelred Ricks to U. Simpson Tate, January 20, 1936,
all in NNC Papers.

ally opposed "to anything which is not strictly labor." Randolph admitted "frankly" that Webster was "not sold on the Congress." Noting that the BSCP's annual National Negro Labor Conference for 1936 had to be postponed because of the NNC, Randolph remarked that "Brother Webster . . . never warmed up to this." Webster's attitude caused at least one NNC member to call him "a bastard"; Randolph, nevertheless, suggested that Davis approach Webster and try to "sell" him on the NNC.[71] Winning Webster's active support would be a key to the success in Chicago of the later March on Washington Movement.

Despite participation by individuals, the NNC had a problem forging a coalition of black organizations from its inception. Although there was initial enthusiasm, it quickly became obvious that the sponsoring groups feared one another's infringement on their own programs, thus making the divisions among them greater than any unifying factor. The black church was the first group in the NNC coalition to become openly dissatisfied. After they had contributed financially to the organization, church leaders voiced vigorous resentment that the names of no well-known preachers were found among the selection of persons to "strike keynotes or champion causes."[72] The reluctance of the NAACP to become a sponsor presented an even-greater obstacle to the federated organization. Although the NUL actively participated, the NNC leaders felt the necessity of NAACP cooperation. Pressured by some of his own staff members to become more involved in economics, NAACP head Walter White nevertheless retained reservations about John P. Davis stemming from the NAACP's financial disputes with Davis' previous organization.

The Call to the First Congress was designed to alleviate organizational fears of displacement: "The NATIONAL NEGRO CONGRESS will be no new organization, nor does it seek to usurp the work of existing organizations." In a personal letter to White, Davis assured him the NNC in no way intended to supplant the "fine work" of the NAACP. Alluding to their past problems, Davis also reassured White that endorsement of the NNC would entail no greater financial contribution than the NAACP cared to make. Despite such reassurances, the association remained con-

71. Randolph to Davis, December 28, 1935, Eleanor Rye to Davis, August 27, 1936, Rye to Davis, [after August 27, 1936], all *ibid.*
72. Chicago *Defender*, February 15, 1936.

cerned about organizational autonomy. Fresh from conflict with the Communist party over the Scottsboro case, the NAACP was apprehensive of the NNC's left-wing backing, and its board of directors decided to neither participate in nor endorse the NNC.[73]

White's fears of "duplication" received confirmation when the NNC made the fight for antilynching legislation a priority measure for 1938. The NNC decision to enter the antilynching field was undoubtedly prompted by the fact that "like the NAACP, the Congress had discovered that the crusade against lynching was the surest way to raise badly needed funds." This policy decision not only upset the NAACP but caused dissension within the NNC ranks; to those belonging to both groups, the issue became a test of organizational loyalty.[74]

Despite those problems, Randolph constantly tried to make peace between the two groups. Although White refused to meet with NNC officials on the antilynching issue, Randolph and White managed to maintain their cordial personal relations. While repudiating Davis, NAACP officers excused Randolph's affiliation with him, apparently feeling Randolph had been taken in by Davis' "trickery."[75] Thus while giving him a wider audience for his ideas, affiliation with the NNC did not jeopardize Randolph's prestige with the established race-advancement organizations.

Still, the relations between the NAACP and the NNC illustrated the problems inherent in a coalition of black groups. The two organizations appeared to enjoy complementarity of resources, with the NNC able to contribute economic expertise and to tap a labor constituency that the NAACP had no other way of reaching, while the NAACP was able to supply middle-class adherents and a more steady source of income. Yet gains for the NNC were perceived as losses by the NAACP, which feared the younger organization as a potential threat to its influence in the black community and as a competitor for the always-short supply of available funds.

73. Call for National Negro Congress, 1936 [should be 1935], Davis to White, December 20, 1935, both in NAACP Papers; Zangrando, *NAACP Crusade Against Lynching*, 99–101.

74. Wolters, *Negroes and Great Depression*, 365; Zangrando, *NAACP Crusade Against Lynching*, 80–83, 110; Telegram, Arthur Huff Fauset to Davis, March 19, 1938, in NNC Papers; White to Gertrude B. Stone, March 29, 1938, in NAACP Papers.

75. See, for example, Randolph to White, June 22, 26, 1937, both in NAACP Papers; Randolph to Davis, May 11, 1938, in NNC Papers; note signed J. W., appended to form letter from Randolph dated December 7, 1937, in NAACP Papers.

From the NNC's inception, however, money, clerical help, and other assistance came from white and racially mixed groups. Largely because the organization experienced so much difficulty in obtaining funds, it drew toward a closer alliance with the CIO and the Communist party. Affiliation with the CIO meant a definite sum of money ("$50,000 every two weeks" for the Chicago branch) could be depended on to meet expenses, so by December, 1936, Davis had begun to place primary emphasis on CIO work.[76]

Although Communists neither dominated nor controlled the NNC's sponsoring committee in the organizational stage, they were prominent in the NNC from the outset. Communist ability to provide organized forces, experienced personnel, and a variety of skills assured the party a powerful role. Even before the First Congress took place, rumors of association with the Party abounded, prompting the organizers to declare, "We are affiliated with no other political organization, and we would suggest that such rumors be disregarded." The high visibility of the Communists almost caused cancellation of the First Congress in Chicago.[77] But since the NAACP would not be pushed into taking a more aggressive stance on black economic problems, black intellectuals like Randolph, Bunche, and Granger, who were also economic activists, had little choice in their search for allies. Besides, they realized that Communists during the United Front era played a role in prodding the American conscience on racial equality similar to that played by Randolph within the AFL.

Prior to the summer of 1939, the Communist party did not interfere overtly in the working of the NNC because the two organizations shared the same goals. The situation changed, however, when the party line abruptly shifted following the signing of the Nazi-Soviet pact in August, 1939. Instead of pressing for a united front, the Communists now attacked Roosevelt's pro-Allied foreign policy stand.

Randolph's address to the Third Congress in April, 1940, indicated that he was unaware that the NNC had become totally dominated by the

76. ANP Release, February 15, 1936, pp. 2–3; Memorandum to the Board of Directors on the National Negro Congress from Mr. Wilkins, March 9, 1936, in NAACP Papers; Eleanor Rye to Davis, August 12, 1936, Randolph to Davis, September 10, 1936, both in NNC Papers.

77. U. Simpson Tate to F. Griffin, December 24, 1935, in NNC Papers; Chicago *Defender*, February 8, 1936; ANP Release, February 15, 1936, p. 5.

Communists. In response to condemnation of the NNC as a Communist front, Randolph said, "We brand this charge as false." The fact that the NNC supported some policies and movements that the Communists supported did not prove that the organization was Communist, according to Randolph. Instead it might "prove that the Communists propose some policies that are sound." Asserting that "Negroes cannot afford to add to the handicap of being *black* the handicap of being *Red*," Randolph stated that he personally "would not be a member of the Negro Congress, or any other organization which was a Communist Front," and urged the delegates to do everything possible to remove the Communist stigma from the NNC in the public mind.[78]

But during the debate on the resolutions, Randolph learned that Communists indeed controlled the Congress. A resolution condemning the administration's foreign policy was passed by an overwhelming majority after a speaker who tried to defend Roosevelt was hissed and booed.[79] Over Randolph's objections, the Third Congress also passed a resolution to accept a proposal made by John L. Lewis to cooperate with Labor's Non-Partisan League, a political action group founded by Lewis and other CIO leaders in 1936. Despite his gratitude to Lewis for helping the porters' union, Randolph protested that acceptance of the proposal would split the mass action of the NNC, and to show his sincerity, he added that he would be just as opposed to tying the NNC to the AFL. But it was too late. The Communist-packed Third Congress was anti-Roosevelt and pro-CIO.

After the passage of the antiadministration resolutions, Randolph refused reelection as president of the NNC. He noted that rather than disproving the charge that the NNC was a Communist front, "the Congress has brilliantly succeeded in giving the charge every appearance of truth and validity. I am convinced that until the stigma of the Communist Front is wiped from the Congress, it will never rally the masses of the Negro people. . . . The American Negro will not long follow any organization which accepts dictation and control from the Communist Party." Noting that over one-quarter of the 1,200 delegates were white, Randolph added: "The American Negro will not long follow any organization which accepts dictation and control from any white organization. . . . I am un-

78. A. Philip Randolph, Pamphlet, *The World Crisis and the Negro People Today,* n.d., 19, 23–24.
79. New York *Times,* April 29, 1940.

alterably opposed to having a Negro organization, which is supposed to be fighting the battles of the race, depending for its main income upon a source outside the Negro people themselves."[80]

Although Randolph realized that "where you get your money you also get your ideas and control," he was never able to solve the dilemma this truism posed for a minority-group spokesman. If a black leader decided upon an alliance with a dominant-group organization, he risked the danger of corruption of goals and principles or even outright takeover of his movement, as Randolph learned from his experience with the NNC. The difficulty arose because the relationship was not a partnership of equals, but rather one of client to patron. Alternatively, if a black leader decided against an alliance with the white majority, he was then faced with the almost insurmountable obstacles of paucity of skills and resources, and inaccessibility to decision-making power in the minority community. Afro-Americans had faced this quandary since emancipation. As interracial organizations, both the NAACP and the NNC were ultimately subject to their white benefactors. The liberal patrons of the NAACP, however, were willing to train a cadre of blacks with the necessary skills and, in time, turn the leadership of the organization over to them.[81] In contrast, the Communist patrons of the NNC were only interested in utilizing the organization for their own purposes.

Understanding that the goals of the patrons were not always identical to those of their client, Randolph believed that "salvation for a race, nation or class must come from within. Freedom is never granted; it is won. Justice is never given; it is exacted." Nevertheless, he displayed a kind of schizophrenia regarding white allies. On the one hand Randolph decreed: "In very truth, the Negro must save himself. He must depend on his own right arm." On the other, he qualified his assertion by adding, *"together with the cooperation of his true white friends."*[82] Thus the predicament: The powerless black minority on its own could not mount an effective movement for liberation; some aid from the dominant group appeared to be a necessity. The key was finding a white ally, as Randolph thought he

80. A. Philip Randolph, "Why I Would Not Stand for Re-election in the National Negro Congress," *American Federationist* (July, 1940), 24–25; *Black Worker*, May, 1940; New York *Times*, April 29, 1940; *Black Worker*, August, 1940, p. 4.

81. See Weiss, "From Black Separatism to Interracial Cooperation," 76, for support of this view. See also Meier and Rudwick, *Along the Color Line*, Chap. 5.

82. A. Philip Randolph, "Negro Congress Urges Co-Racialists to Organize Themselves for Democracy," *New Leader*, May 11, 1940. Emphasis added.

had for the porters, who would allow the minority-group leaders to maintain control of their own movement.

Randolph was physically incapacitated during most of the NNC's active period, the strenuous fight to obtain recognition of the BSCP from Pullman having taken its toll on his health. He had some input in decision making during the early days of the NNC, although he was too ill to attend the First Congress and his address had to be read by a stand-in.[83] His union activities also prevented him from becoming deeply involved with the routine workings of the organization. While Davis supplied the day-to-day leadership, Randolph was more of a figurehead, his association with the NNC intended to give the group an air of respectability and to enable the organizers to capitalize on his reputation. Prior to the Third Congress, Randolph willingly played this role by entreating influential members of the NAACP and the NUL to engage in "closer cooperation" with the NNC.[84]

Given Randolph's illness and the demands of his union organizing, editorship of the *Black Worker,* and civil rights work both inside and outside the AFL, it is not difficult to understand how the NNC could have been subverted without his knowledge. Why the harassed Randolph took on the added responsibility of the NNC in the first place is in part explained by George Schuyler, who asserts that Randolph accepted the presidency of the NNC because, despite his notoriety, he "had never quite been accepted by the NAACP Brahmins up to that time, and he was panting for leadership."[85] But another part of the explanation lies in the fact that Randolph always had a vision of race leadership that extended beyond the porters. When the NNC was proposed, because of its economic thrust it seemed to present the ideal vehicle for the realization of that vision.

The NNC thus marked a transitional stage in Randolph's quest for greater black equality in America. Operating in the depths of economic disaster, the organization attempted to bring all sections of the black

---

83. See *Official Proceedings of the National Negro Congress* (Chicago, February 15–16, 1936), and *Official Proceedings of the Second National Negro Congress* (Philadelphia, October 15, 16, 17, 1937), for decisions taken by the NNC that clearly reflect Randolph's input, and *Black Worker,* August, 1938, p. 1; Randolph to Davis, July 19, 1938, in NNC Papers.

84. See correspondence from Randolph to Walter White and Lester Granger, 1936–38, in NAACP Papers and NUL Papers.

85. Schuyler, *Black and Conservative,* 243.

community together to make unified demands on the government. No one before Randolph had quite visualized American blacks utilizing group pressure to push for their share of the nation's economic pie. His effort to form coalitions among black groups also furthered Randolph's goal of requiring the government to take cognizance of Afro-Americans as a distinct ethnic group on a par with other ethnic groups in American society. The NNC, furthermore, provided Randolph with a nationwide forum to teach blacks his ideas of race protest. The black community realized that here was no old-fashioned defensive leader, but rather a civil rights leader cast from a unique mold and demanding new rights for blacks.

During his early career as a street-corner orator and Socialist party organizer, Randolph had honed his speaking and writing skills. Eloquent statements like "the ineradicable faces of four million mulattoes" provide testimony that there has always been "social equality galore after dark," were unmatched by any other black spokesman of the time.[86] Emerging as the first black labor leader in the country, he molded a unified, disciplined union membership, and forged a lasting alliance with the organized labor movement, learning in the process to play down his socialism in public. Although he was unwavering in his economic beliefs, he put aside his commitment to pacifism, never as strong, during the fight against fascism. Presidency of the NNC gave him practical civil rights experience and also reinforced his animosity toward the Communists. Hence by the end of the 1930s, Randolph was ready to take on the role of civil rights leader.

As Harvard Sitkoff has demonstrated, civil rights emerged as a national issue during the New Deal years.[87] Rather than denying responsibility for unemployment relief and remaining blind to deprivation of civil rights, the many commissions and agencies of the New Deal proved more rational, dependable, and, consequently, more amenable to deciding minority-group issues on their merits than did local authorities and private employers characterized by emotional racism and paternalism. His experience with the National Labor Relations Board on behalf of the porters

86. *Messenger* (March, 1919), 9–10.
87. Sitkoff, *A New Deal for Blacks.* The historiographical debate between Nancy Weiss and Harvard Sitkoff regarding the New Deal record on race relations is extraneous to this work. See Weiss, *Farewell to the Party of Lincoln,* and Sitkoff, *A New Deal for Blacks.*

taught Randolph the advantages of federal intercession, even though bringing cases before federal agencies involved enormous expenditures for poor minority groups.[88]

The New Deal also fostered labor organization, which in turn gave birth to the industrial union movement. Not only were the racial practices of the CIO more liberal, but the exposure given to labor-organizing battles by the popular media brought legitimacy to tactics such as the sit-down strike and picketing—a development that would have great significance for Randolph's later mass action strategies for civil rights. By making labor struggles and their tactics familiar, mass communications helped create a new constituency for organizations emerging in the black communities in response to the overwhelming hardships of the Depression. Young black academics called for a radical reorientation to economic issues, but the old black betterment organizations refused to modify their style. While successful early in the decade at channeling black militancy and popularizing civil rights concerns, the American Communist party later lost credibility among American blacks because of its blind following of Moscow's line on foreign policy.[89]

Randolph, understanding that novel strategies were called for, fused economic concerns with militancy on racial questions. That he came to race leadership through the trade union movement made him a different type of leader; he was not a politician indebted to the city machine that bestowed favors upon him, nor was he a preacher or educator whose institution depended upon the donations of white businessmen to keep its doors open. He did not come up through the ranks of an established, integrated race-advancement group. While his consequent lack of administrative training would plague all his civil rights undertakings, the fact that Randolph achieved prominence as the first black union leader left him essentially unencumbered in terms of either traditions or debts to white patrons. Time would prove that the trade union alliance had its own drawbacks, but that was not at all apparent in the 1930s. In the meantime, he was free to strike out in new directions.

88. See Weiss, *Farewell to the Party of Lincoln*, 62.
89. Sitkoff, *A New Deal for Blacks*, Chap. 6.

II / Let the Negro Masses March

Randolph transcended the debacle of the NNC, and his career reached its zenith on two fronts in the early 1940s: first, wartime demands for rail service brought the BSCP to its peak of influence, and second, he became an acknowledged civil rights leader. Taking advantage of the wartime atmosphere that created a need for unity on the home front, Randolph utilized the Afro-Americans' most potent weapon, mass manpower, to force concessions from the president of the United States. Coming to the fore at a time when black anger at discrimination and unemployment reached the boiling point, Randolph was able to capitalize on "situational charisma." In a time of acute adversity his normally nonmessianic personality invoked a charismatic response, and his leadership was perceived as a means of salvation from distress.[1]

Not coincidentally, Randolph's rise to prominence coincided with unprecedented change in the black community. By the hundreds of thousands, black men and women left the farms of the rural South for the more lucrative defense jobs of the urban North, and thousands more joined the armed services. But the arrival of large numbers of Afro-Americans in northern cities intensified white racism, which in turn fed black militance. Randolph took advantage of this black anger in the early 1940s, as he had earlier utilized the turbulence of the Depression, to found his own equality movement. His first rights organization displayed both the strengths and weaknesses of his leadership style as it foreshadowed the ideologies and strategies of the midcentury civil rights movement.

1. Tucker, "The Theory of Charismatic Leadership," 69–94.

By the fall of 1940, the American economy, fueled by war contracts, was beginning to emerge from the Depression. The defense boom helped whites, but Afro-Americans, denied the opportunity to apply for defense jobs because of racial discrimination, remained on the relief rolls in inordinant numbers. Government-instituted training programs excluded blacks with the rationale that it was foolish to train them; even those with training were not considered for skilled positions. Afro-American resentment reached fever pitch as black soldiers were drafted under a discriminatory quota system, trained in segregated camps, and assigned to menial duties. If unfortunate enough to be stationed in a southern town, black troops found their loyalty repaid with insults and brutality. The Red Cross even segregated black blood.

In September, 1940, shortly after passage of the Selective Service Act, Randolph, Walter White of the NAACP, and T. Arnold Hill of the NUL met with President Roosevelt to discuss discrimination against blacks in the armed services and defense industries. They came away without any tangible gains, although the president promised to investigate discriminatory methods.[2] Afro-American frustration increased following the conference, and the black press intensified the bitter tone with which it delineated the facts of black deprivation. More than 250,000 new defense jobs were closed to Afro-Americans regardless of their qualifications; moreover, they were denied placement even in unskilled jobs. Only 240 of 107,000 workers employed in the aircraft industry were black. The 56 St. Louis factories that had been awarded war contracts employed an average of only 3 blacks each. In response to a United States Employment Service inquiry, more than 50 percent of the defense industries questioned stated they would not hire blacks. Although building contractors begged for construction workers, they refused to consider some 75,000 experienced black carpenters, painters, plasterers, cement workers, bricklayers, and electricians. When blacks demanded the elimination of the union color barrier at Boeing Aircraft in Seattle, the district organizer for the International Association of Machinists resisted, saying, "Labor has been

2. See Walter White to David Niles, September 19, 1940, Telegram, White to General Edwin M. Watson, September 20, 1940, Watson to White, September 19, 1940, Confidential Memorandum for General Watson from S.T.E. [Steven T. Early], September 19, 1940, all in FDR Papers; Walter White, *A Man Called White* (New York, 1948), 187–88. For the exchange of letters between Randolph and Roosevelt on the statement of War Department policy, see *Black Worker*, November, 1940, p. 3.

asked to make many sacrifices in the war and has made them gladly, but this sacrifice [the admission of black members] is too great."[3]

Thus, despite acute labor shortages, the color bar held fast as labor unions, management, and the government all systematically excluded blacks from job opportunities. Both former liberal white allies and the administration had become preoccupied with winning the war and ignored the Afro-American job crisis. While black antagonism was on the rise, the white press remained silent on the issue.

When the meeting with Roosevelt failed to produce results, Randolph concluded that he and other black leaders had exhausted the conference method of handling black problems; new strategies were imperative. "I think we ought to get 10,000 Negroes and march down Pennsylvania Avenue asking for jobs in defense plants and integration of the armed forces. It would shake up Washington," Randolph told Milton Webster. He conceived of the march as a show of black mass power so enormous the government could not ignore it. The idea was not different in kind— there had been marches before—but it differed significantly in scope. Because blacks were "supposed to be just scared and unorganizable," such a march, Randolph anticipated, "would wake up and shock official Washington as it has never been shocked before."[4]

Envisioning participation from all segments of the black community and from all sections of the country, by March, 1941, Randolph was educating readers of the *Black Worker* to his plan. He built his new movement of protest and pressure by explaining its aims and urging support in speeches and articles in the black press, which, with the exception of the Pittsburgh *Courier,* was generally supportive. According to the Chicago *Defender,* "This is the time, the place, the issue and the method."[5]

The White House had been alerted in January that Randolph had suggested a black march on the Capital. Yet, despite intense interest and activity within the black community, the government did not manifest any concern and refused to grant the Afro-American leaders another meeting with the president in the spring. Then Randolph sent letters to Roosevelt

3. Murray Kempton, *Part of Our Time* (New York, 1955), 249; Roi Ottley, *New World A-Coming* (New York, 1943), 289–90.
4. Dufty, "A Post Portrait," December 30, 1959; Randolph to author, July 13, 1973; Chicago *Defender,* February 1, 1941.
5. Ira F. Lewis to Randolph, June 9, 19, 1941, both in NAACP Papers; Chicago *Defender,* June 21, 1941.

and other government officials requesting them to address the marchers
at the Lincoln Memorial following the march, making the administration
realize it could no longer pretend the march threat did not exist. Word
came from "as high as the cabinet itself, that this proposed march is disturbing the administration."[6] Randolph was introducing new rules into
the old clientage politics game. Blacks were not supposed to make demands; they had always begged in the past. The white decision makers,
accustomed to dealing with blacks as clients, did not know how to react
to pressure tactics. When Roosevelt finally called Randolph to Washington in an effort to force cancellation of the march, he made certain Walter
White was summoned too. White was an old client; the power structure
knew how to deal with him.

Since Randolph planned to keep his march racially exclusive, its revolutionary implications immediately became apparent. The idea that masses
of blacks would be brought into one of the most segregated cities in the
country shocked and frightened the white community. When Eleanor
Roosevelt demanded to know how Randolph proposed to feed and house
his black marchers, Randolph answered he assumed they would register
in hotels and order dinner in restaurants; his job was merely to bring in
the marchers.[7] The Roosevelts feared the march would result in a race
war in the nation's capital and prove an embarrassment to a country that
held itself up as a model of democracy.

Although the administration did not realize it, there were definite limits to Randolph's militancy. Whether caused by fear of a mass black invasion of the segregated city, or concern about possible Communist infiltration, or perhaps the same desire to manage and orchestrate an acceptable
spectacular that would surface in later marches, there were behind-the-
scenes efforts toward careful supervision of the proposed march. Randolph formed the March on Washington Committee as the organizing
vehicle for the march. He emphasized "complete organization," thereby
implying that "the power to control the March" was of "paramount im-

6. William J. Thompkins to Honorable Edwin M. Watson, January 23, 1943, White to
Roosevelt, March 13, 1941, Memorandum from Edwin M. Watson to Honorable William
McReynolds, March 14, 1941, Memorandum from McReynolds to Watson, April 8, 1941,
Watson to White, April 8, 1941, Randolph to Honorable Franklin D. Roosevelt, May 29,
1941, Randolph to William S. Knudsen, June 3, 1941, all in FDR Papers; Roy Wilkins to
Dr. John A. Singleton, June 12, 1941, in NAACP Papers; Black Worker, August, 1941, p. 1+.
7. Kempton, Part of Our Time, 251; Dufty, "A Post Portrait," January 3, 1960.

portance." To this end he requested that the Washington branch of the committee seek out churches and schools to feed the marchers at cost at the same time that an image of black invasion of lily-white Washington restaurants and hotels was being conveyed to the dominant power structure. As in subsequent marches, the committee wanted veto power over all slogans, banners, and statements of purpose. The committee also reserved to itself the selection of battalion chiefs and deputy inspectors both at the point of assembly and throughout the line of march.[8] The white world, however, knew nothing of these precautions.

Encouraged by the favorable response in the black community, Randolph raised his estimate to 100,000 marchers, whereupon the president enlisted Eleanor Roosevelt and Mayor LaGuardia of New York, a friend of Randolph's, to try to talk him out of the march. When they failed, Randolph and Walter White were summoned to Washington, where Roosevelt asked them to stop the march in return for his personal promise for better treatment of blacks. Randolph, however, refused to call off the march without a tangible concession.[9]

The proposed march had the twin goals of desegregation of the military and the opening to blacks of jobs in defense industries. Although he was not promised desegregation of the armed services, Randolph's pressure tactics elicited Executive Order No. 8802, which brought into being the wartime Fair Employment Practices Committee (FEPC). In exchange, Randolph agreed to call off the March on Washington. Although it was not "the most significant and meaningful United States declaration affecting Negroes since the Emancipation Proclamation" Randolph proclaimed it to be, the FEPC resulted in some economic improvements for many Afro-Americans. As no one can ever know how many blacks would actually have marched, historian Lerone Bennett, Jr., called Randolph's ma-

8. Memorandum, n.d., in APR Files; Minutes of Meeting of Subcommittee to Draft Program for "March on Washington," April 23, 1941, Minutes of Sub-Committee Meeting on "March to Washington," April 10, 1941, both in NAACP Papers.

9. Stephen Early to Wayne Coy, June 6, 1941, in FDR Papers. See draft and letter by Eleanor Roosevelt to Randolph, June 10, 1941, in ER Papers; Telegram, Randolph to The President, June 16, 1941, Memorandum for the President from E.M.W. [Edwin M. Watson], June 14, 1941, Memorandum for General Watson from FDR, June 14, 1941, Memorandum, Wayne Coy to Steve Early, all in FDR Papers. Roosevelt was apprised of the demands sought by the march movement before he met with Randolph and White. See Proposals of the Negro March-on-Washington Committee: To President Roosevelt for Urgent Consideration, June 21, 1941, in FDR Papers.

neuver "one of the most brilliant power plays ever executed by a Negro leader, if not the most brilliant."[10]

But discontent over the cancellation quickly surfaced in the black community. Once aroused, militancy was not easily quelled. True to his proposal to have various segments of the community represented in the march, Randolph had instituted a separate Youth Division. Led by Richard Parrish of the Association of Negro College Students in New York, the Youth Division was more radical than the parent organization, unwilling to compromise with the establishment, and the most unhappy about losing its chance to march. The young militants accused Randolph of selling out to Roosevelt and suggested that, rather than canceling the march, it merely be postponed for ninety days. Older critics remained skeptical of industrial compliance with the rulings of an FEPC that lacked enforcement powers. Author Roi Ottley, calling the executive order valueless, went so far as to state that Randolph had betrayed his followers.[11]

Although Randolph called the Youth Division "more sonorous than sound," the disappointment of the young blacks, together with censure from other sectors, indicated more than a little dissatisfaction with his compromise, and he felt compelled to answer his detractors. In an article entitled "Why and How the March Was Postponed," Randolph insisted that the main goal, the issuance of an executive order, had been achieved. Elimination of discrimination in the armed services had not been the primary aim; gaining jobs in national defense was more important, Randolph maintained, and the marchers would have appeared ridiculous marching when the primary objective had been met. In fact, the march committee had earlier given consideration to calling off the march if Roosevelt came through with an executive order, but had been unable to reach a decision.[12]

Randolph rationalized his action by insisting that the march had not been called off, merely "postponed." He asserted: "I don't want anyone

10. Randolph, quoted in Allan Morrison, "A. Philip Randolph: Dean of Negro Leaders," *Ebony* (November, 1958), 108; Lerone Bennett, Jr., quoted in Garland, "A. Philip Randolph," 33.

11. Walter White vigorously defended Randolph's actions. See White to New York Youth Division, July 14, 1941, in NAACP Papers; Roi Ottley, "Negro Morale," *New Republic,* November 10, 1941, pp. 613–15. See also White to Clifford Morgan, February 13, 1942, in NAACP Papers.

12. Randolph to White, July 21, 1941, in NAACP Papers; A. Philip Randolph, "Why and How the March Was Postponed," *Black Worker,* August, 1941, p. 1+: See Minutes of Local Unit of Negro March-on-Washington Committee, June 14, 1941, in NAACP Papers.

to think I called off that march on Washington permanently. That's still our ace in the hole." When the FEPC became a reality, Randolph announced he would maintain the threat of a march as a "watchdog" to keep the government from backsliding on its commitment.[13]

Still desiring to be a prime mover in the civil rights struggle, rather than disband the organization he had built, in July, 1941, Randolph made the decision to perpetuate it. Realizing that the idea of a mammoth march would not be feasible for a nation at war, Randolph searched for a dramatic protest symbol that would have the same appeal and exert the same pressure as the march. "I am convinced," he wrote, "that no little ordinary effort will be effective. Whatever is done must be big, colossal and dramatic." Ultimately he conceived the idea of rallies so huge they would prove to the administration that the black community was indeed united and prepared to push for its rights. Randolph planned to stage a series of these giant protest meetings in key cities "in an all-out effort to win the democratic rights for Negroes now during the war." Although a rally projected for Washington was never held, the meetings in the summer of 1942 in New York, Chicago, and St. Louis were enormously successful.[14]

Planning for the rallies represented an organizational feat. The *Black Worker* was utilized for propaganda, and the black communities in the target cities were inundated with leaflets, stickers, and posters. In New York and Chicago, Randolph employed a blackout scheme on the night of the rally that proved effective. He requested that all outside lights on apartment buildings, stores, and places of amusement be put out during the demonstration, and dark shades drawn over windows in homes. In New York, signs reading "Between 8 and 10 P.M., June 16th, we shall be 'DARK, DRY, SILENT'" were placed in merchants' windows, announcing their cooperation in the "voluntary" blackout, and the names of those complying were printed in the Amsterdam *Star News*. The headline of the *Black Worker* read, "Blackout Harlem, June 16th!" Black social and civic organizations supplied publicity, and Harlem pastors announced

13. Randolph, quoted in William A. H. Birnie, "Black Brain Trust," *American Magazine* (January, 1943), 94–95; Randolph, quoted in Louis Kesselman, *The Social Politics of FEPC: A Study in Reform Pressure Movements* (Chapel Hill, 1948), 20.

14. Randolph to Ira F. Lewis, April 14, 1942, in APR Files; *Black Worker*, March, 1942, p. 4. Randolph's correspondence indicates that he had trouble finding a place to hold a mass meeting in Washington, but apparently planned to use the ball park, September 4, 1942 (Randolph to White, July 24, 1942, in NAACP Papers).

the blackout from their pulpits. Picked representatives were on hand to see that the blackout was observed. "Thus, on this historic night," Randolph wrote, "will dark Harlem dramatize the economic and political blackout through which our people still stumble and fall in their too-slow progress toward the light in half-free America." According to Ellen Tarry, the plan was so successful that "Harlem was like a deserted village. Every man, woman, and child who had carfare was in Madison Square Garden."[15]

The movement reached the pinnacle of its popularity at the Madison Square Garden rally. The program consisted of a musical pageant and a play by Dick Campbell, *The Watchword Is Forward.* But the evening was hampered by too many speakers, each of whom spoke for so long that five hours elapsed, and Randolph was unable to deliver his own address. He nevertheless wrote a Chicago colleague that the meeting was "beyond all expectations."[16]

The black clergy endorsed Randolph's requested blackout for the June 26 rally at the Chicago Coliseum and urged their congregations to participate in the thousand-voice choir. Employing the theme "Marching for Victory on Two Fronts" to connect the fight for black civil rights at home with the fight against fascism abroad, a parade of floats planned for the Sunday preceding the rally turned out to be "spectacular." Randolph also obtained support from civic and fraternal groups and businessmen, an "encouraging" number of whom agreed to cooperate in blacking out their businesses. The Chicago *Defender* backed the event editorially, stating that the blackout typified the blackout of democracy in the American attitude toward Afro-Americans.[17]

Coming just ten days after the Madison Square Garden event, the Chicago rally was a huge success. The crowd of 12,000 that overflowed into the street represented a cross section of the black community, including many from the working classes. The choir sang, and Campbell's play was again presented. Because there were fewer speeches, Randolph was able to deliver his address, threatening that if the president did not issue a proclamation abolishing government Jim Crow, "Negroes are going to march

15. *Black Worker,* June, 1942, p. 1; Ellen Tarry, *The Third Door: The Autobiography of an American Negro Woman* (New York, 1955), 192.
16. Tarry, *Third Door,* 193; Julius J. Adams, *The Challenge: A Study in Negro Leadership* (New York, 1949), 40–130; *Interracial Review,* XV (July, 1942), 99; Randolph to Halena Wilson, June 22, 1942, in BSCP Papers, CD.
17. Chicago *Defender,* June 6, 13, 20, 27, 1942.

and we don't give a damn what happens." "Surely Negroes can't be expected to fight for democracy in Burma," he maintained, "when they
don't have it in Birmingham." [18]

In Chicago, Randolph appeared to be on the way toward building the
"significant movement" of his dreams.[19] Nevertheless, at the St. Louis
rally held less than two months later, on August 14, it became apparent
that the momentum had slowed. Attendance was down to 9,000 persons,
and the length of the blackout diminished to fifteen minutes—from 9:00
to 9:15 P.M.

Since a mere threat to march did not constitute a movement, Randolph
had submitted the blueprint for a permanent, racially exclusive organization with a tight hierarchical structure in the fall of 1941. The reorganization, he emphasized, was effected to meet the desire of local committees
to have definite regulations. By December, Randolph moved to transform
the March on Washington Committee into a dues-paying membership organization, the March on Washington Movement (MOWM).[20]

The MOWM developed as Randolph's personal vehicle—a fact that
led to increasing rebuke from the old-line black leadership and the black
press, one columnist even referring to Randolph as "Fuehrer."[21] Criticism was directed not only at his autocratic rule and the all-black membership policy but also at the apparent lack of a concrete program and
the unpatriotic tenor of the organization. The name of the group was also
criticized as it became increasingly clear a march was unlikely ever to
take place.

Detractors' accusations of despotism were not unjustified: Randolph's
dictatorship was an integral part of the organization. Initially Randolph
did not bother with democratic trappings such as electing delegates to

18. *Ibid.*, July 4, 1942. Randolph claimed 16,000 present. See A. Philip Randolph,
"Why Should We March?" *Survey Graphic* (November, 1942), 488–89.

19. Yet Randolph could not get an appointment to see Roosevelt regarding armed-forces
discrimination on July 4, 1942. See Frank Kindon to Major General Edwin M. Watson,
June 22, 1942, Memorandum for Mrs. Roosevelt from FDR, June 24, 1942, M. H. McIntyre
to Frank Kindon, Esq., June 24, 1942, all in FDR Papers; *Black Worker*, August, 1942,
p. 1; St. Louis Scrapbook, BSCP Papers, CD.

20. Minutes, National Committee of Negro March on Washington, July 2, 1941,
Richard J. Thomas To Randolph, October 31, 1941, Randolph to Dear Friend, December 12,
1941, all in APR Files; Randolph to Dear Friend, July 12, 1941, January 10, 1942, both in
NAACP Papers; "MOWM Establishes Permanent Organization," n.d., in APR Files.

21. George S. Schuyler, "Views and Reviews," Pittsburgh *Courier*, July 17, 1943.
Schuyler, an old associate from the radical days of the *Messenger*, subsequently turned conservative and became critical.

congresses to discuss issues, decide on policies, and elect leaders. Rather, upon making the decision to become a membership organization, the MOWM passed a motion that the "autonomy of the local branches of the Movement be circumscribed by the executive chairman" and all fund raising be placed in his hands. Rumors began to circulate that the executive committee met only when Randolph called it into session and it had no veto power; "Randolph is free to do anything he chooses," one observer noted. An informant advised Roy Wilkins of the NAACP, "At the present time Randolph's opinion is practically law in that everybody is anxious to follow him." His control even reached into the branches, as Randolph personally selected the officers for the New York local.[22]

Some insiders, like Richard Parrish, complained early on about the autocratic organization. Parrish wanted the MOWM to hold a yearly national convention with the members of the executive committee deciding "broad lines of policy," thereby making Randolph responsible to them. Not only would such a procedure be more democratic, Parrish pointed out, but it would also "tend to develop a national Negro leadership of men capable of administering national jobs."[23]

In part to answer these criticisms, and in part to give members the feeling that they were participating in policy making and the choice of leadership, Randolph called the Detroit Policy Conference in September, 1942, to "deal with goals, methods and tactics."[24] In actuality, the purpose of the conference was to plan for a convention in Chicago, projected for the spring of 1943. The Detroit Policy Conference proved to be significant, however, because it marked an ideological change for the MOWM.

Whereas the Detroit conference was deliberately kept small, the 1943 Chicago convention, ultimately called the WE ARE AMERICANS, TOO! Conference, was planned as the first national convention of the now-institutionalized organization. As such, it should have attracted thousands of participants, but Roy Wilkins, acting as an observer for the

22. Minutes of Executive Committee, March on Washington Committee, December 19, 1941, in APR Files. For a model of leadership of a democratic organization, see Yonathan Shapiro, *Leadership of the American Zionist Organization, 1897–1930* (Urbana, 1971), 270–71; Memorandum to Mr. White from Mr. Wilkins: Supplementary report on the March on Washington convention, July 8, 1943, Wilkins to White, June 24, 1942, both in NAACP Papers; Memorandum, Dr. L. M. Ervin to Randolph, January 14, 1942, in APR Files.

23. Richard Parrish to Randolph, December 17, 1941, in APR Files.

24. Randolph to Lester B. Granger, September 9, 1942, in NUL Papers.

NAACP, reported no more than seventy-five functioning delegates. Various mass meetings associated with the convention attracted larger numbers, in part because they had been well advertised by loudspeaker trucks along Chicago's South Side. There was always a problem getting delegates to travel to a convention at their own expense; Randolph, however, blamed wartime travel difficulties for the poor showing.[25]

By the time of the WE ARE AMERICANS, TOO! Conference the NAACP saw the MOWM as a rival organization; thus Wilkins could not be considered an unbiased critic. Nevertheless, his is the only available account that gives details of the conference. According to Wilkins, "a considerable number" of the few delegates that attended came from the BSCP, while some others came from NAACP branches. Still others came as lone individuals, rather than representing organized units of the MOWM. Wilkins thought the conference poorly organized, with sessions starting late, running over time, and failing to address the scheduled topics.[26] Clearly the enthusiasm and organization that had marked the mass rallies were gone. Following the Chicago convention, which ended July 4, 1943, the MOWM declined rapidly.

Although it eventually disintegrated, the MOWM remains important in Afro-American history because its struggles over philosophy, tactics, alliances, leadership, and finances foreshadowed both the promises and problems of the midcentury drive for civil rights. Ideologically and strategically, the two most provocative components of the MOWM were Randolph's all-black membership rule and his recommendation of mass, nonviolent civil disobedience. Because of his previous experience with Communist takeover of the NNC, the obvious explanation for Randolph's decision to keep the movement racially exclusive is that he thought it would help prevent Communist infiltration and co-optation. According to Charles Houston of the NAACP, "One of the main reasons for the present policy of exclusion of all white people from participation is the desire to make it impossible for the charge of Communism to be leveled

25. Memorandum to Mr. White from Mr. Wilkins: March on Washington Convention in Chicago, July 7, 1943, in NAACP Papers; Randolph to Pauli Murray, May 17, 1943, in APR Files.

26. Memorandum to Mr. White from Mr. Wilkins: March on Washington Convention in Chicago.

at the undertaking." Randolph's own words also give credence to this view: "We do not want Communists in the organization for the reason that they penetrate such movements for the sole purpose of dominating them in the interests of Soviet Russia."[27]

Coalition with the NAACP served to strengthen anti-red rhetoric as the association bore the scars of its own battles with the Communists in the 1930s. Wilkins pushed maximum NAACP branch involvement in the march on the grounds it would "prevent a certain effort on the part of Communists to seize control and gum up the works." Communist infiltration became such an overriding concern that one member of the March on Washington Committee suggested the movement not use the word *demand* for fear of being "dubbed 'red.'" Walter White's obsession with the Communist menace was so great it made him reluctant to call off the march in the event Roosevelt capitulated to their pressure because he was concerned Communists would take over the march machinery for their own purposes.[28]

More in-depth analysis of Randolph's utterances, however, reveals that his reason for keeping the movement racially homogeneous was more complex than mere anticommunism. From the beginning Randolph defended excluding whites, not only as insurance against Communist takeover, but also as a necessity for enhanced black self-esteem. Blacks had a special problem since "only [they] are jim-crowed in America and they more than anyone else feel the pain and embarrassment and insult of segregation and discrimination." Randolph insisted blacks "can and must be relied upon to take the initiative and assume the responsibility relentlessly, ceaselessly, and uncompromisingly to fight for the destruction of Jim-Crow." Likening Afro-Americans to other ethnic and minority groups, he argued that only Jews could fight anti-Semitism, and "Why should Negroes expect to be different?"[29]

Randolph saw that a black-led, black-financed, black-run organization would help provide Afro-Americans with the self-confidence they so desperately needed. "The essential value of an all-Negro movement such

27. Charles H. Houston to Randolph, May 20, 1941, in NAACP Papers; New York *Times*, July 18, 1943.
28. Wilkins to Dr. John A. Singleton, June 12, 1941, in NAACP Papers. Channing Tobias said, "Demand is a CP-Copyrighted word." See Minutes of Local Unit of Negro March-on-Washington Committee.
29. Randolph to Dear Walter, May 19, 1941, in NAACP Papers; Press Release, National Headquarters MOWM, in St. Louis Scrapbook, BSCP Papers, CD.

as the March on Washington is that it helps to create faith by Negroes in Negroes. It develops a sense of self-reliance with Negroes depending on Negroes in vital matters. It helps to break down the slave psychology and inferiority-complex in Negroes which comes and is nourished with Negroes relying on white people for direction and support." Randolph wanted to see "a million Negroes organized—not to get jobs for one or two big Negroes—but to advance the total economic, political, educational and social interests of the Negro." Organizing such numbers would force the Republican and Democratic parties to give blacks "equal and fair consideration. There will no longer be the need of seeking the ear of a so-called big white friend in either . . . Party; Negroes will have the power to demand and take their rights." [30]

Since the distinction between the racial exclusivism of Randolph in the 1940s and the racial chauvinism of Marcus Garvey's Back-to-Africa movement in the 1920s was not always obvious, Randolph was forced to caution participants of the necessity of "steering clear" of "Black Nationalism." No matter how similar they appeared, the MOWM was "not akin" to "so-called" "Back-to-Africa Movements" because the final goal of the MOWM was "to secure full integration of Negro citizens into all phases of American life on a par with other citizens." Thus Randolph defended his use of segregation to obtain the ultimate end of integration—a contradiction his detractors did not hesitate to point out. Charles Houston, for example, opposed the exclusion of whites because he did not believe that "Negroes can win the battle for integration and citizenship by themselves. What success Negroes have had in the past has been due in large part to their ability to interest and enlist other persons in their cause." Houston reminded Randolph, "Exclusion of white people solely on the grounds of race would be the color bar in reverse, the very thing you have fought against so long in the A. F. of L." [31]

Roy Wilkins thought the "greatest single mistake" of the Chicago convention lay in its adoption of the constitutional provision excluding whites; the membership simply could not understand the inconsistency of protesting against lily-white labor unions and advocating an all-black

30. A. Philip Randolph, "Keynote Address to the Policy Conference of the March on Washington Movement," in Broderick and Meier (eds.), *Negro Protest Thought in the Twentieth Century*, 201–10; *Black Worker*, May, 1942, p. 1+.

31. *March on Washington Movement: Proceedings of Conference Held in Detroit, September 26–27, 1942*, p. 37, and Charles H. Houston to Mr. A. Philip Randolph, May 20, 1941, both in NAACP Papers.

movement *"against Jim-Crow."* Wilkins noted deprecatingly, "In one breath, they call for integration of the Negro into American life and in the next breath they refuse membership to persons who want to further that integration simply because those persons happen to be white." Most columnists for the black press similarly attacked the idea of racial "isolationism," or reverse Jim Crow.[32]

While he gave the fear of Communist takeover and the objective of building black self-esteem as the reasons for keeping the MOWM racially exclusive, Randolph had another motivation that he did not discuss openly: his continuing desire to "create a significant movement." Although his "Garvey Must Go" campaign successfully disposed of Garvey in the 1920s, it did not help Randolph build a mass movement of his own. Randolph realized his Socialist economic theories lacked appeal for the black masses, whereas Garvey's racial chauvinism had brought him enormous numbers of followers. Thus, once having decided to build an independent, permanent MOWM, Randolph also settled upon racial exclusivism as a temporary expedient to gain a mass following. Short-term racial separatism was not uncongenial to him, for Randolph always vacillated between integrating his groups and keeping them all-black.

Randolph conceived of the other prominent component of the MOWM, mass, nonviolent direct action, as a fusion of Gandhi's Satyagraha with the sit-down strike of the industrial union movement. Spelling out his developing ideas for utilizing nonviolent civil disobedience as a means of protest against Jim Crow at the Detroit Policy Conference, he began by praising Gandhi's success in India with mass civil disobedience and noncooperation. But more in keeping with his personality and background, Randolph also extolled the precedent of labor strikes in general and the example of the CIO sit-down strikes in particular. "Demonstrations of great masses of workers in strikes on the picket line, is the chief strategy of the trade union movement. It has gotten results and will continue to get results," he maintained.[33]

Like racial exclusivism, the mass action tactics Randolph advocated did not represent a new departure for him. Early in his career, while the

32. Memorandum to Mr. White from Mr. Wilkins: March on Washington Convention in Chicago; S. W. Garlington, "Generally Speaking," Amsterdam-New York *Star-News,* July 17, 1943; "Did 'March on Washington' Err in Barring Whites as Members?" Kansas City *Call,* July 17, 1943, in BSCP Papers, CD.

33. Randolph, "Keynote Address"; A. Philip Randolph, "A Reply to My Critics," Chicago *Defender,* July 3, 1943.

Messenger was still in its radical phase, Randolph had advised blacks to join the Industrial Workers of the World, among other reasons because "the Negro must engage in direct action." [34] He continued to recommend direct mass action, even cooperating with the Communists in employing the technique during the United Front years, and he utilized it most successfully with the threatened march. But with the Detroit Policy Conference in the fall of 1942, Randolph introduced a subtle pacifist emphasis, which became more pronounced in succeeding months.

Randolph's direct action program advocated organizing Afro-Americans into a hierarchical structure of block systems directed by divisions. Such mobilization was necessary, he argued, for blacks to develop mass power, "the most effective weapon a minority people can wield." At the same time, Randolph began to stress a series of small marches on local city halls and councils to awaken the black masses and center public attention on the grievances and goals of the race. Even more important, these small marches would provide blacks with training and discipline for the more strenuous struggle of a march on Washington. This time a new twist was added to that elusive march: picketing of the White House and maintenance of the picket line until the country and the world recognized that blacks had come of age and would sacrifice all to be counted as free men.[35]

Building the new mass movement upon local bases of small units would provide the opportunity for more individual involvement, Randolph reasoned. In a preview of later-day "consciousness raising sessions," divisions were to serve as "Negro mass parliaments" where day-to-day problems such as police brutality and high rents could be debated and action taken. In meetings to be held at least twice a month, every black "should be made to feel his importance in the *Negro liberation movement*." Through these "parliaments" the voiceless and helpless "little men" would become articulate.[36]

Randolph's plan showed sensitivity to the problems of ghetto blacks. Although unemployed, for the first time they would, according to Ran-

34. Editorial, "Why Negroes Should Join the IWW," *Messenger* (July, 1919), 8.
35. See St. Louis Scrapbook, in BSCP Papers, CD; Randolph, "Keynote Address"; Randolph to Dear Friend, January 10, 1942, in NAACP Papers; *March on Washington Movement: Proceedings of Conference Held in Detroit*.
36. Pamphlet, *National March on Washington Movement: Policies and Directives*, St. Louis Scrapbook, in BSCP Papers, CD; Randolph, "Keynote Address"; *March on Washington Movement: Proceedings of Conference Held in Detroit*. Emphasis added.

dolph, experience "a thrill from a sense of their importance and worth-whileness." In these sessions the "forgotten black man" could rise and tell about "jobs he sought but never got, about the business agent of the union giving him the brush-off, how he had gone to the gates of defense plants only to be kept out while white workers walked in, how he cooled his heels in an office and finally was told with a cold stare, 'no more workers wanted' or how the government employment services would not permit him to enroll as a skilled worker but only as a porter or janitor or how he was denied entrance into certain government training courses for skilled defense jobs." Randolph concluded, "In very truth, in the March On Washington, little men can tell their story their own way."[37] Randolph's "mass parliaments" were thus directed specifically toward the alienated ghetto resident overcome by a sense of powerlessness. Through the meetings, the estranged could develop a degree of group "integration," with empathy and mutual understanding among group members.

Randolph's strategy utilized white friends to ask for a table in a restaurant, a hotel room, or admission to a place of amusement. If blacks were subsequently denied admittance, blacks and whites were to join together and request a conference with the manager, giving him a copy of the civil rights law of the state if one existed. Picketing or a sit-down strike would result if such a conference were denied. If the trespassing law was invoked by the proprietor, the policy of the MOWM was for the demonstrators "to stand their ground in said restaurant even to the point of being thrown out physically." Realizing these techniques of civil disobedience required training, the MOWM was prepared to coach adherents.[38] Thus Randolph's movement anticipated the student sit-ins of the early 1960s.

But before engaging in any form of direct action, Randolph emphasized, all the resources of negotiation should be exhausted.[39] The policy of the MOWM was not to fight back if violence ensued; every participant was pledged to nonviolence, even in language. One was not to seek to collect damages if one were hurt; that should be considered part of the price. Such practices on the part of the individual represented a significant departure from the direct mass action that Randolph had earlier advocated and that had proved so effective in the threatened March on Washington. The use of interracial teams and small-scale actions, in fact, was the technique pacifists from the Fellowship of Reconciliation (FOR)

37. Randolph, "A Reply to My Critics," Chicago *Defender*, June 12, 1943.
38. *Ibid.*, June 19, 26, 1943.
39. Randolph, "March on Washington Movement Presents Program for the Negro," 150.

employed in their newly organized secular civil rights group, the Congress on Racial Equality (CORE).

Randolph was condemned for his strategy of nonviolence, especially by the Pittsburgh *Courier,* which charged him with "irresponsible talk about suicidal civil disobedience and mass marches which never materialize." Feeling compelled to defend his position, Randolph published a series of articles in the Chicago *Defender.* Appearing from shortly before until shortly after the Chicago convention in the summer of 1943, these articles presented the most definitive statement of Randolph's philosophy at the time. The goal of the MOWM, he stated, was complete equality— economic, political, social, and racial—with desegregation of industry, government, housing, education, and public accommodations. Achievement of this freedom required "struggle, sacrifice, suffering," for "power resides in the masses and they must be organized and mobilized and disciplined to struggle for equality." For too long blacks had depended on the processes of written persuasion without throwing themselves into actual physical motion against Jim Crow. "Non-violent good-will direct action" was "based upon the theory of the common unity of all peoples and the possible modification of behavior patterns by a process of reconditioning through the word and the deed, but fundamentally through the deed." [40]

By December, 1942, Randolph had devised I AM AN AMERICAN TOO! Week as a broad, nationally coordinated program of nonviolent civil disobedience in an effort to abolish Jim Crowism throughout America. The scheme projected actions against the federal government, local governments, and especially southern railroads and schools. Randolph requested sermons and editorials on the theme of black citizenship from both the black and white communities and suggested that black organizations throughout the country participate in I AM AN AMERICAN TOO! Week "as a symbol of the struggle of the Negro for the status of first class citizenship." Randolph wanted the project, which was based on the premise that "a citizen is morally obligated to disobey an unjust law," to have the effect of a massive boycott. [41]

This proposal was a direct response to the white community's I AM AN AMERICAN Day. Proclaimed by Congress in 1940, I AM AN AMERICAN Day

40. Pittsburgh *Courier,* May 3, 1943, quoted in Chicago *Defender,* June 12, 1943; Randolph, "A Reply to My Critics," June 19, 26, 1943.

41. *Black Worker,* December, 1942; St. Louis *Argus,* January 8, 1943; Pittsburgh *Courier,* January 9, 1943; *Black Worker,* January, 1943, p. 1; clipping, February 6, 1943, in St. Louis Scrapbook, BSCP Papers, CD.

set aside the third Sunday in May for the celebration of citizenship. Randolph's campaign, designed as a reminder that blacks were only second-class citizens, was to have been held concurrently with the national holiday in 1943. Unfortunately, the plan lost its impact when the conference planned by the MOWM was postponed because of financial difficulties.[42]

When the WE ARE AMERICANS, TOO! Conference was finally held in Chicago in the summer of 1943, the delegates made the decision to actually march on Washington, but they agreed to leave the time for holding the march to the discretion of Randolph and the national officers. In the meantime, the leadership recommended smaller local marches on city halls and state capitals to emphasize the demands of the MOWM. It became apparent that these small marches, together with small-group, non-violent direct actions against Jim Crow restaurants and theaters, were to replace the mass civil disobedience campaign.[43]

Meanwhile, CORE, which had been formed in the spring of 1942, also attempted to apply nonviolent civil disobedience to the race problem. James Farmer became the director and Bayard Rustin an organizer of CORE. Farmer's original memorandum recommending the establishment of the new group had suggested an organization to stimulate racial equality based upon the combination of Satyagraha and the sit-down strike. At its inception CORE utilized only small-scale direct action techniques, whereas Randolph envisioned massive, nationwide civil disobedience campaigns. Increasingly, though, Randolph began advocating both large- and small-scale direct actions, and in the summer of 1943, he predicted that "an important part of the future strategy and technique of the Negro must be in the field of demonstration, both nonviolent mass activity and disciplined non-violent demonstration of small Negro and white groups for civil and economic justice."[44] The latter, of course, sounded almost identical to the program of CORE.[45]

42. The name was also changed; it became WE ARE AMERICANS, TOO!
43. Memorandum to Mr. White from Mr. Wilkins: March on Washington Convention in Chicago.
44. George M. Houser to Miss Juanita Morrow, July 7, 1948, in CORE Papers; Broderick and Meier (eds.), *Negro Protest Thought in Twentieth Century*, 210; Randolph, "A Reply to My Critics," July 3, 1943.
45. Lawrence Wittner states that FOR loaned Farmer and Rustin to Randolph to assist him in steering the MOWM along Gandhian lines (Wittner, *Rebels Against War: The American Peace Movement, 1941–1960* [New York, 1969], 64–65). At least one observer believed Rustin was responsible for the entire nonviolent program at the Chicago convention. See *Labor Action*, July, 1943, in St. Louis Scrapbook, BSCP Papers, CD.

Judging from his shift in emphasis, one may reasonably conjecture that Randolph was being influenced by CORE pacifists who joined the MOWM, as well as by the wartime atmosphere that made large-scale demonstrations less feasible. The influence, however, was reciprocal. In their study of CORE, August Meier and Elliott Rudwick maintain that the MOWM provided "a key inspiration for CORE people." Not only did the march movement demonstrate "the power inherent in nonviolent direct action" by forcing the creation of the FEPC, "but it also encouraged CORE's founders in their hopes that their own organization had the potential of becoming a mass movement."[46]

The primary difference between CORE and the MOWM lay in their constituencies, CORE being "quite deliberately and as a matter of principle, thoroughly interracial" while the MOWM restricted its membership to Afro-Americans. Randolph himself called this distinction one of the "major differences" between the two movements. The racial chauvinism of the MOWM, in fact, caused a debate within the CORE organization as to whether CORE should support Randolph's endeavors, in much the same manner that CORE's interracialism made the MOWM leaders leery of collaboration. Any qualms on CORE's part, however, were quickly settled in favor of cooperation, which, in the words of Farmer, was "the only sensible procedure." Farmer's primary reservation stemmed from his belief that Randolph had adopted civil disobedience on the grounds of political expedience rather than out of conviction. Farmer nevertheless recognized as invaluable the education along nonviolent, direct action lines that Randolph and the MOWM could provide for both blacks and the wider American public.[47]

Farmer was correct. Unlike the pacifists in FOR and CORE, the atheist Randolph did not have the religious fervor required by Satyagraha, which derived from Gandhi's religious belief in the capacity of truth and love to triumph over even violent oppression.[48] Randolph alone at this period,

46. August Meier and Elliott Rudwick, *CORE: A Study in the Civil Rights Movement, 1942–1968* (New York, 1973), 15.

47. James Farmer to Alistair Cooke, August 28, 1962, in CORE Papers; Randolph to author, September 29, 1972; Meier and Rudwick, *CORE*, 11; Randolph to George M. Houser, January 5, 1945, Houser to Randolph, February 25, 1944, Randolph to Houser, March 6, 1944, all in APR Files; James Farmer to George Houser, February 5, 1943, Houser to Farmer, February 13, 1943, both in CORE Papers.

48. Erik Erikson, *Gandhi's Truth: On the Origins of Militant Nonviolence* (New York, 1969), 414–34.

however, saw the advantage of separating out the nonviolent, goodwill, direct action aspect of the doctrine from its religious setting, and encouraging its use as a political technique by which American blacks could gain their civil rights.

By keeping his organization racially exclusive, Randolph avoided any danger of co-optation by his new pacifist supporters. But FOR was unable to contribute much in the way of membership or finances since pacifism appealed only to a relatively small number of intellectuals of both races.[49]

There were thus two groups working in the early 1940s to educate blacks to nonviolent direct action: the MOWM, which built on the base of the porters' union and by 1942 attempted to reach out to lower-class blacks, and tiny CORE, which at this early period was an elitist interracial organization. The MOWM remained the only group based upon all-black mass action and addressing itself primarily to economic problems, particularly of the urban ghetto resident.

Randolph's turn toward a pacifist ideology revealed itself to be problematic. Although the middle class had provided the organization and leadership of the proposed 1941 march, the idea had allure that transcended class, and many of the poorest blacks had come to idolize Randolph. With the rallies in 1942, Randolph made a conscious effort to appeal to lower-class blacks, but as he became increasingly interested in nonviolence as a technique, and his followers began to realize there might never be a march, they became disenchanted and the mass base of his movement began to dissolve. Nonviolence was a difficult concept even for the educated, and the degree of self-discipline it demanded was not easily elicited from the masses, as the later civil rights movement discovered. When Randolph began advocating it, the concept of civil disobedience to gain civil rights was strange to American blacks and whites alike, and the common belief was that "someone has talked him into the idea that he is a kind of Gandhi of the Negroes."[50]

Unfortunately, along the way Randolph neglected the maxim that to

49. For FOR's reaction to its newfound allies, see A. J. Muste to Randolph, January 11, 1943, in APR Files; James Farmer and A. J. Muste to White, February 1, 1943, White to Farmer and Muste, February 4, 1943, both in NAACP Papers.

50. Thomas Sancton, "Something's Happened to the Negro," *New Republic*, February 8, 1943, p. 177.

communicate with the rank and file, leaders must enunciate limited goals in terms that are easily comprehensible. In the early days of the movement, Randolph appeared to understand the necessity for single-mindedness. "Without an issue which is clear, understandable and possible of realization, the masses cannot be rallied. The masses cannot comprehend and will not respond to an omnibus program with a multiplicity of aims or abstract ideologies," he declared. The proposed march had two clear, concise goals, but after its cancellation and his decision to maintain the march movement as a bureaucratized organization, Randolph appeared to forget his own exhortations against omnibus programs and wistful ideas. It is unlikely that many of the followers who came into the movement expected the discipline and complex ideology with which Randolph subsequently confronted them. A number of contemporary observers perceived the shift in emphasis from militant mass action to nonviolent pacifism as causing dissension at the Chicago convention and the decline in participation in the MOWM.[51]

Despite the exclusionary rule, Randolph never totally gave up the idea of cooperation with white allies who were "progressive, liberal and sound." Maintaining that the MOWM was well aware of the dangers of Negro racial chauvinism and wanted to work with all white groups or individuals in sympathy with its program, Randolph wrote Walter White, "It's farthest from my mind to suggest any policy of discrimination against white people because they are white." Racial exclusivism was a means, not an end. The MOWM preached the doctrine of self-reliance to blacks, but that did not rule out "collaboration with other groups, white or otherwise, that seek to wipe out jim-crow." What was important was that

51. Nelson W. Polsby, *Community Power and Political Theory* (New Haven, 1963), 137; *Black Worker*, August, 1941, p. 2; *The Militant*, July 10, 1943; Harry Allen, "Unity with Labor—The Only Hope for MOW," *Labor Action*, July, 1943; David Coolidge, "We Need a Program for Action by the MOW," *Labor Action* (July, 1943), in St. Louis Scrapbook, BSCP Papers, CD. Wittner, in *Rebels Against War*, states that the civil disobedience program was popular with the Chicago convention delegates, but the material in the St. Louis Scrapbook, BSCP Papers, CD, indicates it caused a great deal of dissension. Roy Wilkins' informant also pointed to the nonviolent, goodwill, direct action program as the cause of much dissension. See Memorandum to Mr. White from Mr. Wilkins: Supplementary report on the March on Washington convention.

blacks run their own liberation movement. "Salvation for the Negro must come from within. Our friends may help us. They cannot save us."[52]

Interestingly, Randolph's racial policy did not upset his small coterie of white liberal supporters as much as it did his black critics and allies. Norman Thomas, Roger Baldwin, A. J. Muste, Morris Milgram, J. Holmes Smith, and Lillian Smith, among others, issued a press release expressing their conviction that white exclusion did not indicate "a narrow black nationalism." Rather, they agreed "that at this stage of their development" blacks needed "to assert a kind of sturdy independence in certain areas in order to prove to themselves and others thaty [*sic*] they are competent to handle their affairs without white leadership." These white liberals realized that the adoption of nonviolent direct action as a strategy made it imperative to confine membership to those who suffered the indignities of race discrimination, because only they would be willing to engage in and accept the consequences of such actions.[53]

To give credence to its statements about willingness to collaborate with liberal white supporters, the MOWM attempted to organize a group called Friends of the March on Washington. But the practice, at Randolph's insistence, of allowing black-run groups to make their own "mistakes and blunders" and "move forward haltingly" toward higher standards of competence and discipline seemed too inefficient to the white Friends. Nancy and Dwight MacDonald, for example, said they became attracted to the MOWM because of its courageous stand for black rights: "It stands head and shoulders above other Negro groups in that respect." They nevertheless felt compelled to point out the organization's defects, the foremost of which was that it worked from the top down instead of from the bottom up: "So far as we can see, policy is decided entirely by Mr. Randolph, who lacks the time to give it the attention it deserves." Randolph dominated the organization, "not because he wants to do so, but because initiative and responsibility [are] not properly delegated to subcommittees." They argued, "There is, especially in the National Office, an unhealthy degree of leader-worship of Mr. Randolph," which

52. Randolph, *World Crisis and the Negro People Today*, 25–28; A. Philip Randolph, "Why I Would Not Stand for Re-election," 24–25; *Black Worker*, May, 1940; "March on Washington Movement—What Do We Stand For," n.d., in APR Files; Randolph to Dear Walter [White], May 19, 1941, in NAACP Papers; Randolph, "A Reply to My Critics," June 12, 1943; *Black Worker*, May, 1943, p. 1+.
53. Press Release, August 19, 1943, in APR Files.

"paralyzes action and prevents an intelligent working-out of policy." Although the MacDonalds had personal regard for E. Pauline Meyers, the executive secretary of the MOWM, they deplored her ineffectiveness and complained about the "gross inefficiency" in the national office that caused "the most tremendous waste of time and energy." There was no systematic central planning; organization was "almost non-existent," the MOWM's structure was "undemocratic and confusing," and it lacked a regular periodical to keep the membership informed.[54] Moreover, according to the MacDonalds, the MOWM failed to develop strong local branches that could mount independent demonstrations.

The MacDonalds also complained that although the MOWM talked of using nonviolent direct action, it made no plans to put the tactic into effect, and since the strategy was never tried out, it could not be intelligently discussed at the Chicago convention. Indeed, the MOWM did not do much beyond preparing for the convention, "and doing this in the most wasteful and ineffectual way," with longwinded "conferences" and "vague statements." Furthermore, while the Friends of the March on Washington was designed as a group of white sympathizers, the members were given no clear idea of what they could do to help.[55]

By white standards, the MacDonalds presented a cogent analysis of the problems besetting the MOWM. Yet their criticisms provided a good illustration of the pitfalls inherent in a minority-group alliance with middle-class white liberals. Dominant-group members of social movements seeking to change the subordinate status of ethnic minorities inevitably tried to assume decision-making positions and impose their standards of efficiency and punctuality. This tendency was at odds with Randolph's approach, derived from his belief that the progress of a minority-group liberation movement "must come from its own successes and defeats."[56]

Since the white Friends had a strictly limited association with the MOWM, of necessity Randolph had to look to the black community for

54. Friends of the March on Washington Movement Program, April 5, 1943, Randolph to Mr. & Mrs. Dwight MacDonald, July 20, 1943, both in APR Files; Nancy and Dwight MacDonald, "Two Outsiders Look at the M.O.W.," June 20, 1943, in APR Files. J. Holmes Smith and Winifred Raushenbush were also among the Friends.

55. Nancy and Dwight MacDonald, "Two Outsiders Look at the M.O.W."

56. Marx and Useem, "Majority Involvement in Minority Movements," 81–104; Randolph to Mr. & Mrs. Dwight MacDonald, July 20, 1943, in APR Files.

allies. The older, bureaucratized black uplift organizations, the NAACP and the NUL, complemented Randolph's charisma. Although they did not have access to great wealth, they had a steady income and fairly large membership roles of middle- and upper-class blacks. Their initial affiliation was not an accident, for Randolph actively sought the cooperation of their leaders. At Walter White's suggestion, Randolph called a conference on April 1, 1941, to coordinate plans to secure a more equitable share of defense employment for blacks. This meeting provided Randolph with a platform from which to introduce his March on Washington plan to the old-line black leadership. To cement his relationship with White, Randolph invited the NAACP leader to make the principal speech at the Lincoln Memorial after the march. The fact that he was elected to the NAACP's national board of directors in 1940 and received the association's Spingarn Medal for 1941 attests to Randolph's success in courting the older helmsmen in the early days.[57]

Predominantly conservative, the established leaders had little previous experience with mass action protest movements and only reluctantly went along with Randolph. The head of the Armstrong Association in Philadelphia, for example, hesitated before joining the march movement because he perceived it as a pressure movement. The Armstrong Association preferred "to emphasize activities along the lines of education and reconciliation, rather than along contentious lines," although its chief confessed to coming under some criticism for failing to participate in more action-oriented activities.[58] The Detroit and Pittsburgh branches of the NAACP actively opposed participation for similar reasons.

The prevailing mood of the black masses was so desperate, however, that even the old-line leaders realized they had to take some action, and the NAACP board of directors, after much discussion, voted to participate. Walter White talked to Randolph almost daily, and by June, 1941, the NAACP was "urging our branches everywhere to cooperate" to make

57. Randolph to Dear Walter, March 18, 1941, White to Dear Philip, March 20, 1941, Randolph to Dear Walter, March 27, June 2, 1941, all in NAACP Papers. See Dufty, "A Post Portrait," December 30, 1959; Kempton, *Part of Our Time*, 249. White was subsequently invited to be a principal speaker at the New York and Chicago mass meetings. See Randolph to White, May 20, 1942, White to Randolph, March 21, 1942, both in NAACP Papers; "Randolph to Board," *Crisis*, XLVII (February, 1940), 53; *Black Worker*, July, 1940, p. 3.

58. Form letter to the board members of the Armstrong Association of Philadelphia from Executive Secretary Wayne L. Hopkins, May 9, 1941, in ULP Records.

the demonstration "monster" and "an overwhelming success."[59] Lester Granger, who had become executive secretary of the NUL, acted as an individual and not on behalf of the NUL in becoming a member of the original sponsoring committee of the march. "Randolph's immense prestige among all classes of Negroes," Granger recalled, made the idea of the march "something more than a pretentious notion." Granger was undoubtedly constrained by his position at the NUL, which depended on white employers to provide jobs; consequently, he remained more conciliatory toward the administration than either Randolph or White.[60] The tenuous coalition nevertheless managed to hold together through the early days of the FEPC.

From the beginning, however, Randolph's decision to keep his march movement racially exclusive caused problems for the interracial NAACP and NUL. The black community in the early 1940s was not as torn by nationalist-integrationist ideological warfare as it had been during the Garvey era, twenty years earlier. Yet Randolph's bid for greater black independence made the NAACP and NUL self-conscious about their own dependence on white patrons and sparked debate over the place of white members in a black organization. The District of Columbia branch of the NAACP, one of whose prime movers was a white woman, solved its predicament by refusing to participate in the march movement so long as it adhered to "the policy of excluding other than Negroes."[61] Other branches found themselves rent with conflict over the issue.

Racial exclusivism was merely one source of disgruntlement. Despite Randolph's protestations that the march movement represented a complementary, rather than a rival, black rights group, his institutionalization of the MOWM, the ten-cent dues requirement, and the hiring of Meyers as executive secretary acted to excite the suspicions of his allies in the older betterment organizations. As early as the spring of 1942, some branch heads were questioning the wisdom of NAACP participation in

59. See Memorandum from Walter White for files, June 16, 1941, in NAACP Papers; White, *Man Called White*, 189–90; NAACP to All Branches, May 12, 1941, "March on Washington," June 26, 1941, Wilkins to Dr. John A. Singleton, June 12, 1941, all in NAACP Papers; *Black Worker*, May, 1941, p. 4.

60. Granger to John T. Clark, February 10, 1943, in ULP Records; Granger, quoted in Garfinkel, *When Negroes March*, 39; Minutes of Local Unit of Negro March-on-Washington Committee.

61. John Lovell, Jr., to Mr. Thurman Dodson, May 7, 1941, White to Dear Philip, May 13, 1941, White to Dear Gertrude [Mrs. Gertrude B. Stone], all in NAACP Papers.

Randolph's proposed mass rallies, despite White's opinion that "the more pressure there is on Washington the better." [62]

The dilemma presented the staid NAACP by Randolph's militant posture and newfound popularity did not go unnoticed by outsiders. "Randolph is the man most worshipped by the Negro rank and file now," trumpeted columnist Horace Cayton. White, however, defended his commitment of the NAACP to the MOWM project, saying, "I don't think the people of the country would approve our refusing to cooperate in a worthwhile movement because it might endanger our own position or because we were not the sole initiators." White was concerned that the association would have a difficult time explaining why it did not participate if the MOWM rallies turned out to be as large as predicted. [63]

Cayton perceptively noted that whereas White seemed to go "all the way" with Randolph, Roy Wilkins was "much more cagey about the Association's losing its identity in this upsurge of mass feeling that has frightened the more conservative of his members." Wilkins became even more concerned after the success of the Madison Square Garden meeting in the summer of 1942. Jealous of the MOWM's financial and organizational success, Wilkins was at a loss as to the proper course the NAACP should pursue in regard to the upstart group. To adopt the traditional NAACP attitude that the new movement was of no importance was bound to fail, and claiming that the association's prestige or membership could not be hurt by it seemed inadequate. Rather, Wilkins preferred to see "some scheme" worked out "whereby we can work with them, absorb them, or get along in some fashion until we can see how the wind is blowing." Wilkins admitted he would like the support of Randolph's backers for the NAACP and "would be willing to go to considerable lengths to get them in the fold." Although White shrugged off predictions that the MOWM would steal the play from the NAACP and insisted Randolph had "given full credit to the Association in all his speeches and statements," he was apprehensive enough to send out a new public relations release aimed at improving the NAACP's image. [64]

62. White to Oscar C. Brown, March 20, 1942, *ibid.*

63. Horace R. Cayton, "Tail Wags Dog: Cayton Believes Randolph May Steal Play from NAACP if Association Doesn't Wake Up," Pittsburgh *Courier,* September 25, 1942; White to Daisy E. Lampkin, April 6, 1942, in NAACP Papers.

64. Cayton, "Tail Wags Dog"; Roy Wilkins to White, June 24, 1942, White to Lampkin, April 6, 1942, Memorandum to Miss Crump from Mr. White, April 29, 1942, all in NAACP Papers.

Always concerned about overlapping jurisdictions, the NAACP soon came to suspect that the MOWM was out to replace it—a suspicion not without some basis in fact during the heyday of the march movement. When NAACP members who were also executive committee members of the MOWM received an invitation to the Detroit Policy Conference in the fall of 1942, their suspicions were confirmed. The announced plans for the Detroit meeting, which included drafting a constitution and by-laws to determine the movement's structure and government and the election of national officers, "seemed to indicate that the March on Washington is to become a permanent organization instead of a coalition of agencies cooperating during the war emergency." When it gave its original endorsement, the NAACP had not envisioned the march movement being transformed into an enduring institution. Furthermore, NAACP members perceived the Eight Point Program now proposed by the MOWM as "duplicat[ing] existing organizations."[65]

Indeed, the MOWM's agenda, calling for an end to Jim Crow in American life, legislation to enforce the Fourteenth and Fifteenth amendments, abolition of segregation in the military, a permanent FEPC, withholding of federal funds from agencies that discriminated in using them, and minority-group representation at the peace conference negotiating the post-war settlement, differed little from that of the NAACP. Consequently, the NAACP's board of directors decided that it would treat the MOWM as it did other permanent membership organizations: It would cooperate on specific issues to be decided on an individual basis.[66]

In the eyes of the established black organization leaders, both Randolph's prominence and the MOWM itself constituted potential threats to their leadership positions and represented competition for the perennially short supply of funds in the black community. The leaders were also afraid a bluff like the march threat would not work a second time. When it subsequently became apparent that the institutionalized MOWM could not sustain its earlier popularity, the leaders of the old-line black advancement groups intensified their attacks on Randolph. In an article

65. Eardlie John to Dear Member, August 3, 1942, Memorandum from Mr. White to Mr. Wilkins—and the Staff, August 11, 1942, Wilkins to White, June 24, 1942, Relationship of NAACP to March-on-Washington Movement, in Board of Directors' Minutes, September 14, 1942, all in NAACP Papers.
66. Eight Point Program of March-on-Washington Movement, in NAACP Papers; Relationship of NAACP to March-on-Washington Movement.

for *Survey Graphic,* Randolph stated that the black leadership had united behind the MOWM's drive for jobs and justice, but by the time the piece appeared, in November, 1942, this assertion was no longer true. Although an open break was avoided on both sides, the withdrawal of support became apparent as neither the NAACP nor the NUL sent representatives to the Detroit conference. Lester Granger became disaffected after participation in the Madison Square Garden meeting convinced him "that the March on Washington was experiencing serious problems of organization and membership constituency which must be settled before I would wish further affiliation either as an individual or as an official representative of the League." Walter White reminded Randolph that participation by NAACP executives in a conference to form another organization was not possible without the board of directors' consent.[67]

In a manner reminiscent of NNC attempts to woo the NAACP in the late 1930s, Randolph refused to give up on the idea of cooperation. As the Detroit meeting was held in part to answer critics' charges that the MOWM had no effective program, a report on the conference was sent to the NAACP with the hope that its board would "reconsider the question of close relations." Then Randolph requested that White sign the Call for the WE ARE AMERICANS, TOO! Conference. Since the conference was planned to decide on the structure and future activities of the MOWM, on whether a mass march should actually be staged and if so when, and on the details of a civil disobedience campaign, White referred Randolph's request to the NAACP board. The board in turn appointed a committee to discuss with Randolph the problem of a rival organization—an embarrassing task since Randolph was a fellow board member.[68] The board finally circumvented the issue by deciding it would con-

67. Randolph, "Why Should We March?" 488–89; *March on Washington Movement: Proceedings of Conference Held in Detroit;* Granger to John T. Clark, February 10, 1943, ULP Records; Granger to Randolph, September 1, 1942, in NUL Papers; White to Randolph, September 3, 1942, in NAACP Papers. Despite his objections to a permanent, duplicating MOWM, White was reluctant to intervene directly to prevent its formation. See White to Alfred Baker Lewis, September 21, 1942, in NAACP Papers.

68. Minutes, Board of Directors meeting, April 12, 1943, Report on March on Washington Policy Conference prepared by Pauli [Murray] and sent to White, October 6, 1942, both in NAACP Papers; Extract from Minutes of the Board [NAACP], February 8, 1943, in APR Files; Memorandum from the Secretary to the Board of Directors, February 8, 1943, Minutes, Board of Directors meeting, February 8, 1943, White to Arthur B. Spingarn, Esq., February 11, 1943, all in NAACP Papers.

sider NAACP participation only if the MOWM became a federated organization and not an individual membership group—an action effectively ruling out NAACP affiliation.

By the summer of 1943, Wilkins noted that the programs of the NAACP and the MOWM were identical; the only difference lay in their methods. The MOWM believed in "mass action" and charged that the NAACP was not a "mass organization." Wilkins admitted that there was much sentiment "against the traditional programs and methods" of his association, especially among "racial chauvinists," who directed considerable criticism at white occupation of principal offices. He feared, with justification, that the MOWM would trade on this chauvinistic approach.[69]

Randolph tried to allay the concerns of the older rights organizations, emphasizing: "Certainly, it is not the intention of this movement to carry on any work that is a duplication of that which is being done by the NAACP or the National Urban League. . . . There is no need for any new movements among Negroes doing the same things that are being done by existing groups." In *National March on Washington Movement: Policies and Directives,* a pamphlet sent by the national MOWM headquarters to the local branches between the time of the Detroit Policy Conference and that of the Chicago convention, Randolph reiterated his position, promising cooperation with existing agencies and no duplication of functions. The MOWM, he maintained, sought only "to demonstrate the techniques of militant mass pressure in the field of minority problems where other techniques have broken down." White, nevertheless, interpreted Randolph's protestations to mean that "while the March on Washington Movement does not want to duplicate existing organizations, it has decided to do so." The program of the MOWM, argued White, "is almost completely a duplication of what the N.A.A.C.P. has been advocating and working for during the last thirty-four years."[70]

69. Memorandum to Mr .White from Mr. Wilkins: March on Washington Convention in Chicago. There were many critics of NAACP policy at this time. See, for example, Ray W. Guild to White, April 5, 1943, Pauli Murray to George S. Schuyler, July 31, 1942, Alfred Baker Lewis to White, September 18, 1943, all in NAACP Papers.

70. Randolph to White, September 9, 1942, in NAACP Papers; Pamphlet, *National March on Washington Movement: Policies and Directives; March on Washington Movement: Proceedings of Conference Held in Detroit;* White to Judge William H. Hastie, September 21, 1942, in NAACP Papers.

Rumors began to circulate publicly about a growing breach between the NAACP and the MOWM. Ultimately White did not speak, and the NAACP spurned participation in the Chicago convention. The association also declined to distribute the pamphlet Dwight MacDonald had written for the MOWM, *The War's Greatest Scandal: The Story of Jim Crow in Uniform*. Although White admitted the pamphlet was "well done," he realized that it was designed primarily to promote the MOWM and argued, "There is no sound reason why we should buy and distribute promotional literature of a duplicating body."[71]

Milton Webster posed still another obstacle to cooperation between the two organizations. NAACP members were alienated by his prickly personality and open criticism, even as members of the NNC had earlier been offended by his attitude. However, despite his displeasure over Webster's censure of the NAACP, White accepted Randolph's explanations and refused to allow mere personality conflict to "affect our complete unity of purpose and action." Randolph in turn agreed not to press large NAACP contributors for donations to the MOWM. "I assure you I would not be a part of anything that would either serve to diminish contributions to the NAACP or to reflect unfavorably upon its work and officers because I am as interested in its growth, progress and influence as an agency for advancement of our group as you are," Randolph pledged.[72]

Treason was yet another charge leveled against the MOWM by the old-line organization heads. Although the MOWM demonstrations avoided advocating treason, Randolph clearly designed them to appear disruptive, thereby threatening the government's need for unanimity during the wartime crisis. Disregarding its slogan, concerned black leaders greeted the proposed I AM AN AMERICAN TOO! Week with cries of "unpatriotic," and accused Randolph of "Marching Against the War Effort." In reply to these "misleading comments," Randolph asserted that "the MOWM is unequivocally back of the war effort and seeks the victory of the United Nations."[73]

71. Morris [Milgram] to White, December 1, 1942, Memorandum to Mr. White from Mr. Wilkins, May 21, 1943, and penciled notes thereon, White to Randolph, June 11, 1943, Telegram, Wilkins to White, June 23, 1943, Memorandum to Mssrs. White and Wilkins from Mr. Konvitz, June 9, 1943, and handwritten note from WW thereon, all in NAACP Papers.

72. Daisy Lampkin to White, April 7, 1942, White to Randolph, April 9, 1942, Randolph to White, April 10, 17, 1942, all in NAACP Papers.

73. *California Eagle*, July 15, 1943; Press Release, "The March on Washington Movement and the War," January 29, 1943, in APR Files.

Yet Randolph's rhetoric gave critics much grist for their mill. He stressed that white victory at the expense of black rights would not be tolerated, although he did not oppose the United States' entry into World War II on principle as he had its entry into World War I. "Negroes made the blunder of closing ranks and forgetting their grievances in the last war. We are resolved that we will not make that blunder again," he affirmed. Before Pearl Harbor he recommended that the United States "do everything to help the Allies win the war short of going to war." Even a confirmed pacifist could not contemplate accommodation to Fascist racist principles, but the old Socialist cautioned blacks not to be deceived. "This is not a war for freedom. . . . It is a war to maintain the old imperialistic systems. It is a war to continue 'white supremacy' . . . and the subjugation, domination, and exploitation of the peoples of color. It is a war between the imperialism of Fascism and Nazism and the imperialism of monopoly capitalistic democracy." Such statements as "this war need not be a world movement of reaction. The people can make it a Peoples' Revolution" frightened conservatives.[74]

As rumors of conflict between the black rights groups spread, well-meaning observers warned against the danger of the federal government getting "the idea that Negro forces are split and cannot work together effectively in demanding their rights now." For his part, Randolph continued to press for harmony of the "Negro High Command" during the "War Emergency," as he had in the 1930s; cooperation was particularly important if he were to keep up the fiction that the MOWM enjoyed unified support. Toward this end he entreated the leaders of other black groups to participate in a symposium organized to suggest methods to effect the abolition of Jim Crow "now." At the meeting, as he delineated the magnitude and complexity of the problems confronting Afro-Americans, Randolph lamented the lack of a coordinated, well-defined policy among organization heads to grapple with the issues. He wanted consultation and periodic meetings of top leaders for objective, realistic discussions of policy and strategy regarding broad national issues.[75] Randolph, however, envisioned himself as head of this "Negro High Command," and

74. Randolph, quoted in Kesselman, *Social Politics of FEPC*, 20; *Black Worker*, June, 1940, p. 4; Morrison, "Randolph: Dean of Negro Leaders," 111; Randolph, "March on Washington Movement Presents Program for the Negro," 134–35.

75. Morris Milgram to White, December 1, 1942, in NAACP Papers; Press Release, December 3, 1942, in APR Files; E. Pauline Meyers to Roy Wilkins, May 20, 1943, in NAACP Papers.

the other leaders were not willing to grant him that status. Organizational jealousy precluded group coordination in the 1940s as it had in the previous two decades, and would continue to do so in the 1950s and 1960s.

Why did Randolph maintain the MOWM, given the opposition it engendered from the established rights organizations? Many observers would accuse Randolph of "panting for leadership," like George Schuyler earlier. While the desire for power and influence undoubtedly played a part, a multiplicity of factors entered into Randolph's decision. Mistreatment of black soldiers continued without letup and without punishment. Although the FEPC had made some gains, by and large the predicament of blacks was only slightly improved: industry granted token employment, but the pattern of blacks in menial, low-paying occupations remained unbroken. Truly the FEPC did need a "watchdog." But Randolph's primary purpose in keeping the MOWM going was that it approached the black problem in America in a different way. It aspired to be "a mass movement" and looked for its support "among the great mass of working class and rural Negroes." It favored "bolder, more direct action than some other Negro organizations," basing its approach on the belief that the fight for black rights "must be conducted on a much broader, more political basis." Randolph refused to condemn other black organizations but argued it was "not enough to fight isolated instances of injustice, not enough to do research and educational work."[76]

Although their organizations parted company, Randolph and White retained a personal relationship of warmth and mutual regard. It was White who insisted the BSCP should be reimbursed for out-of-pocket expenses incurred in setting up the threatened march in 1941 because it had already contributed through Randolph's "leadership and unselfish service far more than could be measured in dollars and cents." Subsequently defending Randolph to a critical NAACP contributor, White said, "We do not have any person in the race or out of it who, in my opinion, is more honest, intelligent, uncompromising and unselfish than he." White agreed to NAACP support for the mass rallies because of his faith in Randolph's judgment. Answering critics who questioned the wisdom of the associa-

76. Memorandum to Mr. White from Mr. Wilkins, September 1, 1942, in NAACP Papers; March on Washington Movement—What Do We Stand For.

tion's participation, White emphasized, "Philip Randolph is absolutely straight and we need never fear anything from him."[77]

When Horace Cayton's Pittsburgh *Courier* column suggested dissension between Randolph and White in the summer of 1942, White wrote to Randolph, "If he thinks that he or anybody else can create any friction or jealousy between you and me he is even nuttier than I think he is." Somehow White even convinced others in the NAACP not to let their bitterness at Randolph's having set up a rival organization interfere with their recognition of his ability. White's persuasiveness is shown by the fact the NAACP board of directors elected Randolph as a vice-president in 1946.[78]

Thus Randolph became an acknowledged civil rights leader, his rise to preeminence facilitated by the black community's militance and anger over discriminatory treatment. Randolph's failure to remain in the forefront resulted from his liabilities as a leader, which surfaced in the MOWM. One drawback was his difficulty in concentrating all his energies on one cause. Part of the reason he could not give sufficient attention to the MOWM, for example, was that while he was planning for the mass rallies in the summer of 1942, he was also involved in trying to save Odell Waller from execution in Virginia. Waller, a black sharecropper convicted of killing his landlord, had pleaded self-defense on the grounds that the landlord threatened him when he tried to get his fair share of the crop, which his family needed to keep from starving. Randolph thought the Waller case represented "a test case for American democracy" because it raised the constitutional question of "whether a man convicted by a jury from which his whole economic class has been deliberately excluded can be rightly said to have been tried by a jury of his peers." Randolph's contention that the poll tax debarred poor blacks from the jury selection list received support from liberal white journalists. Declaring "Odell Waller Must Not Die," Randolph designated the June, 1942, issue of the *Black Worker* a "Special Odell Waller Issue," despite the fact that the mass rallies were scheduled to take place in June and their success depended upon maximum publicity. He also requested that black churches throughout the country set aside Sunday, May 31, to pray for Waller.[79]

77. White to Randolph, August 25, 1941, Randolph to White, September 4, 1941, White to Clifford Morgan, February 13, 1942 [dictated February 4, 1942], White to Randolph, April 29, 1942 [dictated April 27, 1942], White to Daisy E. Lampkin, April 6, 1942, all in NAACP Papers.

78. White to Randolph, July 27, 1942, January 21, 1946, both in NAACP Papers.

79. "Democracy Demands Justice: Case of Odell Waller," *Christian Century*, June 3, 1942, pp. 717–18; *Black Worker*, June, 1942, p. 1.

Wanting to force a showdown on the poll tax, Randolph encouraged the BSCP to give strong moral and financial backing to the Workers' Defense League (WDL) effort to save Waller. Randolph and his followers threatened to throw a picket line around the White House, and they accused the president of "lack of sensibility" to Afro-American problems and of allowing the southern bloc in Congress to maintain a stranglehold that inhibited Roosevelt's "humanitarian approach." Although they warned of greater black discontent and militancy, the president refused to meet with them, and government pressure forced them to cancel their picket line.[80]

Despite the combined efforts of Randolph and the MOWM, the largely white WDL, and the NAACP, Waller was executed on July 2, 1942. The MOWM and the WDL then quickly organized a silent protest parade to take place in New York City on July 25. The conception for the parade was dramatic: Following the precedent of the 1917 silent parade of blacks in New York, the march was to be accompanied by the sound of muffled drums. The participants would wear black armbands to protest the execution of Waller as well as the continued existence of the poll tax and lynching in the South. After Randolph announced the parade, however, he placed Pauli Murray in charge and left town. The New York branch of the MOWM was just recovering from its successful Madison Square Garden rally and had disbanded its committees. The membership was not disposed to march in the streets, and Murray was left without an organizational base or money. Consequently, only about four hundred blacks, augmented by some one hundred whites, actually paraded—a rather poor showing even with the short notice.[81]

Organizational friction prevented the silent-march planners from putting forth their best efforts. Although they were bound by Randolph's commitment to work in harmony with the WDL now that there "was not enough time to do anything more," MOWM members feared their group would be "swallowed up" by the WDL. Resentment ran so high that MOWM officers never acknowledged the instrumental role played by

80. Randolph *et al.* to Roosevelt, July 17, 1942, Telegram, Randolph and White to Roosevelt, July 1, 1942, both in FDR Papers. On July 4, 1942, the Chicago *Defender* incorrectly reported that Randolph headed a committee that met with the president July 1, 1942. Randolph was, in fact, unable to make an appointment with the president even when he tried for a third time in August (Telegram, Randolph to Roosevelt, August 1, 1942, Telegram, M. H. McIntyre to Randolph, August 6, 1942, both in FDR Papers).

81. Interview with Pauli Murray, October 15, 1984; Pittsburgh *Courier*, August 1, 1942.

the WDL in preparing for the parade. Thus another of Randolph's attempts to work cooperatively with whites proved less than successful, even though he had always enjoyed good relations with the Socialist WDL and its national secretary, Morris Milgram, who was one of his closest white colleagues. The experience with the silent parade served to harden Randolph's resolve to keep the MOWM all black. There were other interracial groups, he reasoned, and it was necessary to restrict the MOWM's membership "to show the world that Negroes can do things to help themselves without the assistance of others."[82]

As Randolph's time was so divided, he was forced to depend on his able group of lieutenants, although he only reluctantly shared authority with them. Milton Webster was crucial both in getting the Chicago unit of the MOWM started and in the subsequent success of the Chicago mass rally. Webster later became disaffected, however, as he perceived the march movement taking too much of Randolph's attention away from the BSCP. At any rate, once Webster was appointed to the FEPC, his services were lost to the institutionalized MOWM.[83]

Both the threatened march and the bureaucratized MOWM depended largely on the BSCP for their secondary leadership—indeed, some thought too much so. C. L. Dellums was head of the Western Division of the MOWM, and another BSCP member, T. D. McNeal, was chairman of the St. Louis Division, the most active and militant branch. Dr. Charles Wesley Burton, who headed the Chicago office of the MOWM, had worked with Randolph as head of the Chicago region of the NNC and enjoyed the personal backing of Webster. When Randolph proposed B. F. McLaurin, international field organizer of the BSCP, for national secretary of the MOWM, one national committee member commented, "Ben is a swell fellow but do you think it wise to have another Brotherhood man as nat'l officer."[84] Lacking Webster's administrative ability, McLaurin could not perform the intermediary function for the MOWM as efficiently as Webster did for the BSCP.

In addition to problems with alliances and secondary-level leadership,

82. Call Meeting of the March on Washington Movement, July 7, 1942, in APR Files; Robert Early, Jr, to the N.A.A.C.P., July 13, 1942, Pauli Murray to George S. Schuyler, July 21, 1942, both in NAACP Papers; St. Louis Scrapbook, in BSCP Papers, CD.
    83. See, for example, Minutes, Chicago Division meeting, April 30, June 22, 23, 24, 25, 1942, all in BSCP Papers, CD.
    84. Penciled note on Randolph to Members of the National Committee of the March on Washington Movement, March 30, 1942, in APR Files.

financing proved a recurring obstacle. Randolph proclaimed: "If it costs money to finance a march on Washington, let Negroes pay for it. If any sacrifices are to be made for Negro rights in National Defense, let Negroes make them," but others were skeptical about his ability to draw financial help from a black community only slowly emerging from the Depression. Even the most conservative estimates, based on the use of volunteer stenographers, required a substantial outlay for the threatened march in 1941. Funds were so tight that Walter White was reluctant to spend the extra money required to fly to Washington from the NAACP convention in Houston, which would have ensured his arriving in time for the march. Yet Randolph's fund-raising schemes were the usual button sales, attempts to obtain contributions from individuals and organizations, and collections in churches on a designated Sunday.[85] Certificates "suitable for framing" were also sold for one dollar each.

Through the sale of ten-cent buttons and whatever other methods they could devise, local March on Washington committees were expected to raise funds to help pay for their marchers' expenses. They were also expected to send half the amount raised to the national steering committee. Thousands of buttons were actually sold, over 15,000 distributed in less than a week in New York City alone. Nevertheless, by June 18, Randolph was forced to admit to White that "the monies have not come in in the volume we need," and to suggest that the NAACP and the BSCP each "provide $500.00 for use on the day of the march."[86]

After the cancellation of the march, a financial report issued by the national steering committee showed that the sale of buttons actually brought in $900. Small donations ranging from one dollar to $975 were received from individuals and organizations, with the largest single contribution, as would be expected, coming from the BSCP. Although its board of directors authorized only $100 initially, the NAACP had contributed $543 by the time of the August accounting.[87]

85. Black Worker, March, 1941, p. 4; Minutes of Meeting of Subcommittee to Draft Program for "March on Washington"; Randolph to Dear Walter, May 6, 1941, White to Dear Philip, May 14, 1941, both in NAACP Papers; Minutes of Sub-Committee Meeting on "March to Washington."

86. See "Suggestions for Developing Local Committee," in NAACP Papers. A Saturday in May was set aside as button day (Bulletin, Negro March-on-Washington Committee, May 22, 1941, in APR Files; Randolph to Dear Walter, June 18, 1941, in NAACP Papers).

87. Black Worker, August, 1941, p. 2; Robert E. Turner, Memories of a Retired Pullman Porter (New York, 1954), 138; White to Dear Philip, May 9, 1941, in NAACP Papers.

The following year, to help erase the looming $4,000 deficit incurred by the mass rallies, Randolph requested that the NAACP increase its pledge. The March on Washington Committee needed a headquarters, a telephone and electric service, workers, typewriters, a printing press, and all the other paraphernalia of a modern pressure movement. The NAACP reluctantly complied; in addition, White used his personal contacts to help Randolph solicit contributions in Chicago, despite the protests of NAACP members that this would hamper the association's fund-raising activities there. At one point White himself questioned the expenditure of so much money for a single rally without "a constructive follow-up program."[88] How to channel the energy released by his dramatic demonstrations would prove to be another recurring problem that Randolph was unable to resolve.

The collection at the Madison Square Garden rally in 1942 amounted to $1,371.69 from 23,000 persons. Contributions and ticket sales, at twenty-five cents each, were enough to pay expenses, making the New York meeting a rare financial success. One of the ushers for the WE ARE AMERICANS, TOO! Conference recalled passing wastebaskets to take up the collection, which provided most of the money to finance the movement there. Organizers also sold advertisements in souvenir programs distributed at the meeting. Subsequently accused of disloyalty, Randolph felt called upon to refute the charge that the Madison Square Garden rally was subsidized by Nazi funds. Every dime of the expense for the extravaganza had been contributed by blacks, he maintained, with the exception of money originating from some tickets bought by liberal white organizations, presumably Socialist-led groups like the WDL.[89]

Following the mass rallies, the MOWM began to experience greater financial difficulties. By the time he called a meeting to discuss plans for the May, 1943, WE ARE AMERICANS, TOO! Conference, Randolph noted the MOWM was "without funds." The financial shortage caused him to postpone the conference, which consequently did not take place until after the Detroit race riot of June 20, 1943. The projected cost of the convention was $12,000. Lacking other prospects, members of the

88. Randolph to White, April 14, 1942, Eardlie John to White, April 17, 1942, White to Dear Daisy [Lampkin], April 2, 1942, all in NAACP Papers; White to Randolph, April 21, 1942, in BSCP Papers, LC.

89. Eardlie [John] to White, Saturday after June 17, 1942, Report of Finance Committee, MOWM, August 7, 1942, both in NAACP Papers, LC; Interview with Leroy Shackelford, Jr., November 9, 1972; Randolph, "Why Should We March?," 488–89.

national conference committee personally put up money for office rent. Despite the desperate need, the committee had trouble devising novel fund-raising methods. It settled on having ministers take up "after collections," asking "boosters" to contribute $5 or more, sending out personal appeal letters, and selling advertisements for a souvenir journal. In addition, participants in the week-long program of special events accompanying the conference were to wear identifying caps made of blue crepe paper, which the local units could buy from national headquarters for six cents each and sell for ten cents, with the profit remaining in the local treasury to finance local activities.[90]

A dollar registration fee was charged for the Chicago convention, with admission for the mass meetings and programs placed at twenty-five cents. Although the convention raised between $7,000 and $10,000, another problem arose: A large percentage of the proceeds slipped away from the national office because of inadequate organization and control.[91]

By the fall following the WE ARE AMERICANS, TOO! Conference, the MOWM was in dire financial straits. It owed $2,000 and had only $86 on hand. The executive committee secured a loan to underwrite the organization for a six-month period, but received payment of only three pledges. The committee then sought suggestions "for putting the Movement on a sound financial basis," meanwhile deciding to cut back on expenditures and activities. Of foremost importance, saying that she had "not been as successful as had been hoped and expected," the committee decided to dispense with the services of Meyers as executive secretary and save her $200-a-month salary. Yet without a full-time national secretary, the MOWM lost any pretense to the status of a nationwide black rights organization.[92]

90. MOWM Financial Report, September 26, 1942–July 1, 1943, Randolph to Thurman L. Dodson, April 27, 1943, both in APR Files; E. Pauline Meyers to the St. Louis Branch MOWM, May 3, 1943, in BSCP Papers, CD; Minutes of National Executive Meeting, MOWM, May 14 & 15, 1943, Randolph to Dear Friends, May 24, 1942, MARCH-ON-WASHINGTON MOVEMENT, all in APR Files; Randolph to White, June 12, 1943, in NAACP Papers; Memorandum to Mr. White from Mr. Wilkins: March on Washington Convention in Chicago. The hats had a red, white, and silver band with the slogan WE ARE AMERICANS—TOO! Defeat Hitler-Mussolini and Hirohito—By enforcing Constitution and Abolishing Jim-Crow."

91. Memorandum to Mr. White from Mr. Wilkins: Supplementary report on the March on Washington convention; Wilkins to Dear Walter [White], July 1, 1943, in NAACP Papers.

92. Aldrich Turner to each member of the National Executive Committee, November 11, 1943, McLaurin *et al.* to Randolph and to Mr. A. L. Thomas, November 10,

A budget of $10,000 was projected to keep the organization going from August, 1943, to the end of 1944. Randolph and other loyalists made personal contributions to the cause, but they were not sufficient to keep the organization afloat.[93] With the exception of St. Louis, most branches of the MOWM had fallen into decline by 1944. Consistently the most militant, the St. Louis branch had notable success in producing 5,000 jobs by desegregating industrial plants and public service companies. It also organized effective demonstrations against racial segregation at lunch counters and department stores, as well as boycotts and picketing of offending businesses. Yet in the winter of 1944, B. F. McLaurin complained that no monies had been received from the St. Louis branch since the Chicago convention, even though the National Office was finding it increasingly necessary to rely on the local units for support.

Acknowledging the "number of individuals who would be very happy to see the organization fold up," McLaurin nevertheless exuded confidence that the MOWM would "be able to stem the tide." By the fall of 1945, however, Randolph was enmeshed in other activities and no longer interested in maintaining the MOWM. In the fall of 1946, he pointed out that its origins and history stamped the movement as an "emergency war organization which fulfilled an important and vital mission," and suggested a conference to discuss its possible dissolution. Still, the little nucleus of the devoted clung to the MOWM, although the organization could not even support a conference called to consider its future in June, 1947. "For obvious reasons," it became necessary to postpone the conference until the following fall.[94] Thus the MOWM gradually faded away.

In 1942 Roy Wilkins had prophesied that a permanent MOWM would ultimately fail because "a steady dependable source of regular income has to be built up if an organization is to live." Merely to hold semi-monthly forums at which a collection would be taken up was too pre-

---

1943, both in APR Files; St. Louis Scrapbook, BSCP Papers, CD; Aldrich Turner to B. F. McLaurin, November 12, 1943, E. Pauline Meyers to Randolph, December 2, 1943, both in APR Files.

93. Audit Report, March on Washington Movement, August 1, 1943–December 31, 1944, dated April 19, 1945, in APR Files. The New York Division and National Office accounts are difficult to separate in this audit.

94. B. F. McLaurin to St. Louis MOWM, February 21, 1944, in St. Louis Scrapbook, BSCP Papers, CD; B. F. McLaurin to All Local Presidents, March on Washington Movement, September 6, 1945, Randolph to Dear Fellow Marcher, September 10, 1946, McLaurin to Dear Friend and Co-Worker, June 9, 1947, all in APR Files.

carious a way to raise money to guarantee office rent, mailing expenses, and salaries. Wilkins' prediction proved to be all too accurate. Even with the BSCP contributing some $50,000 over the years, the activities of the MOWM were continually circumscribed by inadequate funding—a constraint Randolph found almost impossible to overcome in all his rights organizations.[95]

Still, Randolph did something no black had ever done before: He pressured the president of the United States into making concessions to the black community, an achievement historian Harvard Sitkoff has characterized as contributing to the emergence of civil rights as a national issue. Thus, if only temporarily, Randolph was elevated to the position of charismatic leader. Although the Chicago *Defender* initially dismissed Randolph's march proposal—saying, "To get 10,000 Negroes assembled in one spot, under one banner with justice, democracy and work as their slogan would be the miracle of the century"—and Randolph himself was uncertain people would actually march, his followers nevertheless believed his prediction of 100,000 blacks marching on Washington.[96]

There is no doubt that in the early 1940s Randolph had the qualities of a charismatic leader. He was handsome, tall, imposing in stature and bearing, and possessed of a magnificent speaking voice. His delivery had been carefully honed through the years through his experience as a Shakespearean actor, a Socialist street corner orator, and finally a public speaker on behalf of unions and black civil rights. Although an atheist himself, Randolph never ceased to include biblical imagery in his speeches and writing. Exposed in his youth to the oratorical style of black preaching, he utilized to good effect the repetitive cadence of the black preacher:

> Hence, let the Negro masses speak!
> Let the Negro masses march!
> Let the Negro masses fight![97]

Randolph sometimes drew on speeches already familiar to his audience. From Abraham Lincoln came, "Now we are engaged in a great world revolution testing whether this nation or any nation so conceived

95. Wilkins to White, June 24, 1942, in NAACP Papers; Kempton, *Part of Our Time,* 252; Embree, *Thirteen Against the Odds,* 229.
96. Sitkoff, *A New Deal for Blacks,* 309; Chicago *Defender,* February 8, 1941.
97. *Black Worker,* March, 1941, p. 4.

and so dedicated can long endure." He adapted phrases from Franklin Roosevelt: "Freedom from want! Freedom from fear! Freedom from Jim Crow!" and "Dear fellow Negro Americans, be not dismayed by these terrible times. You possess power, great power."[98] These "Rooseveltisms" gave a legitimacy to the call to march on Washington that it might not otherwise have had. Further, they created in the minds of the listeners images of their own personal Roosevelt, in the form of Randolph, leading them from depression to prosperity.

Pageantry was yet another device Randolph employed; his mass rallies relied on spectacle in a manner reminiscent of Marcus Garvey. At the Madison Square Garden rally, for example, Randolph "was escorted through the auditorium by a hundred Pullman porters in uniform. A chef in white cap and apron marched at the head of the procession while fifty maids formed the rear guard." Randolph was tumultuously greeted as the audience rose to its feet and applauded while the BSCP's marching band played the union's song, "Hold the Fort for We Are Coming."[99] Randolph's manipulation of this type of dramatic symbol was important in attracting a large following.

Randolph continually pushed his followers into more militant types of behavior by emphasizing that they should "Fight for Freedom" and "Pay for Equality of Rights." He said they "Must Storm" Madison Square Garden and the Chicago Coliseum, and urged them to show "Manhood," "Courage," "Guts," and "Determination." Urging "Wake Up Negro America!" he listed black "demands" rather than requests as had the old-style leaders. In planning for the Chicago mass meeting, he cautioned against "any spiritual song that indicates resignation or weakness."[100]

But Randolph enjoyed only situational charisma, originating with the masses of blacks arriving in the urban areas. The newcomers triggered virulent white racism, which in turn fed black anger and militance. According to Richard Dalfiume, "Mass militancy became common among American Negroes in World War II," a development that "was personified by the MOWM and was the reason for its wide appeal. Furthermore,

98. *Ibid.,* May, 1943, p. 4; Pamphlet, *Why Should We March?,* in NAACP Papers; *Black Worker,* May, 1941, p. 4.

99. Theophilus Lewis, "Plays and a Point of View," *Interracial Review* (July, 1942), 111; Dufty, "A Post Portrait," January 3, 1960.

100. See, for example, Handbills for Mass Meeting at Madison Square Garden, in NAACP Papers; Randolph to Neva Ryan, May 22, 1942, in APR Files.

older Negro organizations found themselves pushed from below into militant stands."[101] But while rallies and talk about marches worked in the short run, over a longer time span they did not help Randolph paper over differences with the established black rights groups. The NAACP and the NUL were willing to join in an *ad hoc* coalition with Randolph to march on Washington; they were not willing to tolerate the continuation of a rival organization competing for the scarce assets of the black community. With time, the divergence of goals and strategies became too great to breach. The NAACP and the NUL were still dependent on white patrons for skills, additional financial support, and entrée to the decision-making apparatus of the dominant community. They were still run by the old black bourgeoisie, men with prestige but little power, whose approach Randolph rejected. The moment had arrived, he believed, for Afro-Americans to break free of such dependence on whites.

Given the time and place, Randolph's schemes of colorful mass rallies and local blackouts had much to commend them. They took advantage of modern urban conditions. They were easily comprehensible, and putting them into practice required neither a great deal of money nor long-term dedication or sacrifice. Building on the slim resources of the ghetto, they attracted many previously unaffiliated lower-class blacks. Despite some lip service to the contrary, the MOWM was not created—and made no serious attempt—to reach tenant farmers and sharecroppers located throughout the South. Rather, Randolph's pressure tactics required concentrated numbers of enfranchised Afro-Americans, and the MOWM was designed to take advantage of the huge concentrations of blacks in the largest northern ghettos.[102]

At first the masses flocked into the movement, but industrial discrimination was only slightly abated by the tangible achievement of the march threat—the FEPC—and the armed services continued to be segregated. Tension in the black community remained high, even after the United States entered the war. Although Randolph inaugurated the MOWM to respond to these conditions, many of his followers believed that a movement incorporating the word *march* in its name should indeed march. Yet, paradoxically, the idea of a mass protest march against the federal government during wartime seemed treasonous. No matter how loudly

101. Richard M. Dalfiume, *Desegregation of the U.S. Armed Forces* (Columbia, Mo., 1969), 122–23.

102. Richard J. Thomas to Randolph, October 31, 1941, in APR Files.

Randolph proclaimed loyalty with his slogan "Winning Democracy for the Negro Is Winning the War for Democracy," the MOWM retained a slightly unpatriotic tone.

Then, in the fall of 1942, Randolph began proposing small-scale, non-violent actions to gain greater rights for Afro-Americans. By this time, in critical need of manpower, the nation's war industries had begun hiring more blacks. The initial response among blacks to the lifting of economic distress was a lessening of militancy; impeding the war effort began to seem as unpatriotic to blacks as it did to whites.

Increased black employment brought additional migration to the industrial cities, however, resulting in competition with whites for some jobs and, more important, scarce housing as the overcrowded ghettos began to overrun their boundaries. These provocations fused together and led to a wave of race riots in the summer of 1943, the worst of which occurred in Detroit on June 20. The Chicago convention of the MOWM, which began on June 30, proved ill timed. The outbreaks seemed to confirm the predictions of Randolph's critics, both black and white, that civil disobedience advocated by "militant" leadership would lead to racial conflict. In addition to the stigma of disloyalty, the nonviolent MOWM now had to contend with the accusation that it was promoting violence as well. Thus, by the time the Chicago convention opened, the climate was no longer conducive to an MOWM based on nonviolent, direct mass action tactics, and the first trial of mass civil disobedience in this country was aborted. As Harvard Sitkoff has demonstrated, the racial violence of the bloody summer of 1943 caused black leaders to retreat from militancy and instead seek aid from white liberals for congressional and court battles.[103] The opportunity to build an all-encompassing civil rights movement provided by wartime needs for unity and manpower had passed.

The loss in following Randolph suffered as a result of routinization of his organization, the change to an abstract ideology, and the altered atmosphere of a country engaged in world war all contributed to the decline of the march movement at the same time that membership in the older, more moderate NAACP reached a new high.[104] Time would show,

103. White, *Man Called White*, 226–67; Robert Goldston, *The Negro Revolution* (New York, 1968), 195; Harvard Sitkoff, "Racial Militancy and Interracial Violence in the Second World War," *Journal of American History*, LVIII (December, 1971), 661–81.

104. Zangrando, *NAACP Crusade Against Lynching*, 171.

however, that the employment of political pressure and nonviolent, direct mass action as techniques to gain greater equality had much merit for a minority group lacking in power and influence. Randolph's adoption of these tactics came, as his pacifist coalition supporters in FOR realized, not from any religious belief, but rather from the pragmatic conviction that nonviolent civil disobedience was an effective political weapon. Randolph had the strategy, but the black community did not possess the means to implement it. Civil disobedience was too ideologically oriented to appeal to a people laboring to support their families; they needed immediate gains, not elusive causes.

Although the wartime atmosphere was not conducive to the sustained success of the MOWM, the 1940s would prove pivotal to Afro-American fortunes. Randolph designed his march movement to take advantage of the war-induced demographic changes, the significance of which few others at the time appreciated. The MOWM had a profound effect on the future generation of civil rights leaders, many of whom first became race conscious and received their organizational training under Randolph's tutelage. Bayard Rustin, active in the Youth Division, James Forman, who credited the march movement with making him aware of the race issue, Pauli Murray, who honed her writing skills in movement work, and the porter E. D. Nixon, who later became the initial organizer of the Montgomery bus boycott, were among those substantially influenced by the MOWM.[105] The legacy of the march movement lies in the legitimacy it gave to the ideology of civil disobedience among the young. They would grow up convinced of the efficacy of nonviolent direct mass action as a strategy to gain greater rights for Afro-Americans.

105. James Forman, *The Making of Black Revolutionaries* (New York, 1972), 30.

III / Fair Employment and Politics

The crowning achievement of Randolph's march threat was Executive Order No. 8802, establishing the FEPC. In the public consciousness Randolph's name was synonymous with the FEPC, and to the black masses the agency became a panacea that would alleviate all their problems. In the view of one historian, the FEPC was one of the "most significant creations of the Roosevelt Administration"; another claimed it "constituted the most important effort in the history of this country to eliminate discrimination in employment by use of governmental authority." [1] Although it was only a temporary wartime measure, the FEPC did to some extent increase the number of Afro-Americans in fields of employment theretofore closed to them. It also created an awareness in the leaders of American industry that they had a responsibility to the public in their employment practices. Above all, the FEPC proved Randolph's thesis that properly applied pressure would yield practical dividends, and that the threat of direct mass action was the correct tactic to use on an executive sensitive to public opinion.

Randolph tailored his methods to take advantage of the changing condition of Afro-Americans. As slaves blacks had been completely dependent on their masters for the necessities of life. During Reconstruction, the federal government had helped provide the freedmen with jobs, education, and personal safety, but after the Compromise of 1877, when the South was left to handle its "Negro problem" in its own way, blacks were forced to revert to dependence on their white employers for support and protection. In the process they developed patron-client relationships with

1. Winifred Raushenbush, "Green Light for the FEPC," *Survey Graphic* (December, 1943), 501; Louis Ruchames, *Race, Jobs, and Politics: The Story of the FEPC* (New York, 1953), 22.

their sponsors. This situation began to alter somewhat with the social welfare measures of the New Deal, as the government began to take responsibility for the well-being of its citizens, but as young black intellectuals like Ralph Bunche were quick to point out, New Deal measures did not always work to the advantage of Afro-Americans.[2]

Randolph's achievement of the FEPC contributed to a reorientation wherein blacks began to look first to the federal government, rather than to wealthy white patrons, on matters affecting their welfare. The New Deal had sparked a shift in black political allegiance from the Republicans to the Democrats while the war had instigated another "Great Migration" of blacks from the rural South to the urban North. Randolph early realized the problems inherent in too great a black dependence on the federal government and the Democratic party. He was confronted by the reality of Afro-American powerlessness as he endeavored to turn the temporary wartime FEPC into a permanent agency through the National Council for a Permanent Fair Employment Practices Committee. The drive for permanent legislation hinged on a lobbying campaign in Congress, but unlike the administration, the legislative branch proved invulnerable to mass action tactics. The direct action strategy itself fell victim to anti-Communist paranoia during the cold war. Additionally, Randolph compounded his difficulties in obtaining a permanent FEPC by his self-defeating political machinations.

At the FEPC's inception, Randolph requested that he and Walter White be consulted regarding appointments. Randolph declined to serve himself, saying he desired to continue his efforts with the MOWM; furthermore, he was afraid that if he took a place on the committee, "it would seem to indicate a selfish end being accomplished." Randolph's dislike of administrative detail probably figured in his decision as well. After his refusal of a position, the MOWM national committee, anticipating that the most serious problems the FEPC would face would "hinge around" union issues, chose Milton P. Webster as their candidate because of his

2. Kilson, "Political Change in the Negro Ghetto, 1900–1940s," 177. For the effect of New Deal economic measures on Afro-Americans, see John B. Kirby, *Black Americans in the Roosevelt Era: Liberalism and Race* (Knoxville, 1980); James O. Young, *Black Writers of the Thirties* (Baton Rouge, 1973); Bunche, "Programs of Organizations," 543; Bunche, "A Critical Analysis of Tactics and Programs," 308–20.

"experience and skill in handling difficult labor situations."[3] Webster turned out to be a great asset to the FEPC and the only person to continue to serve when it was reorganized as the Second President's Committee on Fair Employment in 1943.

Following the issuance of the executive order, a clause prohibiting discrimination had been placed in all defense contracts, and the committee began its work of receiving and investigating complaints of violations on account of race, color, religion, or national origin. Thus not only Afro-Americans, but other minorities as well, took advantage of the FEPC. From the beginning it was deluged with complaints, more than six thousand filed in a year's time. Although the committee had no power to institute punishment, and although it was disinclined to recommend cancellation of war contracts because of the national emergency, its existence had a salutary effect on the employment status of blacks, some companies even changing their policies to avoid having to explain them. The number of black civil servants increased, and the types of positions open to them improved.[4]

The FEPC held a series of public hearings in Los Angeles, Chicago, and New York. Just before the MOWM-sponsored Madison Square Garden rally in 1942, it was announced that the FEPC would "invade" the South with hearings scheduled for Birmingham in June. But when the FEPC field office opened there, stories circulated that its real purpose was to establish "social equality."[5] Rumors abounded that the administration was systematically replacing white soldiers with blacks in Alabama army camps and that in time the black garrisons would take over the state. As FEPC workers recognized, this was the same type of propaganda that had been used to keep unions out of the South.

The Birmingham hearings marked the zenith of the FEPC. Having created it under duress, Roosevelt failed to give the committee the strong backing it needed to be effective. In July, 1942, he transferred the FEPC from his executive office to the War Manpower Commission, where it came under the direct supervision of Manpower Commissioner Paul V. McNutt. The FEPC had annoyed top government officials by insisting that they put an end to discrimination in their own agencies, and black

3. Randolph to Roosevelt, June 30, 1941, in FDR Papers; Minutes, National Committee of Negro March on Washington, July 2, 1941, in APR Files.
4. Ottley, *New World A-Coming*, 302; Franklin, *From Slavery to Freedom*, 439.
5. John Beecher, "8802 Blues," *New Republic* (February 22, 1943), p. 249.

leaders considered the move a bow to reactionary southern pressure. The leaders were apprehensive that the move would result in a conflict of interest, reasoning that the War Manpower Commission could not contemplate punitive action against an employer while asking him to speed up production. Randolph pointed out that the FEPC would be unable to investigate the departments of which it was now a part or the head of the department that supervised it.[6]

Northern industrial interests and white trade unions had had a surreptitious hand in the move, according to labor reporter John Beecher. Led by Randolph, the outcry from black leaders, Jewish organizations, and other liberal groups forced the president to make a public statement that the shift was made with "the intention to strengthen—not to submerge—the Committee, and to reinvigorate—not to repeal—Executive Order 8802." Subsequent events, however, bore out Randolph's fears. After they spent thousands of dollars in months of careful preparation, black organizations were told that McNutt had intervened to indefinitely postpone railroad hearings that had been scheduled for January, 1943. McNutt later claimed that his intervention came at White House direction.[7]

In a rare display of agreement, black leaders, realizing that their pressure powers were greater with the president than with Congress, insisted that the FEPC remain an independent agency responsible directly to Roosevelt. The combined group protest over McNutt's policies was so vociferous that the president removed the FEPC from McNutt's jurisdiction on May 27, 1943, again made it part of his executive office, and gave the committee sufficient funds to function independently. The pressure had been effective. A new executive order, No. 9346, established the Second President's Committee on Fair Employment, consisting of six part-time members and a full-time chairman. The reconstituted FEPC was mandated "to promote the fullest utilization of all available manpower, and

6. Eardlie John to The President of the United States, August 16, 1942, in NAACP Papers; A. Philip Randolph, "The Negro in American Democracy," *Social Action,* January 15, 1943, p. 26.

7. Beecher, "8802 Blues," 250, 248; Telegram, Randolph to Eleanor Roosevelt, January 27, 1942, Telegram, Randolph to Mayor Fiorello LaGuardia, August 6, 1942, LaGuardia to Roosevelt, August 10, 1942, M. H. McIntyre to LaGuardia, August 14, 1942, all in FDR Papers.

to eliminate discriminatory practices."[8] It was empowered to make recommendations to federal agencies, the president, and the War Manpower Commission, to hold hearings and take appropriate steps to eliminate discrimination, and to utilize the services and facilities of other private and public organizations. In addition, the antibias clause the FEPC inserted in government contracts was extended to subcontracts.

The Second President's Committee should have been able to do a more effective job, and indeed expanded its operations to fifteen field offices, but its enforcement system broke down when the president and cooperating agencies failed to back up the committee by invoking sanctions. Government officials did not want to interfere with war production. Furthermore, the FEPC had difficulty making the United States Employment Service and the War and Navy departments take the no-discrimination clause seriously.[9]

After its reconstitution, the FEPC rescheduled the railroad hearings for November, 1943. As a result of the committee's findings, new FEPC chairman Malcolm Ross ordered the southern railroads to stop discrimination and to give blacks an equal chance at almost all jobs, including that of fireman. Although there was a shortage of firemen on the railroads, because of company and union collusion unemployed blacks, even though trained, were not hired for the job.[10]

Aware of the problem much earlier, in March, 1941, Randolph had started the Provisional Committee to Organize Colored Locomotive Firemen. Utilizing BSCP money, the committee began suing the all-white Brotherhood of Locomotive Firemen and Enginemen for damages. To garner publicity and financial contributions and to increase pressure, Randolph also organized the Citizens Committee to Save Colored Locomotive Firemen's Jobs. Because he believed famous names helped attract

8. *Black Worker*, July, 1943, p. 1; Telegram, Randolph to Roosevelt, July 2, 1943, M. H. McIntyre to Randolph, July 5, 1943, Randolph to McIntyre, July 15, 1943, all in FDR Papers; Raushenbush, "Green Light for FEPC," 501; San Diego *Informer*, June 11, 1943.
9. Ruth P. Morgan, *The President and Civil Rights: Policy-Making by Executive Order* (New York, 1970), 51; Randolph to White, November 18, 1943, NAACP Papers; Telegram, Randolph to Roosevelt, November 1, 1943, James F. Byrnes to Randolph, November 10, 1943, Telegram, Randolph to The President, December 27, 1943, all in President's Personal File, FDR Papers.
10. "FEPC Vs. the Railroads," *Time*, December 27, 1943, p. 18.

attention, he made Mayor LaGuardia of New York chairman and persuaded Eleanor Roosevelt to serve as honorary chair.[11] His efforts on behalf of the black firemen presaged the strategies Randolph would later
employ to gain permanent FEPC legislation.

Meanwhile, Ross's order elicited a predictable reaction from the southern carriers: They argued that employment of blacks as stewards would
mean social equality, and employment of blacks as engineers and trainmen would "interfere with the prevailing manners and customs of the civ-
ilization of the section" where the carriers operated. The FEPC ridiculed
these arguments and issued sweeping orders against railroad employment
discrimination. When the carriers continued to defy orders, the president,
rather than declaring that they must comply, appointed a committee to
work out ways to handle the directives. Without a personal commitment
to black equality and preoccupied with the war effort, Roosevelt viewed
preserving his coalition of northern urban political machines and conservative southerners as more compelling than fighting discrimination.
Backed by the FEPC, however, Randolph's Provisional Committee began
to win its legal cases against the southern carriers and white unions. In
1944, the Supreme Court outlawed the antiblack deal between the white
Brotherhood of Locomotive Firemen and Enginemen and the railroads,
and the union was forced to pay off the pending suits.[12] Thus Randolph
was instrumental in proving the effectiveness of the Second President's
Committee.

But the executive order would expire with the coming of peace. Randolph realized that maintenance of the FEPC after the war was a necessity
if blacks were not to be thrown out of their bitterly won, higher-status
jobs to make room for returning white soldiers. Since the omnibus program of the all-black MOWM had not had significant impact, in 1943
Randolph founded the single-issue, racially integrated National Council
for a Permanent FEPC. He anticipated that the fight to make the FEPC
permanent would also aid the Second President's Committee "by giving it
more moral strength" and helping it to "ward off some of its enemies."[13]

11. Lester Velie, "The Porter Who Carried Hope to His Race," *Readers Digest* (May,
1959), 125; *Black Worker*, September, 1941, p. 4.

12. Pittsburgh *Courier*, December 4, 1943; Lester Velie, *Labor U.S.A.* (New York,
1959), 214; "The Supreme Court and Racialism," *Nation*, December 30, 1944, p. 788.

13. Press Release, September 23, 1943, in APR Files; Randolph to White, September 28,
1943, in NAACP Papers.

For the first three years of its existence the FEPC had not been dependent on congressional approval, for it received its appropriations from the president's emergency war funds. Also, segregationists had failed in their attempt to "smear" the FEPC by congressional investigation. But when, in the spring of 1944, the president sent Congress his first request for a congressional appropriation of $500,000 for the agency, southern advocates of white supremacy, together with sympathetic northerners in Congress, saw their first opportunity to abolish the FEPC. That its opponents thought it more important to kill the FEPC than to win the war seemed clearly demonstrated to the agency's supporters by the vote on the omnibus War Agencies Appropriations Bill. When southerners failed to strike the FEPC out of the measure, they voted against passage of the entire bill, thereby denying funds to war-related agencies as well as to the FEPC.[14]

The hearings on the FEPC revealed mounting opposition. Detractors argued that the legislation was unconstitutional and represented a violation of the freedom of the employer to hire those whom he chose; they said blacks were inferior; and they indicated that the aim of the bill's sponsors was to abolish segregation by abrogation of state laws. As opponents gained strength, they resorted to race baiting and claimed the legislation was inspired by Jews who wanted to take away the jobs of boys fighting overseas. Misrepresenting the way the law would work, virulent southern racists urged whites to reassert their rights. Southern white "liberals" (and some northerners) said they deplored discrimination, but its alleviation required "gradualism"; the immediatism of the FEPC would only retard the development of harmonious relations between the races.[15]

The FEPC appropriations bill eventually passed both houses of Congress, but only after the adoption of a restricting amendment proposed by Senator Richard Russell of Georgia. The Russell amendment prevented the use of the president's emergency funds for more than a year for any agency created by executive order. It would now be necessary to seek congressional appropriations for all executive expenditures, and the FEPC was faced with extinction if a recalcitrant Congress refused to fund it. In 1945 President Roosevelt requested a $599,000 appropriation for the

14. Report of the National Council for a Permanent Fair Employment Practices Committee, June 30, 1944, in NAACP Papers.
15. *Ibid;* Report to the Nation, May 22, 1945, in Phileo Nash Files, HST Papers.

FEPC, slightly more than that of the previous year, but in the interval between the request and congressional action on it, he died. As the war appeared to be drawing to a close, legislation to create a permanent FEPC was introduced into both houses of Congress, and predictably southern senators mounted a filibuster. Finally a compromise was agreed upon that cut the FEPC appropriation to $250,000 and stipulated that the agency must terminate either when those funds ran out or at the close of the fiscal year, July 1, 1946, unless a bill for a permanent FEPC was passed. Thus for the first time the existence of the Second President's Committee was tied to permanent legislation.[16]

With the end of the war in August came rapid reconversion from war to peacetime production. As an emergency war agency, the Second President's Committee had no jurisdiction over the converted industries, and all but three FEPC regional offices were closed by December 15. When a Senate-House conference committee denied funds for a final FEPC report requested by President Truman, the Second President's Committee closed its offices in May, 1946, and used what was left of the year's appropriation to compile a final report, which showed that during their short life the two meagerly supported President's Committees had "satisfactorily settled" nearly five thousand cases by peaceful negotiation.[17]

The FEPC had thus begun slow progress toward improving the economic situation of blacks. Where the war industries had employed only 3 percent nonwhites in 1941, they employed 7.2 percent by January, 1944. But Chairman Ross revealed that blacks were not secure in their gains. "The Negro," he said, "has made practically no advance in any industry which is basic to the peace-time economy. The real problem is to see that the Negro finds employment in the new peace-time industries." Blacks were not likely to find such employment without government protection for minorities. Early reports indicated that the reconversion brought a return to the prewar pattern of discrimination: In some sections of the country 50 percent of job descriptions contained discriminatory provi-

---

16. Report to the Nation, July 16, 1945, in Nash Files, HST Papers. No roll call vote was taken on the compromise proposal in the House. The National Council thought this was because those in favor were not eager to be recorded.

17. Telegram, Anna Arnold Hedgeman to Walter White, November 13, 1945, in NAACP Papers; Press Release, May 3, 1946, Nash Files, HST Papers; Morgan, *President and Civil Rights*, 51.

sions. The final FEPC report revealed and documented "increasing dis-crimination in employment since the war in eleven American cities."[18]

Randolph's tour of the country in the fall of 1945 confirmed these findings, as he observed mounting black unemployment and predicted "inevitable violence." He deplored the fact that reconverted industries were returning "to their old habits of discriminating against Jews and Catholics, Negroes and Mexicans. Their policy once more is to divide the worker and build cheap labor markets."[19] In an effort to head off disaster, Randolph concentrated on his National Council for a Permanent FEPC.

The idea of a movement for a permanent FEPC with strong enforce-ment powers had been discussed in Washington in February, 1943, at the Conference to Save FEPC. The National Council for a Permanent FEPC was formally created at a second Conference to Save FEPC, held in Sep-tember of that year and attended by one hundred delegates representing fifteen organizations and states. A budget was drawn up, a constitution drafted, and the wording of bills to establish a permanent FEPC discussed.[20]

In addition to permanent legislation, Randolph had two other primary goals for the National Council—preventing blacks from losing employ-ment when the wartime FEPC passed out of existence, and aiding the Sec-ond President's Committee in its remaining days. He and other support-ers of a permanent committee wanted more than the continuation of the wartime agency: They wanted the new FEPC to have sufficient funds and power to be effective; they wanted an "FEPC with 'teeth.'" Proponents of permanent legislation realized, however, that to win broad support with adequate funding and authority required majority acceptance of the prin-ciple of federal action to prevent discrimination in employment.[21]

Further objectives of the National Council were promoting the estab-

18. Report of the National Council for a Permanent Fair Employment Practices Com-mittee; Press Release, November 26, 1945, *Michigan Chronicle,* April 5, 1947, both in Nash Files, HST Papers.

19. Press Release, October 18, 1945, in Nash Files, HST Papers.

20. Call to Save the FEPC Conference, in St. Louis Scrapbook, BSCP Papers, CD; Call for Conference, National Council for a Permanent FEPC, January 4, 1944, in ULP Records; The National Council for a Permanent F.E.P.C,. 1943, in NAACP Papers.

21. Press Release, September 23, 1943, in APR Files; Randolph to White, September 28, 1943, Hedgeman to White, July 21, 1944, Memorandum on the Need for Immediate Re-placement of the Present FEPC . . . , October, 1944, Summary of the Scope, Powers and Limitations of the Bill for a Permanent Fair Employment Practices Commission . . . , n.d., Digest of Proposed Fair Employment Practices Act, n.d., all in NAACP Papers.

lishment of equal opportunity in employment; securing hiring on the basis of skills and experience; obtaining equal wages for the same work; and securing the right to promotion within an industry regardless of race, creed, color, or origin. Perhaps most important, the National Council planned a campaign to educate the public to the necessity for equal employment opportunity.[22] The council's officers wanted federal legislation to come under the constitutional authority of Congress and the permanent FEPC to have jurisdiction over industries and unions engaged in interstate commerce as well as agencies of the national government. They anticipated that state legislation to carry the principle into intrastate enterprises would follow.

Looking for someone with a conservative reputation to lend prestige to his new organization, Randolph settled on the Reverend Dr. Allan Knight Chalmers of the Broadway Tabernacle Church. Randolph and Chalmers were elected cochairmen at an early meeting. Randolph, the functioning chairman, wielded the most power in the National Council; Chalmers merely lent his name.[23]

In the beginning the National Council existed primarily on paper; it operated out of the BSCP office in New York, which was managed by one secretary. Realizing that he could not conduct a successful lobbying campaign from New York, as soon as the FEPC bill was introduced into the House, in January, 1944, Randolph took steps to establish a headquarters in Washington. He appointed Anna Arnold Hedgeman, who had been active in the MOWM, as executive secretary. The National Council finally opened its Washington office in February, 1944, after surmounting the problem of finding quarters for its racially diverse staff in the segregated capital.[24]

Since the National Council would represent all minority groups, Randolph reluctantly acquiesced to the necessity of making it both interracial and a federation of civil rights groups. He projected the council as a clearinghouse for all organizational work on behalf of permanent FEPC legislation, thus avoiding duplication of effort and enabling coordination

22. CONSTITUTION, n.d., in NAACP Papers.

23. Eleanor Roosevelt turned down Randolph's request to serve on the National Council. Randolph and Chalmers to Mrs. Franklin D. Roosevelt, November 18, 1943, Eleanor Roosevelt to Randolph, November 24, 1943, both in ER Papers.

24. Alice Stark to Randolph, November 5, 12, 1943, both in APR Files; Randolph to Wilkins, February 24, 1944, in NAACP Papers.

of lobbying activity. Consequently, when the Second President's Committee was involved in its appropriations battle with Congress, the National Council set aside its own work on behalf of permanent legislation to help the temporary agency in its funding fight.[25]

When first established, the Washington office of the National Council worked mainly through its cooperating organizations, which sent material through their own channels to their own local units for consideration and action. But the National Council "soon realized that it was necessary to establish our own local councils," and so Randolph began building local organizations for the purpose of applying pressure locally, as he had in the BSCP and the MOWM.[26] The National Council staff in Washington aided communities in establishing state and local FEPC councils, helped with programming and education, distributed literature, and provided speakers. The BSCP and the MOWM shared with Randolph the greater part of the responsibility for establishing local permanent-FEPC councils.

The MOWM organized the New York City council that sponsored the large Madison Square Garden rally in February, 1946. Despite obstacles, Randolph's followers began many local councils in the South; Randolph himself set up the New Orleans council while attending the 1944 AFL convention there.[27] These southern locals capitalized on the more progressive attitude toward race relations exemplified by organizations such as the Commission on Interracial Cooperation and the Southern Conference for Human Welfare.

In theory the local councils were to be interracial, interfaith, and "truly representative of the community." The National Council suggested that a prestigious person in each community be made chairman and emphasized that the FEPC bill was "to be for the protection of all minorities and not just for the Negro." The local councils were to make contacts with congressmen in their district and urge them to support the bill for a permanent FEPC. They were also to send local delegations to Washington to secure commitments from individual congressmen to break fili-

25. Randolph and Rev. Dr. Allan Knight Chalmers to Wilkins, February 29, 1944, Hedgeman to White, May 29, 1944, both in NAACP Papers.

26. Minutes, Strategy Conference, National Council for a Permanent FEPC, February 22, 1946, pp. 5, 10–11, in BFM Papers.

27. Press Release, August 11, 1945, in Nash Files, HST Papers; Press Release, January 20, 1945, in APR Files.

busters and committee logjams. Most important, of course, they were to raise money for the National Council. As part of their program the local units promoted "FEPC Sundays," on which ministers were asked to preach about the FEPC and take up collections for it. Philadelphia even celebrated an "FEPC Week."[28]

Yet the National Council displayed contradictory attitudes about the role of the local councils. On the one hand, Randolph pointed out the importance of giving local councils a sense of participation in all phases of the effort and not merely using them as a source of funds; on the other hand, the National Council under his direction tried to maintain tight control by setting up its own regional representative system. Thus Hedgeman admonished Dr. Charles Wesley Burton in Chicago, *"Please do not organize any local councils,"* and by the late 1940s, the national office employed field representatives to do most of the local organizing.[29] But because the National Council was a federated agency, the local units often resented Randolph's intrusion. This attitude contrasted with that of organizations completely under his control, like the BSCP and the MOWM, which always sought the presence of "the Chief" to give legitimacy to their local groups. Although Randolph was careful to give the provincial leaders sufficient autonomy in local decision making to keep them content, Anna Hedgeman, lacking his political skills, was more abrasive in her treatment of regional leaders, thereby provoking animosity toward the national office.

Since the BSCP and the MOWM were instrumental in establishing so many local councils, there was a great deal of commonality of intermediary leadership between the organizations, particularly on the local level. B. F. McLaurin, Thurman Dodson, and Aldrich Turner, all closely involved with the local councils, came from the MOWM, as did Hedgeman. With the National Council depending so heavily on white support, the plethora of black leaders became another source of resentment.

Because passage of permanent legislation would require votes from both Democrats and Republicans, the National Council endeavored to project a nonpartisan image, and the organization's 1943 statement of

28. "Is Your Community Interested in a Permanent Fair Employment Practices Committee?" n.d., in NAACP Papers; Kesselman, *Social Politics of FEPC*, 195–97.

29. Minutes, Executive Committee Meeting, July 2, 1947, in APR Files; Hedgeman to Dr. Charles Wesley Burton, August 27, 1945, in BFM Papers; Manual of Strategy, October, 1945, in NAACP Papers.

principles included quotations from both President Roosevelt and his Republican opponent, Wendell Willkie. As would be expected of a Randolph enterprise, the council rejected support from the "extreme left wing." Susceptibility to red-baiting became more pronounced later in the decade as the cold war fastened its grip on the country. All who championed liberal causes found themselves vulnerable to accusations of disloyalty while their groups were smeared with charges of Communist domination. The National Council, consequently, objected vigorously when far-left congressman Vito Marcantonio of New York was selected to be a spokesman for the FEPC on the radio, and insisted the organization "has never had the support of the extreme left, does not want it and will not accept it."[30] Despite these statements and Randolph's anti-Communist credentials, the civil rights cause in general and the National Council in particular remained suspect.

The drive for permanent legislation formally began at a Washington conference held January 20 and 21, 1944, in an atmosphere of continued defiance of the Second President's Committee directives by the railroad brotherhoods and the southwestern carriers. The supporting groups, which had been broadened to include civic, church, liberal, educational, and even some labor organizations, pledged to work for action by Congress to attack the problem of discrimination at home. They argued elimination of racism in the United States would provide a symbol to all oppressed peoples of the world and convince them of the sincerity of America's determination to implement the Four Freedoms as quickly and effectively as possible.[31]

Randolph had planned to use the black vote as a lever in the 1944 elections to press for passage of permanent FEPC legislation. His hopes were dashed when the House Labor Committee voted to postpone completion of hearings on the bill until after the election. This decision, together with the refusal of the House Appropriations Committee to grant funds to the Second President's Committee, and the Rules Committee's action in January, 1945, to prevent House consideration of permanent legislation, indicated a "vicious intent to kill FEPC altogether" in the view of the Na-

30. Outline of Principles: The National Council for a Permanent FEPC, October 1943, in NAACP Papers; Randolph and Chalmers to the Members of the Board and All Cooperating Organizations, March 29, 1948, Randolph and Chalmers to Edgar Kobak, March 12, 1948, both in Nash files, HST Papers.
31. Kesselman, *Social Politics of FEPC,* 31–32.

tional Council's officers.[32] The stalling provided evidence that a majority in the House did not favor the FEPC and was unwilling to face a vote on the issue.

Aware that the same entrenched economic interests were against both employment legislation and any changes in the racial status quo, Randolph pinpointed the opposition as coming from "the solid south and open shop business interests." The FEPC, however, suffered not only from the antagonism of determined and organized southerners but from the apathy and uncertainty of its supporters.[33]

Before the temporary wartime committee expired in the fall of 1945, Randolph tried to make an appointment to see President Truman to discuss permanent legislation. Randolph reasoned that since Truman had pledged to carry out his predecessor's program, he needed information from persons who had worked with Roosevelt on formulating the executive order. Unsuccessful in getting the appointment but encouraged by Truman's response, Randolph again requested a meeting with the president in February, 1946, but was again turned down. At this time, however, Truman publicly expressed support for permanent FEPC legislation—an action that prompted an appreciative telegram from Randolph.[34]

In January, 1945, bills proposing creation of a permanent FEPC had

32. FLASH, September 20, 1944, in NAACP Papers; Telegram, Randolph to Roosevelt, September 20, 1944, in President's Personal File, FDR Papers; Telegrams, Randolph to Roosevelt and Honorable Thomas E. Dewey, August 25, 1944, both in NAACP Papers. Roosevelt finally granted an interview with the black leaders on the issue after Eleanor Roosevelt interceded. See Memorandum for The President from Jonathan Daniels, September 28, 1944, Telegram, Walter White to General Edwin Watson, September 27, 1944, White to Watson, September 25, 1944, Memorandum for Major General Edwin M. Watson from Jonathan Daniels, September 11, 1944, Telegram, Randolph and White to The President, September 5, 1944, Memorandum for Watson from Daniels, September 6, 1944, Memorandum for Miss Thompson from Roberta, September 29, 1944, Eleanor to General Watson, July 5, 1944, Memo for General Watson from E.R., June 17, 1944, Memorandum for Roberta Barrows from ld, June 20, 1944, General Watson from ld, July 6, 1944, all in FDR Papers; Hedgeman to White, June 5, 1945, Telegram, Randolph and Chalmers to White or Wilkins, June 2, 1945, both in NAACP Papers; Hedgeman to Dear Friend, July 21, 1945, in NAACP Papers.

33. Telegram, Randolph to White, December 28, 1945, in NAACP Papers; Will Maslow, "FEPC—A Case History in Parliamentary Maneuver," *University of Chicago Law Review* (June, 1946), 422.

34. Randolph to Charles Ross, August 31, 1945, Telegram, Randolph to Mr. Conley [sic], September 6, 1945, Telegram, Matthew J. Connelly to Randolph, September 10, 1945, Telegram, Randolph to Connelly, September 29, 1945, Randolph to President Harry S. Truman, September 29, 1945, Connelly to Randolph, October 4, 16, 1945, Randolph to Connelly, October 10, 19, 1945, all in Official File, HST Papers; Randolph to HST, Febru-

been introduced into the House, but rather than recommend a House vote on the bill, the House Rules Committee, after much stalling, had produced only a tie vote. According to several observers, the tie was the result of collusion between southern Democrats and Republican members of the committee. The National Council then held a strategy conference in February to devise ways to push the bill through the Seventy-ninth Congress. Nevertheless, the bill's sponsor, Congresswoman Mary Norton of New Jersey, could not get enough signatures on her petition to have the bill discharged from the Rules Committee, nor was she successful in utilizing a Calendar Wednesday strategy. Thus the House phase of the effort to secure the approval of the Seventy-ninth Congress for a permanent FEPC came to an end.[35]

The National Council held another strategy conference in September, 1945, where conflict developed over legislative tactics. Some council members continued to favor the "House first" approach, but with the bill being held up in the Rules Committee, the National Council announced the "unprecedented step" of seeking an FEPC vote in the Senate first. In the traditional treatment of minority legislation, bills were passed in the House only to be killed in the Senate. Passage in the Senate would put the FEPC issue to the House at a time when all of its members were up for reelection the following year. Commitments to the FEPC in the Senate and the strength shown there during the appropriations fight for the Second President's Committee made the council hopeful for success. Its members reasoned that failure in the Senate would not hurt the situation in the House, although success might help.[36]

But this strategy proved no more effective. In addition to the threat of a southern filibuster, the National Council became concerned that a voluntary FEPC bill introduced by Senator Robert Taft would draw considerable Republican support away from an FEPC with enforcement powers. In the end Taft did not push his voluntary bill, and the National Council's

ary 13, 1946, Connelly to Hedgeman, February 19, 1946, in Nash Files, HST Papers; Telegram, Randolph to Truman, January 5, 1946, Truman to Randolph, January 10, 1946, Memorandum, David K. Niles to Honorable Matthew J. Connelly, January 10, 1946, all in HST Papers.

35. Call for Conference, February 7, 1945, Hedgeman to White, June 5, 1945, Telegram, Randolph and Chalmers to White or Wilkins, June 2, 1945, all in NAACP Papers; Ruchames, *Race, Jobs, and Politics*, 202.

36. Hedgeman to Dear Friends, August 29, 1945, in NAACP Papers; *Black Worker*, August, 1945, p. 3; Press Release, November 26, 1945, A Call for Early Congressional Action on Permanent FEPC Legislation, November 23, 1945, both in Nash Files, HST Papers.

bill, as predicted, was subjected to filibuster. A cloture vote failed by eight votes, signaling the end of FEPC legislation for the session. The major legislative effort of the National Council had ended in failure, and Randolph no longer seemed invincible.[37]

Following the Senate filibuster, the National Council called still another strategy conference, in early 1946, at which Randolph recommended a march on Washington and a conference with the president. Randolph wanted a commitment from Truman to place the administration forces behind the measure "so that when we bring it up in this Congress, we won't have the dilly-dallying we had when it came up before." Anna Hedgeman tried to point out the flaws in the idea of marching on Washington. A march, she argued, "should mean that you have in your hands Congressional district representatives from every district in your states. Remember, getting masses of people together isn't the answer. Those masses of people must have behind them the votes which count and which maneuver the situation as well." When Randolph and Roy Wilkins continued to push for a march, Hedgeman insisted on publicizing it as an "inter-racial, inter-faith, trade-union march." She reminded Randolph and Wilkins that although the black minority had produced the executive order, the wartime committee's experiences showed there were other minorities also facing discrimination, and it was important to keep them involved.[38]

After this strategy conference, the Mass Rally to Save FEPC was held at Madison Square Garden on February 28, 1946. Although the president declined Randolph's invitation to speak, he sent a personal message to be read by the secretary of labor, who was one of the speakers. Truman told Randolph he regarded "Fair Employment Practice Legislation as an integral part of my reconversion program," and in contrast to Roosevelt, he pledged to continue efforts to bring it before Congress.[39]

37. Telegram, Chalmers and Randolph to White or Wilkins, February 6, 1945, Hedgeman to Wilkins, February 15, 1945, both in NAACP Papers. See also Donald R. McCoy and Richard T. Ruetten, *Quest and Response: Minority Rights and the Truman Administration* (Lawrence, Kans., 1973), 33.

38. Minutes, Strategy Conference, National Council for a Permanent FEPC, February 23, 1946, pp. 268, 270–71, in BFM Papers.

39. Randolph to Truman, January 24, 1946, Telegram, Randolph to Truman, January 25, 1946, Truman to Randolph, February 4, 1946, Matthew J. Connelly to Mary H. Blanchard, February 18, 1946, Memorandum for Mr. Niles from Connelly, January 29, 1946, Statement of the President for F.E.P.C. Rally, February 28, 1946, all in Nash Files, HST Papers; Truman to Randolph, February 6, 1946, Official File, *ibid.*

Nevertheless, in his address Randolph told rally participants that FEPC legislation had not been enacted because of the failure of the administration to "place its full force" behind the bill: "Although the President must be credited for his splendid statements for the Bill," words were not sufficient to counter the "unholy alliance" of southern Democrats and northern Republicans. Randolph pledged that FEPC supporters "shall rigidly apply the rule of rewarding our friends and punishing our enemies," and he called for "a silent non-violent march down the streets of the nation's capital if Congress fails by June 30th to enact fair employment practice legislation." By this time, however, the council was in financial trouble, and the proposed march never materialized.[40]

Both Randolph's image and that of the National Council had been tarnished by the congressional defeat. The Chicago *Defender*'s reference to the "long-hibernated National Council" indicated the derision with which the black press now viewed the organization. The *Defender* noted that the group had finally "come out of its shell and started casting about for non-partisan sponsorship" when Randolph and Chalmers announced that the National Council would present bills for permanent legislation to the Eightieth Congress at the earliest opportunity.[41]

While a congressional victory continued to elude the National Council, Truman issued an executive order providing an FEPC for the federal government in 1948 in an attempt to woo the black vote. The strategy worked; blacks supplied an important component in Truman's unexpected reelection. With a Democratic majority in Congress again, when the president announced his Fair Deal in 1949, both he and civil rights proponents anticipated progress on the permanent FEPC bill as well as other prominority measures. Nevertheless, in early February a Senate filibuster developed, this time not over the FEPC itself, but over an effort to change cloture rules to make it easier to shut off debate. Liberals had come to believe that only by eliminating the filibuster could they get reform legislation past intransigent southern senators. The cloture vote lost by a narrow margin, however, demonstrating once again that neither Democrats nor Republicans had much interest in passing the FEPC legislation.[42]

40. A. Philip Randolph, Address to Madison Square Garden Rally, February 28, 1946, in BFM Papers; *Black Worker*, March, 1946, p. 1.

41. Chicago *Defender*, February 28, 1947.

42. Zangrando, *NAACP Crusade Against Lynching*, 200–201.

Early in January, 1949, Randolph revealed that a deal had been struck whereby the Dixiecrats promised to support repeal of the Taft-Hartley Act if no real fight for civil rights legislation were made. Under these circumstances Randolph decided that the Senate rules must be altered if FEPC were to be enacted. Consequently he urged blacks to deluge Congress with calls and telegrams in support of the rules change in order to abolish the use of the filibuster as an anti–civil rights weapon. In March, Randolph wrote an open letter to Truman, declaring that the president must step into the civil rights fight. He asserted that he was in constant contact with mass opinion, and if FEPC legislation was not passed, Afro-Americans would feel "let-down"—a feeling that could be reflected in the 1950 congressional campaign. "It is well nigh axiomatic that the instinct to live in human beings regardless of race or color . . . is so strong that they will fight for the right to work in order to live," noted Randolph, and predicted that unless Congress remedied the situation, "it is apparent that color wars may beset and plague our country in a recession or depression period." [43]

Meanwhile, the NAACP decided that Randolph's National Council was inadequate and, in November, 1949, formed the National Emergency Civil Rights Mobilization, with Roy Wilkins as chairman. The NAACP could not bring itself to give priority to an FEPC bill over anti-lynching and anti–poll tax legislation and thus had been dissatisfied with the National Council for some time. [44] Theoretically concerned with all civil rights issues, the Emergency Civil Rights Mobilization planned to coordinate efforts of racial, ethnic, labor, religious, and political groups on the civil rights legislation front.

Unlike the NAACP, Randolph deemed his approach—making the FEPC a top priority while at the same time working to increase black registration and voting—appropriate. Although he saw no need for another organization, he believed that passage of a federal FEPC bill was too important to obstruct with internecine strife and agreed to full cooperation. The new organization requested that delegates from all over the country come to Washington and petition for passage of FEPC when Congress reconvened in January, 1950. When four thousand persons arrived to

43. *Black Worker,* February, 1949, p. 2; Randolph, "An Open Letter to President Truman," 6; A. Philip Randolph, testimony on behalf of FEPC, May 17, 1949, in *Black Worker,* May, 1949, p. 1.
44. See Zangrando, *NAACP Crusade Against Lynching,* 190.

stage an intensive three-day lobbying campaign, Truman met with them and said he was making every possible effort to get FEPC legislation passed.[45]

But the FEPC fell victim to postponement when the legislature reconvened in January, in part because the European Recovery Program required quick action. The FEPC bill was brought up between work on other business, but was greeted each time with a filibuster. One observer declared, "FEPC is being postponed to death"; another noted it was obvious "that everybody wants civil rights as an issue but not as a law."[46] By spring the Emergency Civil Rights Mobilization no longer had illusions of victory. Stating that it considered itself only a temporary organization, it ended its brief life by merging with the National Council in March, 1950.

After the FEPC defeat that year, Truman made no further major effort to secure civil rights legislation. With the onset of the Korean War in June, without waiting for approval from the National Council's executive committee, Randolph called on Truman to issue an executive order comparable to Roosevelt's creation of the FEPC in 1941. Such an emergency agency, Randolph argued, would be "not only a soundly practical measure of enlightened self-interest but also a moral necessity." Randolph had hoped the president would embody FEPC in his message to Congress, but Truman was hampered by the Russell amendment, adopted in 1944. The funds Roosevelt had been able to utilize under his war powers were not available to Truman.[47]

By 1951, the tenth anniversary of the original FEPC order, Randolph realized there was no possibility of passage of FEPC legislation and be-

45. New York *Times*, January 17, 1950.
46. Francis Biddle, chairman of Americans for Democratic Action, quoted in Alonzo L. Hamby, *Beyond the New Deal: Harry S. Truman and American Liberalism* (New York, 1973), 345; Arthur Krock, quoted in Ruchames, *Race, Jobs, and Politics*, 209.
47. Morgan, *President and Civil Rights*, 35; New York *Times*, September 11, 1950; Telegram, Randolph to The President, July 17, 1950, in General File, HST Papers; Telegram, Randolph to The President, December 14, 1950, in Nash Files, HST Papers; Minutes, Executive Committee meeting, National Council, July 20, 1950, in APR Files; Randolph to Truman, February 21, 1950, Memo, C.G.R. to Dr. John R. Steelman, February 27, 1950; Randolph to David Niles, April 5, 1950, Memo for Honorable John Steelman from Niles, April 25, 1950, Truman to Randolph, May 1, 1950; all in President's Personal File, HST Papers. After the Korean War began, Randolph wrote again, thinking Truman might wish to speak to the BSCP convention (Randolph to Niles, August 7, 1950, Randolph to Honorable Herbert H. Lehman, August 4, 1950, both in President's Personal File, HST Papers).

came more vociferous in his demands for an executive order. Still cognizant of the importance of the black vote, the president responded by ordering the creation of the Committee on Government Contract Compliance.[48] Lacking enforcement provisions, however, the order was solely dependent on persuasion and conciliation.

Meanwhile, black leaders and their white allies were determined that Senate rules allowing bills to be filibustered to death must be changed. The National Council's executive committee unanimously approved the suggestion of labor leader Walter Reuther to establish a committee to work for abolition of the filibuster rule. Another new organization was developed for this purpose, the Leadership Conference on Civil Rights, which took as its slogan "ABOLISH RULE 22 in '52." Randolph was one of a number of civil rights leaders in the Leadership Conference. This campaign also failed, however, and the FEPC issue lay dormant until the next spurt of civil rights legislative activism late in the decade. Proponents of equal employment opportunity realized there was little chance of government involvement in employment practices under the new Eisenhower administration. Devoted to free enterprise and against any form of "coercive" federal regulation, including integration of the military, Eisenhower was also aware that civil rights advocates bore the taint of being leftist as Senator Joseph McCarthy and his repressive tactics reigned supreme. During the ten years liberals had pushed for FEPC legislation, the House Rules Committee had never approved a bill for floor debate and a vote, and no FEPC bill had ever come to an actual vote in the Senate.[49]

What went wrong? Why was the National Council unsuccessful in obtaining a permanent FEPC? The council endeavored to overcome the antipathy engendered by new groups through becoming a federated organization and, in a manner reminiscent of the NNC and the MOWM, strove to assure potential supporters that it was not a permanent organization and would dissolve once its goal was obtained. A struggle for power and

48. Executive Order No. 10208, December 3, 1951; Morgan, *President and Civil Rights*, 28.

49. Arnold Aronson to Walter Reuther, December 21, 1951, in APR Files; Garfinkel, *When Negroes March*, 170; Robert Fredrick Burk, *The Eisenhower Administration and Black Civil Rights* (Knoxville, 1984), especially Chap. 5; Morgan, *President and Civil Rights*, 36.

prestige developed between the cooperating organizations, nevertheless, prompting Anna Hedgeman to complain about the problems caused by the complexity of unsuspected rivalries among the supporting groups.[50]

The NAACP's board of directors voted that Walter White accept membership in the National Council in October, 1943, after Randolph assured White the group would be "independent of any organization." Lester Granger of the NUL argued there was no need for "another National Committee on the subject" of the FEPC but agreed to present the matter to his executive board. He pledged cooperation "from time to time in taking action on specific questions as they arise," but since the NUL always resisted lobbying and pressure tactics, it did not give the National Council much support.[51]

As early as the fall of 1944, White became disenchanted with the National Council and commented to NAACP attorney Thurgood Marshall, "We have got to draw the line somewhere and make a decision soon about the various Randolph organizations which are proposing to handle general legislation, legal defense and other matters about the Negro." The exasperated White continued, "They propose to duplicate the work of the NAACP in whole or in part and then turn around and want us to use our funds, branches, personnel and general machinery to do the job in whole or in part."[52]

In an attempt to combat such criticism, Randolph reported on plans for a "complete reorganization of the Council" at a meeting of the national board of directors in November, 1946. He said that functional committees had been set up to simplify the various activities of the council, a director was being selected to conduct a nationwide fund-raising campaign, and a committee of lawyers was at work drafting the bills. As part of the reorganization, Elmer Henderson assumed the job of executive secretary with the assistance of Paul Sifton; Henderson, however, was never given as much responsibility as Hedgeman had had. The leadership of the council became more representative, with the NAACP playing a

50. MANUAL OF STRATEGY; Anna Arnold Hedgeman, *The Trumpet Sounds: A Memoir of Negro Leadership* (New York, 1964), 93. There are factual errors in Hedgeman's books, so one must be careful in using them.

51. Memo from RR to Mr. White, October 18, 1943, Randolph to White, September 28, 1943, both in NAACP Papers; Granger to Morris Milgram, February 12, 1943, in NUL Papers.

52. Memorandum to Mr. Marshall from Mr. White, September 23, 1944, in NAACP Papers.

larger role and Jewish agencies contributing financial support. Arnold Aronson of the American Council on Race Relations was named secretary of the executive committee and Roy Wilkins chairman. Together they shared direction of the council, and since both were professional administrators, it functioned more efficiently under their leadership.[53] But greater efficiency had no noticeable effect on pushing through permanent FEPC legislation.

Inadequate financing was an important factor in the National Council's poor showing. Randolph utilized all the promotional techniques he had devised for the MOWM to promote permanent FEPC legislation, including the sponsorship of mass rallies, at which collections were taken up. The rallies featured high caliber entertainment and famous personalities sympathetic to the cause. For example, at the Madison Square Garden rally in 1946, which drew a crowd of 19,000, Eleanor Roosevelt and Mayor LaGuardia spoke, the Katherine Dunham dancers performed, and stage and screen stars participated in a skit portraying the continuous fight against bigotry and job discrimination. Sometimes the cost of the rally exceeded the receipts. Some demonstrations, however, were quite successful, such as a meeting in the Kansas City municipal auditorium that netted $4,000 from eight thousand people. Nevertheless, the funds were never sufficient, and as a result the National Council's lobbying activities were circumscribed. David Dubinsky of the International Ladies Garment Workers Union, the original chairman of the finance committee, set up an initial budget of $25,000, of which the first $5,000 was pledged by November, 1943. The council mounted an FEPC button drive and sold FEPC stamps, but stamps and buttons could not raise enough money to keep the council afloat.[54]

In the summer of 1944 the National Council projected a budget of at least $100,000 to carry on its educational function and to push for permanent legislation. To this goal the NAACP had contributed $225 by the

53. Press Release, [stamped November 18, 1946], in APR Files. Aronson was also affiliated with the National Community Relations Advisory Council and later became secretary of the Leadership Conference on Civil Rights.

54. Ralph G. Martin, "FEPC Rally," *New Republic,* March 18, 1946, p. 380; *Black Worker,* March, 1946, p. 8; Randolph to Matthew J. Connelly, October 19, 1945, in Official File, HST Papers; Winifred Raushenbush to The Conference Against Race Discrimination, Dear Member, November 26, 1943, in NAACP Papers; News from Washington, November 20, 1945, in Nash Files, HST Papers; Press Releases, January 20, 1945, December 29, 1944, both in APR Files.

fall. The chairmen complained that although they wanted the FEPC bill brought up before January, they were "handicapped for lack of operating funds." As a result of local council activities, the National Council received some financial support from southern communities. The Chicago division of the BSCP contributed $500, and other divisions also made contributions, but there was still not enough money to mount an effective campaign. Consequently, the strategy conference in February, 1946, took up the problem of fund raising. Randolph objected to a proposal to charge one dollar per council member and issue membership cards because if the council solicited memberships it "would be in competition with other membership organizations." Through his efforts and those of other members of the board of directors, the council obtained $15,000 in contributions from trade unions, religious and civic organizations, and "public spirited individuals."[55]

Despite these efforts the National Council remained in deep financial trouble. In January, 1946, Hedgeman wrote Randolph, saying she could not handle legislative, educational, and administrative duties and also raise funds. Although Randolph did not answer her letter, she claimed that he verbally agreed to take charge of fund raising. Indeed, at the strategy conference, he remarked, "It is my responsibility to see to it that the funds are here to run this movement."[56] Hedgeman maintained that once Randolph assumed responsibility for fund raising, the professional staff could no longer interpret the council's need to the public.

By the summer of 1946, incurred obligations amounted to roughly $18,000, and the need for money was imperative. Hedgeman was forced to inform the staff that unless funds were forthcoming immediately, she had "no alternative" but to resign and terminate their services. Thereupon she advised Randolph that his "total disregard" of her continual notification of impending financial needs made her task an impossible one. Just when the council was beginning to secure commitments to its cause, Hedgeman lamented, "We must now abandon it simply for lack of

55. Your National Council for a Permanent FEPC Reports on the Headlines, July 1, 1944, Receipt, August 4, 1944, Hedgeman to Wilkins, September 18, 1944, Chalmers and Randolph to Dear Friend, October 6, 1944, all in NAACP Papers; Report to the Nation, May 22, 1945, in Nash Files, HST Papers; Minutes, Chicago Division meeting, April 30, 1945, in BSCP Papers, CD; Minutes, Strategy Conference, February 23, 1946, pp. 286–87, News on the FEPC Bill, August 14, 1947, Los Angeles *Sentinel*, June 19, 1947, all in Nash Files, HST Papers.

56. Minutes, Strategy Conference, February 23, 1946, p. 300.

funds and permit some other organization to carry it to fruition." In reply to her outburst, Randolph merely complained that the telegram she sent cost him $11.47. Although having to close the offices was "unfortunate," Randolph said, "it seems to me unavoidable." In his typical fashion, he passed the unpleasant task of dealing with Hedgeman on to another member of the executive committee.[57]

Hedgeman said nothing to the public of the National Council's financial troubles; rather, she indicated in a press release that the council was not effectively using the established political affiliations necessary for the enactment of permanent legislation. "Therefore," Hedgeman stated, "I have no choice except to resign." The executive committee clearly was not adverse to this decision: Her resignation was submitted August 2, but accepted as of August 1.[58]

Of course, Hedgeman's resignation did not alleviate the council's financial problems. In the summer of 1947, Paul Sifton, the new director of legislation and public relations, complained that his effectiveness had been reduced from the beginning because of "lack of funds for stenographic, clerical, research and writing personnel." He added that he was not willing to continue in an organization that might lose the fight because it was inadequately financed, planned, organized, staffed, and coordinated. "If the National Council is to be operated as a Washington peanut stand with a stuck whistle, I want to check out, with all friendship and best wishes, with the recessing of Congress." But, Sifton insisted, if the council were adequately funded, he would "be willing and proud to continue."[59]

Sifton defended the National Council against criticisms of the way it handled the congressional hearings. He insisted the council had planned a "rather thorough" job of coverage, reporting, analysis of testimony, and press releases for the hearings, but "principally because of lack of funds for staff, it was not possible to deliver as we had planned and hoped." Sifton was never supplied with the service operation he had expected when he accepted the job, and *the principal reason was money.*" The National Council was so short of funds that mail was held up for lack of postage. Sifton's secretary became ill after three weeks on the job and left. Even though he considered a secretary the "absolute minimum for any

57. Day Letter, Hedgeman to Randolph, July 15, 1946, Randolph to [Nathaniel] Minkoff, July 19, 1946, both in APR Files.
58. Press Release, September 4, 1946, in Nash Files, HST Papers.
59. Memo, Paul Sifton to Roy Wilkins, June 30, 1947, in APR Files.

efficiency of operation," the financial stringency made replacing her impossible, and he had no assistant for press releases, hearing coverage, or contact.[60]

When Elmer Henderson took over as executive secretary, he too was plagued with the shortage of funds and outstanding debts. In addition, Henderson "lacked the close, current co-operation of the Council officers and committee members." One observer maintained that many of the council's troubles were caused by the fact that "with the exception of Arnold Aronson, no one outside the paid staff has given close day-to-day concern to the Council's affairs"—although, the critic granted, on occasion Randolph and a few others gave "emergency aid in raising funds."[61]

Insiders defended the inability of the National Council to take a more active role in the filibuster fight along the same lines: The council was "completely bankrupt insofar as the question of taking on paid staff is concerned." Aronson called the situation "discouraging" and recommended "long-range planning and programming," but he, too, was unable to come up with a solution to the financial problem.[62]

Sifton wrote Wilkins in November, 1949, that he had heard rumors of the NAACP's desire to start a new organization to bypass the National Council. Since practically all the interested organizations were members of the National Council, Sifton argued, the existing council could best perform "the central co-ordinating function." Nevertheless, if some of the groups were unwilling to delegate the job to the National Council and support it financially, the participating agencies still had a moral responsibility to use part of the funds they had pledged to a 1950 FEPC fight to meet the obligations the National Council had incurred in 1949.[63] But as had happened with the NNC, over time the member groups became less willing to share with the parent body.

In part the constituent organizations were reluctant to contribute because Randolph's autocratic rule left them little participation in decision making. As one insider noted, "One cannot expect cooperation from organizations which are not permitted *participation in policy decisions.*"[64]

60. Sifton to James H. Anderson, [July, 1947], Memo, Paul Sifton to Randolph, "Remarks in July 11, 1947, letter from James H. Anderson," both *ibid.*
61. [?] to Thurman L. Dodson, December 24, 1947, in APR Files. The BFM Papers show about $21,000 in assets and liabilities for 1947.
62. Arnold Aronson to Thurman L. Dodson, March 21, 1949, in APR Files.
63. Sifton to Wilkins, November 15, 1949, *ibid.*
64. Press Release containing letter from Sidney Wilkinson to Randolph, August 27, 1946, in Nash Files, HST Papers.

Blacks were over represented, and Randolph's hand-picked loyalists dominated the executive committee. As the National Council remained unsuccessful in obtaining permanent legislation, dissension increased, especially among other minority groups supporting the FEPC movement. When the council leadership was broadened after the legislative failure in 1946, however, the action did not have noticeable impact on the attainment of a fair employment law.

FEPC historian Louis Kesselman ascribed the failure of the NAACP and the CIO to make greater contributions to the FEPC drive in large measure to Randolph's failure to share responsibility with their top leaders.[65] Although this was true of the NAACP early on, in the end the older organization wrested leadership of the National Council from Randolph. With the CIO, Randolph consistently tried to maintain good relations, as his correspondence shows. The BSCP even sent a check for one thousand dollars to the United Auto Workers in 1946 to aid their strike against General Motors.[66] The primary problem with CIO participation in the National Council came from the organization's preoccupation with postwar strike activity and absorption in cleansing itself of Communist influence.

Since the National Council was inaugurated as a federation, in theory it should not have had to undergo the evolution from charismatic authority to bureaucratized organization. Yet in practice it underwent precisely this type of institutionalization. In the beginning Randolph's control was so complete, according to Kesselman, it could "almost be said that Randolph was the National Council." Kesselman believed that Randolph's "personality and his experience have not prepared him well for leadership of a reform movement containing widely diverse groups," and Randolph's single-handed management of the BSCP had "not conditioned him to share policy-making and leadership with others."[67]

The National Council experienced the same problems of a federated agency that the NNC had previously encountered. Randolph's desire to prevent black identity from being submerged in an interracial alliance made for strained relations with the white cooperating groups, and traditional black organizational jealousy meant less than wholehearted coop-

65. Kesselman, *Social Politics of FEPC,* 35–37.
66. See correspondence in ALH, and *Black Worker,* March, 1946.
67. Kesselman, *Social Politics of FEPC,* 35–37.

eration from black allies. After the National Council proved ineffective in gaining permanent legislation, the cooperating agencies began to contest actively for control over the organization. But once there was a plurality of leadership, the council came no closer to its goal. Congress proved more resistant to pressure than the executive branch, and the postwar surplus of industrial manpower made the exclusion of blacks from jobs more desirable than ever to many congressmen. In addition, the developing cold war with its concomitant domestic anti-Communist hysteria did not provide a congenial atmosphere for reform legislation.

Randolph's civil rights leadership suffered not only from the FEPC setbacks but from his unwillingness to give up stewardship of the BSCP. Union organizing kept him traveling most of the time, and since he was reluctant to delegate authority, his organizations were chronically starved for full-time administration as well as for adequate funding. Randolph's associates in the MOWM had earlier perceived the conflicting demands on his time to be a problem and urged him to devote his attention to civil rights. Noting that so many followers had dropped out of the MOWM that "just a thread holds us together," one participant wrote in 1944, "Mr. Randolph I have asked you in vain to take leave from the Brotherhood and come on and give us the kind of leadership that only you can give and the kind that Black America is thirsty for. *You alone.*" Layle Lane, an employee of the Teachers' Union and one of Randolph's top aides in the MOWM, wrote him in 1944, "Either you must find a way to give definite direction to the March during the next few months or a group must be given the responsibility for making decisions and carrying them on without interference." Lane's demand that programs be under the control "of March people and not those personally selected without any advice or consultation with March officers" indicated her resentment of Randolph's dictatorial rule.[68]

Over all, the management of the National Council did not differ markedly from that of the MOWM. One observer expressed "the very strong feeling that you (Mr. Randolph) should personally take a hand in organizing the Washington office," but this Randolph was never willing to do. The diversion of his energy and his lack of administrative ability prompted Kesselman to charge that "confidence in Randolph's generalship was not

68. A. J. Johnson to Randolph, February 24, 1944, Layle Lane to Randolph, April 27, 1944, both in APR Files.

great," which had an "adverse effect upon staff morale." Anna Hedgeman, for one, complained that she found contact with potential "big givers" fruitless because of the "apparent lack of responsibility in planning ahead for a national program." [69]

Randolph's autocratic style was resented by National Council members, as it was by Lane and other MOWM workers. When Sidney Wilkinson, Hedgeman's white assistant, resigned over Hedgeman's "forced" resignation from the council, she wrote Randolph, "To you, who have spoken for human rights it must be obvious that those rights have been violated by the summary dismissal of the staff of the National Council for a Permanent FEPC without even a formal statement of appreciation for services rendered over a period of two and a half years." Wilkinson admonished Randolph, "It has been my conviction that, in order to promote fair employment, it must be practiced, and I do not think you and the Administrative committee of the National Council have complied with this fundamental principle." [70]

Some of Randolph's coworkers also took issue with his ambivalence over the interracial nature of the National Council. Even though his fear of Communist takeover remained unabated and he still believed blacks should run their own organizations, Randolph had bowed to the necessity of making the council interracial because many of the complaints submitted to the FEPC came from other minority groups, especially Jews. Wilkinson, for one, however, thought Randolph did not grasp the significance of a "truly integrated staff" and found it "regrettable that 'minority' leaders sometimes make it difficult for members of the so-called 'majority' group to actually function in programs which fundamentally benefit all of our fellowmen." She believed "*all* Americans must share in the responsibility for securing enactment of a Federal FEPC, and no one 'minority' group leader should make the mistake of trying to wage the fight single handed." She also thought that Randolph did not comprehend "the strength that arises from an executive committee which is given real opportunity to formulate policy and the authority to carry it out." [71]

69. Memo, Paul Sifton to Randolph, re "Remarks in July 11, 1947, letter from James H. Anderson"; Kesselman, *Social Politics of FEPC*, 222; Day Letter, Anna Arnold Hedgeman to Randolph, July 15, 1946, in APR Files.

70. Press Release containing letter from Sidney Wilkinson to Randolph, August 27, 1946, in Nash Files, HST Papers.

71. *Ibid.*

Louis Kesselman accurately assessed the problems caused by Randolph's authoritarian rule, but some of his other criticisms are subject to debate. Kesselman believed Randolph's ideological intransigence made his hatred of Communists so intense that he went out of his way to exclude them from the FEPC movement even though their short-range objectives may have been identical. Consequently, according to Kesselman, the National Council suffered when labor unions and black and white reform organizations that leaned toward the Communist viewpoint or abhorred ideological warfare refused to give the council their full support. Kesselman, however, failed to acknowledge that as the United States became more involved in the cold war, Randolph's reputation as an anti-Communist crusader inhibited efforts of the National Council's opponents to smear it as a "Communist front" group, although they never ceased trying to do so. Historian Robert Wiebe has called attention to the tendency among "local Americans" to equate all postwar changes they disliked with communism. Small-town whites in particular did not differentiate between black demands for greater equality and Communist subversion. Under these circumstances Randolph's refusal to countenance Communist influence in the National Council can only be considered as advantageous, even though the national fear and equation of social change with radicalism made passage of permanent FEPC legislation highly unlikely.[72]

Kesselman characterized Randolph as a "political butterfly" flitting from reform to reform but not staying with any for long.[73] While involved with the National Council, Randolph was still head of the MOWM as well as the BSCP and the Committee to Organize Colored Locomotive Firemen; in addition, he continued to edit the *Black Worker*. He extended himself further by participating in efforts to form a third political party and an organization to desegregate the armed forces. Small wonder, then, that he was unable to give the National Council proper attention.

But full blame for the failure of the National Council to obtain permanent FEPC legislation cannot be placed on Randolph, for other factors

---

72. Kesselman, *Social Politics of FEPC*, 222; Robert H. Wiebe, "White Attitudes and Black Rights from Brown to Bakke," in Michael V. Namorato (ed.), *Have We Overcome? Race Relations Since Brown* (Jackson, Miss., 1979), 150–51.

73. Kesselman, *Social Politics of FEPC*, 222. Randolph made a concession to demands on his time when he appointed Theodore E. Brown managing editor of the *Black Worker* in April, 1946.

also played a role. The council displayed all the weaknesses of a minority organization. The ethnic bloc vote strategy devised by Randolph worked to extract an executive order from a chief executive whose election was contingent on the electoral college vote piled up in the large-city states. Enactment of congressional legislation, however, depended on pressure and lobbying activities among legislators spread throughout the country. Neither Jews—the primary white ethnic group represented by the council—nor blacks possessed sufficient nationwide influence or voting strength to exert adequate pressure on Congress. And because the National Council's goal of fair employment practices involved a reordering of economic priorities, the dominant group resisted moral suasion. Americans, especially in a time of unprecedented prosperity for the majority, were not amenable to changes in the economic status quo. As we have seen, domestic response to the deepening cold war also worked against social change.

Thus, quickly as Randolph's star had risen, within a few years it began to descend. Randolph's image became tarnished, first from the attempt to routinize his charisma within a bureaucratic MOWM, and then from association with the National Council for a Permanent FEPC. Both groups declined as a result of the transition to institutionalization, of problems with their intermediary leadership, and of Randolph's attempt to single-handedly hold onto the reins of power, as well as of events in the larger society over which he had no control.

Randolph always believed political power was Afro-Americans' most potent weapon. Urging blacks to press for passage of a permanent FEPC bill before the 1944 election, he pointed out that "in ten or twelve states the balance of power lies in the hands of the Negroes and they can determine the trend of the election."[74] Indeed, the black vote was the National Council's principal form of pressure; always short of funds, it could offer little in the way of campaign contributions to congressmen. The council could only threaten individual candidates and the established parties with loss of the black vote or hold out the promise of black support.

After the *Smith* v. *Allwright* Supreme Court decision outlawing the

74. Press Release, September 1, 1944, in APR Files.

white primary in Texas in 1944, Randolph began an educational campaign through the BSCP and the pages of the *Black Worker* to encourage southern blacks to register and vote. He saw that enlarging the black vote would strengthen the lobbying power of the National Council.[75] Prompted by his efforts and those of liberal interracial organizatons such as the Southern Regional Conference and the Southern Conference for Human Welfare, as well as the NAACP, blacks began voting in the South in larger numbers than they had since the end of Reconstruction. But while his work on behalf of black registration was helpful to the National Council, Randolph's own political behavior in the 1940s often militated against passage of permanent FEPC legislation. Politically, his two primary problems were, first, that in his efforts to form a black political bloc he employed rhetoric that sounded racist to white supporters of the National Council and, second, that his continued affiliation with, and advocacy of, the Socialist party undercut the council's attempt to pressure the Democratic party.

In part because he feared that New Deal economic policies fostered excessive Afro-American dependence on the Democrats, Randolph recommended forming "a race political bloc" at the Chicago convention of the MOWM in 1943. He wanted to see blacks build a powerful, nonpartisan bloc reaching from local communities to the national scene. Although he did not advocate blacks leaving their respective parties, Randolph hoped that when questions of concern to Afro-Americans arose, they would "express their united political strength regardless of party politics on the issue." Politicians respected votes, and there were fifteen million Afro-Americans in the United States. True to form, Randolph insisted, "Such a political bloc should be financed by Negroes entirely, for he who pays the fiddler calls the tune."[76]

After the convention, Pauline Meyers suggested that Randolph call a National Non-Partisan Political Conference for Negroes to meet in New York. Meyers wanted the political bloc to be "something more than talk": She thought it should provide concrete action on poll taxes, white primaries, and southern congressmen. Whether Meyers' ideas had any influence on Randolph or his actions were simply a logical extension of his

75. Press Release, April 9, 1944, *ibid.*
76. A. Philip Randolph, "A Reply to My Critics," Chicago *Defender*, July 17, 1943.

recommendation to the Chicago conference is unknown, but Randolph decided to go ahead with such a conference the following summer to discuss the proper strategy for blacks in the 1944 presidential campaign.[77]

The proposed platform decided on at a preliminary planning conference in January included abolition of armed forces discrimination and segregation, enactment of a permanent FEPC law, enforcement of the Fourteenth and Fifteenth amendments, and black representation at the peace conference—many of the same goals enunciated by the MOWM. The rhetoric was militant: "The Negroes of the United States of America are determined to attain their adulthood as participating citizens in the national political life during the year 1944. As long as we remain second-class citizens, promises and charity are our portion, but we demand that we be dealt with as first-class citizens." Blacks, therefore, should band together in a bloc "to struggle for our rights through the means provided by a democratic form of government."[78]

Just prior to the 1944 Republican National Convention in Chicago, Randolph issued the Conference Call to a National Non-Partisan Political Conference for Negroes under the auspices of the MOWM to review Afro-American political history, assess the present status of blacks, and chart their future progress. In addition to the proposed program promulgated in January, the demands in the call also included federal aid to education and a national commission on race. To ensure enforcement of the Fourteenth and Fifteenth amendments, the call suggested setting a standard of 60 to 65 percent participation by eligible voters in a state as a requirement to maintain congressional representation. Furthermore, the call recommended establishing a ballot commission within the Department of Justice to which appeals regarding violations of the amendments could be made—a suggestion that would become a reality twenty years later. Blacks needed organization to obtain compliance with these demands and enable them to bargain most advantageously with both political parties for fair treatment, Randolph argued. At the same time they should work out a strategy whereby they could launch independent ac-

77. Pauline Meyers to Randolph, August 12, 1943, in APR Files; Press Release, January 7, 1944, *ibid.*; Randolph to Wilkins, January 31, 1944, in NAACP Papers. Addressed to "My dear Phil" and signed "Love, Pauline," Meyers' letter displayed the warmest feelings any female colleague ever showed toward the impersonal Randolph.

78. See Charles Wesley Burton to Randolph, April 30, 1944, Press Release, "MOWM Plans a National Negro Non-Partisan Political Conference," January 7, 1944, National Statement of Non-Partisan Political Bloc of Negroes, n.d., all in APR Files.

tion because "no matter how much we are promised by others our surest safeguard is to be in a position to serve ourselves effectively."[79]

The conference, followed by a Sunday mass meeting, was held in Chicago on June 25 and 26, 1944. In his speech to the participants Randolph argued, "There is no fundamental difference between the Republican and Democratic Parties so far as Negroes and labor are concerned. They are truly tweedledee and tweedledum." Thus "the sound political strategy" for blacks would be to submit a set of minimum demands to both the Republican and the Democratic conventions and their candidates. He also proposed waging an educational campaign, *"with funds supplied by Negroes alone,"* to inform blacks of the record and position of the parties and their candidates. Black voters should free themselves from party labels "and support men and measures that will enhance the position of the Negro in the post-war era," he maintained. A statement was issued to both political parties listing the conference demands, which, to Randolph, represented "an absolutely minimum program on which ALL Negroes can and should agree."[80]

The Non-Partisan Political Conference involved all the regulars from the MOWM and the BSCP. Milton Webster and T. D. McNeal of the BSCP were scheduled to appear on the program, along with Ralph Bunche of the administration's black brain trust and Earl Dickerson of the FEPC. Randolph's disciples concurred with his desire to keep the conference all black, although Layle Lane thought the organizers should make an exception for the Sunday mass meeting. To invite representatives of the major political parties to appear on that day's program, Lane argued, would "help draw a crowd as well as put the parties on the spot."[81]

The conference presented the usual financial problems, and as usual Randolph was too busy to give fund raising top priority. Since the conference planners needed between $8,000 and $10,000 to hire a hall and get out publicity, Lane suggested that Randolph contact "key people," "wealthy men of our race to find out how much they would give or

79. Conference Call to National Non-Partisan Political Convention of Negroes, in St. Louis Scrapbook, BSCP Papers, CD; Sponsors to Dear Friend, [stamped February 10, 1944], in NAACP Papers.

80. St. Louis *American,* July 6, 1944; *Black Worker,* July, 1944, p. 2+, 3; A. Philip Randolph, "Message of Greeting," in Souvenir Program to the Non-Partisan Political Conference, in St. Louis Scrapbook, BSCP Papers, CD.

81. "Tentative Program" of Non-Partisan Political Conference, Layle Lane to Randolph, May 7, 1944, both in APR Files.

pledge." When Randolph failed to respond, Lane tried again: "While I know you are extremely busy I believe only you Mr. Randolph can approach some of the well-to-do men in our group and ask for donations." But Randolph's other commitments prevented him from devoting full attention to ensuring a large turnout for the convention.[82] Yet the weakness of the civil rights plank in the Democratic platform showed that he had correctly anticipated the danger of being "taken for granted" by the Democrats.

Whether because of the contradictions ensuing from openly supporting a racially exclusive political movement and the interracial National Council at the same time, or because of financial difficulties, or because of Randolph's failure to stay with the movement, or his subsequent involvement in third party activity, the newly formed nonpartisan political bloc dissolved after the 1944 election. Most blacks continued to see their interest aligned with the Democratic party, and their failure to become a cohesive political bloc in the manner Randolph envisioned increased the difficulty of making the major political parties responsive to Afro-American group interests.

During this same period, Randolph passed up the opportunity to become a politician himself. In 1944 both the Amsterdam *News* and many Harlem groups tried to persuade him to run against Adam Clayton Powell in the newly created twenty-second congressional district, which would give Harlem its first black congressman. Layle Lane, among others, believed it imperative that Randolph run because the person elected from the new district would be considered by both whites and blacks as "the outstanding Negro leader." That mantle had not been placed on Congressman William Dawson of Chicago, Lane pointed out, because he was not of Randolph's caliber and had been handpicked by the Democratic machine. But "the candidate from the new Harlem district will not be picked except by Negroes themselves and will be more directly an expression of Negro aspirations and intentions," Lane believed. If no "bigger man" ran, the election was already conceded to Powell despite his "opportunistic and selfish" nature. Powell's election would mean not only national leadership for him, but entrée by Powell's following, "including

82. Lane to Randolph, March 21, 1944, Randolph to Charles Wesley Burton, May 26, 1944, Lane to Randolph, May 7, 1944, Burton to Randolph, May 23, 27, 1944, all *ibid.*

Communists." Thus, Lane urged Randolph, "you can't afford to let down the Negro masses or abdicate the leadership in such a crucial time as this."[83]

Lane, of course, also hoped that Randolph's congressional candidacy would have a salutary effect on the declining fortunes of the MOWM. Indeed, she urged Randolph to consider his decision in light of its effect on the march program. Not all Randolph's colleagues agreed with Lane, however; some were afraid he would be lost to the cause away in Washington. Halena Wilson, head of the BSCP women's auxiliary, undoubtedly reflected the general BSCP view when she wrote Randolph describing how pleased she was that he had declined to make the race against Powell.[84]

Publicly, Randolph stated that he could render greater service to his race outside of Congress and that his lifelong commitment was to the porters' union. The "pay-off" necessary to get ahead in public office, Randolph said, "may involve compromises of various types which may strike at the basic convictions, ideals and principles that one has held dear all of his life." Indicating that he could support neither the domestic nor the foreign policies of the major parties, he also made it clear that he could not accept the nomination from the Communist-dominated American Labor party. Disinclined to give up the sinecure of union leadership for the uncertainty of political life, Randolph probably also considered his distaste for administration in deciding to turn down the proffered nomination.[85]

Although he declined to run for office himself, Randolph subsequently became involved in the founding of a third political party. He had always believed the United States needed an ideologically based party similar to the Labor party in Great Britain. The formation of a workers' party, Randolph reasoned, would add political strength to the coalition of outgroups that he hoped to forge. In the 1920s, after the *Messenger* had left

83. New York *Times*, April 13, 1944; Lane to Randolph, March 19, 1944, APR Files. For a discussion of Powell's relationship with the Communists, see Naison, *Communists in Harlem*.

84. Lane to Randolph, April 27, 1944, in APR Files; Halena Wilson to Randolph, June 2, 1944, in BSCP Papers, CD.

85. New York *Times*, April 19, 1944; Chicago *Defender*, May 6, 1944; New York *Times*, June 16, 1946; Randolph to Morton Goodman, April 14, 1944, in BSCP Papers, LC; Randolph to A. J. Johnson, March 7, 1944, in APR Files.

its radical phase, Randolph saw hope for a progressive movement in the presidential candidacy of Robert La Follette. But La Follette did not go out of his way to attract black voters in 1924, and by the following year Randolph had turned his attention to organizing the porters. When John P. Davis considered promoting a national Farmer-Labor party through the NNC in 1936, Randolph declined to be part of the organizing committee because he belonged to the Socialist party. He nevertheless presented a resolution calling for a Farmer-Labor party to the AFL convention that year, arguing it would give labor a voice in the determination of legislation affecting its interests.[86] In 1940, Randolph objected to John L. Lewis' proposal that the NNC cooperate with the CIO's Non-Partisan League on the grounds that such cooperation amounted to a first step toward possible participation in a third party movement if the platforms and nominees of the major parties were not acceptable. Still, he continued to promote a labor party through the years, although the AFL displayed little interest in the project.

After the Democratic defeats in the congressional elections of 1946, however, the political situation in America raised Randolph's hopes that the time might be right for a workers' party. A series of appalling racial incidents caused President Truman to create the Commission on Civil Rights, and going beyond its instructions, the commission submitted a report, *To Secure These Rights*, in the fall of 1947, that called for complete overhauling of the civil rights laws to secure equal rights for blacks and their full integration into all aspects of society. Taking his cue from advisers who thought the black vote would be important in the forthcoming presidential election, Truman sent a civil rights message to Congress in February, 1948, calling for elimination of the poll tax, a law making lynching a federal crime, an FEPC, and elimination of segregation in interstate travel. Although the proposals fostered optimism among civil rights partisans, they, not unexpectedly, elicited southern political fury. Truman took no further action, hoping that the rhetoric alone would be sufficient to satisfy black demands and that his inaction would appease southern Democrats. Both Democrats and Republicans wanted to woo the black vote in 1948, but the Republican-controlled Congress, with support from southern Democrats, decided to back no civil rights legislation

86. Randolph to John P. Davis, June 10, 1936, in NNC Papers; *Black Worker*, December, 1936, p. 1.

with the exception of a weak antilynching bill. They anticipated that this bill would ease pressure for passage of the more rigorous anti–poll tax and FEPC bills.[87]

Meanwhile, Truman's reaction to the postwar wave of strikes had alienated some sections of the labor movement. In particular, labor leaders resented that Truman asked Congress for emergency power to break strikes in any industry in which the federal government had an interest. When a railroad strike threatened to paralyze the nation's transportation system in the spring of 1946, the president proposed inducting strikers into the army and imprisoning officers of striking unions who failed to obey a return-to-work order. Significantly, in 1947 Truman vetoed the Taft-Hartley Act—a revision of the labor laws to curb unionism. His veto was overridden, and his strong stand on the railroad strike continued to brand the president as antilabor in some quarters. For his part, Randolph argued Truman's position should "open the eyes of labor, farm and co-operative leaders to the impossibility of continuing the wornout tradition of a two-party system in which neither party serves the interest of the people." Despite the Democratic convention's adoption of its entire platform, labor remained ambivalent about Truman. Blacks and white liberals were also disgruntled by his inaction on the civil rights front. Noting the loss of these key constituencies, along with most other knowledgeable observers Randolph thought Truman could not possibly win reelection in 1948. The results of electoral reprisals against anti-FEPC congressmen in the 1946 elections had been disappointing, and, Randolph pointed out, the country typically turned reactionary in a postwar period.[88]

Concern over unemployment, which always affected blacks hardest, the new specter of atomic power, and renewed American imperialism made Randolph decide independent political action was urgent. He invited Walter White and other liberals to a meeting in November, 1945, to discuss the possibility of forming a democratic-socialist party. Randolph then accepted the chairmanship of the National Educational Committee

87. U.S. President's Commission on Civil Rights, *To Secure These Rights* (1947); Harvard Sitkoff, "Harry Truman and the Election of 1948: The Coming of Age of Civil Rights in American Politics," *Journal of Southern History*, XXXVII (November, 1971), 597–616; William C. Berman, *The Politics of Civil Rights in the Truman Administration* (Columbus, Ohio, 1970); White to Honorable Wayne Morse, April 22, 1948, in NAACP Papers.

88. Joseph G. Rayback, *A History of American Labor* (New York, 1966), 387–402; Garfinkel, *When Negroes March*, 156.

for a New Party, which was backed by liberals, cooperators, and farmers who thought that neither the administration nor the existing parties were responsive to the needs of the people. The new group projected itself as antifascist, pro-democratic, and in favor of a planned economy. The National Educational Committee planned to work "against the threat of monopoly capitalism to economic plenty, freedom and peace," and thus stood for a collectivist social democracy to go beyond the New Deal.[89]

A Call to American Progressives for an unpublicized conference to meet in Chicago was issued in February, 1946. In addition to Randolph, among those backing the proposed party were Samuel Wolchok, president of the United Retail, Wholesale and Department Store Employees, CIO; Simeon Martin, president of the Michigan Farmers Educational and Cooperative Union; H. L. Mitchell, president of the National Farm Labor Union; John Dewey; Walter Reuther; Norman Thomas; and David Dubinsky.[90] The meeting took place April 7 and 8, and was attended by 125 delegates from sixteen states. The National Educational Committee, however, decided not to become involved in the 1946 congressional and state elections.

In May, 1946, the committee met again, this time in Detroit, to start an educational campaign for the new party, by now called the People's party. Randolph became chairman of the committee, and John Dewey was made honorary chairman. Representatives of the CIO and United Auto Workers were among the thirty persons attending, but names of those present were not made public "because some of them did not wish to be identified as yet." Participants denied they intended to actually form a third party, stating the group "organized simply for the purpose of carrying on an educational campaign for a People's Party and for the principles upon which such a Party should be based." They wanted merely to help "build sentiment for a new party when the time is ripe." Yet Randolph argued that the call of A. F. Whitney, president of the Brotherhood of Railroad Trainmen, for the defeat of Truman in 1948 should be accompanied by action for "a new victorious political party of the common people, based on a democratic planned economy." The group decided to

89. Randolph to White, November 14, 1945, in NAACP Papers; New York *Times*, May 5, 1946.

90. A Call to American Progressives, and Randolph to James Carey, February 6, 1946, both in ALH.

open a national office in Chicago and projected another conference for December, 1946.[91]

The "Provisional Declaration of Principles," part of an article published in the *Antioch Review* in the fall, stated that although the group did not intend to become a party, it did propose to stimulate discussion for a new political alignment to counteract the bipartisan congressional coalition of reactionary Democrats and Republicans that was preventing the adoption of progressive measures. The declaration set forth many ideas for government involvement in the economy that would be developed more fully in Randolph's Freedom Budget of 1966. Basically, the declaration argued that the achievements of science and technology had made it possible for the dream of a good life for all to come true.[92]

The National Educational Committee's foreign platform embraced the ideals of worldwide democratic and economic development. Accused of being a Communist front, it claimed the Communists had spread such rumors because they were "conspiring to capture for themselves the rising sentiment for independent political action. . . ."[93] Extending its strictures against imperialism to cover the Soviet Union, the group rejected the spheres-of-influence doctrine as a "thinly disguised form of colonial and political domination" that could only lead to future wars, and called on the United States to support "the liberal, democratic rights of people anywhere in the world, and to insist that other nations respect those rights." Even voicing such sentiments in cold war America, however, made the group suspect in many quarters.

According to historian Alonzo Hamby, the National Educational Committee represented the last effort of an indigenous American radicalism to change the structure of American politics and thereby open up new vistas of reform. The committee had impressive leadership but could not muster the numbers needed to gain power in democratic politics. Primarily made up of intellectuals and heads of groups with small constituencies, the

91. "Ideas for a New Party," *Antioch Review*, VI (Fall, 1946), 449–72; New York *Times*, May 5, 30, 1946. Other members of the group were Lewis Corey, research director; Jack McLanahan, secretary; Pearl Willen, treasurer; and Mary Martinson, administrative secretary. See David Dubinsky and A. H. Raskin, *David Dubinsky: A Life with Labor* (New York, 1977), 284, for George Meany's attitude toward a third party.

92. "Ideas for a New Party," 449–72.

93. New York *Times*, May 5, 1946.

National Educational Committee bore little resemblance to Randolph's longstanding dream of a coalition of outcasts.

Hamby argued that the new party proposed by the committee "could succeed only if the Democrats continued on the path to disintegration," and for a while it looked like the Democratic party was indeed in a state of dissolution. A substantial split occurred at the 1948 convention when northern liberals insisted on putting a strong civil rights plank in the platform in accordance with Truman's own civil rights message earlier in the year. Appalled at the vigorous civil rights stand, state's rights Democrats slated their own presidential candidate, Strom Thurmond. Truman thus was faced with the loss of many traditional southern Democratic votes to the Dixiecrats, and "all of a sudden," civil rights became "an issue big enough to split a great national political party."[94]

The party further splintered when Truman's former secretary of commerce, Henry Wallace, became the presidential candidate of the newly organized Progressive party. Wallace wooed the black vote by campaigning for a program of domestic social reform, and appealed to leftists by coming out against Truman's hard line toward the Soviet Union in foreign affairs. Initially Wallace brought many liberals over to his new party, but most subsequently became disillusioned over what they saw as Communist subversion of the movement. Although he praised it for pressing for peace and fighting against bigotry, Randolph condemned the Progressive party because it was controlled by Communists. He also denounced the Wallace party because it represented progressive capitalism "à la Roosevelt," which, claimed Randolph, "the record shows never solved the crisis of unemployment."[95]

The split in the Democratic party, however, relieved Truman of the need to cater to the extreme southern bloc that had strangled Roosevelt's freedom of action on civil rights. When the president called Congress back into special session, he was praised by Randolph, who attempted to convince him that the issuance of executive orders abolishing armed forces segregation and instituting fair employment practices for the federal government would rob both Wallace supporters and the Republicans of the civil rights issue. Such action, Randolph said, would "win the admiration, respect, and support of not only the minority groups but a

---

94. Hamby, *Beyond the New Deal*, 139, 140; Des Moines *Sun Register*, August 15, 1948.

95. ANP Release, August 18, 1948, p. 30.

powerful section of independent and liberal voters in the nation. . . .
[Y]ou have nothing to lose, but everything to gain." Truman's advisers
also subscribed to this course of action. Hence, in an effort to gain the
black vote, without which he could not win the election, Truman issued
the two executive orders Randolph requested.[96]

Following its establishment in 1946, the National Educational Committee for a New Party had made few headlines, and even some of its
founders despaired of its future. With the apparent disintegration of the
Democratic party in 1948, however, there was renewed talk of a political
realignment following the election. In an interesting turn of events, after
Truman issued the two executive orders Randolph announced publicly
that he was voting for Norman Thomas "because a strong socialist vote
may serve as a basis for the organization of a national third party based
upon sound socialist principles which will make for peace, plenty and
freedom." At a BSCP Labor Education Institute in August, Randolph
called on his listeners to follow his example and vote the Socialist ticket
in November. "The Democratic and Republican parties are controlled by
the economic royalists of the country who have little in common with
98% of the American people," he argued. Their record showed that since
the end of Reconstruction neither party had seen fit to pass even minimum civil rights legislation. "The Socialist party, on the other hand, has a
program which is economically sound; its record on civil liberties and social legislation is commendable; and it is controlled by the common
people, intellectual liberals and progressives. A million votes for Norman
Thomas," Randolph urged, "would be the greatest boon for a truly progressive third party of farmers and labor."[97]

In the election, the Dixiecrats on the right and the Progressives on the
left canceled each other out. Failing to heed Randolph's advice, most
blacks stood by Truman. Labor, having nowhere else to go, came back
into the fold, and it combined with the black vote to give Truman three
pivotal states and the presidency. Indeed, blacks supported Truman with
more than their votes. The Chicago *Defender* pleaded with its readers not
to let him down: "For every dollar the Dixiecrats withhold from the campaign chest of the President, Negroes will give ten," the paper pledged,

96. Telegram, Randolph to Truman, July 16, 1948, in APR Files; Sitkoff, "Truman and
Election of 1948," 614.
97. Hamby, *Beyond the New Deal*, 264; A. Philip Randolph, "Why I Voted for Norman
Thomas," *Black Worker*, November, 1948, p. 6; ANP Release, August 18, 1948, p. 30.

and organized a fund-raising committee for Truman.[98] The majority of blacks did not forget his historic civil rights message to Congress nor his executive orders.

The victory of the Democratic party in 1948 aborted any chance the National Educational Committee may have had to establish a new party. But Randolph continued to hold his old dream of a political party based on ideology and, at the AFL convention in November, spoke of the need for a labor-oriented third political party. Randolph called it "the principle of the third force or middle of the road methodology of the British Labor Party, as the way, without violence and bloodshed, to a new social order of security and freedom, peace and justice." The AFL should study, explore, and develop a twelve-year plan to build such a party, said Randolph, but the other delegates perceived the election results as a major victory for labor and overwhelmingly rejected his plan.[99]

Upon cursory examination, Randolph's political behavior in the 1940s appears self-defeating. But it actually illustrates his vacillation between pragmatism and idealism. On pragmatic grounds, Randolph should have concentrated on forming a cohesive black political bloc within the established parties to pressure Truman and the Democrats. Instead he disregarded his own advice and succumbed to his idealistic vision of a black-white laboring class alliance, thereby weakening the force of the black vote by trying to influence it openly on behalf of Norman Thomas and the Socialists. Although his actions seemed contradictory, since the power of a black mass vote was the only political weapon in his arsenal, Randolph acted on the hope of realizing a democratic socialist commonwealth that ultimately, he believed, would bring the greatest benefits to Afro-Americans.

Randolph's efforts to found a third party based on the ideology of democratic socialism were consistent with his conviction that the primary need of blacks was economic security, and the best method of obtaining such security was through a proletarian class alliance. His affiliation with the National Educational Committee, therefore, was an attempt to implement a coalition of the out-groups in American society—blacks, laborers, Socialists, and small farmers—as an effective pressure group. Convinced blacks were discriminated against for social and economic,

98. Memorandum to Mr. White from Mr. Moon, November 19, 1948, in NAACP Papers; Editorial, "Let's Put Up or Shut Up," Chicago *Defender,* July 31, 1948.
99. *Black Worker,* December, 1948, p. 1.

rather than racial, reasons, Randolph thought the Afro-American was not held down and oppressed because his skin was black; rather, the color of his skin made it easier for him to be singled out to do the "world's dirty-work." There was no natural basis for this kind of race prejudice; it grew artificially, nurtured by various exploiting groups to further their own interests. The black problem, therefore, could not be solved by blacks themselves but was dependent on the resolution of the basic social and economic problems of the age.[100]

Randolph came to his third-party activity through the socialism of the labor movement, whereas most of the other leaders of the National Educational Committee came from middle-class, intellectual Socialist backgrounds. Although the two Socialist traditions were not identical, in theory their goals were the same, making Randolph's vision of a bloc of out-groups not at all unrealistic. But the majority of Afro-Americans were no more interested in a third party based upon ideology than was the AFL. Most black Americans, like most white Americans, wanted to participate in the American capitalist system, not eliminate it. Unlike Randolph, they saw their problems as resulting from racism, not the economic system. In the 1940s, as in the 1920s, Randolph's political and economic ideas appealed to only a few black intellectuals; they did not address the perceived needs or desires of the larger black community.

Randolph's politics were so convoluted they defied any simple categorization. Manning Marable labeled him an "anticommunist" and argued that the fear of communism shared by Randolph, the NAACP, and other middle-class blacks made them "unwitting accomplices" of the Truman administration's cold war domestic policy. Marable viewed Randolph's antipathy toward communism as stemming primarily from a desire to obtain the support of anti-Communist liberals and the Truman administration in the post–World War II period when, in fact, Randolph had turned against the Communists in the post–World War I era primarily because he blamed them for the breakup of the *Messenger* editorial staff. Although there may be some merit in Marable's assertion that "by serving as the 'left wing of McCarthyism,' Randolph, White and other Negro leaders retarded the black movement for a decade or more," it is more likely that Randolph's activities, combined with other forces pressing for change—such as the Southern Regional Council, formed in 1944,

100. "March on Washington Movement—What Do We Stand For," n.d., in APR Files.

the resentment of discrimination among returning black soldiers, the achievement of independence by black African nations in the 1950s and 1960s, and the progress through the courts of NAACP suits against segregation—prepared the soil for a more militant equality movement to take root.[101]

Randolph's efforts on behalf of a permanent FEPC placed him at the forefront of what would later become an effective alliance of racial minorities, organized labor, and religious and political liberals. The constant agitation of Randolph and the National Council helped educate white Americans to the need for greater fairness in hiring practices at the same time that the NAACP's victories in the courts began weakening the wall of legal segregation. The mass migration of black Americans to the urban areas gave them political weight that politicians operating on the national level could no longer ignore. Although the efforts of Randolph and other black leaders did not bring equality in the 1940s and early 1950s, they laid the foundation on which the midcentury civil rights movement would build.

101. Marable, *Race, Reform and Rebellion*, 21–33.

IV / "Don't Join a Jim Crow Army"

Originally, Randolph's aborted March on Washington had two goals: the opening of defense jobs to Afro-Americans and the integration of the military. Abolition of segregation in the armed services remained an unfulfilled aim. That blacks were expected to shoulder arms for their country on a segregated basis continued to be a constant reminder of their inferior status.

Still ambitious to lead a major movement, when his role was lessened after the reorganization of the National Council for a Permanent FEPC, Randolph directed his energies back into the military desegregation struggle, believing that "the end of military jim crow is the basic key to smashing all discrimination." Once accustomed to integrated facilities in the service, Randolph reasoned, black recruits could be forced back into a segregated civilian society only with difficulty. Whites opposed to a nonsegregated military shared Randolph's view. One southern newspaper commented editorially that although it did not consider blacks unfit to fight and die for their country, mixing races in the armed forces "may have far-reaching social consequences, the extent of which we are not now prepared to say."[1]

Taking advantage of the president's effort to obtain passage of a peacetime draft bill—a first for the United States—Randolph endeavored to pressure Truman into issuing an executive order integrating the armed services. In 1947 and 1948, Randolph launched a two-pronged attack to achieve his goal. His first movement, the Committee Against Jim Crow in Military Service and Training, employed traditional legal methods; his

1. A. Philip Randolph to Charles Buchanan, October 18, 1948, in APR Files; Editorial, Charleston *News and Courier,* quoted in Lee Nichols, *Breakthrough on the Color Front* (New York, 1954), 116–17.

second, the League for Non-Violent Civil Disobedience Against Military Segregation, begun because of the initial failure of the first, urged youths to resist induction into a segregated military establishment. Another attempt of Randolph's to use nonviolent civil disobedience against a vulnerable president, the league further educated the public in the techniques of noncooperation. The league also drew Randolph into a fragile coalition with the pacifist FOR—an alliance that soon began to show the strain of the divergent goals of its component groups.

The contradiction of fighting fascism on a racially segregated basis had caused a crisis of morale for blacks in the military during World War II and resulted in emotional problems after the war that transcended even the need for jobs. In the postwar period, blacks continued to be taken into the service under a limited quota system and separated on the basis of race at induction centers. Although they trained with white troops, they rode Jim Crow trains and lived in segregated barracks. Black soldiers could buy only at the Negro PX and see films only in segregated post theaters. Any attempt to protest abuse suffered at the hands of prejudiced officers usually led to court-martial.[2]

Since he believed the issue to be so crucial, while the nation was still at war Randolph again asked President Roosevelt to issue an executive order abolishing armed forces segregation. When the president failed to comply, Randolph made military integration one of the themes of the MOWM conference in the summer of 1943. Incensed that the European war was being fought by two separate armies, one black and the other white, in July, 1944, Randolph induced his faltering MOWM to sponsor a telegram and letter-writing campaign urging Roosevelt to issue a national proclamation abolishing segregation and discrimination in the armed forces.[3] But the MOWM by then had lost much of its influence, and, not surprisingly given the political realities of the time, the president declined to act.

Even earlier, in April, 1943, the MOWM had published a pamphlet, written by Dwight MacDonald, entitled *The War's Greatest Scandal!*

2. Marjorie McKenzie, "Pursuit of Democracy: Reaction to Randolph's Stand Exposes Division of Opinion Within Race," Pittsburgh *Courier*, April 12, 1948; Walter White to Honorable Wayne Morse, April 14, 1948, in NAACP Papers.

3. Press Releases, September 8, 1943, July 14, 1944, St. Paul *Recorder*, May 12, 1944, all in St. Louis Scrapbook, BSCP Papers, CD.

The Story of Jim Crow in Uniform. It was this publication that Walter White and the NAACP declined to distribute. Declaring "Jimcrow in uniform must go!" the pamphlet was an argument for civil disobedience based on the thesis that the government could not arrest thirteen million people. MacDonald's essay had been prompted by the Winifred Lynn case. Lynn, a soldier and brother of Conrad Lynn, a civil liberties attorney, brought a writ of habeas corpus against the United States Army, charging his Jim Crow status was illegal. The MOWM joined the American Civil Liberties Union (ACLU) in support of the soldier because Randolph believed the Lynn issue would become the "Twentieth Century Dred Scott Case." When the Lynn Committee to Abolish Segregation in the Armed Forces, an interracial group devoted to the defense of blacks who refused to serve in a Jim Crow military establishment, was formed, Randolph became active in the organization.[4]

Randolph's first attempt to organize a formal movement of his own to abolish army Jim Crow came in the spring of 1945. Together with Willard Townsend of the United Transport Service Employees, CIO; Morris Milgram of the WDL; and Winifred H. Kerr, cochairman of the Lynn Committee, Randolph called a conference in New Jersey "to Formulate a Program of Action to End Race Segregation and Discrimination by the Armed Service." Randolph suggested a "plan of action" to the delegates to bring pressure to bear against the government, claiming, "The basic root of this problem is the federal government; its major agency, the Army." In addition to encouraging publicity on the way army segregation affected the spirit of the country and asking liberal congressmen to draft a bill abolishing this area of segregation, Randolph also wanted to embarrass the American delegation at the organizing conference of the United Nations in San Francisco by holding protest meetings and picketing.[5]

Obliged to defend his formation of a new organization, Randolph argued that the Lynn Committee was not equipped to cope with the extensive program he envisioned against the entire scope of military segregation. But Randolph's projected budget of $100,000 for the new organization

---

4. Pamphlet and Letter from Pauline Meyers, April 17, 1943, in St. Louis Scrapbook, *ibid.*; George S. Schuyler, Carey McWilliams, and Randolph to Dear Friend, [prior to 1945], in CORE Papers. See also Memorandum to Mr. Marshall from Mr. White, September 23, 1944, to Mr. White from Thurgood Marshall, September 25, 1944, both in NAACP Papers.

5. Press Release, January 5, 1945, Minutes of Proceedings of Conference, April 28, 1945, both in APR Files.

was clearly beyond the means of the black community, and he was forced to turn to the white community for support. Fresh from organizational competition in the MOWM, Randolph emphasized that his new group would not duplicate the work of existing agencies or function as a membership organization, but rather would devote itself to handling specific cases of discrimination. Whether because his projected budget was unrealistic, or because an attempt to obtain financial aid from the ACLU failed, or because he became too involved in the push for a permanent FEPC law, or because he failed to obtain cooperation from preexisting groups—or because of a combination of these factors—Randolph's initial effort to put together a movement solely to combat army segregation never got off the ground.[6]

Then, in March, 1946, the army released the Gillem Board Report, a new study on utilization of black manpower and a practical plan for implementation of its findings. To the disgust of black leaders, the report did not call for any major changes and only slightly alleviated the longstanding army policy of discrimination and segregation. Recruitment of black soldiers, in fact, had to be suspended for six months in 1946 because the army's traditional 10 percent quota of Afro-Americans had been filled.[7]

In February, 1948, prompted by the report of the Commission on Civil Rights, Truman gave his well-known civil rights address to Congress. No sooner had the president delivered his message, however, than Randolph began castigating him for failing to couple his words with action to institute immediate equality in the armed services. Randolph argued that blacks "would see through the hypocrisy of the Eightieth Congress if it passed even a model Fair Employment Practices Bill and then herded 18-year-old youths into jimcrow garrisons commanded by bigoted generals." He called for a "crack down on this new-style lynch party which would surrender Negro boys to Mississippi Army officers without legislative safe-guards."[8]

Randolph actually began considering action against what he termed "*a government sponsored program of jimcrow*" in late September, 1947. He called a meeting of black leaders in October to organize an "Emer-

6. Roger Baldwin to Randolph, May 23, 1945, *ibid.*
7. The Gillem Board Report, "Utilization of Negro Manpower in the Postwar Army Policy," was issued as War Department Circular No. 124, April 27, 1946. See Richard J. Stillman II, *Integration of the Negro in the U.S. Armed Forces* (New York, 1968), 34–36.
8. Press Release, February 5, 1948, in CORE Papers.

gency Committee Against Military Jimcrow," for "militant *action*" on the issue. The Committee Against Jim Crow in Military Service and Training, with Randolph and black New York Republican Grant Reynolds as cochairmen, came out of this meeting. As with Chalmers and the National Council, Randolph hoped that Reynolds—a former minister and World War II army chaplain who ran for Congress as a Republican against a Communist-supported candidate in Harlem in 1946, and by 1948 was New York State commissioner of corrections—would lend respectability to the endeavor. In their capacity as coheads, and claiming to represent two hundred black leaders on the committee, Randolph and Reynolds tried to make an appointment with the president. They did not see him, but the pair did receive a promise from the Democratic National Committee that a statement against a segregated draft act would be issued.[9] The statement, however, never materialized.

When it became apparent that the dominant power structure would not take action without being pressured, Randolph and Reynolds sponsored a conference of black spokesmen, in February, in an effort to rally forces to fight against a draft that would institutionalize the Jim Crow system far into the future. Although they had begun what they thought would be a long-range fight for abolition of segregation in the military, Randolph and Reynolds felt the issue was placed on an "immediate and urgent" agenda when Truman called for Universal Military Training (UMT) in March, 1948.[10]

Action to banish segregation in any proposed draft had been a prime recommendation of the Civil Rights Commission and was considered of utmost importance by the black helmsmen, but abolition of Jim Crow had been deleted from the original UMT bill at the request of the army.

9. Randolph to Layle Lane, September 3, 1947, in APR Files; Randolph to Gloster Current, October 2, 1947, in NAACP Papers; Randolph to Harry S. Truman, December 28, 1947, Reynolds and Randolph to President Harry S. Truman, December 10, 1947, Matthew J. Connelly to Randolph, January 7, 1948, Randolph to Truman, January 12, 1948, all in Official File, HST Papers. Randolph was at the AFL convention in San Francisco when the meeting of black leaders was held in his office on October 10; Grant Reynolds presided in his absence. Randolph later claimed the appointment with Truman was not granted because the president had no intention of issuing an executive order abolishing segregation in the military, and he knew they would request such action (Press Release, February 5, 1948, in CORE Papers; Randolph to J. Howard McGrath, February 2, 1948, in JHM Papers).

10. Reynolds and Randolph, Notice of Emergency Conference, January 8, 1948, in APR Files; "Crisis in the Making: U.S. Negroes Tussle with Issue of Resisting a Draft Law Because of Racial Discrimination," *Newsweek*, June 7, 1948, p. 29.

Randolph and Reynolds therefore conferred with the Republican and Democratic leaders of both houses of Congress and initiated what seemed like endless correspondence with all the senators and representatives. "No assurances of an anti-segregation policy were forthcoming," however.[11]

Randolph and Reynolds were finally received at the White House on March 22. Unknown to them, the president had refused their proposed earlier meeting because his advisers wanted to make certain that the pair would not be able to claim that his civil rights message to Congress came as a result of their visit. During their meeting, Randolph and Reynolds urged the president to insist on antisegregation and pro-civil rights provisions in any UMT program. Randolph informed Truman "that Negroes are in no mood to shoulder a gun for democracy abroad so long as they are denied democracy here at home. In particular they resent the idea of fighting or being drafted into another Jim Crow army."[12] The president was clearly upset by Randolph's militancy.

Randolph and Reynolds concluded from the meeting that Truman would not push desegregation. On March 31, they were to testify before the Senate armed services committee, and realizing the publicity potential, Randolph first "exclusively" advised columnist Drew Pearson that he would drop the civil disobedience bombshell. In the course of their testimony, the pair warned that unless all forms of racial discrimination were prohibited in the proposed UMT, they would advise young men to resist induction. Randolph made it clear that passage of a Jim Crow draft could result in a mass civil disobedience movement along the lines of the one in India against British imperialism. "I personally pledge myself," he added, "to openly counsel, aid and abet youth, both white and Negro, to quarantine any jimcrow conscription system."[13]

Under prodding, Randolph told Senator Wayne Morse that he would counsel civil disobedience even if the country were at war. When Morse stated that such a step could lead to his indictment for treason, Randolph replied that he expected nationwide terrorism against blacks refusing to go into service, and that he would be willing to face such indictment "on

11. See Randolph to Harry S. Truman, February 27, 1948, in Official File, HST Papers; Grant Reynolds, "A Triumph for Civil Disobedience," *Nation*, August 28, 1948, p. 229.

12. Memo for Honorable Matt Connelly from David K. Niles, January 20, 1948, in Official File, HST Papers. At this point Randolph and Reynolds claimed the support of 73 cooperating organizations. See Press Release, February 5, 1948, in APR Files; *Hearings*, 687.

13. Randolph to Drew Pearson, March 26, 1948, in APR Files; *Hearings*, 688.

the grounds that we are serving a higher law than the law which applied the act of treason to us when we are attempting to win democracy." Recalling the event later, Reynolds observed that only after he and Randolph gave their civil disobedience "ultimatum" did the senators come "to life" and "realise that here was something new to contend with." Reynolds believed the proposal "startled" white America. "We informed the nation and the world that segregation was reaching an unbearable point." [14]

Neither Randolph nor Reynolds was included when the first secretary of the combined defense establishment, James V. Forrestal, invited black leaders to participate in a National Defense Conference on Negro Affairs in April. Forrestal convened the conference to seek advice on how the government could utilize Afro-Americans in the armed forces. From his point of view, the meeting failed since the black spokesmen refused to aid in working out a program within the framework of segregation. The consensus of the group was that, while they were not ready to say what action blacks should take if they were segregated in the army in another war, they would not put themselves on record as opposed to the Randolph-Reynolds statement. Moreover, the organization heads maintained that the responsibility for any draft resistance movement lay with America's failure to practice the democracy it preached; Randolph had been forced into his protest by the deplorable conditions black recruits encountered. [15] At a press interview during the conference, the black statesmen expressed doubt that the country could fight another war on a segregated basis. Even though they were not ready to endorse his action, the leaders made it clear they were glad Randolph had taken his civil disobedience stand.

The black organization heads had undoubtedly been pushed into their uncooperative position by the attitude of the army. The secretary of the army had called segregation in the armed forces a wise policy. And in the UMT hearings, much to his later regret, World War II hero General Eisenhower stated that, since blacks were less educated, segregation was desirable as it gave less qualified blacks opportunity for promotion that they would not have if forced to compete with better-prepared whites.

14. *Hearings*, 691; New York *Times*, April 1, 1948; A. J. Muste to Honorable Wayne Morse, April 28, 1948, in APR Files; Reynolds, "Triumph for Civil Disobedience," 228.

15. Pittsburgh *Courier*, May 1, 1948; Minutes of Press Conference on Negro Affairs, April 26, 1948, Sadie [T. Mossell Alexander] to Lester Granger, April 28, 1948, both in NUL Papers; New York *Times*, April 27, 1948; ANP Release, May 5, 1948.

The conference with Forrestal thus marked a turning point after which black leaders felt pressured into adopting a more militant public posture.[16] Yet the very convening of the committee proved that Randolph's previous efforts had borne fruit. The political presence of blacks had been institutionalized and formalized to the point where the military realized that Afro-American reaction must be taken into account.

When Randolph argued that the existence of segregation in the largest federal enterprise undermined black efforts to make headway in civilian life, particularly in endeavors to get business to conform to fair employment standards, the armed forces countered they should not be expected to take the lead in establishing new social patterns in the country. The military was faced with a difficult dilemma: If it continued segregation, it confronted the possibility of mass resistance by young blacks; if it abolished segregation, it risked mass resistance from a large segment of white youth, particularly those from the South.[17]

On May 7, Randolph and eight followers marched in front of the White House distributing buttons inscribed with the admonition "Don't Join a Jim Crow ARMY." Randolph carried a sign emblazoned with his slogan: "If we must die for our country let us die as free men—not as Jim Crow slaves." He warned that the poster march would be followed by preparation for a civil disobedience movement "if Congress should enact a Jim Crow conscription program."[18]

Meanwhile, amendments were being offered to the draft bill working its way through Congress. Senator Richard Russell of Georgia tried to insert a provision entitling men to choose to serve only with members of their own race. Seeking to exhaust all other possibilities before resorting to a civil resistance program, the Committee Against Jim Crow arranged for Senator William Langer, a Republican from North Dakota, to introduce amendments lifted bodily out of the report of Truman's Civil Rights Commission. The fact that no prominent liberals aided Langer during the

16. Minutes of Press Conference on Negro Affairs; Pittsburgh *Courier*, April 10, 1948; "Mr. Randolph's Statement by Walter White," April 22, 1948, in NAACP Papers; Dwight D. Eisenhower Testimony, *Hearings*, 995–96; L. D. Reddick, "The Negro Policy of the American Army Since World War II," *Journal of Negro History*, XXXVIII (April, 1953), 194–215; E. Frederic Morrow, Interview by Dr. Thomas Soapes, February 23, 1977, pp. 15–17, Oral History Transcripts, Dwight David Eisenhower Library, Abilene, Kans.

17. "Crisis in the Making," 29.

18. The buttons were white with green lettering (APR Files; New York *Times*, May 8, 1948).

four days of debate, even though it was only a month before the political party conventions, disheartened Randolph, as did the Republican party command that "brazenly and cynically" tabled six of Langer's seven amendments. Since the liberals let him down, Randolph proclaimed that the nature of bipartisan hypocrisy and the "gentlemen's agreement" on civil rights had been exposed. He was horrified when liberal senator Morse rose to state that "neither Congress nor the country is ready for a complete anti-segregation policy." [19]

Randolph and Reynolds then announced that unless Truman issued an executive order banning segregation in the armed forces, they would go ahead with their plans for a League for Non-Violent Civil Disobedience Against Military Segregation. Such action would amount to far more than a one-day march on Washington—defiance of the law could have serious consequences. It was impossible to determine whether the black masses would follow Randolph in this radical protest. For the young, rural, southern black or northern ghetto youth, service, even in a segregated military establishment, provided better living conditions than he could expect at home. [20]

When the Youth Division of the NAACP took a poll of black draft-age college students, however, it found that 71 percent of those polled favored the proposal, and only 15 percent actively opposed it. More than a third, 37 percent, rejected the idea of service in segregated armed forces and expressed themselves as feeling "very strongly" about their position. Even more surprising, 50 percent said they would serve in the event of a war emergency only if segregation were abolished. The NAACP youth secretary was careful to point out that these were the opinions of the "more favored youth of the race": No attempt had been made to ascertain the opinion of the more representative working- and lower-class males. [21] Still, their reactions indicated blacks were disturbed by the army's intransigence, as manifested in the Gillem Board Report. Randolph had exposed an issue that profoundly touched Afro-American sensitivities,

19. New York *Times*, May 13, 1948; ANP Releases, June 2, 7, 1948; A. Philip Randolph, "The Negro's America: The Fight for Civil Rights," *New Leader*, November 13, 1948, p. 5.

20. "Crisis in the Making," 29.

21. NAACP Press Release, June 3, 1948, in NAACP Papers; New York *Times*, June 5, 1948. These findings confirmed those of Theodore Brown, who was dispatched by Randolph to sample the opinions of young draft-eligible blacks on college campuses (Velie, *Labor U.S.A.*, 213).

and he had again anticipated a segment of the black community, middle-class youth of draft age, that was just beginning to find its voice.

Randolph himself picketed both national political party conventions in the summer, carrying a sign that read, "Prison Is Better than Army Jim Crow." He was accompanied by draft-eligible blacks carrying banners proclaiming, "We Will not Register August 15." The combination of electoral realities and Randolph's efforts to obtain antisegregation planks produced declarations against military Jim Crow in both the Democratic and Republican party platforms.[22]

True to his word, Randolph, together with A. J. Muste of FOR, inaugurated the League for Non-Violent Civil Disobedience after the draft act was passed and signed into law in June, 1948, without "safeguards" for black civil rights. Randolph became chairman of the league, and Bayard Rustin and George Houser of FOR were named executive co-secretaries.[23] The organization proposed to encourage young men to oppose draft registration and resist induction into service when the law went into effect.

At a protest meeting in Harlem, Randolph told youths that the aim of the league was to achieve true democracy, not to destroy the government. He announced that plans were being made for protest marches in Chicago, Harlem, and other areas, as well as to picket the registration office in Washington. Randolph insisted that he personally intended to picket the draft headquarters "since I don't want to call upon anyone to do something I am not willing to risk myself."[24]

The league planned to set up small committees in various states to carry out its goals: to establish contact with young men to advise them about refusing to register or be inducted; to obtain lawyers to appear with these young men if and when they were arrested, to make certain they were given a fair trial; and to educate the public that, far from constituting treason, civil disobedience reflected such hallowed traditions of

22. ANP Release, June 21, 1948, p. 22; Dufty, "A Post Portrait," January 3, 1960.

23. Randolph to Truman, June 29, 1948, in Official File, HST Papers. Houser never actively participated in the day-to-day running of the organization ("Questions on Civil Disobedience," June 17, 1948, in APR Files). The new league and the Committee Against Jim Crow overlapped in some ways. For example, Randolph solicited "interested persons" on Committee Against Jim Crow stationary, but enclosed the league pledge and form letter (July 3, 1943, in APR Files).

24. New York *Times,* July 17, 18, 1948; Randolph to David Dubinsky, June 30, 1948, in APR Files.

American protest as the Boston Tea Party's defiance of British law and the underground railroad's defiance of the Fugitive Slave Act.

The league did attempt to set up local committees and to spell out the relationship between these committees and the national organization. Each local was to have a financial committee, a public relations committee, and a committee on morale, and each was to attempt to influence already existing groups.[25] There is no evidence, however, that these plans were successfully carried out during the league's short life. A failure to set up strong local units, unusual for a Randolph movement, occurred despite the presence of some trusted Randolph aides like B. F. McLaurin and Layle Lane on the executive committee, and proved to be one of the league's weaknesses.

Focusing its attention on draftees on the assumption that if the movement was to be effective it would be "cracking 'jimcrowism' in the armed forces," the league distributed anti-Jim Crow buttons and propaganda pamphlets containing a "Civil Disobedience Pledge" to be signed and returned. Signers pledged themselves not to register or be drafted for segregated military service or training and to urge others of all races with similar convictions to follow the same course. Several lawyers from around the country, although not affiliated with the league, pledged support and indicated their willingness to defend those who ran into legal difficulty through following the league's proposals.[26]

One of the first projects of the new league was to propose setting aside Sunday, July 25, as a national day of prayer to ask God to give young men the strength to endure prison and other hardships for their beliefs. League leaders asked the permission of ministers to sign their names to the Call to a Day of Prayer, at the same time assuring the clergymen that this gesture did not commit them to belief in nonviolent disobedience.[27]

When Randolph persisted in placing demonstrations on behalf of black rights ahead of defense efforts during World War II, his behavior had appeared treasonous. In the postwar period, when he threatened noncooperation with new preparedness efforts in response to the cold

25. Bulletin, League for Non-Violent Civil Disobedience, in APR Files.
26. New York *Times*, June 27, 1948; Pledge in APR Files. Randolph was advised confidentially that 307 persons had actually signed the pledge ("The Strength of the Movement for Civil Disobedience Against Military Segregation," n.d., APR Files). The league distributed a list of thirty-two attorneys (APR Files).
27. Randolph and Rustin to Dear Friend, July 3, 1948, in APR Files.

war, Randolph's actions seemed equally unpatriotic. Most blacks thought the security of the United States was essential for their own struggle, and it would be folly to jeopardize that security. Thus Randolph made certain to reiterate his stance against Russian totalitarianism and argued that by opposing racism he was trying to improve the American image abroad. In the face of Soviet propagandizing about Russia's equalitarian racial climate, only changing American policies could strengthen the voice of American democracy in world affairs.[28]

American Communists played into Randolph's hands by condemning his strategy. They called it headline grabbing, claimed that it only spread "division, confusion and defeatism" among blacks, and pointed out the "contradiction of asking for equal rights as a bargain for support of UMT."[29] Communist denunciation, however, made it more difficult for opponents to brand the organization as a Communist front.

Randolph based his argument on legal principles: Afro-Americans should not be deprived of their constitutional rights as men and as citizens because of racial prejudice. As he expressed what the majority of blacks thought and felt about the problem of segregation, most black leaders avoided open repudiation of his scheme, hoping that the threat alone would be sufficient to gain concessions. The NAACP said it would not "advise" young men to follow him, but would give legal aid to those who did. Although most black newspapers and many individuals agreed with Randolph's diagnosis, they rejected his methods as too drastic; as George Schuyler noted, "After all, there ARE worse things than serving in a Jim Crow army!"[30]

The white press for the most part was antagonistic toward Randolph's crusade, although Max Lerner, writing in *P.M.*, called Randolph and Reynolds' congressional testimony "one of the most impressive and courageous statements that has ever been made before a Congressional Com-

28. Reverend J. Raymond Henderson, "An Open Letter to A. Philip Randolph," in ANP Release, August 18, 1948, p. 13; Lawrence R. Sheppard to Honorable Harry S. Truman, April 9, 1948, in General File, HST Papers; *Hearings*, 694.

29. Reddick, "Negro Policy of American Army," 201. See also Frank R. Crosswaith to Editor, New York-Amsterdam *News*, April 19, 1948, in NUL Papers.

30. ANP Release, May 5, 1948, p. 30; *Congressional Record*, 80th Cong., 2nd Sess., Vol. 94, Pt. 4, pp. 4312–18; "Fighting the Jim Crow Army," *Crisis*, LV (May, 1948), 136. See Claude Barnett to Randolph and Reynolds, June 1, 1948, in Claude A. Barnett Papers, Chicago Historical Society; George S. Schuyler, "Views and Reviews," Pittsburgh *Courier*, May 15, 1948.

mittee by any man, white or black." More typical was an editorial in the New York *World Telegram* that accused Randolph and Reynolds of doing "their race and their country a great disservice." Theodore Brown of the *Black Worker* responded to the editorial, "Like most white individuals or organizations you cannot understand the thinking or test the pulse of the Negro people. . . . Greater is the fear of most Negroes in serving or training in the armed services in the Southern sections of this country than that experienced on the firing lines facing a foreign enemy."[31]

A brouhaha resulted when the New York *Times* quoted Randolph, in his capacity as head of the league, as urging draftees to employ four main courses of action: open refusal to register; quiet ignoring of registration; registration, but refusal to be inducted; and feigned illness, the claim of nonexistent dependents, and "other subterfuges." According to the *Times*, Reynolds disagreed with Randolph over these measures and announced that he would continue to seek another conference with Truman and pursue the desired end through legislative and constitutional means. Randolph, however, maintained that the press report had given the wrong impression of both the league's and his personal position. Advising enlistees to employ such "subterfuges" was "absolutely foreign to my mind and could not possibly be a part of my thinking because it would be thoroughly dishonest." Rather, Randolph said, he intended to indicate that draftees were likely to pursue those courses of action, and if they did, the league would be bound to support them "inasmuch as they would be doing so with a view to refusing to serve in a jimcrow army." He and the league merely advised draftees "not to register or be inducted into the armed forces." In view of a later falling-out between Randolph and Bayard Rustin in which Randolph accused Rustin, among other things, of failing to clear press releases, one wonders whether the *Times* misquoted Randolph or was given the information by Rustin.[32]

Advocating civil disobedience brought condemnation of Randolph even from some of the porters. They claimed that Randolph was in no position to voice the sentiments of all black people; indeed, he did not

31. Max Lerner, "The Negroes and the Draft," *Crisis,* LV (May, 1948), 140+, rpr. from *P.M.,* April 11, 1948; Editorial, "Misrepresenting Negroes," New York *World Telegram,* April 1, 1948; *Congressional Record,* 80th Cong., 2nd Sess., Vol. 94, Pt. 4, pp. 4312–18; *Black Worker,* April, 1948, p. 6.

32. New York *Times,* June 27, 1948; Randolph to John Haynes Holmes, July 1, 1948, in APR Files; *Black Worker,* November, 1948, p. 1+.

even speak for the sleeping car porters. One critic demanded that Randolph release a statement to the press immediately retracting his civil disobedience pronouncement or face an attempt to remove him as head of the BSCP. Perhaps because the new campaign was less well organized, or perhaps because they were overage for the draft, or perhaps because of the emphasis on civil disobedience, although most porters supported this movement as they did all Randolph's civil rights efforts, they were less actively involved in the military desegregation struggle than in the MOWM and the permanent FEPC effort. Still, Randolph never relaxed his pressure on the porters to become an instrument of social change. The BSCP, he maintained, had a dual responsibility: the immediate task of developing a higher degree of economic security for its members, and the longer-range task of creating the type of society in which they and their fellow Americans could enjoy abundance and freedom without regard to race, creed, color, or national origin.[33]

In July, 1948, the Committee Against Jim Crow sent a letter to President Truman, over the signatures of Randolph and Reynolds, asking him to set "a moral pace" for the special session of Congress he had recently called. Since the platforms of both parties expressed disapproval of army discrimination, they argued, there was now "a bi-partisan mandate to end military segregation." With the date for registration under the new draft law only a month away, the committee asked for "an alternative beyond submission to a discriminatory law and imprisonment for following the dictates of self-respect."[34]

The importance of the Randolph campaign in helping to swing administration opinion cannot be denied. Subjected to pressure similar to that used on Roosevelt in 1941, in 1948 a vulnerable Truman was fighting for his political life. As already noted, a Democratic party splintered by Dixiecrat disaffections on the right and Henry Wallace's Progressive revolt on the left had relieved him of the need to cater to the southern bloc. Truman could not win without the black vote, and he was being pressured by Randolph on two fronts—on behalf of military desegregation and on behalf of the National Council for a Permanent FEPC. The president, as we have seen, finally capitulated and issued two executive orders: No. 9980,

33. Telegram, Jesse W. Miller to Randolph, April 1, 1948, in APR Files; *Black Worker*, April, 1948, p. 6.

34. New York *Times*, July 17, 1948.

establishing fair employment practices within the federal government, and No. 9981, "establishing the President's Committee on Equality of Treatment and Opportunity in the Armed Services." The orders came on July 26, after the jailing of more than thirty draft resisters and on the eve of the special session of Congress. Senator Russell condemned the orders as "unconditional surrender . . . to the treasonable civil disobedience campaign organized by the Negroes." According to Phileo Nash, Truman's adviser on minorities, the roll of the equal rights directives in the 1948 election showed "the importance of politics in making progress toward American ideals."[35]

Whether by design or by inadvertence, however, the wording of Executive Order No. 9981 was ambiguous; it stated simply, "There shall be equality of treatment and opportunity for all persons in the armed services without regard to race, color, religion, or national origin." Objections were promptly raised in black circles that the order prohibited discrimination rather than segregation. Writing the president to that effect, Randolph also issued a press release stating that since the executive order had apparently not eliminated segregation, "the League shall relentlessly continue its struggle." Randolph also wrote the major political party leaders, saying he still hoped the president would outlaw racial segregation in the army, as that was the only solution acceptable to the majority of Afro-Americans.[36]

In response, Truman dispatched his chief spokesman, Senator J. Howard McGrath, to confer with Randolph and Reynolds on August 1 to clarify the meaning of the order. The black leaders questioned Truman's objectives: Was it his intention that segregation be eliminated from the armed forces? Was it his intention that the committee provided for in the executive order be civilian and function on the basis of nonsegregation as official policy? Did the president intend to lend the full authority of his

35. *Ibid.*, July 27, 28, 1948. Joseph L. Rauh confidentially revealed to Randolph that Leon Henderson, national chairman of Americans for Democratic Action, had requested that Truman issue an executive order (Joseph L. Rauh, Jr., to Randolph, July 22, 1948, in APR Files; Nichols, *Breakthrough on the Color Front*, 88). For the text of the orders, see *Code of Federal Regulations*, Title 3—The President, 1943–48 Compilation (Washington, D.C., 1948).

36. Telegram, Randolph to Truman, July 30, 1948, Bayard Rustin to Truman, July 27, 1948, both in HST Papers; Chicago *Defender*, July 31, 1948; ANP Release, August 11, 1948, pp. 30, 27; St. Clair Drake to Randolph, August 7, 1948, in APR Files.

office to see the necessary machinery established to put the committee's recommendations into effect? Above all, would selective service come under the purview and directives of the executive order to achieve the goal of nonsegregation?[37]

McGrath assured Randolph and Reynolds that segregation, as well as other discriminatory practices in the armed services, was unequivocally banned under the new order. McGrath also clarified the role of the president's advisory committee to be appointed under the order; a civilian group, it was to function on the basis of nonsegregation as official policy. Truman subsequently appointed what appeared to Randolph to be a "strong body" of five whites and two blacks to the committee, headed by Charles Fahy, former solicitor general. "Inasmuch as nonsegregation in the armed services is now the announced policy of the Commander-in-Chief," Randolph and Reynolds stated, "we can now place in storage the League for Non-Violent Civil Disobedience Against Military Segregation."[38]

The pair formally discontinued their civil disobedience campaign on August 18, 1948, explaining that they "were morally obligated" to do so. Randolph and Reynolds were now willing to accept the president's assurances of desegregation "in order to prevent any American youth from languishing in jail. . . . Candor compels us to state that the President's Executive Order, even before the subsequent clarification of its intent, understandably reduced the number of men prepared to surrender their freedom." Without the sentiment of the people and other leaders behind their movement, Randolph and Reynolds could not carry on. They could not fight complacency. "Once an organization has forced the government to initiate action on an issue, it is difficult to convince the public that the problem is not solved," they admitted. The pair believed that the president's order and further "clarification" represented a substantial gain, although it was not wholly satisfactory. "My position is that no Order or law made by man is perfect. That is why laws are amended and constitutions revised. However," Randolph insisted, "this Executive Order is a step in the right direction upon which it is possible to build for the future." Roy Wilkins later credited Randolph's threatened draft resistance campaign with helping to push Truman to integrate the military services.

37. Memorandum, Grant Reynolds to Senator J. Howard McGrath, August 1, 1948, in APR Files.
38. *Black Worker*, August, 1948, pp. 1, 8.

In Wilkins' words, "The draft resisters of the Vietnam era may not have known it, but Randolph was their spiritual and historical father."[39]

With military desegregation, as with his previous antidiscrimination movements, although Randolph received the publicity, he did not carry out the campaign alone. For a minority to take on the military establishment, the cooperation of white allies was necessary. Randolph's problem was finding dominant group support for action that sought to radically overturn social relations in the country.

In 1943, when he ventured to mount a civil disobedience campaign through the MOWM, Randolph had attempted an alliance with pacifists in FOR and its offspring, CORE. After the forging of the alliance, the MOWM had declined in significance; Randolph, however, maintained his contacts with the pacifists, even writing the foreword to a CORE pamphlet, *Erasing the Color Line*. It was natural, then, that he should turn to CORE for aid in the military desegregation struggle. CORE had some initial doubts about cooperating with the Committee Against Jim Crow in the fall of 1947 when Randolph called for a demonstration of black ex-GIs, because "CORE engages only in interracial projects as a matter of policy." Members were also concerned that Randolph's group, not CORE, would receive credit for the demonstration. Still basking in the publicity the organization had received for its Journey of Reconciliation to desegregate buses in the upper South the previous spring, CORE was particularly sensitive on this score. As CORE went on record against UMT at its convention, in part because of the segregation aspect, Action Director William Worthy, Jr., urged the CORE executive committee not to make "a fetish of 'interracialism'" and to support Randolph's crusade. Worthy inclined toward support for Randolph since he was an official of the New York Council for a Permanent FEPC, and the two had worked together. Worthy would subsequently become executive secretary of the Committee Against Jim Crow. But his support was personal; most CORE members who did not also belong to FOR did not follow his lead.[40]

39. Randolph to Mrs. Barnett, October 5, 1948, in APR Files; *Black Worker*, August, 1948, p. 1; Randolph to Charles Buchanan, October 18, 1948, Randolph to Reverend J. Raymond Henderson, August 24, 1948, in APR Files; Roy Wilkins with Tom Mathews, *Standing Fast: The Autobiography of Roy Wilkins* (New York, 1982), 202.

40. Bill Worthy, Confidential Memo to CORE Executive Committee on U.M.T., [Fall, 1947], in CORE Papers; Meier and Rudwick, *CORE*, 45–46.

After Randolph's congressional testimony in March, 1948, Bayard Rustin, fresh from the Journey of Reconciliation and also race relations secretary of FOR, announced that he would organize disciplined cells across the nation to advise individuals on draft resistance and to provide spiritual, financial, and legal aid to resisters. Rustin pointed out that America had told the German people at the Nuremberg trials that men are individually responsible for their acts and are not to be excused for following unjust demands made by their governments. He and three other CORE pacifists, Worthy, James Peck, and George Houser, the last a white Methodist student leader, announced they would not only support Randolph by refusing to fight but "from now on [would] pay no taxes to support a jimcrow Army." All four had participated in the Journey of Reconciliation and concluded that it would be inconsistent to give financial support to the same principle in government that they risked their lives to challenge on privately owned buses.[41]

Immediately after his Senate testimony, FOR pacifists rushed to Randolph's aid. A. J. Muste, head of FOR, urged support for Randolph, calling him "unquestionably the most important anti-communist leader among Negroes." Muste reminded FOR members that Randolph was personally a "pacifist" and had "frequently and consistently urged the pacifist way of reconciliation and non-violence" as a policy to gain black rights.[42]

The coalition between FOR and Randolph's movement was tenuous from the beginning. The pacifists were against any type of military conscription, whereas Randolph's more narrow objective was to eliminate Jim Crow from what he thought was an inevitable selective service bill. The members of FOR expressed concern that "objection to the Jim Crow draft . . . waters down our pacifist witness" since "the worst thing about the army is not that it is Jim Crow but that it is an army." In their point of view, the more democratic the army's practices, the more likely it would

41. "Negro Youth Leader Pledges Support to Randolph Civil Disobedience Program," April 11, 1948, in NAACP Papers; "Statement on Refusal to Continue the Payment of Taxes to Support the Racially Segregated Armed Services of the United States, the Production of Atom Bombs and the Current Armament Race," April 14, 1948, in APR Files. This statement, signed by Houser, Peck, Rustin, and Worthy, was on blank paper without a letterhead. See also Randolph to Editor of Associated Press, April 21, 1948, in CORE, Papers; Meier and Rudwick, *CORE*, 46.
42. A. J. Muste, Non-violent Action in Connection with Jim Crow in the Armed Forces, [Spring, 1948], in CORE Papers.

be to survive as a social institution, and hence, the worse for pacifist "dreams of a nonviolent world order."[43] Randolph, however, repressed any doubts he may have had about divergent goals and eagerly welcomed his new colleagues, hoping they would stimulate a bandwagon effect.

FOR could hardly remain indifferent to Randolph's attempt to apply the techniques and philosophy of civil disobedience to an important social problem. As Muste pointed out, those who hoped to build a Gandhian movement had to be inside it, "even though the movement itself and many of its members may not theoretically go all the way with us on the issue of war." A desire developed among FOR members to make clear that their objections to conscription and war would not be diminished if Jim Crow were eliminated from the army. They recognized, however, that segregation in and of itself was a violation of a basic principle of the Fellowship since it humiliated "the spirit of the individual human being." Even though FOR was against the military, segregation should be opposed there as insistently as anywhere else; "there is something peculiarly abhorrent about the idea of forcing men into an allegedly democratic army engaged in an alleged conflict against racism and totalitarianism when that army itself rests on a racist basis."[44]

FOR also justified its involvement on the grounds that if Randolph's civil disobedience movement grew in numbers, there was the danger that it might become violent, and FOR had a responsibility to see "that violence is prevented and that the spirit and methods of non-violence are taught to people engaged in a conflict against evil." Furthermore, Jim Crow was such a basic element in the American social system that its elimination from the armed forces "would almost certainly have revolutionary effects in many sectors of American life."[45] Randolph's crusade, therefore, represented too good an opportunity for the Fellowship to miss.

Because of the philosophical differences that existed between FOR and the Committee Against Jim Crow, Muste suggested setting up an independent organization, an "Action Committee" designed specifically to carry out the civil disobedience campaign. The League for Non-Violent Civil Disobedience, therefore, was actually Muste's idea. He reasoned that, once a draft law was on the books and civil disobedience amounted

43. Memorandum, Charles Lawrence to Bayard Rustin, Bill Worthy, and George Houser, [Spring, 1948], *ibid.*
44. A. J. Muste to Elver A. Barker, May 27, 1948, *ibid.*
45. *Ibid.*

to violation of the law, it would be better to have an organization composed entirely of people fully committed to the concept. He and other pacifists thought that true adherence to nonviolence gave one the "spiritual armor" that was necessary for civil disobedience; without such a commitment the movement could not be successful, they believed. Because civil disobedience was not "a weapon to be used lightly or without thorough preliminaries and precautions," Muste saw the necessity of having a functioning action committee rather than one that left the making and carrying out of decisions to one or two staff members; recruiting, training and supporting civil disobedience volunteers required full-time vigilance.[46]

Since, in Muste's opinion, Randolph was the "key person" in the movement, a "basic requirement" for FOR participation was that Randolph serve as chairman of the new action committee. Rustin had already spent a good deal of time enlisting people to serve on the committee, and some of his colleagues had undertaken other necessary preparatory steps. Rustin had even drafted a letter asking attorneys to agree to represent civil disobedience volunteers. But before he released Rustin and Houser from their FOR duties to devote themselves full-time to the civil disobedience effort, Muste wanted a firm commitment from Randolph to stay with the cause and make "a genuine effort to build the movement to become a real force and back up the young men participating in it."[47] Randolph acquiesced, and the League for Non-Violent Civil Disobedience came into being.

When Randolph subsequently called off the civil disobedience campaign, the pacifists became bitter, believing he had failed to keep his promise. They argued that issuance of the executive order had proved the efficacy of the civil disobedience campaign; if "cold water" was poured on the campaign now, it would "lead the administration to the conclusion that it has outmaneuvered the opponents of military segregation who are willing to go the whole way." They were also afraid that calling off the campaign would leave individuals who were committed to noncooperation without support.[48]

46. Memorandum, Charles Lawrence to Bayard Rustin, Bill Worthy, and George Houser, [Spring, 1948], in CORE Papers; Muste to Randolph, June 9, 1948, in APR Files; Orval Etter to Dear Friend, April 5, 1948, in CORE Papers.
47. Muste to Randolph, June 9, 1948, in APR Files.
48. George M. Houser to Randolph, August 18, 1948, *ibid.*

James Peck, for one, was shocked that Randolph planned to abandon his civil disobedience stand. Such action, he maintained, would be playing into the hands of Truman, who by his "meaningless" order hoped to garner black votes in the coming election and at the same time undermine the civil disobedience movement. Peck thought Randolph's argument that the movement did not have a sufficient number of adherents was "completely invalid": Any pioneering movement was bound to be limited in numbers, but that did not mean it was ineffective. Peck cited the Journey of Reconciliation as an effort by a small group that received national publicity and claimed, "The same would be the case with civil disobedience to army jimcrow." Peck and the other pacifists accused Reynolds of "just riding along so long as it suited his political ambitions." They thought Randolph, on the other hand, was "a man of integrity." Peck argued, "For you to abandon the civil disobedience stand now, on the eve of registration, would be a tragic sellout of us, who pledged ourselves to the movement and of the entire Negro people. I beg you to reconsider." [49]

The executive order thus brought to the fore the previously suppressed differences in philosophy between Randolph and the pacifists, and caused a schism in the leadership of the league. Because desegregation was only one of their goals, the pacifists wanted to continue agitation, hoping to educate the public to the evils of militarism per se. In their prepared statement announcing abandonment of the league, Randolph and Reynolds found it necessary to "dissociate" themselves from some key league people, headed by Rustin, who were not yet ready to compromise with the establishment. Rustin claimed that he wanted to keep the league going until the last vestige of discrimination had been removed and until the protestors who refused to register for the draft had been released from jail. In mid-August, Rustin called a press conference of his own prior to Randolph and Reynolds', at which he bitterly denounced Randolph, declaring, "On the face of it the executive order does not abolish segregation, even with the President's so-called clarification statement." [50]

49. Jim Peck to Randolph, August 15, 1948, *ibid.* See also Adams, *The Challenge,* 40–41.
50. *Black Worker,* August, 1948, p. 8; New York *Times,* August 19, 1948. See also ANP Release, August 23, 1948; "Randolph Withdraws from Anti-Jimcrow League," *Fellowship,* XIV (October, 1948), 34. Rustin was later ashamed of his actions and avoided Randolph for two years, assuming that Randolph was angry with him. Randolph, however, ignored Rustin's indiscretion, and when they met again, simply said, "Hi. Where have you been?" (Interview with Leroy Shackelford, Jr., November 9, 1972).

Rustin and his supporters declared that Randolph and Reynolds had "made a grave and tragic mistake." Calling the executive order "a weasly worded, mealy mouthed sham" that only confused the issue, the dissidents noted a lack of response to the call for civil disobedience and blamed it "*in large part*" on "*a justified lack of faith in leaders who fail to follow through.*" The dissenters renamed their group the Campaign to Resist Military Segregation and pledged continued agitation. Although they lacked funds and by no means constituted a mass movement "as yet," the new organization expected greater participation from local groups "and a long overdue democratization of our structure."[51]

The breach became so great that Randolph and Reynolds felt compelled to issue another statement in November—a castigation of the league's "religious pacifist nucleus" and its use of "unethical tactics." Although the league had initially welcomed pacifists like Rustin and Muste, assuming that their experience would help keep a "potentially violent movement non-violent in spirit and action," it subsequently became convinced the pacifists were using the organization for other purposes. Rustin's unauthorized letters and statements to both major political parties and his violation of the injunction to clear press releases revealed a basic split in ideology and an internal weakness within the league. Randolph personally shared a firm opposition to conscription, whether segregated or not, but believed "that good faith demands above board dealings with draft-age youth and a separation of pacifist aims as such from the anti-Jim-Crow campaign." The league was formed for resistance to a Jim Crow draft, not in opposition to conscription itself, Randolph maintained.[52]

Randolph and Reynolds went on to answer their critics on the abandonment of the league, as Randolph had earlier had to justify calling off the March on Washington. Like all Randolph's undertakings, the league was desperately short of funds. It was so financially weak, in fact, that Randolph had advanced $800 out of his own pocket since the passage of the draft bill—a sum representing almost the entire amount raised by the staff. The league workers, faced with launching a revolutionary movement with a deficit in excess of $1,000, thought proceeding without resources would be reckless and fatuous: "The civil disobedience technique would have been discredited in the beginning, and our hopes of using it

51. Mimeo sheet, "We Have a New Look," n.d., in APR Files; Bayard Rustin to Honorable Harry F. [sic] Truman, August 20, 1948, in Official File, HST Papers.
52. Black Worker, November, 1948, p. 1+.

again in other fields would have been in vain." Randolph and Reynolds had also been criticized for revealing that the league did not have a "mass following." They responded that years of experience had proven to them the futility of attempting to build movements without "complete candor and integrity." There had not been time between March 31 and August 30 "to build a mass revolutionary movement"; the failure was the fault neither of the technique nor of the organizers. The executive order had been obtained despite public apathy and press antipathy because "our program was morally unassailable."[53]

It was not easy to educate the masses in the concept of civil disobedience, but Randolph and Reynolds' eagerness to disband the league also reflected the fact that internal dissension had rendered it largely ineffective. A major cause of the league schism was behind-the-scenes friction between Rustin and Worthy, as the two contested for financial control and power.[54]

Appalled over the depth of the rift in the movement and the bad feelings resulting from Randolph's press release denouncing the pacifists, Houser wrote Randolph, "If those of us who believe in nonviolence can't come to some kind of agreement with one another, how can we ever expect nation-states to solve their differences short of war?" He understood that there could be honest differences in analysis and strategy, but the questioning of motives was a tragic turn of events, something that "seems to have crept into this whole affair, probably on both sides." The only reason he and the other pacifists had issued their statement about not calling off the civil disobedience campaign, according to Houser, was to let those who wished to take the position know they had support; he, at least, did not mean to imply that Randolph had deserted the cause. For his part Houser had no illusions about building a strong movement after Randolph and Reynolds pulled out; "we lost our opportunity for a real campaign because of the internal split which existed in the League almost from its very inception. We were able to put our whole energy neither into the civil disobedience aspect of it nor into the legislative work." Although he was not certain how far the movement would have gone even if there had not been inner strife, the important aspect of the campaign in his view was that it educated the public to the value of civil disobedience.[55]

53. *Ibid.*; ANP Release, August 25, 1948, p. 23.
54. Memo, John Swomley to William Worthy, September 4, 1948, in APR Files.
55. George M. Houser to Randolph, March 30, 1949, *ibid.*

Another pacifist, John Swomley, indicated that his hesitation about FOR joining the movement had been so great that if Randolph had not been in the picture he would have opposed the use of FOR personnel. Pinpointing the persistent weakness of all Randolph's civil rights movements, he noted that Randolph had been "too busy to be in on the week-by-week problems which arose." Once animosity developed between Rustin and Worthy, only careful and consistent supervision could have resolved the conflict, but Randolph's frequent absences had placed the two men "in a position where they had to carry forward the work and make decisions without the advantage of adequate consultation" with Randolph. Unfortunately, Randolph would then be asked to make choices on the basis of biased reports by either Rustin or Worthy.[56] Thus the military desegregation movement suffered, as had his earlier civil rights efforts, from Randolph's multiple commitments.

Unhappy about the split in the movement, Randolph blamed the pacifists for instigating it through their refusal to call off the civil disobedience campaign after the issuance of the executive order. He thought "that an important and valuable moral victory was forsaken . . . for a temporary and transitory advantage," and theorized that the disposition to construe success only as the continuance of the civil disobedience campaign "was responsible for the trouble." For Randolph the essence of Gandhian civil disobedience lay "in faithful adherence to truth, and to moral commitments, even though the full and complete objective of the campaign be not realized." On the one hand he was angry at the pacifists' behavior; he deplored the "reckless manner" in which they handled nonviolent civil disobedience, "taking the form of a rumpus movement," after the leaders officially called off the campaign. Randolph thought such action was "certain to set back the cause of civil disobedience and non-violent good-will direct action among minorities in the United States, for some time," which he regretted because he had "high hopes for the application of the philosophy . . . as a way of abolishing jim-crow." On the other hand, Randolph claimed to harbor no ill feelings toward the "Brothers" opposed to his methods, and he still planned to employ the technique in the future.[57]

56. John M. Swomley, Jr., to Randolph, March 18, 1949, *ibid.*
57. Randolph to Houser, April 26, 1949, *ibid.*

If Randolph had difficulties trying to forge an alliance on behalf of military desegregation with a predominantly white group, he fared little better in his attempted coalition with black groups. Although the established black leaders were in favor of integrating the military, once Randolph made headlines with his civil disobedience proposal and attempted to mount a new membership movement, organizational jealousies and competition once more surfaced. The NAACP's and the NUL's reservations about actively participating in Randolph's campaign were based on tactical, rather than ideological, grounds. Reflecting their moderate-to-conservative constituencies and bases of support, the two leading black rights organizations equivocated in their assistance as they had earlier with the MOWM.

Lester Granger noted in his weekly column for the Amsterdam *News* in April, 1948, that whether or not Randolph's civil disobedience statement was wise, it was morally justified. Despite years of Afro-American protest, official Washington had done nothing to challenge the army policy of segregation. Still, Granger was concerned that pacifists might merely use Randolph's crusade to further their own cause, that enemies of black progress might use Randolph's statement as "proof" that blacks were not true Americans and could not be trusted, and that Communists "opposed to our present foreign policy" might jump on Randolph's bandwagon. Granger pointed out that Randolph's position carried to its logical conclusion required not participating in any facet of a Jim Crow style of life. But, the columnist believed, the biggest problem with Randolph's proposal was the inconsistency of, on the one hand, asking for an FEPC law because "our racial interest is the common national interest" and, on the other, declaring that national defense is of no concern to blacks "until and unless it is carried out in a democratic fashion."[58]

Granger was also afraid that Gandhian tactics would not work in America. The Indian people were a majority in their own land, acting against an alien and infinitesimal white minority, whereas blacks were a small minority in the United States, "acting against an entrenched majority in possession of all the political, economic and military controls." While it took "guts" to be a martyr in Randolph's fashion, it took "an

---

58. Lester Granger, "Battle-Ax and Bread," Amsterdam *News*, April 13, 1948; Granger to Max Malmquist, April 27, 1948, in NUL Papers.

equally strong, though different kind of guts" to abjure martyrdom, Granger maintained. Based on his analysis, the official statement issued by the NUL noted that the organization "would view with grave concern the adoption of the course of resistance advocated by Messrs. Randolph and Reynolds," because the country needed unity during a time of international crisis and because this tactic "would weaken the foundation of law upon which our democratic processes rest."[59]

Not all NUL board members concurred with Granger's cautious approach. Realizing that the league could not officially advocate civil disobedience, some board members were nonetheless pleased with Randolph's more militant stance. They pointed out that since Granger by this time was acting as an adviser to Secretary of Defense Forrestal, any derogatory statement about Randolph's movement coming from the NUL would appear to have been unduly influenced by the government: Indeed, Granger's participation in drafting the NUL statement amounted to conflict of interest. Public dissent from Randolph and Reynolds' position by the NUL appeared to another board member to be circumscribing traditional American freedom of thought and expression.[60]

In contrast to Granger, Walter White told Randolph he would "follow the Voltairean philosophy of fighting for your right to say what I know you honestly believe," even though he disagreed with Randolph's stand on civil disobedience, "chiefly as a matter of practicality." White explained to the dominant community that the NAACP would not disassociate itself from the labor leader because "Randolph is highly regarded in the Negro community as a man of integrity. He is regarded as selfless and incorruptible. He is no self-seeking opportunist. He will not ask others to make sacrifices which he himself is unwilling to make. Negroes believe in him and his opinion carries weight among them."[61]

Officially, the NAACP neither supported nor condemned Randolph's stand. The association agreed, however, to give legal assistance in par-

59. Granger to Malmquist, April 27, 1948, Revised Draft of Statement to be Issued by the National Urban League, [April, 1948], both in NUL Papers.
60. Sidney [Hollander] to Granger, April 20, 1948, William H. Dean to Granger, April 28, 1948, Sadie [T. Mossell Alexander] to Granger, April 28, 1948, all in NUL Papers.
61. Walter White to Randolph, April 21, 1948, Walter White to Victor F. Reuther, June 22, 1948, Draft of Letter to Senator Morse for Mr. White's Signature, April 7, 1948, all in NAACP Papers.

ticular cases that fell within its rules "with respect to discrimination because of race or color or the denial of civil rights in general." The NAACP would not go so far as to recommend to fellow Afro-Americans "that they should not defend their country if it is in danger," but protested Senator Morse's suggestion that Randolph be tried for treason. White tried to interpret for Morse exactly how "fed up with segregation in the armed services" blacks really were, and expressed the hope "that sufficient courage can be mustered by the government to do the simple thing which will make unnecessary and unthinkable any campaign of civil disobedience. That simple act is to wipe out segregation forthwith." Morse had charged on the floor of the Senate that the NAACP encouraged Randolph's position. That was not true, said White; rather, Randolph derived his encouragement "from the righteous resentment of Negroes against the national hypocrisy which preaches democracy while practicing vile forms of racism." Morse, one of the more liberal senators on the race question, was himself a member of the NAACP's board of directors, although he threatened to resign if the association supported Randolph's civil disobedience proposal.[62] Playing upon cold war fears, the NAACP pointed out that continued segregation would lead to low morale and lack of fighting spirit among black troops "in the conflict that seems imminent," even if blacks would not follow Randolph to the point of draft resistance. The Communists, after all, did not practice racial discrimination—a fact they effectively publicized among the black masses.

Despite the NAACP's cautious defense of Randolph, the association became concerned that it was being "smothered" and was consequently fading into the background when Randolph's congressional testimony received so much publicity. Roy Wilkins even considered NAACP sponsorship of a demonstration in Washington by veterans against military Jim Crow to "give some punch to our protest." The association eventually set up its own Council to Abolish Segregation in the Armed Forces

---

62. White to Wilson A. Head, August 2, 1948, Memorandum to Mr. White from Mr. Wilkins, March 31, 1948, Memorandum to Mr. White, Mr. Moon, from Mr. Wilkins, Telegram, White to Senator Wayne Morse, April 1, 1948, White to Morse, April 18, 1948, "U.S. Should Make Civil Disobedience Unnecessary—White," April 15, 1948, Walter White, "Mr. Randolph's Statement," April 22, 1948, White to Morse, April 22, 1948, NAACP Press Release, April 22, 1948, Draft of Letter to Senator Morse for Mr. White's Signature, April 7, 1948, all *ibid.*

to counter Randolph's civil disobedience program and set October 16, 1948, as "D-Day" in Harlem. The NAACP wanted the area to "close down completely" for several hours in mass protest against army segregation—a strategy clearly borrowed from Randolph, and one that he had pioneered in conjunction with the mass rally at Madison Square Garden in 1942.[63]

As with the NUL, not all NAACP branches concurred with national office policy. A member of the Decatur branch, for example, thought that because Randolph was a vice-president of the NAACP, he should be censured by the national board so that his remarks would not bring "criticism upon the organization unnecessarily." Another member argued that blacks should take pride as a race in wanting all-black military units. Thus, although the NAACP did not openly dissent from Randolph, the organization gave him only limited support in the military desegregation struggle. Walter White's personal loyalty to Randolph, however, remained as strong as ever. It was White who wired Defense Secretary Forrestal to "suggest and urge" that Randolph be invited to participate in his conference on utilizing Afro-Americans in the military. White advised Forrestal, "Mr. Randolph's prestige and integrity are such that I believe it would be difficult to explain ignoring him to the large public which trusts him." On the other hand, Granger, Forrestal's adviser, recommended not inviting Randolph since his method was "not one of discussion, but of intransigent position."[64]

Randolph's militant stand gave punch to the protest of the more moderate black betterment groups. Still, with their confused and sometimes conflicting reactions, the old-line leaders were grateful when Randolph and Reynolds decided to call off their civil disobedience campaign. The Chicago *Defender* also applauded their action, saying the pair demonstrated "sound statesmanship" to abandon the cause once the Truman administration had thrown its full weight behind abolition of Jim Crow.[65]

---

63. Memorandum to Mr. White from Mr. Wilkins, April 9, 1948, *ibid.*; ANP Release, August 23, 1948, p. 1.

64. Marie G. Baker to White, April 1, 1948, Signed, Veteran, June 9, 1948, Telegram, Walter White to James Forrestal, April 21, 1948, Lester Granger to Walter White, April 23, 1948, all in NAACP Papers.

65. Lester B. Granger to Randolph, October 5, 1948, in APR Files; Chicago *Defender*, August 28, 1948. The editor of the *Defender* was on the fund-raising committee for Truman's reelection. The *Crisis* also promoted Truman's reelection. See, for example, "A Look at the Candidates" LV (January, 1948), 9, and "Wallace's Southern Tour" LV (October, 1948), 297.

The *Defender* editors, like so many other established Afro-Americans, had never been convinced of the effectiveness of Gandhian techniques in America.

After the disbanding of the League for Non-Violent Civil Disobedience, Randolph redirected his attention to the Committee Against Jim Crow. At this time Worthy won over Rustin in the battle for Randolph's confidence, and was appointed executive secretary. The original plan was for the committee to continue to monitor Executive Order No. 9981 and report to the people on its implementation, since it would not automatically change the pattern of segregated black and white units. "On the contrary, the Brass Hats will obey the Order only if the public demands compliance," Randolph emphasized. Hence the committee engaged in a variety of activities, among which were sponsoring "unofficial" inspection trips to military installations to check their compliance with the president's order, initiating a campaign to end racial segregation and discrimination in the National Guard in the northern states, and continuing to press for a congressional investigation of armed forces' racial policy. In addition, Randolph thought the committee should work to abolish Jim Crow laws affecting servicemen in the southern states. He believed segregation could not long endure on the civilian front once black soldiers experienced treatment as equals in public facilities.[66]

The committee's most important activity was to conduct Commission of Inquiry hearings to reveal the effects of discrimination on the psyche of black soldiers. The initial hearing took place in Washington in May, 1948, before Forrestal's meeting with the black leaders. In fact, many knowledgeable observers thought Forrestal arranged his conference to counteract the publicity given the hearing and its revelation of the country's poor record regarding minorities during the war. After looking into the wartime treatment of black soldiers, the commission made recommendations to Congress for provisions on complete integration of Afro-

66. *Black Worker*, November, 1948, p. 1+; Fund-raising letter, October 21, 1948, Draft, Prospects of Committee Against Jim Crow in Military Service and Training, September, 1948, Bill Worthy to Randolph, November 26, 1949, all in APR Files; Randolph and Reynolds to Truman, November 28, 1949, General File, HST Papers; Press Conference, August 18, 1948, in APR Files; New York *Times*, August 23, 1948; ANP Release, August 23, 1948, pp. 14–15; Reynolds and Randolph to Louis Johnson, January 15, 1950, in APR Files.

Americans into the military. The first hearing also took up the issue of the quota system and other barriers to black enlistment.

The commission was made up of prominent black and white individuals personally solicited by Randolph. At the first hearing, Randolph made an opening statement wherein he argued that whites had little conception of the physical and psychological aggression against black GIs during World War II, and Reynolds provided the commission with secret Jim Crow army orders and court-martial transcripts. All subsequent Commission of Inquiry hearings built upon the Washington model.[67]

In addition to the Committee Against Jim Crow, Truman's Fahy committee also worked for implementation of the executive order throughout 1949. The navy and air force soon satisfied the Fahy committee, but the army, with the largest percentage of black personnel, utilized delaying tactics. General Omar Bradley, the new army chief of staff, said he still favored segregation among the lower echelons. "The Army is not out to make any social reforms," declared Bradley. "The Army will put men of different races in different companies. It will change that policy when the nation as a whole changes it."[68]

The Fahy committee eventually achieved a compromise whereby the army committed itself to gradual integration but refused to abandon its 10 percent quota for blacks. This compromise prompted Randolph to comment that the army obviously still did not intend to abolish either its racist restrictions or segregation. Resisting pressures for its termination, the Fahy committee retained Truman's support and continued to press until it finally achieved a change in army policy in January, 1950: Blacks with special skills would now be "assigned to any . . . unit without regard for race or color." The Committee Against Jim Crow also worked for abolition of the quota. Truman finally intervened and secured the army's acquiescence in mid-March, 1950, but only after a secret agreement was signed stating that the quota system might be reinstituted if the new policy resulted in some unspecified "disproportionate balance of racial strength."[69]

67. Memorial of Commission of Inquiry into the Effect of Discrimination and Segregation on the Morale and Development of Negro Soldiers, [April, 1948], in APR Files; ANP Release, May 3, 1948, p. 19; *Black Worker*, July, 1949, p. 6.

68. Omar Bradley, quoted in Chicago *Sun-Times*, July 30, 1948.

69. Randolph, quoted in New York *Times*, February 15, 1950; Nichols, *Breakthrough on the Color Front*, 96; Hamby, *Beyond the New Deal*, 343.

Such concessions notwithstanding, the army, the last branch of the military to launch an all-out assault on discrimination, did an about-face in three years—from almost complete segregation to a situation in which more than nine of every ten blacks were serving in racially mixed units. The army would never have moved toward nonsegregation so quickly had the Korean War not broken out in June, 1950. General Bradley admitted, "The war hastened Army integration by at least ten years."[70]

Acting as a watchdog over an intransigent institution like the army, together with engaging in its other activities, was full-time work for the Committee Against Jim Crow. There remained the perennial problem of financing, however—to carry out its projected program and to provide for publicity and public education.[71] Faced with the task of raising funds from a poor black constituency, by the late 1940s Randolph was more inclined to solicit white financial aid than he had been earlier in the decade. Ironically, the government crackdown on Communist activity in the cold war era, while running roughshod over civil liberties, lessened the threat of Communist takeover of liberal movements, thus removing one objection to acceptance of dominant-group support. Achievement of the goal of integrating the armed forces would itself provide a heightened black self-image, thereby eliminating another reason for keeping the movement all-black. The League for Non-Violent Civil Disobedience did not have much success in attracting contributions for its campaign, which was perceived as too radical by the dominant community; for the Committee Against Jim Crow, which appeared more moderate, however, Randolph was able to tap white sources.

In the black community Randolph resorted to the familiar fund-raising methods of asking church leaders to take up special collections and selling "Don't Join a Jim Crow Army" buttons "at whatever sum a person wishes to contribute." Randolph also attempted to obtain funds from unions and appealed to David Dubinsky of the International Ladies Garment Workers Union for the money to put together and distribute another pamphlet on military Jim Crow. Then Randolph reconsidered foundation support—the Garland Fund, after all, had helped him start the *Black Worker*—even though he had been unsuccessful at tapping foundation funding in 1945 for his first movement against army Jim

70. Nichols, *Breakthrough on the Color Front*, 201, 97.
71. Draft, Prospects of Committee Against Jim Crow.

Crow. In 1948 he applied to the Robert Marshall Civil Liberties Trust on behalf of the Committee Against Jim Crow, requesting that the trust contribute $2,000 of a projected $3,280 budget to help finance the committee's Commission of Inquiry hearings. This figure was greatly scaled down from the $100,000 budget Randolph had projected for his similar movement three years earlier. Although the commission's hearings had proven their value, Congress still failed to make an official investigation; thus the Committee Against Jim Crow was needed to fill the void, Randolph argued. The committee had financed the initial hearings out of its own "extremely low treasury" but needed additional funding to continue the work, he maintained.[72]

Randolph also applied to the ACLU for financial aid, but Granger replied negatively when ACLU chief Roger Baldwin requested his opinion of the merits of Randolph's proposal. Granger was upset in part because Randolph and Reynolds "never bothered to sit down in council session with representative Negroes whose interests and experience equal, where they do not overmatch, those of the co-chairmen." Admitting there was a need for a scientifically developed program to reach whites who were uninformed about or hostile to integration, Granger argued a $3,280 budget could not make much of a contribution toward solving the problem. But more important, in his opinion, was the impossibility of the Committee Against Jim Crow disassociating itself in the public mind from the draft resistance movement, despite Randolph's statement to the Senate committee that he spoke as an individual.[73]

When he canceled the civil disobedience campaign in August, Randolph promptly informed the Marshall Trust and reminded it that the program of noncooperation was "executed under the auspices of an organization entirely separate from the Committee Against Jim Crow." Randolph also emphasized the necessity for the continued existence of the committee; past experience with the FEPC proved the need "for an alert group of citizens to monitor and police" the executive order.[74]

72. Randolph to Reverend James Robinson, May 13, 1948, in CORE Papers; Randolph to David Dubinsky, June 30, 1948, Randolph to Mrs. Richard J. Walsh [Pearl Buck], March 24, 1949, Randolph to Max Sherover, March 28, 1949, all in APR Files; Randolph to Philip Murray, August 15, 1949, Files of the Office of the Secretary-Treasurer of the CIO, ALH, Randolph to Simon Gross, [application for funding dated June 5, 1948], in APR Files.
73. Baldwin to Granger, June 24, 1948, Granger to Baldwin, June 29, 1948, both in NUL Papers.
74. Randolph to Simon Gross, August 19, 1948, in APR Files.

Philanthropic foundations are usually conservative institutions, but the Commission of Inquiry hearings were essentially a noncontroversial activity and one directly connected with the denial of civil liberties. Thus, unlike his previous attempt, Randolph's effort to receive aid from the Marshall Trust was successful. Encouraged, he submitted another application early in 1949 asking for an additional $8,100 to carry on the hearings on a broader scale.[75] Experience with the Marshall Trust proved that foundation money could be obtained for civil rights causes, provided the tactics employed did not appear too militant.

Although he initially did not support the committee's bid for financial assistance, Granger changed his mind after Randolph canceled the civil disobedience campaign, and he made a personal contribution to the second Washington Commission of Inquiry hearing, held in January, 1949.[76] The legal work of the Committee Against Jim Crow was not militant and did not bring headlines, nor did it bring a mass influx of members; hence it did not represent a threat to the NUL.

To supplement the grant from the Marshall Trust, Randolph decided to ask twenty "key leaders" and friends to contribute one hundred dollars each to the Committee Against Jim Crow to put it on a sound financial basis. In addition, the committee endeavored to raise funds locally for Commission of Inquiry hearings. Borrowing a technique Randolph employed with the National Council, the local committees invited key persons in the community to an informal gathering in someone's home, where Randolph would say a few words and urge support of the program. Randolph also tapped his trade union contacts and worked to obtain the support of prominent personalities.[77] As always, however, he attracted more publicity than cash.

Even after the cancellation of the civil disobedience campaign and the disbanding of the League for Non-Violent Civil Disobedience, finances, which had played a part in the dissension between the Committee Against Jim Crow and the league, remained a problem. Although Randolph and Muste were at odds over its abandonment, they worked jointly to clear

75. Application to Marshall Trust [before March, 1949, hearings in St. Louis], *ibid.* Theodore Cross incorrectly states that Randolph "never accepted funding from white foundations" (Cross, *The Black Power Imperative: Racial Inequality and the Politics of Nonviolence* [New York, 1984], 40).

76. Randolph to Granger, December, 20, 1948, in NUL Papers.

77. Randolph to Charles Buchanan, October 18, 1948, Randolph to A. W. Dent, March 31, 1949, Randolph to G. C. Garren, February 28, 1949, all in APR Files.

up the league's liabilities of roughly $1,200. To this end, Muste drafted a fund-raising letter claiming that the executive order resulted largely from the civil disobedience campaign. The letter was apparently ineffective as Randolph and Muste sent out another form letter in December, 1948, again requesting money to pay the league's bills. The controversy over who should be responsible for the league's debts continued into the New Year. Although Randolph thought all former league members should bear the burden, predictably he wound up paying many of the bills out of his own pocket.[78]

The onset of the Korean War marked the end of both the Fahy committee and the Committee Against Jim Crow, but the beginning of a truly integrated United States military establishment. Under pressure of the war, the army made great strides toward abandoning its Jim Crow policy, even desegregating schools in the South for the children of military personnel.[79] Ironically, from the most segregated institution in the nation, the integrated military became the realm wherein Afro-Americans enjoyed the greatest equality in the country—a factor that would separate blacks from liberal young whites during the later Vietnam War era. Building on his earlier efforts, Randolph's civil disobedience movement played a vital role in bringing about this major social change. Although this latest campaign did not provide Randolph with his coveted mass movement, under his guidance the poor black minority had succeeded in utilizing its primary asset, manpower, to pressure the most powerful institution in the country, the military, to alter its discriminatory policies. In the process it further educated the American public, black and white, on the techniques of noncooperation.

Randolph was less involved in the day-to-day workings of this movement than he had been in either the MOWM or the National Council for a Permanent FEPC. William Worthy actually wrote many of the letters

78. Draft Letter, Muste to Randolph, September 14, 1948, Randolph to Muste, September 22, 1948, Form letter, December 13, 1948, Randolph to Muste, January 26, 1949, all *ibid.* Randolph's files contain much correspondence with Muste over the league's bills. It was finally decided to await Rustin's return to the country before a discussion of payment of the debts (Randolph to Muste, February 4, 1949, *ibid.*).

79. Reddick, "Negro Policy of American Army," 214–15. For a less sanguine view of the integrated military, see Burk, *Eisenhower Administration and Black Civil Rights,* Chap. 2.

and press releases that Randolph merely signed or approved. Besides his lack of availability, internal value conflicts also made Randolph's leadership less effective than it might have been. Pragmatism appeared to win over idealism in funding issues, whereas idealism held sway in politics. The army desegregation struggle, no less than the permanent FEPC battle, was affected by Randolph's political activities. Certainly his campaigning for Norman Thomas and the socialists did not make President Truman kindly disposed toward Randolph or his causes. Nevertheless, Randolph's efforts in the late 1940s had sufficient impact to prompt historian William Berman to claim that Truman's issuance of Executive Order No. 9981 "was not simply an exercise in good will, but rather the product of political pressure applied by A. Philip Randolph, Walter White, and others at a time when a presidential incumbent needed all the support he could muster in states with the greatest votes in the electoral college."[80]

Once again Randolph had successfully employed civil disobedience to demand new rights for blacks. The military desegregation movement was not a mere protest against prevailing conditions or the request of favors for a few chosen ones. In large part because of Randolph's activities, patron-clientage politics was dead and the black political presence had been institutionalized. Randolph correctly perceived that if the demand for equal treatment in the military were met, the consequences would be enormous for blacks in all sectors of American life. The importance of the movement lay in Randolph's attempt to implement civil disobedience in a national forum, thereby demonstrating its effectiveness as a technique to gain black rights. The lesson was not lost on many of the participants in Randolph's campaign—men like Bayard Rustin, James Peck, and James Farmer, who would play important roles in the midcentury civil rights movement.

Randolph's campaign was the widest use of civil disobedience thus far attempted in the United States. Service integration was a single, clearly delineated issue and thus proved an excellent target for mass, nonviolent, direct action tactics. "Agitation for racial justice broke out of traditionally respected bounds on March 31, and I, for one," Grant Reynolds concluded, "do not believe that Negroes will ever again be satisfied with the mere issuance of educational and propaganda material or with the hat-in-the-hand approach to members of legislative bodies or to the White

---

80. Berman, *Politics of Civil Rights*, 239.

House itself." Rather, Reynolds predicted, blacks would "cast their eyes around" to find other areas of segregation where a program of non-compliance might be feasible. He suggested for consideration "schools in the South, intra-state Jim Crow transportation, and segregated public facilities."[81] Nonviolent direct action was eventually employed in all these areas, but only in one community at a time, never on the large, nation-wide scale with centralized direction envisioned by Randolph.

Although Randolph and Reynolds foresaw the use of civil disobedience in other areas of the black equality movement, neither the black masses nor the old-line leadership was ready for the tactic. The administration's capitulation to the pair's demands made it impossible to know whether a civil disobedience campaign would actually have gained countrywide support. One may conjecture, however, that the civil rights movement would probably not have erupted in the late 1940s, even if Randolph had not disbanded the League for Non-Violent Civil Disobedience. Although the Korean War was unpopular, social reform movements fared poorly during any war, and the subsequent witch hunts of the McCarthy era created an even less congenial atmosphere for radical or innovative methods.

Nevertheless, Randolph's appeals to philanthropic foundations, labor unions, and liberal whites to support the military equality drive foreshadowed the coalition that would finance the civil rights movement of the late 1950s and 1960s. And the publicity given Randolph's direct action tactics further educated the public, both black and white, to the merits of civil disobedience as a viable strategy for Afro-Americans to extract concessions from the dominant power structure.

81. Reynolds, "Triumph for Civil Disobedience," 229.

V / The Preliminary Civil Rights Marches

> *By what logic can it be argued that you can legislate for dis-*
> *crimination but cannot legislate against it?*
> —*A. Philip Randolph, 1952*

The military desegregation campaign was one of several attempts made by both Randolph and CORE to employ nonviolent civil disobedience. The March on Washington Movement of the early 1940s, CORE's Journey of Reconciliation in 1947, and the army integration struggles all worked to slowly gain wider acceptance for the direct action strategy. The victory of the NAACP in the school desegregation case *Brown* v. *Board of Education of Topeka, Kansas* in 1954 contributed to a climate of rising expectations in the black community. Although the atmosphere engendered by the cold war, the Korean War, and the McCarthy inquisition was not conducive to the spread of radical movements and methods, discontent with the restrictive status quo increased to the point that Afro-Americans became ready to embrace Randolph's method of nonviolent direct mass action.

These early demonstrations of noncooperation on behalf of equality combined with a variety of other circumstances to create the preconditions for the modern civil rights movement. Black Africans' fight against their colonial rulers made American blacks self-conscious that they were not doing more for their own liberation. The Southern Conference for Human Welfare disintegrated during the cold war because of charges of Communist infiltration, but the old Commission on Interracial Cooperation was transformed into the Southern Regional Council in 1944. Thus reinvigorated, the council provided a vehicle for cooperation with liberal white southerners. The demographic distribution of Afro-Americans changed, not only because of the movement of southern blacks to the North, which increased the number of blacks in the North from 2.4 to 6.4 million between 1940 and 1950, but also because of the movement of blacks out of the rural areas and into the cities of the South. Whereas they had been concentrated primarily in the rural Black Belt, by 1950 blacks constituted 39 percent of the population of Montgomery, Alabama, and 41 percent of Birmingham. Also, while they were still segregated and discriminated against, blacks in southern urban areas were forming social networks, the most important of which was the black church. In their houses of worship blacks could congregate without fear of retaliation from white employers. Even the NAACP allied with religious groups in the South because churches often provided the only available meeting places, and ministers often supplied local branch leadership.[1]

In the North, blacks continued to enjoy the widening economic opportunities resulting, in many cases, from the militant protest activities of the war years. Sensing the change in mood and determined to thwart white southern resistance to integration, Randolph mounted a series of marches in the nation's capital in the late 1950s in an effort to demonstrate the mass power of a united black race. Ironically, rather than impressing the dominant community with the force of a solid Afro-American front, Randolph's Prayer Pilgrimage and youth marches had the effect of redirecting his emphasis on blacks attaining their own liberation to a greater dependence on white support.

Randolph played a large role in stiffening the determination of Afro-Americans to fight for their civil rights. During the heyday of the MOWM, he had called for blacks in the South to "march in groups of a thousand or more at a time on the city halls," and for "all-out mass demonstrations" to wipe out the poll tax and white primary system. "Negroes must realize the necessity of winning the right to vote in the South," he insisted. Since the dominant power structure would not willingly reallocate resources, he argued, "Freedom must be won by Negroes. It will not be granted. Justice must be exacted; it will not be given." Above all, Randolph demanded new opportunities for blacks, not only as participants in the economic and political contest, but as "members of the policy making bodies that make the rules of the game."[2]

---

1. August Meier and Elliott Rudwick, *From Plantation to Ghetto* (3rd ed.; New York, 1976), 262; Marable, *Race, Reform and Rebellion*, 41; Aldon D. Morris, *The Origins of the Civil Rights Movement: Black Communities Organizing for Change* (New York, 1984), 41.
2. *Black Worker*, May , 1942, p. 1+.

During the declining period of the MOWM, his efforts to procure permanent FEPC legislation, and the campaign to desegregate the armed services, Randolph continued to educate the porters, through the *Black Worker*, to the importance of struggling to achieve greater equality. He discussed the "moral and political importance" of a strong, vigorous civil rights movement in the United States and pointed out the "paradox" of black troops fighting for democracy in Korea while denied it in Washington. Since segregation was enforced by law, "By what logic can it be argued that you can legislate for discrimination but cannot legislate against it?" In August, 1952, in anticipation of the forthcoming presidential election, the *Black Worker* featured a two-page supplement, "The Negro's Battle for Civil Rights," in which Randolph argued, "The battle for civil rights is the battle for the recognition of the dignity of the human personality of all men and women regardless of race, color, religion, national origin or ancestry." For blacks not to fight for civil rights was "tantamount to refusing to fight to be recognized as human beings." Furthermore, Randolph maintained, the country must grant full citizenship to blacks because unless it built "a moral and spiritual, as well as material arsenal of democracy" the United States would be limited in its role as a world leader.[3]

The *Black Worker* counseled its readers to make a candidate's civil rights stand the test for giving him their vote in the upcoming election. Randolph again recommended that rather than give allegiance to either party, blacks and other minorities should vote for the lesser of the two political evils, at least until labor built its own party. The 1948 election had shown that blacks in strategic states could play a decisive role in the election of a president; "thus, Negroes need to put down their begging policy tin cup, and present their demands for political concessions." Randolph stressed the methods of mass demonstrations and registering and voting in maximum numbers as being most effective in helping blacks obtain their desired equality measures.[4]

The Supreme Court's 1944 *Smith* v. *Allwright* decision had outlawed the white primary in Texas and, by implication, in the other southern states as well. As a result of this decision, Randolph's educational campaign, and voter-registration efforts by the NAACP and other groups,

3. *Ibid.*, July, 1952, p. 1, August, 1952, pp. 4–5.
4. *Ibid.*, August, 1952, p. 5.

southern blacks had begun making some inroads in obtaining the franchise, although the dominant community remained largely unaware of their efforts. In 1946, for the first time thousands of blacks in Mississippi and Georgia participated in Democratic primaries. Through Randolph's prodding, the People's Defense League, sponsored by many AFL and CIO unions, maintained "voter" schools to teach blacks to surmount voting obstacles, and launched a drive to register 50,000 New Orleans blacks to vote in the primary.[5]

Randolph continued to insist that the porters' union financially back movements to improve the condition of Afro-Americans. The BSCP donated $3,000 to the NAACP's Legal Defense and Educational Fund in December, 1953, to aid in bringing school desegregation cases before the Supreme Court. Elated at the favorable *Brown* decision in 1954, the BSCP sent another $1,000 to the fund in 1955. The May, 1956, edition of the *Black Worker* ran a full-page advertisement urging, "Don't Let Down Your Brothers and Sisters in Dixie!!" If each member of the BSCP would contribute an hour's wage, or $1.50, to fight segregation in the South, the journal's editor urged, $18,000 would be raised, and blacks would be helping to finance their own liberation movement.[6]

When Rosa Parks was arrested in December, 1955, in Montgomery, Alabama, for sitting in the white section of a bus, the first person she called for help was E. D. Nixon, head of the local chapter of the NAACP, of which Parks was a former secretary. An organizer of the Montgomery division of the BSCP and a disciple of Randolph's, Nixon had been leading the city's blacks in a struggle to gain greater equality from the time of the *Smith* decision. Having paid a $36 poll tax, Nixon tried to register for at least ten years before finally receiving a certificate—and that was only after he had filed one lawsuit and threatened to file another. Organizing the Montgomery Voters League, Nixon began a drive to get other blacks to register. He took a leave from his porter's job to pursue the drive, and proved so successful that 750 blacks appeared before the board of registrars in June, 1944. In 1948 he described himself as being "very busy in this fight for the right to vote for Negroes. . . . I wish that I

5. Press Release, April 9, 1944, in APR Files; Rayford W. Logan, *The Negro in the United States* (New York, 1970), I, 98, 154–57; *Black Worker*, July, 1946, p. 2.

6. *Black Worker*, November 15, 1953, May, 1954, p. 2; A. Philip Randolph, Address under the auspices of Kappa Alpha Psi fraternity, May 23, 1954, rpr. in *Black Worker*, June, 1954, p. 2; *Black Worker*, May, 1956, p. 4.

could sell the people on the one idea of full citizenship and that we could be free if we make up our own minds that we really wanted to be free, but," he lamented, "these crackers here have did a good job of keeping the Negro afred [*sic*] and also keeping him unlearned."[7]

Nixon continued to work closely with Randolph on strategies for obtaining equality, setting an example when he became the first black to file as a candidate in the Democratic primary in Montgomery in May, 1954. With much of his vote coming from the white community, Nixon lost by only a scant ninety-seven votes.[8]

Before Rosa Parks' arrest, Nixon had tried to desegregate Montgomery's buses, but had lacked the proper candidate to set the campaign in motion. Parks, however, had impeccable credentials, and when she was arrested, Nixon immediately began organizing people to stay off the buses. After the success of the boycott the first morning, December 5, Nixon and Ralph Abernathy, a Baptist preacher, decided on a permanent organization to carry on the fight; the Montgomery Improvement Association grew out of their discussion. Because he had to be out of town on Pullman runs, Nixon proposed Martin Luther King, Jr., a resident of Montgomery for only a year, to lead the boycott. When King agreed, the midcentury civil rights movement was born. He proved a most fortunate choice. A brilliant orator and a true believer, King supplied the religious quality lacking in Randolph's intellectualized adaptation of Gandhi's ideas. Thus Randolph's disciple Nixon supplied the spark that ignited the movement and implemented Randolph's strategies.[9]

Frustrated, white southerners retaliated against the boycott with terror tactics. They failed to break it, but succeeded in having King and almost one hundred other blacks indicted on the charge of conspiring to conduct an illegal boycott in February, 1956. At that point the NAACP began to actively support the boycotters and defended their case in the federal court. The conscience of the country was aroused, and help began to arrive from concerned people throughout the nation, black and white. The

7. *Black Worker*, June, 1959, p. 7, March 15, 1954, p. 2+; E. D. Nixon to Halena Wilson, February 10, 1948, in BSCP Papers, CD.

8. *Black Worker*, May, 1954, p. 1.

9. E. D. Nixon to author, December 1, 1972. For the importance of King's newcomer status, see Morris, *Origins of Civil Rights Movement*, 43–44. For Bayard Rustin's contention that the Montgomery episode forged a definite link between Randolph and the subsequent civil rights movement, see Garland, "A. Philip Randolph," 34. For Randolph's assertion that he influenced Nixon, see Randolph to author, July 13, 1973.

BSCP sent money, but sensing "the possibility of its developing into a nonviolent movement all over the country," Randolph, by now having made up his differences with Rustin, urged him to go south to help King organize the movement. It was Rustin who "developed the bag of tricks that sustained" the boycott. Although Nixon did not specifically "request the services" of Rustin, he did "ask for any help that we could get and, of course, when Mr. Rustin came, his services were most welcomed."[10] Thus, even if indirectly, Randolph's presence made itself felt from the beginning of the movement.

Randolph had always advocated closer cooperation between black leaders. Now that the South had finally erupted in civil rights ferment, he wanted to see coordination of goals and strategies extend from the top national personalities to "the grass roots representatives." To this end he arranged a closed conference of black helmsmen, sponsored by the BSCP, in Washington, April 24, 1956, on "The State of the Race." The conference was called in part to deal with problems resulting from a manifesto issued in March by more than one hundred anti-civil rights southern legislators, a so-called Declaration of Constitutional Principles asking their states to refuse to comply with the school desegregation order. The southern manifesto appalled Randolph: It aimed at nullification of the Supreme Court decision by breaking liberal forces away from involvement in the desegregation movement and mobilizing public opinion in favor of southern segregation. Not content with defying federal authority, the manifesto's supporters also wanted to annihilate the NAACP and create a cheap labor market to attract northern antiunion business interests.[11] That those who wanted to keep blacks in subjugation were most often the same persons who were against unionization would enable Randolph to forge the link between the civil rights struggle and organized labor.

At the State of the Race Conference, leaders of diverse black advancement organizations and church, fraternal, and business groups reached a

10. Randolph to Martin Luther King, August 7, 1956, in MLK Papers; Bayard Rustin, *Down the Line* (Chicago, 1971), 263; Coretta Scott King, *My Life with Martin Luther King, Jr.* (New York, 1969), 137–38; Martin Mayer, "The Lone Wolf of Civil Rights," *Saturday Evening Post*, July 11, 1964, p. 76; Thomas R. Brooks, "A Strategist Without a Movement," *New York Times Magazine*, February 16, 1969, p. 111; Randolph to author, July 13, 1973; Nixon to author, December 1, 1972.

11. Theodore E. Brown to Randolph, March 13, 1956, in BSCP Papers, LC; *Black Worker*, April, 1956, pp. 1–2; Telegram, Randolph to King, April 10, 1956, in MLK Papers. Theodore Brown had crystallized many of these ideas in a memorandum to Randolph. See Brown to Randolph, March 13, 1956, in BSCP Papers, LC.

"meeting of the minds" on the problems facing them. Representing some twelve million blacks, they declared the pace of desegregation "too slow" and civil rights progress "inadequate." Throwing their moral and financial weight behind the civil rights fight, they voted to seek an immediate meeting with President Eisenhower on the country's worsening race relations and to strengthen the NAACP by raising two million dollars for its legal and educational program. The black spokesmen agreed to try to increase the NAACP's membership to one million persons, to raise voter registration through voting drives while encouraging blacks to remain uncommitted politically, and to seek unity among Afro-Americans on civil rights by organizing a group of black leaders to meet with NAACP officials. The State of the Race Conference presented to the platform and resolutions committees of the national political conventions a statement on civil rights, which called for abolition of segregation and new civil rights legislation to protect the franchise, and urged passage of fair employment practices legislation.[12] Despite the promise it held for united action, the conference engaged in no further activity after issuing this statement.

Perhaps because of Randolph's advancing age, his personal ambitions had changed. No longer anticipating his own civil rights movement, Randolph was now actively working to increase black support of the NAACP to make it the primary black rights organization. In part his actions were a response to southern harassment, which, following the school integration decision, increased to a level that threatened the very survival of the NAACP. Yet it was still necessary for him to allay the other leaders' fears that he sought to displace them, and to this end Randolph emphasized that he did not intend the State of the Race Conference as a new or permanent organization.[13] This may have been a mistake on two counts. First, the NAACP still did not have an economic program. Second, the State of the Race Conference provided a vehicle to effect coordinated direction of the civil rights movement on a nationwide scale, and Randolph, who did not head a rival organization, was the only leader able to

---

12. "Map, 'State of Race' Confab for D.C.," *Jet*, April 19, 1956, p. 3; "73 Negro Leaders in D.C. Session Seek Immediate Meeting with Ike," *Jet*, May 10, 1956, pp. 4–5; Randolph to The President, May 8, 31, December 29, 1956, June 10, 1957, all in EFM Papers; Randolph to King, January 4, 1957, King to Randolph, January 7, 1957, both in MLK Papers; Statement on Civil Rights Plank for Platforms of the National Republican and Democratic Parties, in BSCP Papers, LC; *Black Worker*, September, 1956, p. 6.

13. *Black Worker*, April, 1956, pp. 1–2.

implement such unification. Once the opportunity presented by the conference slipped by, it would not come again; cooperation among civil rights groups would dissolve into competition for funds, membership, and publicity.

After the conference, Randolph was deeply discouraged by his inability to unite black leadership on a more permanent basis than merely for a one-day meeting. He also felt frustrated at the slow pace of integration in the South and at the lack of commitment to civil rights on the part of the Eisenhower administration. Rather than galvanize the president to action, southern resistance only reinforced Eisenhower's decision not to inflame the situation further. Randolph, who always retained the vision of a march on Washington, chose to mount a series of marches in the nation's capital in an effort to pressure the administration. He still believed the only way to sway public opinion was by dramatic pageantry: "No events in human history more deeply stir and capture the imagination of men and women than the marching of men. Abolish the tread of the soldier down the streets of a city or village and the romance in war will pass." Because of the multitude of issues competing for attention, great causes still had to "be given sharp picturization to secure attention" even from those who would benefit directly from them.[14] As marches fit this criterion, Randolph sponsored a Prayer Pilgrimage in 1957 and a pair of Youth Marches for Integrated Schools in 1958 and 1959. Although the three demonstrations had some limited success, all met with the problems of discord among the sponsoring organizations, concern about Communist subversion, and scarce financial resources.

Early in 1957, when Randolph and Martin Luther King returned from a trip to Africa, they conferred with Roy Wilkins, who had succeeded to secretaryship of the NAACP in March, 1955, after White's death. The trio decided to dramatize black demands through a mass pilgrimage to the nation's capital. Planned as a religious march, a spiritual protest against the white backlash movement in the South, the Prayer Pilgrimage was timed to coincide with the third anniversary of the *Brown* decision to highlight southern intransigence. The sponsors also wanted to demonstrate that blacks were united behind the civil rights bill pending in Congress. Randolph, Wilkins, and King hoped for participation from across the country to symbolize black protest against mounting injustices in the South. A Call for a Prayer Pilgrimage was issued by the cochairmen and

14. *Ibid.*, March 15, 1954, p. 2+.

approved by seventy-three national black leaders in an initial planning meeting in Washington on April 5. Donations of $5,000 were received, and additional pledges of $8,000 were made to back promotion of the march.[15]

The leaders believed that such a demonstration was the only means by which disfranchised southern blacks could exert their influence on a government that failed to guarantee their right to vote and their freedom of expression. The organizers also projected psychological aims for the Prayer Pilgrimage, arguing it would provide an outlet for the frustrations of southern blacks and thus minimize the possibility of violence. They feared that violence would dissipate the reservoir of goodwill "built by the nonviolent nature of the southern struggle." At the same time, they hoped the Pilgrimage would offer northern blacks a means of participation "other than by providing money," thereby reducing the resentment of southern blacks who saw themselves as "bearing the brunt of the struggle." The Pilgrimage would "demonstrate that the discipline and dignity in mass action" that characterized the struggle in the South were "properties of all Negro groups."[16]

The emphasis of the Prayer Pilgrimage underwent subtle change from chastising President Eisenhower for failing to go south to speak out on behalf of law and order to advocating passage of the civil rights bill pending before Congress. The leaders, who justified the change by stating that the "center of gravity" had shifted from violence in the South to Congress, wanted to avoid the appearance of harassing the popular president while Randolph was still trying to obtain an interview with him.[17]

The Prayer Pilgrimage for Freedom took place on May 17, 1957. Thousands of civil rights advocates met at the Lincoln Memorial in a three-hour demonstration to observe the third anniversary of the Supreme Court's desegregation decision, to prove they were united in demands for civil rights legislation, to protest terror and violence in the South, and to pay homage to the Great Emancipator, Abraham Lincoln. The program consisted of prayers, musical selections, and Scripture readings. The participants hoped that their presence would move the presi-

15. Form letter from Thomas Kilgore, Jr., April 17,1957, in NAACP Papers; "200,000 Plan May Religious 'March' on D.C.," *Jet*, April 11, 1957, pp. 3–4; *Black Worker*, May 15, 1957, p. 1, July 15, 1957, p. 1.

16. Form letter from Kilgore, April 17, 1967; "200,000 Plan May Religious 'March'"; *Black Worker*, May 15, 1957, p. 1, July 15, 1957, p. 1; Memo Regarding Prayer Pilgrimage, [before March 25, 1957], in NAACP Papers.

17. Memo Regarding Prayer Pilgrimage.

dent to condemn discrimination and "speak out more firmly" on civil rights, and also prompt Congress to call for support of the *Brown* decision. Eisenhower, however, had retired to his Gettysburg farm.[18]

The organizers had anticipated 50,000 people, but the police estimated the crowd at about 15,000, among whom were a few whites. The leaders placed the number closer to 27,000, with the largest group of approximately 10,000 coming from New York City. Randolph was personally responsible for bringing hundreds of trade union members to Washington. The BSCP closed its offices May 17 to enable its staff to attend, and Randolph planned a meeting of the Firemen's Provisional Committee in Washington on May 17 and 18 to bring still more persons to the Capital to swell the crowd.[19]

The Pilgrimage was a dignified affair. The printed program asked that applause be withheld because of the religious nature of the observance. Randolph relaxed the request when he spoke, saying that listeners might show their approval by waving handkerchiefs and saying amen, which they did. Participants received a "Freedom Certificate," proving they had attended to "arouse the conscience of the nation" and "in the spirit of nonviolence, to work for the elimination of racial discrimination and segregation." In Randolph's view, the Pilgrimage "highlighted the quest of human rights so that it became not only national, but world-wide, in interest, scope, and concern." Even W. E. B. Du Bois, who moved steadily toward the left after his return to the NAACP in 1944 and his second expulsion from the organization in 1948, was impressed with the Pilgrimage. Without mentioning Randolph or the other leaders, he admitted that it was not an easy task to bring 27,000 people to Washington, but advised that if the effort were to have lasting effects, blacks in the South must register and vote; only with black political power would the southern social structure change on the local level.[20] Although it is difficult to

18. See "Call to a Prayer Pilgrimage for Freedom," in NAACP Papers; "Leaders Spell Out Aims for Mass Pilgrimage in Washington," *Jet*, May 23, 1957, p. 8; New York *Times*, May 18, 1957.

19. "Prayer Pilgrimage to Washington," *Ebony* (August, 1957), 18–19; New York *Times*, May 18, 1957. The figures for attendance differ. See Coretta King, *My Life with Martin Luther King*, 159, and *Black Worker*, June 15, 1957, p. 1, May 15, 1957, p. 1.

20. Freedom Certificate, Program in NAACP Papers; New York *Times*, May 18, 1957; Julius Lester, *The Seventh Son: The Thought and Writings of W.E.B. DuBois* (New York, 1971), II, 652. Robert Burk suggests that Adam Clayton Powell acted as a White House mole in the planning sessions, keeping the administration informed and advocating re-

gauge the impact of the Pilgrimage on passage of the 1957 Civil Rights Act—the first civil rights act since Reconstruction—the gathering remains memorable because it marked the ascension of Martin Luther King, Jr., to national prominence.

The following September, the president was forced to send troops to Little Rock, Arkansas, to prevent mob violence against students trying to desegregate Central High School. A year after the Pilgrimage and after Eisenhower's unfortunate blunder of advising blacks to be "patient" in their quest for first-class citizenship, black leaders were finally granted a conference with the president on June 23, 1958. Despite the efforts of presidential assistant E. Frederic Morrow, the "token black" in the White House, the meeting took place only after three years of futile attempts. During this time black leaders became increasingly frustrated with the administration's deference to white southern governors.[21]

Although White House staffers fretted over which leaders to invite to the conference, all agreed on Randolph "because he is a respected citizen in whom most Americans have complete faith." Chosen to be the lead-off spokesman for the group by his colleagues, Wilkins, King, and Granger, Randolph "did a masterful job," according to Morrow. In Randolph's opinion, the meeting with the president gave "the Negro a deeper sense of belonging to and being an integral part of the great American family as equals."[22]

Opening the conference by reading the civil rights proposals on which the leaders had agreed, Randolph then presented a nine-point program for action. Its most important recommendations were to organize a White House conference on implementation of school integration and to restore the enforcement sections deleted from the 1957 Civil Rights Act to gain its passage. The compromises had emasculated the bill, and Eisenhower's ambivalence on school integration had fueled southern recalcitrance. Although schools were closed for the summer, the black spokesmen were worried that southern opposition to compliance with the Supreme Court

---

straint. Randolph's actions during the 1941 march, however, indicate that he needed no urging to keep the demonstration under control (Burk, *Eisenhower Administration and Black Civil Rights*, 220).

21. Morrow, Interview by Soapes, 12.

22. King to Randolph, July 18, 1958, MLK Papers; E. Frederic Morrow, *Black Man in the White House* (New York, 1963), 86, 159–60, 218, 233, 226–27; *Black Worker*, July 15, 1958, p. 3.

decision would lead to riots and bloodshed in the fall. The group made its recommendations in the belief that current tensions and anxieties would be eased "if a clear national policy and a program of implementation are established by the Chief Executive of the nation."[23] Claiming to have no quarrel with their objectives, Eisenhower commented largely on strategy and tactics.

Even after the conference, however, the president failed to take positive steps to avoid violence when school opened. Randolph consequently invited one hundred black and white leaders to a conference in New York in September, 1958, to develop strategies to cope with what he viewed as a "crisis" for civil rights, "to discuss concrete proposals" to prevent southern segregationists from taking the offensive, and to decide on ways to hold gains while advancing still further. The initial impetus for the conference came from King, "who appealed on behalf of the embattled leaders of the South," urging that both blacks and whites "organize an expression of support and solidarity" to counter violence against black youths attempting to integrate southern schools. With "unanimous support" the leaders scheduled a Youth March for Integrated Schools in Washington on October 11, 1958. The plan was to march one thousand black and white students down Pennsylvania Avenue, ask for an interview with Eisenhower, and present a petition to both houses of Congress. Before the event took place, Randolph requested that the president receive a few youths at the White House, explaining, "The children's march in Washington was conceived as a method of giving dramatization to the whole civil rights struggle."[24]

At an outdoor rally in Harlem on September 19, Randolph stated that the aim of the youth march was to arouse the conscience of America.

23. *Black Worker*, July 15, 1958, p. 3 (See p. 6 for the complete text of Randolph's statement to Eisenhower); Morrison, "Randolph: Dean of Negro Leaders," 103; Randolph to King, August 19, 1958, Randolph to The President, August 1, 1958, both in MLK Papers. Black leaders were particularly concerned that a federal district judge in Arkansas had granted the state a stay of two and a half years before beginning to integrate its school system (New York *Times*, June 24, 1958; "Negro Leaders Say President 'Lacks Grasp' of Race Problem," *Jet*, July 10, 1958, pp. 8–9; Morrow, *Black Man in White House*, 233).

24. Night Letter, Randolph to 100 Negro and White Leaders, New York City, September 3, 1958, Randolph to Dear Friend, September 11, 1958, both in APR Files; "Jackie Robinson to Head D.C. Youth March," *Jet*, September 25, 1958, p. 10; Randolph to The President, October 10, 1958 [released to Press, October 14, 1958], in APR Files; *Black Worker*, September 15, 1958, p. 1; Louis E. Burnham, "The Spectator: March on Washington," *National Guardian*, November 3, 1958.

Blacks were committed to preventing a revival of post-Civil War conditions, when they were driven from the ballot by terror and subterfuge. "At that time, Negroes were politically and legally defenseless," but today it was different, Randolph noted. Blacks could vote in the North, they had the NAACP to protect their rights, and they had allies in organized labor. "And, above all, the old plantation psychology of fear and submission and docility among Negroes has disappeared, even in the delta of Mississippi, and Negroes are determined to stand upon their feet and fight for first class citizenship, regardless of the fury and savagery of violence against them." But the day following the rally, Martin Luther King was injured by a knife-wielding, apparently deranged black woman as he was autographing copies of his book in Harlem. Although the attack appeared to be unrelated to his civil rights activity, Randolph postponed the youth march until October 25 to allow for enlarged group participation as a "constructive expression of sympathy" for King.[25]

The first Youth March for Integrated Schools, with students parading down Constitution Avenue to the Lincoln Memorial, took place as scheduled on October 25. Randolph, entertainer Harry Belafonte, baseball star and Eisenhower supporter Jackie Robinson, and Coretta King, substituting for her recuperating husband, led the march. The 9,500 black and white students, ranging from fourth grade through college level, came from southern and East Coast cities in chartered buses, private cars, and trains. All had signed a youth pledge composed by Randolph. Attracting more supporters than the sponsors expected, the march took about two hours.[26]

At the high point of the demonstration, Belafonte and a delegation of eleven black and white students were to drop out of the parade to deliver a statement to the president, urging him to announce that school integration "is morally right as well as legally required." But they had no appointment, were denied admission to the White House grounds, were not allowed to see the president's secretary or assistant, and, in Belafonte's words, were given "an undignified reception." Since they represented a

25. *Black Worker*, October 15, 1958, p. 2; Press Releases, September 19, 23, 1958, both in APR Files.
26. Press Release, "Youth March for Integrated Schools," October 25, 1958, in APR Files; "White House Gate Slammed on Youth Marchers," *Jet*, November 5, 1958, p. 4. See Morrow, *Black Man in White House*, 263–64, for his reservations about the march. Estimates of the number of participants vary.

large number of students, they felt entitled to some official form of recognition by the White House and had hoped to hear Eisenhower "express an attitude" on integration "on which he has been silent so long."[27] Belafonte predicted that the rebuff would arouse a "strong feeling of indignation" in both students and "people of the world."

The White House, however, justified its response by claiming that in many cities the march committees had been infiltrated by Communists planning to use the event to berate the president—a powerful argument during the height of the cold war. In answer to critics, Randolph maintained that the call on the White House, even though it took place shortly before the presidential election, was not designed as an embarrassment to Eisenhower or to his administration. Rather, it had been planned as an interracial, interfaith demonstration of student solidarity in support of integrated schools. In his speech at the Lincoln Memorial, Randolph said that the march was intended to dramatize the right of all youth, regardless of race, color, or religion, to receive an education in public schools. He expressed his hope that the march would encourage the public to support the *Brown* decision. Although the administration did not take cognizance of the demonstration, Randolph pronounced it a success because of the pageantry and drama it supplied.[28]

At the conclusion of ceremonies, the audience shouted unanimous approval of a resolution to reconvene in the spring to again push for civil rights laws and their implementation. On November 20, Randolph called a meeting of one hundred leaders at his office to plan a "continuing civil rights youth program." After formal dissolution of the *ad hoc* committee that sponsored the first youth march, a new committee was formed to conduct the Youth March and Petition Campaign in 1959 to achieve the unfulfilled objectives of eliminating violence and achieving the integration of the public schools. The new committee embraced the old and broadened its base of support. Rather than hold the second march on the May 17 anniversary of the *Brown* decision as originally planned, the committee decided to move the demonstration up to April 18 to avoid conflict with the examination schedules of the young participants. April also happened to be the time that Congress was scheduled to consider a

27. "White House Gate Slammed," 4; New York *Times*, October 26, 1958.

28. Morrow, *Black Man in White House*, 263; Washington *Post and Times Herald*, October 26, 1958; New York *Times*, October 26, 1958; A. Philip Randolph, "Why the Interracial Youth March for Integrated Schools?" *Black Worker*, November 15, 1958, pp. 4+, 3.

school aid bill. The change of date greatly pleased the NAACP, which considered May 17 "more or less an 'NAACP Day.'"[29]

Petitions urging the president and Congress to "put into effect an executive and legislative program which will insure the orderly and speedy integration of schools throughout the United States" were distributed by the thousands across the nation. Randolph called on black and white citizens of all faiths to circulate them "through the length and breadth of our land," and do their share "to crystallize and mold the opinions of countless Americans on the great moral issue of our age." In this way, "You will cause the voice of freedom to resound in the capital, and stir the conscience of our government and our legislators." The signed petitions were to be presented to Eisenhower and Congress during the march.[30]

Randolph explained that whereas the first youth march had been a strictly "*regional* demonstration" drawing the bulk of its support from New York, Boston, and Baltimore, the present campaign was designed to be national in scope. Thus he requested various colleagues throughout the country to hold gatherings to bring the youth march to the attention of dedicated young people. He maintained, "The number of marchers in Washington on April 18 will be translated into the number of votes" for the school aid bill on the floor of Congress, and "therefore, every person has a rare opportunity to cast a vote affecting the future of millions of Negro citizens."[31]

The call for the massive petition campaign and youth march was issued by prominent national black and white leaders. The organizers of the second march did not solicit children indiscriminately, nor did they offer to supply adult chaperones as they had in 1958. Rather, the march was restricted to high school and college youth, with exceptions made for children from fourth through eighth grade if accompanied by a parent or designated adult.[32]

The Second Youth March for Integrated Schools took place as scheduled on April 18. The 22,500 marchers chanted, sang, and waved gaily

29. Washington *Post and Times Herald*, October 26, 1958; Telegram, Randolph to T. E. Brown, Ethel Payne, n.d., Reverend Martin Luther King, Jr., Father John LaFarge, S.J., and Randolph to George Meany, January 12, 1959 [same letter to Walter Reuther and Eleanor Roosevelt], Wilkins to Randolph, November 20, 1958, all in APR Files.

30. See BSCP Papers, CD, for copy of petition. Chicago *Defender*, April 4, 11, 1959.

31. Randolph to Miles Horton, February 28, 1959, in APR Files; *Black Worker*, March, 1959, p. 1+.

32. *Black Worker*, March, 1959, p. 1+; Instruction Sheet No. 1, in APR Files.

184 A. Philip Randolph, Pioneer of the Civil Rights Movement

colored pennants and signs bearing slogans such as "Let Freedom Ring," "It's Time for Every State to Integrate," and "Equality Is the Thing That Makes Freedom Ring." They marched from the Mall to the Sylvan Theatre on the Washington Monument grounds, where they were addressed by Martin Luther King and Roy Wilkins. To make evident the link between American blacks struggling for their rights and African blacks fighting off their colonial oppressors, Tom Mboya, chairman of the All Africa Peoples Conference, also spoke.[33]

Once more the organizers endeavored to make arrangements in advance for a committee to be greeted at the White House. President Eisenhower was away on vacation, and Randolph's delegation was denied a meeting with Vice-President Nixon. The president's deputy assistant did meet with Randolph, accompanied by two white and two black youths. The assistant conveyed Eisenhower's best wishes, and the president's statement that he would not be satisfied until the last vestige of racial discrimination had disappeared in the United States. Randolph and the youths gave the deputy assistant their long petition seeking presidential and congressional action for orderly, speedy integration of the nation's public schools. A larger group delivered a similar petition at the Capitol.[34]

After the march, Eisenhower wrote to thank the youth delegation for the petition and promised that his Civil Rights Commission would weigh its recommendations. The president pledged to "take such action as in my best judgement will result in the most constructive progress towards equality of opportunity and the elimination of discrimination that it is possible to achieve"; nevertheless, little executive action was taken on the civil rights front during his administration. E. Frederic Morrow argued that the reason was, not that the president personally was anti-black, but that most of his close friends were from the Deep South. Morrow recalled arriving in Washington as an executive assistant to the Eisenhower administration when the city was still segregated. The president called in the merchants and hotel owners and "told them he wasn't going to have that

33. Randolph claimed that the police estimated the crowd at 26,000. He himself estimated that 35 percent of the marchers were white. In his advance bulletin, he had said he expected 50,000 children to participate (*Black Worker*, May, 1959, p. 3+; New York *Times*, April 19, 1959; Washington *Post and Times Herald*, April 19, 1959).
34. Randolph to Honorable Richard Nixon, March 23, 1959, in APR Files; "Ike Won't See Belafonte with Youth Leaders," *Jet*, April 23, 1959, p. 3; Dwight D. Eisenhower to Randolph, May 25, 1959, in APR Files. Signatures continued to be collected even after the presentation of the petitions.

foolishness." Eisenhower "hoped they would quietly open their places of business to blacks"; if they did not, he would have to take action. According to Morrow, the businesses unobtrusively opened their doors to an interracial clientele.[35]

Historian Robert Burk maintains that the administration's "racial symbolism" and caution on the segregation issue led to an emphasis on voting and other legal rights to the exclusion of the real impediment to black equality, economic problems.[36] The Eisenhower administration could hardly be blamed for its inattention to black economic problems, however, when the main civil rights organizations themselves gave primacy to legal over economic rights. The legal emphasis, in turn, encouraged the belief among white Americans that achievement of racial democracy would require on their part neither sacrifice nor redistribution of wealth, but merely the removal of officially sanctioned discrimination. This belief would have enormous consequences for the course of the civil rights movement in the 1960s.

The demonstrations in the late 1950s sprang from the renewed relationship between Randolph and Bayard Rustin, both of whom treated the misunderstandings that had arisen from the military desegregation effort as an embarrassing incident and never mentioned them again. A new, "symbiotic" partnership, characterized by mutual respect and affection, developed wherein Randolph devised the form of the demonstrations and attracted the followers while Rustin, with his organizational ability, coordinated them. Randolph, at sixty-eight when he proposed the Prayer Pilgrimage, was no longer capable of vigorous leadership on both the civil rights and the labor fronts simultaneously, and was less personally involved in the daily coordination of the youth marches than in his previous civil rights movements. By his own admission, he was less radical than in his youth: When it came down to the wire, he would compromise with the establishment.[37]

Although the marches were successful spectacles, Randolph and Rustin could not find a way to sustain the commitment of participants to work

35. Morrow, Interview by Soapes, 63.
36. Eisenhower to Randolph, May 25, 1959, in APR Files; Burk, *Eisenhower Administration and Black Civil Rights*, 261–64.
37. Interview with Leroy Shackelford, Jr., November 9, 1972; Morrison, "Randolph: Dean of Negro Leaders," III.

for civil rights legislation once the dramatic demonstration was over and they returned home. Randolph tried to implement the Prayer Pilgrimage program by forming the Crusade for Citizenship. Perhaps in response to Du Bois, he conceived the crusade as a nationwide campaign to get blacks to register and vote in every village, hamlet, and city, since sound civil rights legislation would never be won until blacks voted for congressmen who would support it. The effort of the crusade to register five million disfranchised southern blacks was not notable in 1957, however, and the problem of maintaining and utilizing the followers' commitment to the cause remained.[38]

But the Pilgrimage provided Rustin with invaluable experience in orchestrating and controlling a mass demonstration. A twenty-two-square-block area was reserved for parking buses and cars, and some Washington churches, as well as the Uline Arena, served as headquarters. Notices giving "Travel Suggestions for Reaching Washington, D.C." by car, chartered bus, and train were mailed out. The Los Angeles branch of the NAACP independently sent a chartered planeload of people. Rustin had not yet reached the level of sophistication in putting on mass demonstrations he would later achieve. He wisely proposed bringing in one thousand church ushers from Baltimore to maintain order and direct people, but was uncertain as to the need for furnishing ambulances and doctors, and as to the persons responsible for providing chairs or constructing the speakers' platform.[39] Experience with the Pilgrimage and two subsequent youth marches would make him the authority on such tactical problems.

Originally the organizers of the Prayer Pilgrimage wanted to make it clear that each person who went to Washington would be there for only part of one day and would be responsible for any lodging and meals required.[40] But since the planners desired to project an orderly image, they subsequently enlisted black churches in Washington to provide a free light breakfast the morning of May 17 and to serve as gathering places for state delegations. The strategy worked: White observers commented favorably on the "orderly" and "dignified" crowd.

Even more than the Prayer Pilgrimage, the first youth march was a

38. *Black Worker*, August 15, 1957; David L. Lewis, *King: A Critical Biography* (New York, 1970), 93.
39. "Leaders Spell Out Aims," 8–9; "Travel Suggestions for Reaching Washington, D.C.," and Memorandum, Reference to Program for May 17, from Bayard Rustin, April 23, 1957, both in NAACP Papers.
40. Memo Regarding Prayer Pilgrimage.

well-orchestrated demonstration and, considering the short period of time available for planning, represented an organizational feat. Rustin and Stanley D. Levison, a wealthy, left-leaning, white New York attorney, were the coordinators. Sixteen churches served as headquarters. Because of the fear of violence and "crackpot" action from residents of the segregated city against the racially mixed delegation, rigid security measures were taken by the Capital police to protect the children and guard the churches.[41]

All signs and slogans had to be approved by the organizing committee at the beginning of the line of march. The committee even gave examples of approved slogans, such as "2-4-6-8, America Must Integrate." Partisan political banners were prohibited. Since it would be impossible to feed one thousand people at rest stops, participants were advised to carry their own snacks for the trip. A hot lunch and a light supper would be served at churches and union halls for a minimum charge. Buses would depart the Lincoln Memorial at 4:30 P.M. for supper destinations and leave Washington at 6:30 P.M. Each bus was to have a captain and five adults, and all who rode them had to be registered. Five doctors and five nurses would be in the bus caravan. Songsheets with new civil rights lyrics set to familiar melodies and a cartoon book, "The Montgomery Story," were provided to entertain the children on the buses.[42] Again the planning paid off: There was no violence.

By the second youth march in 1959, the organizers were not as concerned that everyone leave Washington before dark, merely cautioning that "groups or individuals planning to stay in Washington over-night should make hotel reservations well in advance." In addition, participants "should provide for their own feed. Groups from the vicinity of Washington, who will be able to get home for a late supper should also not count on the Committee's feeding arrangements," since providing hot meals had turned out to be a prodigious task. The cost of the supper the organizing committee did provide was raised from fifty to seventy cents. The committee also arranged to hire buses, and bus captains from the New York-New Jersey area met the day before the march to coordinate plans.[43]

41. New York *Times*, October 26, 1958; "White House Gate Slammed," 4–5.

42. Youth March for Integrated Schools—Instruction of Signs and Slogans, and Instruction Sheets Nos. 1 and 4—Final Instructions, both in APR Files.

43. Memorandum on Youth March (1959), "Subject: Transportation, Reservations," Final Instructions, and Bayard Rustin to Dear Friend, March, 1959, all *ibid.*

The three demonstrations were thus tightly controlled events, giving the participants no opportunity to roam about the city. Marchers were brought in and taken out of the Capital in one day, and the messages they projected were monitored. The dominant community had nothing to fear from the gatherings.

These demonstrations shared four major concerns with Randolph's previous and subsequent movements: the quest for suitable allies, problems of financing, obsession with Communist subversion, and the anointment of secondary leaders. Perhaps the most provocative aspect of these marches was the coalition Randolph put together to sponsor them. Before the decade was over, he succeeded in forging an alliance between black rights organizations, the black church, white liberals, including religious groups, and organized labor. This coalition would play a major role in future civil rights activity, especially the 1963 march.

The Prayer Pilgrimage was based on an association between the NAACP, "the preeminent mass membership organization," represented by Wilkins; the labor movement, represented by Randolph; and the largely church-based southern civil rights movement, represented by Martin Luther King. When Randolph, Wilkins, and King met in New York on March 26, 1957, each presented a directive from his respective organization advocating some mass civil rights expression. King came as president of the newly inaugurated Southern Christian Leadership Conference (SCLC), which agreed to some type of national demonstration for freedom and civil rights as a protest to the bombings and violence in the South. Wilkins presented the 1956 mandate of the NAACP convention, which called for "some demonstrative action in Washington on the matter of civil rights" and appropriate observance of the third anniversary of the *Brown* decision. Randolph had planned some type of mass action on civil rights in Washington and had had detailed blueprints for such a demonstration for a year. Thus "the Pilgrimage was not the idea of any one of the leaders, but rather developed as a synthesis of the best of the ideas presented by the three." [44]

The alliance with King enabled Randolph to add a new element, the black church, to his old projected coalition of underdogs. Until the Mont-

44. Form letter from Kilgore, April 17, 1957, "200,000 Plan May Religious 'March'"; *Black Worker,* May 15, 1957, p. 1, July 15, 1957, p. 1; Memo Regarding Prayer Pilgrimage; Thomas Kilgore, Jr., Bayard Rustin, and Ella Baker to James Hicks, June 4, 1957, in APR Files. According to Aldon Morris, Randolph influenced the founding of the SCLC (*Origins of Civil Rights Movement,* 83).

gomery bus boycott brought King to prominence, because of his atheistic and anti-institutionalized-church leanings Randolph had never sought to involve the black church in his movements to reach the masses. Still bitter about early ministerial objection to the porters' union and viewing religion as merely a form of otherworldly escapism, Randolph failed to appreciate the church's historic role as a vehicle for black revolt. Still, he had not hesitated to utilize religion in organizing the porters. Whether the absence of churchmen in Randolph's civil rights efforts was his fault or instead stemmed from the fact that the radical economic thrust of his movements was uncongenial to the conservative preachers is unclear. Indeed, Harold Cruse claims that to this day the black church remains politically narrow-minded, intellectually and socially provincial, culturally one-dimensional, economically self-serving, and parochial despite King's rehabilitation of its social image by joining his moral imperative with the issue of equality. It is clear, however, that the affiliation with King brought Randolph access to an enormous new constituency, especially from the South. Their undertakings as partners became suffused with a spiritual quality that movements directed by Randolph alone had lacked. The new alliance did not go unremarked: *Ebony* magazine called it "unprecedented" and predicted that, if preserved, the unique coalition would have a profound influence on both integration and politics.[45]

After years of agitating for civil rights within the labor movement, Randolph also successfully tapped a good deal of organized labor support for the Pilgrimage. In addition to his own BSCP, the International Ladies Garment Workers Union, United Auto Workers, United Steel Workers, Cap and Millinery Workers, Retail Wholesale Workers, and United Transport Service Employees all promised aid. The New York local of the Retail Wholesale Workers alone promised one hundred carloads of participants.[46]

In an effort to avoid organizational jealousy, Randolph and his followers planned the formation of *ad hoc* local committees, whose limited duration would be clear. The sole purpose of the committees, they emphasized, was to send people to Washington and help raise funds for buses and special trains.

To cement the alliance with the NAACP, in his Pilgrimage speech Randolph pledged "uncompromising support" for the association, calling it

45. Cruse, *Plural but Equal*, 258; "Prayer Pilgrimage to Washington," *Ebony* (August, 1957), 17.
46. Press Release, May 9, 1957, in NAACP Papers.

the agency "chiefly responsible" for the Supreme Court's civil rights decisions and warning southern white supremacists "to keep their evil hands off" the organization. Randolph also affirmed unqualified cooperation with the southern struggle against bus segregation "under the inspired leadership of a great church leader and prophet of our times, the Reverend Mr. Martin Luther King." The Pilgrimage thus sought to demonstrate the unity of the black community and its allies—labor, liberals, and the church—behind the 1957 civil rights bill.[47]

Yet no sooner was the Prayer Pilgrimage concluded than stories of dissension circulated, fanned by an article in the Amsterdam *News* accusing Wilkins and the NAACP in particular, but also Randolph and the BSCP, of "dragging their feet" because the Pilgrimage was King's idea alone and his sudden rise to prominence had challenged "the so-called Negro leadership." The author, James Hicks, anticipated a situation that would eventually come to pass, but he did not accurately describe the current scene. Calling the article libelous and "a crude attempt to stir jealousy and rivalry," Wilkins was most concerned about the false picture it projected of the NAACP's role. Emphasizing he had "no wish to quarrel with anyone or any organization," Wilkins sent out a memorandum delineating the efforts of the NAACP in promotion of the Prayer Pilgrimage. Noting that the organization had financially backed the demonstration, he maintained, "No one sinks $9,000 in a project that he hopes will fail. No one spends $9,000 and then 'drags his feet.' No Association utilizes its top personnel from the very first organizational meeting until the final benediction at the Lincoln Memorial if it is 'dragging its feet.'"[48]

The NAACP did seem to be laying its prestige on the line by supporting the Pilgrimage, and Wilkins' cochairmanship gave him a stake in its successful outcome. The record indicates that he acted accordingly. In a special memorandum to nearby branches, Wilkins requested that they "POUR" people into Washington, saying "the good name and reputation of the NAACP" rested on them. Arguing that the Pilgrimage's objectives were identical with those of the NAACP, he emphasized that poor attendance would be regarded as a sign of weakness and would be used to

47. "Statement by A. Philip Randolph to the Prayer Pilgrimage for Freedom at the Lincoln Memorial," May 17, 1957, *ibid.; Black Worker*, June 15, 1957, pp. 1, 3.

48. James L. Hicks, "King Emerges as Top Negro Leader," Amsterdam *News*, June 1, 1957; Wilkins to King, June 4, 1957, Wilkins to Randolph, June 4, 1957, Memorandum, June 6, 1957, Wilkins to Dr. C. B. Powell, all in NAACP Papers.

thwart efforts for civil rights legislation. In another memorandum Wilkins argued that a "gigantic turn-out" would strengthen the fight for the civil rights bill, and outlined a specific program of action for each branch and youth council to follow.[49] Why Hicks made his accusations and where he obtained his information are unclear.

Organized labor, the black church, and the NAACP also worked together to sponsor the first youth march. This time the alliance with the NAACP was strained, perhaps because of financial difficulties originating with the Prayer Pilgrimage or the bad feelings engendered by Hicks. Randolph tried to promote the association by asking the gathering at the Lincoln Memorial to pass a "Resolution on Building the [NAACP's] Youth Membership." For their part, the youth councils and college chapters of the association supported the march with the largest contingency of participants, sending 1,600 marchers from the Eastern Seaboard states. The NAACP also secured bands for entertainment. Gloster Current, director of branches, spoke, and Clarence Mitchell, director of the Washington bureau, aided the BSCP's Theodore Brown in coordinating activities. Still, the national office did not give wholehearted support, and "the report was spread that the NAACP was not cooperating in the Youth March"—a rumor vehemently objected to by Wilkins.[50]

Possibly because of trouble with the NAACP, Randolph made a conscious effort to enlarge and broaden the supporting coalition for the 1959 march and petition campaign. Among the sponsors were fifteen national black and white leaders, including Randolph, Wilkins, King, Harry Belafonte, Jackie Robinson, Reverend Edwin T. Dahlberg, president of the National Council of Churches of Christ in America, and Rabbi Joachim Prinz, president of the American Jewish Congress. Randolph also tried to gain official support from the AFL-CIO and the backing of parent groups and settlement houses. The National Student Association, representing the student governments of over 450 colleges, and the Christian Youth Movement pledged aid. Randolph invited George Meany, new head of

49. Special Memorandum to NAACP Officers, May 1, 1957, To: NAACP Branches, Youth Councils and College Chapters, May 1, 1957, both in NAACP Papers. See also Gloster B. Current to R. D. Robertson, April 17, 1957, Special Memorandum to Branches in: Virginia, Maryland, Delaware, Eastern Pennsylvania, New Jersey, New York, and New England, May 6, 1957, both in NAACP Papers.

50. Press Release, "Youth March for Integrated Schools"; Roy Wilkins to Randolph, November 20, 1958, in APR Files; Memorandum, Herbert L. Wright to Wilkins, October 15, 1958, in NAACP Papers.

the AFL-CIO, Walter Reuther of the United Auto Workers, and Eleanor Roosevelt to become sponsors of the petitions and cochairmen of the organizing committee.[51] Succeeding in appealing to the moral sensibilities of a wide cross section of white America, Randolph gained the backing of major white religious groups for the first time. Because of its interracial leadership, the second youth march reopened the issue of the place of whites in a black movement.

At the November meeting preceding the second march, Wilkins told Randolph that he wanted a clear statement of purpose before he would authorize the NAACP youth director and youth councils to participate, because he believed that several different statements had obscured the objective of the previous demonstration. Since mass lobbying was "looked upon with horror" by the association's legislative agents in Washington, Wilkins doubted the board would approve NAACP participation if the purpose was to pressure for the school aid bill. To help the civil rights campaign in the Eighty-sixth Congress, however, Wilkins promised to solicit the views of organizations participating in the Leadership Conference for Civil Rights for Randolph's "information and guidance." Wilkins also wanted an estimate of the cost of the march and petition campaign; as the NAACP was entering 1959 with a deficit of at least $85,000, finances were of crucial concern. Mindful of criticism that it did not fully cooperate in the 1958 demonstration, the NAACP pointed out that over 10,000 of its youth and student members had attended the march.[52]

Always concerned about rival groups, Wilkins became disturbed at a business meeting following the second march when he detected an "unmistakable sentiment . . . for some kind of continuing body, not only until the collection of signatures [for the petitions] could be finished, but until 'next year.'" He wrote Randolph, "The NAACP assisted in the financing of the Youth March with the understanding that it was a loose coalition of groups interested in providing an opportunity for young people of both races to express themselves on school integration." Wilkins emphasized, "We did not intend either last year or this year to finance the setting up of a continuing permanent organization or semi-permanent organization. We have our own permanent and continuing NAACP youth

51. *Black Worker*, March, 1959, p. 1+; Reverend Martin Luther King, Jr., Father John LaFarge, S.J., and Randolph to George Meany, January 12, 1959 [Same letter to Walter Reuther and Eleanor Roosevelt], in APR Files.

52. Wilkins to Randolph, November 20, 1958, Herbert L. Wright to Bayard Rustin, May 5, 1959, both in APR Files.

group." Sensing interest in a Washington youth lobby, Wilkins added that the NAACP would not finance it "or any other lobby in Washington" because the association had its own Washington bureau, which had functioned since 1941.[53]

Randolph tried to assure Wilkins that the 1959 march was "an ad hoc project" that would terminate upon the completion of the petitions. With his eye on long-term goals requiring the NAACP's cooperation, Randolph defended the youth march, noting it "exceeded the expectations of all of us, from the point of view of its dimensions and significance." Randolph was anxious to maintain the *ad hoc* principle in developing future demonstrations for civil rights and wanted to retain the cooperation of the participating organizations.[54] This was not an easy task. He obtained the NAACP's cooperation in the marches, not because he enjoyed the same warm personal relationship with Wilkins that he had had with Walter White, but rather because he went out of his way to praise the association's achievements publicly and to encourage young people to enroll in and support its program. The board, through Wilkins, expressed its appreciation to Randolph, who continued as a vice-president of the association. Still, the NAACP never entirely rid itself of the fear that Randolph intended to set up a rival group.

Financial arrangements were a continuing source of discord between Randolph and the NAACP. The cost of the Prayer Pilgrimage was projected at $24,000, which included salaries for the national director, Harlem minister Thomas Kilgore, Jr., and the clerical staff, telephone, telegraph, office supplies and postage, and $5,500 for promotion. In the winter of 1957, coorganizers Ella Baker and Bayard Rustin, with the assistance of Stanley Levison, laid out detailed plans for the Pilgrimage. They anticipated that the planning session to be held in April would raise a sufficient sum of money not only to set up headquarters but also to provide for literature, stenographers, and administrative personnel, as well as funds for travel use. Hoping to stimulate contributions by asking for them in the form of loans, they decided to provide a few thousand dollars "to start the pledges rolling" and planned a collection at the Pilgrimage to recover the expenditures.[55]

A collection was not taken up at the Lincoln Memorial, however, and

53. Wilkins to Randolph, May 26, 1959, *ibid.*
54. Randolph to Wilkins, June 5, 1959, *ibid.*
55. Budget, n.d., NAACP Papers; Memo Regarding Prayer Pilgrimage.

expenses ran higher than expected—the cost of advertisements in the black press alone amounting to $3,204. In addition to providing a secretary, the NAACP spent $7,000 on advertisements and general promotion, while the BSCP provided free office space and staff services for eight weeks. Through his personal efforts, Randolph obtained the endorsement and financial contributions of the largest trade unions, including $250 from the Fair Practices and Anti-Discrimination Department of the United Auto Workers. The BSCP and King's Montgomery Improvement Association each contributed $1,000 to the demonstration. Despite these efforts the Pilgrimage ran into debt, leaving Randolph and Wilkins to struggle with unpaid bills. A bus transit bill for over $1,000 was still outstanding a year later.[56] The NAACP was displeased with this drain on its resources.

The first youth march was on a more sound basis financially. Instead of making contributions to overhead, churches were urged to invest their money and energy in sending busloads of young people to Washington. Maida Springer raised several thousand dollars from labor unions. The Meat Cutters Union collected 1,000 pounds of meat, which made it possible to serve almost 6,000 people at 50¢ a meal. With aid from the churches in Washington, the organizers limited the debt on food to $300. As of October 31, there was a $1,300 balance in the march account, with only a few small bills outstanding. Thus the organizers were not left with a crushing debt as they had been after the Prayer Pilgrimage, making a second youth march seem like a feasible undertaking.[57]

To the dismay of the organizers, however, the actual cost of the 1959 demonstration far exceeded the projected budget of $16,000. To help defray expenses, organizers sold space in the souvenir program book to be presented to President Eisenhower along with the petition.[58] Signs for the buses and for marchers to carry were sold for 25¢ each.

After the march, Randolph complained to Wilkins of the "troublesome paradox" that "the great dimensions of support and activity have

56. Memo to Mr. Moon from M. Ward, May 31, 1957, in NAACP Papers; *Black Worker,* May 15, 1957, p. 1, July 15, 1957, p. 1; "D.C. Pilgrimage Prods Solons on Civil Rights, Snubs Reds," *Jet,* May 30, 1957, pp. 4–7; Randolph to Wilkins, August 22, 1957, Wilkins to Randolph, September 3, 1957, both in NAACP Papers.

57. Financial Report for Youth March 1958, n.d., "Proposed Budget for Petition Campaign and Washington Demonstration," n.d., both in APR Files. Maida Springer later worked in the Chicago branch of the A. Philip Randolph Institute.

58. "Proposed Budget for Petition Campaign"; Gerald D. Bullock, General Chairman, Youth March for Integrated Schools, n.d., in BSCP Papers, CD.

not produced corresponding volumes of cash." Since they had asked the churches only to supply buses and had not appealed to NAACP branches for contributions, Randolph proposed that the association share the debt by providing another $2,000; this would make a total of $4,000, "and there would be no further call on you." Randolph claimed that the additional outlay was necessary if the NAACP was not to be left with a pressure situation "such as followed the Pilgrimage." Wilkins complied with an additional $1,500, which raised the total national NAACP contribution to twice the amount originally set aside by the board, and he absolved the local branches of any further levy.[59]

For his part, Randolph congratulated the staff for its "extraordinary achievement in consummating a project of such unprecedented historic dimensions on so small a budget." The feat was accomplished by the "dedicated labors" of volunteers who had gathered 400,000 petition signatures and helped to "overcome the problem of limited finances." Boasting that the combined efforts of the campaign workers had brought 26,000 young people to Washington on a budget of only about $28,000, Randolph urged participating groups to turn over any funds remaining in their treasuries and to solicit contributions so that the project could be terminated on a financially sound basis.[60]

Randolph's incessant demands on the NAACP for money to finance his schemes, as well as the ever-present fear among the association's officials that his popularity would overshadow the credit given to the NAACP, caused constant tension between the staid Wilkins and the charismatic Randolph. In the long run, therefore, Randolph remained dependent on the BSCP's financial support for his civil rights activities. He endeavored to educate the porters to the necessity of backing the youth marches, explaining that despite the NAACP's notable victories in the courts on behalf of public school integration, "The civil rights revolution is heading for a grave crisis of roadblocks." Federal power was needed to enforce the laws, and Randolph designed the youth marches to pressure the administration into using its power to uphold the rights of the black minority.[61] But Eisenhower, convinced of black inferiority, was less amenable to such

59. Randolph to Wilkins, April 8, 1959, Wilkins to Randolph, April 14, 1959, both in APR Files.
60. Randolph to Dear Friend, April 23, 1959, Press Release, September 8, 1959, both in APR Files.
61. Randolph, "Why the Interracial Youth March?"

pressure than either Roosevelt or Truman, and the marches were notably unsuccessful in this aim.

Although they differed on other issues, Randolph and the NAACP displayed a similar paranoia about Communist subversion. They thus took steps to try to keep the "Reds" out, with the dual aim of preventing their movements from being smeared as Communist fronts and of maintaining internal control. They issued a warning that Communists would try to infiltrate the Prayer Pilgrimage, but the New York newspapers failed to carry it. Because of the perceived threat, all activities were scheduled to take place at the Lincoln Memorial, and no picketing, walking with posters, or lobbying was authorized. Should such demonstrations occur, they were not under the auspices or with the approval of the Pilgrimage committee, the organizers warned. Notwithstanding the precautions, individuals not connected with the Pilgrimage sold pennants, and Communist party leaders were present in the crowd. In his speech, Randolph warned his audience about the dangers of communism, saying, "We know that Communists have no genuine interest in the solution of problems of racial discrimination but seek only to use this issue to strengthen the foreign policy of the Soviet Union." Despite expectations that they would try to capitalize on the event, the Communists remained quiet and, with the exception of Randolph's speech, were ignored.[62]

The organizers also worried about Communist infiltration of the youth marches. According to E. Frederic Morrow, a 1958 government report indicated that the march committees in many cities had been infiltrated by Communists, who planned to use the event to denounce the president. This report provided the basis for Eisenhower's refusal to become associated with the 1958 march in any way. Because of reports that Communists would attempt to subvert the 1959 demonstration, the organizing committee issued a policy statement declaring that the march was nonpartisan in character and would neither solicit nor accept financial support or participation from any political group. The organizers urged all partisan political groups to refrain from distributing material along the line of march. Since "certain groups have not complied with our request" in the past, it was necessary to dissociate the march from all such "partisan political activity and literature." Ignoring the disclaimers of the or-

62. Kivie [Kaplan] to Roy Wilkins, May 13, 1957, Wilkins to Kaplan, May 16, 1957, Statement by Roy Wilkins, May 10, 1957, Statement by Randolph, all in NAACP Papers; "D.C. Pilgrimage Prods Solons," 6.

ganizers, Communists ranged through the crowd at the Washington Monument distributing copies of their paper, *Workers World*.[63]

After the march Wilkins was angered by the remarks of a Hunter College representative who sharply criticized Randolph's anti-Communist sentiments. In a letter to Randolph, Wilkins stated adamantly, "We will have nothing further to do with any movement that is not clearly and unequivocally anti-communist."[64] Maintaining a coalition with the NAACP thus had the effect of reinforcing Randolph's own anti-Communist stance and creating undue fear of infiltration and inordinate concern with image in the cold war era. But the overzealous anticommunism of the march leaders makes the administration's explanation of its nonparticipation, fear of Communist influences, appear specious.

Because so many of the directors of the youth marches came from the BSCP, they reflected the continuity of intermediary leadership that characterized all Randolph's undertakings. Lieutenants would follow their captain from one campaign to another, as is illustrated by the Prayer Pilgrimage. Among those on the national organizing committee, E. Pauline Meyers was an old associate from the MOWM.[65] Charles Wesley Burton had cooperated with Randolph even earlier, on the NNC, before coming to the MOWM. Theodore Brown first became acquainted with Randolph in the March on Washington Movement. After working as a porter while putting himself through college, Brown began to help Randolph with editorial duties on the *Black Worker* in the 1940s. Although Randolph was suspicious of Adam Clayton Powell's Communist following, he and Powell had worked together on projects in Harlem since the 1930s. Cleveland Robinson would soon help Randolph organize the Negro American Labor Council and later succeed Randolph as head of that organization. Other secondary leadership was supplied by Martin Luther King, who brought his loyal lieutenants Ralph Abernathy and Fred Shuttlesworth with him, and the NAACP branches.

Continuity was also displayed in the 1958 youth march leadership. Honorary chairmen for the march, in addition to Randolph, King, and Wilkins, were Jackie Robinson, Daisy Bates, and Mrs. Ralph J. Bunche,

---

63. Morrow, *Black Man in White House*, 263; Walter L. Kirschenbaum to Bayard Rustin, March 26, 1959, "Policy Statement," both in APR Files; Washington *Post and Times Herald*, April 19, 1959.

64. Wilkins to Randolph, May 26, 1959, May 23, 1957, April 14, 1959, all in APR Files.

65. Apparently she did not blame Randolph for her forced resignation from the MOWM.

making the first youth march one of the few occasions Randolph gave recognition to women. B. F. McLaurin was coordinator; assistant coordinators were Bayard Rustin, Stanley D. Levison, Reverend Callendar, and Maida Springer. Among those responsible for publicity were James Peck and James Hicks—the bad feelings aroused by the latter's article in the Amsterdam *News* apparently overcome. Frank Crosswaith and Charles Zimmerman were among the chairmen; Ella Baker, James Farmer of CORE, Reverend Thomas Kilgore, Jr., from the Prayer Pilgrimage, Pauli Murray from the MOWM, and Ashley Totten of the BSCP were on the organizing committee. The children's committee was headed by Anna Hedgeman, formerly of the National Council for a Permanent FEPC, who also had made up her differences with Randolph. Socialist Michael Harrington and Richard Parrish of the Harlem Labor Committee were student advisers.

Many of the officials from the first youth march held similar positions in the second. Among the secondary leaders were Father LaFarge, Harry Emerson Fosdick, and Charles Zimmerman as cochairmen, Anna Hedgeman on the finance committee, Ethel Payne and James Hicks on the publicity committee, Maida Springer, B. F. McLaurin, and Cleveland Robinson on the labor committee, and Richard Parrish on the youth committee, the same position he had held in the 1941 march. McLaurin was one of three treasurers, and Rustin and Herbert L. Wright, youth secretary of the NAACP, were the coordinators. It is a tribute to Randolph's integrity that once people enlisted in one of his causes, they usually remained as associates in subsequent undertakings.

The marches of the late 1950s, however, suffered from lack of focus and diversity of goals, as well as dissension among the sponsors. It is debatable whether their achievements justified the efforts. Certainly integration of public schools in the South did not proceed any faster because of them. Yet six days after the Prayer Pilgrimage, Randolph and King were granted a conference with Vice-President Nixon as a substitute for their long-sought meeting with Eisenhower.[66]

The Prayer Pilgrimage had been timed to coincide with legislative consideration of the civil rights bill, and though it may be impossible to establish a definite causal relationship between the demonstration and passage of the bill, undoubtedly the presence of so many Afro-Americans

66. Rustin prepared a six-point memorandum to assist the two leaders in formulating their requests (Lewis, *King*, 93–94).

demanding action could not be completely ignored. As already noted, during the congressional debate the portion of the bill giving the attorney general clear statutory authority to enforce constitutional as well as voting rights was deleted to obtain passage of the measure. When it was finally passed in September, 1957, black leadership divided over whether to accept the weakened bill, with Randolph among those urging rejection. Eisenhower, however, signed the act, which, though generally regarded as insufficient, set precedent for the stronger civil rights measures of the 1960s as it acknowledged the federal government's responsibility to uphold minority rights. While Republicans and Democrats argued over which party should get credit for passage of the bill, Randolph maintained that the growing political power of Afro-Americans was responsible.[67]

A less concrete effect of the Pilgrimage was the favorable reaction it produced in the dominant community. One white newscaster stated that racial bigots would have difficulty denigrating "the power of a respectable and respectful gathering of American citizens in clean shirts and chic dresses whose chief, if not only, weapon is the law and the undownable dignity of the human individual it is supposed to protect." To this observer the Pilgrimage represented "a force of faith which refuses to be stopped by violence or even subtle sabotage."[68]

Certainly the demonstrations had a profound emotional impact on the participants, many of whom asked Randolph to plan still another march. A typical reaction came from a woman quoting Rustin: "On October 25 we came here 10,000 strong and didn't see anybody. . . . We doubled the number and gained admittance. Come with 50,000 and Eisenhower will be in Washington. When we come with 100,000 Congress will sit in special session. With 200,000 the Congress, the President and the Supreme Court will all be in Washington." Most participants were inspired to look forward to another event. Others were disappointed by the scarcity of onlookers and wondered about the lack of media coverage and the fact that Congress was so poorly represented among the spectators.[69]

A group of students from Brooklyn College, participants in the youth march during what has been characterized as the decade of student apathy, wrote Randolph, "This is the first time in over a decade that college

67. "Rights Bill Splits Negro Leaders: Given Slight Chance for Passage," *Jet*, September 5, 1957, pp. 4–5; *Black Worker*, February, 1957, p. 1.
68. "Edward P. Morgan and the News," May 17, 1957, in NAACP Papers.
69. Rubye H. Gill to Randolph, July 11, 1959, Ellen Lurie and Preston Wilcox to Randolph, May 18, 1959, both in APR Files.

students have been able to raise themselves above the stifling atmosphere of conformity and the tragic indifference to vital issues so prevalent in the academic world and to demonstrate for so great a moral cause." They paid tribute to his leadership as "a source of real inspiration to us and to millions of our fellow students. . . . Our energy has been too excited, our conviction too strong, our cause too great for us to tolerate repeated injury to our dignity, to yours, to that of the Negro people and of the fight for equality in America."[70] Randolph thus succeeded in reaching the younger generation through the drama of his mass demonstrations.

As the country geared up for the 1960 presidential campaign, Randolph charged both major political parties with being "evasive and devoid of sincerity on civil rights issues." At a Carnegie Hall salute in his honor in January, 1960, Randolph called for a march on the national political conventions to present the "concrete demands and just grievances of the Negro people" and to demand positive action on civil rights issues. He thought that such a project would mobilize race power and demonstrate the awareness of Afro-Americans that they held "the balance of power in many key states." Rustin, still the tactician behind Martin Luther King, directed King to write to the Republican and Democratic parties, requesting a hearing on the proposals the civil rights leaders wanted included in the 1960 party platforms.[71]

Combining Rustin's suggestion with Randolph's scheme, Randolph and King read a call to "March on the Conventions Movement for Freedom Now" at the BSCP headquarters in June, 1960. They suggested that 10,000 pickets attend the national political conventions to voice the frustration of southern students, whose demands were thwarted "by inert government, by an ingrained indifference to the democratic ideals of equal-

70. Ruth Stack, *et al.* to Randolph, October 31, 1958, *ibid.* Rachelle Horowitz, one of these students, later became Rustin's executive secretary, after the founding of the A. Philip Randolph Institute.

71. *Black Worker,* January, 1960; New York State Department of Labor, "Memo: A. Philip Randolph," *Industrial Bulletin,* XXXIX (January–February, 1960), p. 2+; Lewis, *King,* 123–24. For problems between Congressman Powell and Rustin that forced the latter to sever ties with the SCLC, see Brooks, "Strategist Without a Movement," 111, and Lewis, *King,* 131. Rustin then went to Ghana, but returned to organize the 1960 election project (Rustin to Randolph, November 5, 1959, in BSCP Papers, LC).

ity and freedom." The pair concluded, "Government, far from meeting the needs of the times, has retreated." They noted that school integration had virtually ground to a halt; six years after the Supreme Court decision, only 6 percent of southern black students attended integrated classes. Furthermore, they argued, congressmen of both parties conspired to deprive blacks of their right to vote. Although the 1960 civil rights bill extended the 1957 act by providing for the appointment of federal referees to safeguard voting rights, it had passed only after a lengthy filibuster and placed the overwhelming burdens of prosecution for voting violations on blacks rather than on those who oppressed them. "Both parties must be held responsible for this sellout, not only of the Negro people, but of American democracy as a whole," the two leaders maintained.[72]

Randolph and King wired prominent community leaders of both races in Los Angeles and Chicago that they intended to represent, at the party conventions, the millions of blacks denied the right to vote in the South and to request a forthright declaration from the candidates and parties that "racial segregation and discrimination in any form is unconstitutional, un-American, and immoral." Without such a declaration Afro-Americans would remain doubly disfranchised—first, because they were barred from the polls and, second, because they were denied political representation through the existing parties. The pair threatened a mass march on the conventions to serve notice that blacks would no longer endure such double disfranchisement and that "no party which ignores the just demands of over 18 million people can look to a long future." They planned to present a list of questions to the candidates and to demand specific answers and a program of implementation. To show solidarity with the newly emerged student sit-in movement, Randolph and King said, "The heroic students of the South have shown the way and the least we can do is to carry their demands, and those of all Negroes who are denied the right to vote, directly to the political conventions."[73]

In July, acting on behalf of Randolph and King, Rustin organized a 24-hour vigil outside the Democratic and Republican convention halls "as a living symbol and constant reminder of the student sit-in movement" and the determination of blacks to win their civil rights in the near future. The

72. Statement by Philip Randolph and Dr. Martin Luther King, Jr., Regarding "March on the Conventions Movement for Freedom Now!," June 9, 1960, in BSCP Papers, LC.
73. *Black Worker*, June, 1960, p. 2; New York *Times*, June 10, 1960.

Democratic convention attracted 18,000 pickets and the Republican 10,000.[74]

The March on the Conventions Movement represented another attempt of Randolph's to bring the civil rights issue to the attention of the dominant community. Its effect can be gauged by the actions of John Kennedy after his nomination. Clearly concerned about the black vote, Kennedy decided to bid for it by calling Martin Luther King's wife when King was put in solitary confinement in a Georgia jail for participating in an "illegal" sit-in. Spurning E. Frederic Morrow's advice, Republican candidate Richard Nixon did not react to King's imprisonment, undoubtedly to his later regret, because the black vote proved instrumental in Kennedy's victory.[75]

The March on the Conventions Movement, however, again occasioned discord between Randolph and the NAACP. The association was miffed because it had planned pre-convention demonstrations of its own prior to the press conference at which Randolph and King announced their plans, and resented being assigned a role without having been consulted. Wilkins did not approve of the direct action tactic of a mass picket line both because he thought it unlikely to advance the cause and because he feared it would provide an opportunity for "politically undesirable persons with ulterior motives" to enlist under the pretext of helping the cause. Although the NAACP was interested and willing to cooperate "in any reasonably effective endeavor in behalf of civil rights," it had "the right not to be committed, without consultation, to a specific tactic or course of action," Wilkins emphasized.[76]

By September, Randolph and the NAACP had patched up their differences sufficiently for Randolph, Wilkins, and King to announce the launching of a national nonpartisan crusade to enlist one million new black voters. Randolph was chairman of the crusade committee. His statement, which Wilkins read, pointed out: "In parts of our country, force and violence are our paths to the polls. Elsewhere, nothing but apathy prevents us from voting." Calling on other Afro-Americans to join

74. Press Release, "March on the Conventions Movement for Freedom Now," July 28, 1960, in BSCP Papers, LC; Brooks, "Strategist Without a Movement," 111.
75. Thomas R. Brooks, *Walls Come Tumbling Down: A History of the Civil Rights Movement, 1940–1970* (Englewood Cliffs, N.J., 1974), 155–56; Morrow, *Black Man in White House*, 296–97; Morrow, Interview by Soapes, 18–19, 7–8.
76. Wilkins to Randolph, June 14, 1960, in NAACP Papers.

their crusade, the two noted that although there were more than ten million blacks of voting age, only about five million were registered—and even fewer were likely to vote unless the "crusade for freedom" roused them to their responsibility. But voter-registration drives were expensive, and the new movement was hampered by the leaders' failure to obtain a contribution from the AFL-CIO.[77]

The coalition forged by Randolph and his allies in the late 1950s consisted of black rights groups, white liberals, black and white church groups, and trade unions. It was essentially the same coalition that would back the civil rights movement in the early 1960s. Yet Randolph continued to talk about blacks financing their own movement. As late as 1960 he said, "Negroes must bear the cost of the civil rights revolution. . . . Negroes have no moral right to delegate this responsibility to any other organization in America. . . . They must themselves carry out this mandate of history."[78] Clearly he was still torn between a pragmatic need for dominant group support and the desire to emphasize black pride. Pragmatism won out, and Randolph actively sought greater white involvement in civil rights causes. With the admission of so many whites, Randolph would again be faced with the problem that "where you get your money, you also get your direction and control," which perhaps accounts for his continued vacillation on the issue. In the year that he solidified the new coalition, 1959, Randolph alienated many white liberals in the labor movement by initiating a new, all-black labor group.

Nevertheless, despite Randolph's problems and limitations, when blacks in Montgomery, Alabama, banded together to boycott the city buses in December, 1955, it was his legacy of civil disobedience they implemented. The local leaders did not have to devise new strategies or ideologies. From the threat to march on Washington in 1941 to the philosophical justification for nonviolent direct action worked out in the subsequent MOWM to the attempt to implement civil disobedience to desegregate the military in 1948, Randolph's efforts provided a blueprint.

77. Non-Partisan Crusade to Register One Million New Negro Voters, September 4, 1960, in BSCP Papers, LC; *Black Worker*, September–October, 1960, p. 1; Franklin Williams to Randolph, September 26, 1960, Randolph to Williams, September 27, 1960, both in BSCP Papers, LC.

78. *Black Worker*, June, 1960, p. 1 +.

Young blacks who participated in Randolph's various movements imbibed his race consciousness and became convinced of the efficacy of his tactics; they merely awaited the opportunity to put them into action.

Occurring during a period of unprecedented prosperity for the white community, the midcentury civil rights movement fed on rising expectations that made second-class citizenship more than ever intolerable to Afro-Americans. Although the movement itself presented a challenge to traditional middle-class leadership techniques by utilizing direct action tactics, it was oriented toward such middle-class goals as desegregated housing and places of entertainment and other privileges that blacks believed could only be obtained within the existing economic framework. The civil rights movement demonstrated the power of the federal government, and that was where blacks seeking integration began to place their ultimate faith. They had no revolutionary desire to destroy the institution in which their hopes for salvation rested. Because of his Socialist leanings, Randolph, before any of the other black leaders, would try to reorient the movement toward economic concerns. He alone at this point realized the importance of economic uplift as a prerequisite for social equality.

The Prayer Pilgrimage and youth marches fell within the middle-class protest tradition. Certainly they were conservative in conception compared with the proposed March on Washington in 1941. The later marches were planned as integrated, carefully managed, one-day demonstrations; gone was the idea of a massive assault on the public accommodations of segregated Washington. Where whites were barred in 1941, they were solicited in 1957 and later. In 1941 Randolph and the black community owed little to the federal government, but the executive orders Randolph worked so hard to obtain had the effect of watering down black militancy. Now blacks were making definite gains through the intercession of the executive branch, and they could not afford to jeopardize the government on which they depended for further advances. Consequently, Randolph and other national black leaders realized that they had to set limits on their demonstrations against the federal government. The necessity of cooperating with white liberal groups for lobbying power had the effect of further muting black activism.

The 1950s nevertheless demonstrated the efficacy of nonviolent direct action tactics to gain greater rights for blacks. Once the South erupted in civil rights ferment, in part because of his longtime stress on voter registration in the region, the elder statesman Randolph tried to promote cooperation among black organization heads to decide on a coordinated program of goals and tactics. But the logical leader, Martin Luther King, did not have Randolph's nationwide vision. Restricting himself to isolated demonstrations in small southern cities, King failed to build a potentially far more powerful countrywide movement. Roy Wilkins, the new head of the NAACP, was an administrator; in addition, he did not possess the charisma of either Randolph or King and remained committed to the association's traditional emphasis on legal rights: Under his direction, the NAACP would resist direct action and would not develop an economic program.[79] Thus neither King nor Wilkins had the foresight or creativity to organize a nonviolent civil disobedience movement of national scope. Because he represented organized labor and not a rival rights organization, Randolph was in the best position to promote organizational unity on a nationwide scale. But he was past his prime and becoming increasingly involved in the civil rights fight within the labor movement. Jealousy over organizational prerogatives remained too entrenched to breach, particularly without full-time effort, and the civil rights movement never achieved the unification Randolph envisioned.

79. Vincent Harding argues that King had a vision of a national movement but was prevented by circumstances from implementing it. See Vincent Harding, "So Much History, So Much Future: Martin Luther King, Jr., and the Second Coming of America," in Michael V. Namorato (ed.), *Have We Overcome? Race Relations Since Brown* (Jackson, 1979), 60–73. Aldon Morris, in contrast, maintains that King's SCLC did not even succeed in building a coordinated mass movement in the South during the late 1950s (Morris, *Origins of Civil Rights Movement*, 119). See Wilkins, *Standing Fast*, 237–38, on the NAACP's resistance to change.

VI / The Negro American Labor Council

*Who the hell appointed you as the guardian of all the Negroes
in America?*
— *George Meany to A. Philip Randolph, 1959*

Although Randolph became known as both a labor leader and a civil
rights activist, labor remained the central focus of his career. Indeed, his
position as head of the BSCP was essential to the survival of his civil
rights movements, for the porters' contributions of money and manpower were indispensable. The porters, however, were aging and diminishing in number as the railroad industry fell into decline after World War II.
Thus Randolph expended much energy seeking out other sources of
monetary support. After the AFL merged with the CIO in 1955, the combined federation, through Randolph's efforts, became committed to a
policy of backing racial integration with financial contributions. But
Randolph soon concluded that financial support alone was insufficient:
The AFL-CIO was not doing enough to cleanse itself internally of racial
discrimination. To pressure the labor movement to move faster toward
racial equality, Randolph began a new black labor group, the Negro
American Labor Council (NALC)—his last attempt to forge an all-black
movement.

Relations between organized labor and the black community had deteriorated steadily in the postwar period, in part because the CIO lessened
its earlier commitment to black equality as it became more concerned
with rooting out Communists and merging with the AFL. When George
Meany of the AFL and Walter Reuther of the CIO succeeded as heads of
their respective organizations, the drive for amalgamation began, and
merger terms were agreed on early in 1955. Rumors circulated that the
new federation would have a black vice-president, and observers saw
Randolph as the leading contender. Neither the AFL nor the CIO had a
black vice-president, and it was thought that the gesture would be dramatic evidence of the intention of the merged federation to crusade for

the elimination of Jim Crow. Randolph himself thought it important "that a person of color be placed on the executive council in the new House of Labor" as a demonstration of the democratic character of the trade union movement, not only to Americans, but also to "the teeming millions of color of Africa and Asia."[1]

The merger created an American labor movement of fifteen million members, one and a half million of whom were black. At the first AFL-CIO convention in December, 1955, Randolph and Willard Townsend of the United Transport Service Employees became the two black vice-presidents out of a total of twenty-nine. Randolph had long pushed for unification because he believed "a united, powerful and free trade union movement is a potent ally for all minorities to have in the fight against bigotry and racial intolerance." He predicted that the merged federation would "wage a more effective battle to eliminate economic inequality in our national life" where such inequality was based on color. According to *Ebony* magazine, the election of Randolph and Townsend represented a concession to the growing strength of blacks in the American labor movement. Through the two vice-presidents, the editor argued, blacks would participate in crucial top-level decisions for the first time in history.[2]

Randolph had already pointed to the mutuality of interest between the civil rights struggle and the trade union movement. He had convinced many labor leaders that Afro-Americans and labor shared the same foes— that opponents of racial equality were the same as those who wanted a cheap, docile work force. He had argued that labor had no logical alternative but to join forces with Afro-Americans in the fight against racial oppression: "White labor can never know freedom so long as black labor is in bondage." The White Citizens Councils preached white supremacy, but they were not "as much opposed to Negro rights as they are afraid of the growth and development of a strong and independent trade union movement in the South."[3] Organized labor, therefore, should support civil rights for blacks in its own self-interest since "civil rights are tied up with labor's rights."

1. *Black Worker*, February, 1955, p. 1; A. H. Raskin, New York *Times*, September 20, 1955, rpr. in *Black Worker*, September, 1955, p. 1+. See also *Black Worker*, November, 1955, pp. 1–2, August, 1955, pp. 1–2, December, 1955, p. 2.

2. Chicago *Defender*, February 19, 1955; *Black Worker*, December, 1955, p. 1+; "New Look in Negro Labor," *Ebony* (September, 1956), 25.

3. *Black Worker*, January, 1960, p. 4, May, 1956, p. 1+.

Under the new AFL-CIO constitution, unions could be expelled for corruption and communism but not for civil rights violations—a fact that distressed the black leaders. Not pleased with the Federation's failure to impose definite sanctions against discriminating unions, Randolph nevertheless said that the civil rights program of the AFL-CIO had made "substantial progress."[4] James B. Carey, a member of the International Union of Electrical Workers and a friend of Randolph's, had been chairman of the CIO Civil Rights Committee. He remained in that position in the merged federation, but despite the high hopes of Randolph and other black unionists, the old CIO concern with racial equality failed to emerge.

At first Randolph seemed to make progress toward his goal of a black-organized labor alliance for civil rights. Shortly after the AFL-CIO merger, in the spring of 1956, he persuaded top labor officials to head a special committee to raise $2 million to help fight the civil rights battle. The National Union Civil Rights Committee was formed with George Meany, head of the combined Federation, as chairman and David Dubinsky, of the International Ladies Garment Workers Union, as treasurer. The garment workers began the drive with a $10,000 donation, and Randolph, resurrecting his old idea, pledged that members of the BSCP would each tax themselves $1.50 for the fund. But the AFL-CIO's support for black civil rights disturbed the southern locals, many of which threatened to secede in protest. They said that if they had to choose between remaining southerners and being union members, they would choose to remain southerners. Some labor leaders advocated a "go slow" policy to avert a bolt of the southern unions, but Meany rejected the foot-dragging approach, remarking, "If that is their feeling, let them get out."[5]

After only a year and a half, however, Carey resigned as chairman of the AFL-CIO Civil Rights Committee because it was not moving fast enough. Accusing Meany of countermanding his directives and failing to cooperate in calling a civil rights conference, Carey maintained that he would have more freedom to fight discrimination in labor from the outside, having met only delay and hamstringing in trying to carry out the mandate of the constitutional provision concerning bias.[6] Charles Zim-

4. A. Philip Randolph, To the Editor of New York-Amsterdam *News*, April 30, 1957, in BSCP Papers, LC.

5. *Black Worker*, May, 1956, p. 1+; "Labor Leaders Help Start $2 Million Rights Chest," *Jet*, May 31, 1956, p. 48; "A. Philip Randolph," *American Labor*, I (August, 1968), 51.

6. *Black Worker*, June 15, 1957, p. 2; Chicago *Defender*, June 1, 1957.

merman, vice-president of the garment workers' union, replaced Carey. But blacks objected to Zimmerman on two counts: he was not a member of the executive council, and he was an active member of the Jewish Labor Committee, which might lead to a conflict of interest.

When the AFL-CIO Civil Rights Committee failed to hold a meeting for over a year, Milton Webster, a member of both the committee and its subcommittee on compliance, wrote Zimmerman, in January of 1959, to complain about the lack of interest. Webster noted that when the committee was formed, hopes were high that the group would do something to alleviate the situation of blacks, but clearly their position had not improved. Consequently, Webster predicted, "If some definite and drastic change" was not made, "in justice to our own convictions and to the large number of people in the labor movement who are depending upon us to lead this fight we will have to resort to means outside the AFL-CIO to try to bring about a correction of this situation." Adding, "This is the thing that we are reluctant to do," Webster pledged that he and those for whom he spoke would not take action as long as they believed that the Civil Rights Committee might yet function effectively within the Federation.[7] The action to which Webster alluded was forming a separate black organization within the AFL-CIO.

Randolph had done more than anyone else to bring blacks into the union movement; nevertheless, his previous attempts to form black labor groups in the 1920s and 1930s had not been particularly successful.[8] Although blacks had become an important component of organized labor, discrimination persisted. Criticism of union racial practices had gained momentum in the prosperous postwar period, and by the 1958 NAACP convention, unionist delegates were aroused over the worsening situation. The association would take steps on its own to deal with this dissatisfaction, but Randolph harked back to his old idea of a national black organization based on the model of the Jewish Labor Committee that would enable blacks to protest within the labor movement against the paternalism of "liberal" white leaders and discrimination by unions.

Randolph set the stage for launching such an organization in his address to the 1959 NAACP convention, "The Civil Rights Revolution and

7. Milton P. Webster to Charles Zimmerman, January 2, 1959, in BSCP Papers, CD.
8. See A. Philip Randolph, "The Trade Union Movement and the Negro," *Journal of Negro Education,* V (January, 1936), 57, for the situation in the 1930s.

Labor." He pointed out that the civil rights movement was completing "the incompleted Civil War Revolution by sweeping into the ashcan of history the remnants, vestiges and survivals of the old slave order." The movement sought "to fulfill its historical mission of abolishing the status of second-class citizenship based upon the mythology of racial inferiority." Randolph reminded his audience that not only unions but every institution in America treated blacks as inferiors. "The transformation of relationships of Negro workers in the house of labor," Randolph maintained, "will constitute the second phase of the moral revolution" initiated by the labor movement when it expelled unions permeated by corrupt influences, racketeering, and gangsterism. Thereupon Randolph called for the formation of a new black labor committee "to fight and work to implement the civil rights program of the AFL-CIO." Always mindful of the need for allies, Randolph suggested that every member should also be a member of the NAACP.[9]

After the NAACP convention, Randolph outlined his objectives for the group, stating that its "philosophy, ideals, principles and program . . . stem from the concept that labor leadership is a sacred trust, a great moral responsibility." He promised to seek as members black trade unionists from various crafts and industries. Sounding much as he did in the heyday of the March on Washington Movement, Randolph described the new group as "pro-Negro, although not non-white. It will support pro-labor and pro-civil rights legislation. Recognizing that only within the framework of a democratic society can civil rights and labor's rights exist . . . [we will] unequivocably support and defend freedom and democracy at home and abroad."[10]

Randolph had issued a written call on July 1, 1959, asking black trade union leaders around the country to meet with him to establish the organization. Its goal was to ensure Afro-Americans a more influential role in the shaping of policies and programs of the American trade union movement on all levels. The closed planning session met in New York later that month, immediately after the NAACP convention.[11] In attendance were

9. A. Philip Randolph, "The Civil Rights Revolution and Labor," Address to NAACP Convention, July 15, 1959.

10. Quoted in "A. Philip Randolph," *American Labor*, 54.

11. *Black Worker*, August, 1959, p. 1+; Marshall, *Negro and Organized Labor*, 71. Randolph's ideas for the Negro Trade Union Committee were contained in his statement "The Negro and Organized Labor," in BSCP Papers, CD.

black leaders active in, but not representing, many national and international unions, including the United Auto Workers, Hotel and Restaurant Workers, Building Service Employees, and numerous state, local, and central labor bodies of the AFL-CIO. They expressed concern about the role of the trade union movement in the field of civil rights and the lack of blacks in union leadership positions.

The group decided unanimously to establish machinery to organize a convention for the launching of a permanent black labor organization before the end of the year. Randolph was elected temporary chairman of the new movement, which sought to enroll every black union member in its ranks. He continued to lobby for his new group at the third triennial convention of the BSCP in Chicago in September, 1959. There a resolution was passed in favor of a national Negro labor committee, "the purpose of which shall be to work and fight in the interest of the elimination of discrimination and segregation in the affiliates of the AFL-CIO." [12]

Then, at the 1959 AFL-CIO convention, Randolph announced that he would press for the ouster of unions that had failed to drop their prohibition against blacks. He also demanded liquidation of segregated locals in all unions and proposed a change in the Federation's constitution, making racial discrimination within unions a clear-cut basis for expulsion. Randolph's proposal marked the first time since the merger that the issue of civil rights was brought up at a Federation convention. [13]

Angry debate broke out between Meany and Randolph on the convention floor, caused, at least in part, by Meany's disgruntlement over Randolph's proposed new black labor group. Randolph demanded that the International Longshoremen's Association be required to end discrimination against blacks on the New York waterfront as a condition of readmission to the House of Labor. Meany, furious because Randolph made his charges against the longshoremen from the floor rather than in the executive council, implied that Randolph was merely seeking publicity and suggested that he begin acting like part of the labor movement. Defending his action, Randolph said that he had received a report on the longshoremen from the NUL and had not had adequate time before the convention to present it to the executive council but felt obligated to make it public. Randolph also proposed a resolution calling for expul-

12. *Black Worker*, August, 1959, p. 1+, September, 1959, pp. 4–5.
13. New York *Times*, September 20, 1959.

sion of the Brotherhood of Railroad Trainmen and the Brotherhood of Locomotive Firemen and Enginemen unless they removed their race bars within six months. The two unions, which had been admitted to the AFL-CIO over Randolph's protest, "have had the color bar in their constitutions for over fifty years. How much more time do they want?"[14]

Meany and most of the other white delegates agreed with Randolph in principle but did not want to impose a time limit. For his part, Randolph maintained that the Federation was being "inconsistent" to kick out the teamsters' union for corruption yet not expel the railroad unions for discrimination. If the racial bars were not removed from their constitutions by the next convention, he said, he would introduce a resolution for their immediate expulsion. Apparently his pressure was effective, because the offending passage was ordered removed at the next trainmen's convention.[15]

Randolph and Meany also clashed over Randolph's insistence on the liquidation of all-black locals, even where their members wanted to retain them. Meany declared that a Jim Crow union in existence for many years should have the democratic right to decide if and when it wanted to merge with a white union. Randolph opposed local decision making on this question as again being inconsistent with the policy whereby the Federation expelled Communist-dominated unions and those under corrupt influences. There was no right of decision under the constitution; locals must conform. If a union failed to integrate, it should be expelled—the black union if it refused to merge, the white union if it refused to accept the black union. Racially segregated local unions, Randolph argued, "are just as morally unjustifiable and indefensible when requested by Negro officials and members as when they are arbitrarily imposed upon them by the national or international union." Randolph acknowledged that black officials might be concerned about their fate in a merger, especially where the white membership was larger, but did not think the Federation was "bound to sacrifice the interests of the rank-and-file members to protect a few union jobs."[16]

In a debate that Randolph later described as "colorful and warm,"

14. Milton P. Webster, "Emil Mazey on Civil Rights," in BSCP Papers, CD; *Black Worker*, October, 1959, p. 1; Milton P. Webster to Charles S. Zimmerman, October 23, 1959, in BSCP Papers, CD; *Proceedings of the AFL-CIO Third Constitutional Convention* (San Francisco, September 17–23, 1959), I, 480–99.

15. New York *Times*, September 24, 1959; *Black Worker*, October, 1959, p. 1.

16. Randolph, "Civil Rights Revolution and Labor."

Meany asked Randolph if it was his idea of the democratic process "that you don't care what the Negro members think." When Randolph replied, "Yes," Meany shouted: "That's your policy. Well that's not my policy. I'm for the democratic rights of Negro members to maintain the unions they want. Who the hell appointed you as the guardian of all the Negroes in America?" The NAACP, however, backed Randolph's position that black locals should be eliminated even if their members wanted to keep them.[17]

At a postconvention meeting of the executive council, Meany indicated his readiness to put more teeth into the enforcement machinery for curbing Jim Crow practices in the labor movement. Randolph expressed his confidence that the Federation would proceed more vigorously, but was concerned that the recent controversy would cause "deterioration" in the image of union labor held by the black community. Later Meany maintained that no rift had occurred between Randolph and himself; they did not differ on "ultimate objectives," but rather on methods, procedures, and the pace of the antibias campaign. Meany said that the "press had blown up the incident out of proportion"; he had spoken in "convention language," and as Randolph agreed, "There was no enmity or bitterness" involved. Nevertheless, Randolph asserted: "I will maintain my position. Not only that I will more vigorously step up the fight against segregation in unions. We have the problem of educating some leaders."[18]

Although Randolph and Meany remained close personally, Meany's statements were reported with much indignation and resentment in the black press. For his part, Randolph emphasized: "Negro trade unionists have no intention of coming out of the AFL-CIO because racial prejudice is in it. This would be suicidal folly." He pointed out, "If Negroes followed this logic, they would get out of every institution and movement in the United States since race prejudice is in the church, it is in the government, it is in the schools, industry and sports. Instead of getting out of these institutions because racial prejudice is in them, Negroes must get into these institutions and fight unceasingly and uncompromisingly to drive racial discrimination and segregation out of them."[19]

17. *Black Worker*, October, 1959, p. 1; New York *Times*, September 24, 25, 1959.
18. New York *Times*, September 25, October 6, 1959; "A. Philip Randolph Calls Meany Attack 'Ridiculous,'" *Jet*, October 8, 1959, p. 13.
19. *Black Worker*, October, 1959, p. 1. See, for example, Randolph to the Editor, New York-Amsterdam *News*, April 30, 1957, in BSCP Papers, LC, for Randolph's defense of Meany.

Since he had emerged as the black workers' "guardian," Randolph decided to go ahead with his new black labor group. He called on all the black union officials to meet in November to launch the group and plan a "moral revolution" against race bias in the labor movement. Randolph stated that the purpose of his organization would be "to eliminate all Jim Crow practices and narrow the gap between the fine liberal pronouncements of the labor movement and the actual practices." Arguing that the strain of segregation had forced black trade unionists to develop an organization of their own to fight for the elimination of discrimination and "to secure the status of first class economic citizenship in the labor movement," Randolph maintained that his new organization was twenty-five or more years late. Certainly blacks suffered far more from discrimination than Jews or Italians, yet those groups had found it necessary to form their own labor organizations years earlier. To alleviate AFL-CIO fears, Randolph emphasized: "This is not a labor union. It will not negotiate contracts with employers, nor is it an organization to fight the AFL-CIO or any of its leaders." Rather, the new group would be "pro-AFL-CIO and pro the leaders of the AFL-CIO."[20]

The planners had expected a steering committee of about twenty-five, but in November, 1959, more than one hundred angry, vocal black labor leaders arrived in Cleveland from all over the country to lay plans for a founding convention in Detroit. Randolph, who was cochairman of the New York local council, was named provisional chairman by the steering committee. By now the name Negro American Labor Council had been adopted, and the group was temporarily based in the headquarters of the BSCP.[21] Chapters were established in Detroit, Pittsburgh, Cleveland, Atlanta, Chicago, and six other major cities in addition to New York. The organizers wanted to establish even more chapters to build a strong membership, so that a large body of delegates could attend the founding convention. Chapters were patterned after the Detroit Trade Union Leadership Council, which had been formed two years earlier to protect black union members in the automobile industry.

The call was issued, and one thousand delegates from twenty-six cities attended the founding convention of the NALC in Detroit, May 27–29, 1960. Thus a little less than a year after the blowup between Randolph

20. "Randolph Calls for 'Revolution' Against Race Bias in Unions," *Jet*, November 5, 1959, pp. 18–19; *Black Worker*, October, 1959, p. 2.
21. Dufty, "A Post Portrait," January 3, 1960.

and Meany, a black labor organization had become a reality—a reflection of the growing disillusionment over discrimination in the labor movement. Randolph expected the NALC to provide leadership, programs, and funds for coordinated guerrilla warfare against Jim Crow in labor at every level, from shop steward meetings up to national conventions.

Led by Randolph, the delegates committed themselves to more than a labor organization: They would pursue first-class citizenship and full equality of opportunity for minority groups in every facet of American life. Members would be sought on an individual basis, not as representatives of their unions, and all black trade unionists except Communists were welcome. The council planned to advance the cause of the black unionist on every level—local, state, and federal. Since the small number of blacks in positions of power and responsibility within the labor movement was due in part to a spirit of indifference and a lack of understanding among blacks, as well as to discrimination, the NALC would endeavor to involve the black unionist more completely in the affairs of his community, to acquaint him with political and legislative issues in the areas of labor and civil rights, and to apprise him of the record of his legislators.[22]

The NALC planned to work closely with the trade union movement and other established organizations interested in alleviating problems faced by black workers through eliminating discriminatory wage differentials, hours, and conditions of work; securing the right of union membership for blacks and increasing opportunity for black employment and promotion on the job; encouraging active participation of blacks in executive, administrative, and staff areas of unions; and promoting the election of black unionists as delegates to all trade union conventions. The NALC delegates pledged their opposition to racism, fascism, communism, corruption, and racketeering in the trade union movement and in the council itself. In addition to making American blacks more union conscious, the NALC sought to advance the cause of workers in other countries, especially the emerging nations.[23]

Randolph was elected president, and sixteen men were elected vice-presidents of the NALC. But seventy-five delegates backed a demand that women be represented on the executive board, so an amendment to include two women on the board was passed. Thus eighteen vice-presidents

22. *Black Worker*, February, 1960, p. 1+.
23. *Ibid.*, February, 1960, p. 1+, June, 1960, p. 1+.

were elected in all, although the constitution called for only sixteen. Perceptive observers might have realized that this was a more rebellious group than Randolph's BSCP and predicted trouble ahead.

At first, Randolph advocated that the new labor group's membership be limited to "the Negro members of the national and international unions of the AFL-CIO." Randolph believed that his previous attempts to form black labor organizations had failed because they relied too much on white union leaders for support, and whites "could not be counted on when the chips were down." Consequently, he thought that the new group should be financed entirely by blacks. The exclusion of whites had been debated at length in the period between the New York meeting and the founding convention, and other black leaders agreed with Randolph. But the situation was different from the one in the early 1940s, when Randolph excluded whites from the MOWM. By 1959 Randolph had forged the network of alliances that financially backed his Prayer Pilgrimage and youth marches, and he did not wish to alienate future support for the civil rights movement. He realized that he could not afford to antagonize white liberals in the labor movement. By the founding convention of the NALC, therefore, he had altered his position: Although the council would "seek Negro trade unionists," it would "have no color bar."[24]

While Randolph's paramount concern was the economic disadvantage caused by discrimination, he was not unmindful of the damage caused to the black psyche by racial prejudice, calling it "an affront to the personality" of the black worker. Discrimination, argued Randolph, "disregards [the] self respect" of the black worker, who suffers from "the humiliation that goes with the belief and the concept of racial inferiority" that results from "exclusion from a union because of race."[25] Thus once again Randolph had a twofold purpose for preferring to keep his organization racially exclusive: to make sure it would remain independent, and to increase black self-esteem. But preference gave way to pragmatism. Also, believing that an alliance with organized labor was crucial for the largely laboring black population, Randolph remained as a vice-president of the AFL-CIO. The NALC under his leadership would not be a separatist organization, but rather would be used to pressure the establishment from within.

24. Randolph, "Civil Rights Revolution and Labor"; Marshall, *Negro and Organized Labor,* 71; "Founding Convention Call, Negro American Labor Council, May 27–29, 1960," in *Black Worker,* June, 1960.
25. *Proceedings of the AFL-CIO Third Constitutional Convention,* I, 480–99.

As might be expected, many of Randolph's lieutenants from previous rights groups supplied the secondary leadership of the NALC: Cleveland Robinson became vice-president, Richard Parrish treasurer, and Theodore Brown secretary. Like other organizations Randolph founded, the council formed strong local auxiliaries through extending autonomy in local decision making. It thereby provided the opportunity for powerful intermediary leaders, like Willoughby Abner in Chicago, to emerge on the provincial level.

Randolph displayed the same concern over Communist infiltration of his new labor group as he had with his other organizations. The NALC, he stated, was committed to the philosophy of free, democratic trade unionism and therefore opposed to "Communism and Communists as a menace and danger to the Negro freedom movement and the labor movement." Thus a council member was expelled in 1964 because he was a "self-proclaimed Communist." Stressing that "eternal vigilance is necessary to prevent Communists from infiltrating the black civil rights forces," Randolph reiterated his position that Party members were "not concerned about the advancement of civil rights but only seek, if not blocked, to rule or ruin any movement they can capture."[26]

Randolph thought that the first objective of the NALC should be to secure the compliance of the AFL-CIO's international unions with the Federation's civil rights program by thoroughly investigating every case of discrimination and forcing the AFL-CIO to take action if a complaint was found valid. In addition to overhauling the Federation's racial policy, educating union members, and publicizing the civil rights program, Randolph proposed annual regional civil rights seminars, to be attended by union officials at all levels, "for the purpose of making evident and clear the policy position of the AFL-CIO on civil rights and its importance and value to labor."[27]

The NALC was effective in putting pressure on the unions. "We are in rebellion," said Randolph. "Organized labor will be shaken to its foundation. And, we will not stop until we have not only cleansed labor's house of discrimination but also placed Negro representatives on union policy-making bodies and staffs on the basis of merit and ability." To eliminate any doubt in the public mind, Randolph made the connection

26. Memo, in RP Papers.
27. "Negro Pressure on Unions," *Business Week*, April 30, 1960, p. 139+.

clear: "The NALC reflects within organized labor the same rebellion that finds its expression in the student lunch counter demonstrations in the South." For its part, management was concerned that this black pressure on the unions would have a detrimental effect on productivity—that union hall squabbles over civil rights would erupt inside the plants.[28]

At the next annual convention of the NAACP in June, 1960, Randolph flailed liberals and labor alike for the color bar that kept blacks out of countless union locals. He listed the chief offenders as locals in the building trades and those south of the Mason-Dixon line: locals in the steel and textile industries, and even Walter Reuther's United Auto Workers. "The entire labor movement bears guilt for the existence of racial disadvantage to workers of color," Randolph charged. He also expressed the disappointment of blacks with white liberals: "It is unfortunate that so many of our liberal friends, along with some of the leaders of labor, even yet do not comprehend the nature, scope, depth and challenge of this civil rights revolution which is surging forward in the house of labor and all areas of American life."[29] This criticism of liberal whites would isolate the NALC from the coalition Randolph had built to support civil rights.

To maintain credibility as a viable, functioning group, the NALC sponsored the Workshop and Institute on Race Bias in Trade Unions, Industry and Government in Washington, D.C., in February, 1961. Its purpose was to "inform, awaken, arouse and mobilize the Negro community back of the fight to eliminate discriminatory practices." The NALC wanted to examine the total exclusion of blacks from certain occupations, segregated locals, and separate lines of seniority written into collective bargaining agreements. An economic downturn was gathering momentum, and the unemployment rate for blacks was twice as high as that for whites. Automation was endangering the jobs of skilled workers, as well as diminishing the need for unskilled and semiskilled workers.

When Secretary of Labor Arthur Goldberg addressed the group, he confirmed that 14 percent of blacks were jobless, leading Randolph to conclude that black workers were "victims of a veritable chronic condition of staggering unemployment" that was even worse during the recession because, being primarily unskilled and semiskilled, they were the first discharged. According to Randolph, blacks were victimized by a "conspiracy" among trade unions, industry, and government to block them from apprenticeship programs in the construction industry. Labor should give recognition to "the revolution of rising expectations among all oppressed people" by hastening to stamp out bias within its ranks, he maintained. At least one observer believed that the workshop and institute "profoundly disturbed white AFL-CIO leadership."[30]

In the period following the convention-floor fight with Meany, Randolph had been gradually increasing the tempo of his attacks on the discriminatory policies of the AFL-CIO. Before the March, 1961, quarterly meeting of the Federation's executive council, Randolph announced that he had completed a "code of fair racial trade union practices," which he would submit for the council's consideration. His code called for an end to segregated locals, elimination of racial bars to union leadership, full equality in apprenticeship programs, and new policing machinery to implement the Federation's guarantees of freedom from discrimination. Randolph wanted a six-month time limit on elimination of discriminatory practices by the AFL-CIO and an overhaul of the enforcement machinery to provide for more direct representation of blacks.

The other members of the executive council were becoming increasingly irritated at the vehemence with which the NALC was attacking labor's record in eradicating discriminatory practices. Meany, for one, resented what he called the "separatist" group, and Zimmerman resigned as chairman of the Civil Rights Committee a few weeks after Randolph announced his "code." The executive council was also concerned because Congressman Adam Clayton Powell, chairman of the House Labor Committee, shared Randolph's view. Powell's committee had the power to order public hearings on the exclusion of blacks from the building craft unions working on government projects and the lack of admission of blacks to apprenticeship programs.[31]

After announcing his new code, Randolph said that the Federation's machinery for eliminating Jim Crow had "failed completely" and that Meany had not put the same vigor into the campaign that he had put into the fight against corruption and communism. Meany defended the Federation and charged that the NALC made cooperation impossible by issuing "broadsides" against the AFL-CIO without first checking their validity.

30. New York *Times*, February 18, 23, 1961; Minutes of the Emergency Meeting of the National Executive Board, Negro American Labor Council, May 6, 1961, Randolph to Theodore Brown, November 3, 1960, both in BSCP Papers, LC; "A. Philip Randolph Replies to AFL-CIO Report," *Black Worker*, November, 1961, pp. 4–6.
31. New York *Times*, May 2, March 1, 1961.

He advised the NALC to work with the Federation instead of following the policies of "criticism" and "slander." In reply, Randolph observed that the forces operating to stir rebellion against discriminaton in the labor movement were the same as those working for the overthrow of colonial rule in Africa and encouraging defiance of racial exclusion in the South.[32]

The growing schism between the black community and organized labor reached a critical point with the Theodore E. Brown affair. Randolph had secured the appointment of his protégé Brown as assistant director of the Civil Rights Department of the AFL-CIO in 1956. Brown was "summarily" dismissed from the position in April, 1961, on the charge that he misused his travel credit and made unauthorized trips. Randolph called an emergency meeting of the executive board of the NALC to protest Brown's dismissal.[33] The consensus of the board members was that not only the defense of Brown but that of all black trade unionists was at stake. Randolph pointed out that since the case was an "obvious violation of a long standing trade union principle that no worker be dismissed without a hearing," the firing of Brown was indicative of the "psychological distance" between leaders of the AFL-CIO and the black community.

When Randolph was subsequently presented with convincing evidence of Brown's misconduct, he decided to let the matter drop. It seems obvious, however, that the timing of the allegations against Brown was related to the Federation's anger at Randolph's pressure. Although Brown misuscd his credit privileges, his protestations could not be totally disregarded. He claimed that he first sensed tension in his association with the AFL-CIO after the NALC's founding convention, and he pointed to several significant incidents: when his secretary resigned, he was not given another; his pattern of travel in 1960 was no different from that in previous years, but the AFL-CIO held that some of his trips were advancing the cause of the NALC; and he was told not to attend the NAACP annual convention. Brown claimed that, above all, his support of Randolph's demand that the Federation revamp its racial policies caused his dismissal.

Brown's guilt proved to be immaterial; his dismissal had a galvanizing effect on blacks in the labor movement. The NALC executive board con-

---

32. *Ibid.*, March 1, 1961.
33. Telegram from Randolph, May 2, 1961, in BSCP Papers, LC.

sidered a march on Washington to protest his treatment, and many black trade unionists demanded a break with the AFL-CIO over the issue. Randolph, however, remained firm against all efforts to turn the NALC into a "black federation of labor." Sounding a lot like Meany, Randolph said that the best way to eliminate bias was to "stay inside the A.F.L.-C.I.O. and fight."[34] Clearly Randolph himself was becoming less combative as the NALC's membership was growing more militant.

Formal presentation of Randolph's fair union practices code to the executive council of the AFL-CIO had been delayed from March to June, 1961. At the June quarterly meeting, Meany named a three-man subcommittee of the executive council to analyze Randolph's charges. The subcommittee brought back a "censure" report, saying that Randolph, the Federation's only remaining black vice-president since the death of Willard Townsend, had caused "the gap that has developed between organized labor and the Negro community." On October 12, the executive council moved to adopt the subcommittee's report, with Randolph casting the only dissenting vote. In a far-reaching, harshly worded twenty-page statement, the subcommittee disputed in almost every detail the charges Randolph made of discrimination and racism in AFL-CIO affiliates and of Meany's laxity in fighting for black rights. The report accused the BSCP itself of racism because it had only black staff members and had never attempted to negotiate a nondiscriminatory clause with the Pullman Company. The report also rejected Randolph's proposal that the AFL-CIO adopt a system of penalties against discriminating unions. Randolph was accused of "incredible assertions," "false and gratuitous statements," and "unfair and untrue" allegations.[35]

Meany appealed to Randolph to stop making the Federation defend itself against "baseless charges." To others, Meany observed, "I think we could do a lot with his cooperation, but it seems in the last two or three years he's gotten close to these militant groups and he has given up cooperation for propaganda." That the post of chairman of the Civil Rights Department of the Federation had been vacant for several months, since Zimmerman's departure, contributed to the fallout between Meany and

34. Minutes of Emergency Meeting, NALC; Negro Trade Unionists Move for Reinstatement of Theodore E. Brown, n.d., in BSCP Papers, LC; New York *Times*, May 24, 1961.

35. New York *Times*, May 24, 1961; *Black Worker*, July, 1961, p. 2; New York *Times*, October 13, 1961; "Unions and Discrimination," *Commonweal*, November 3, 1961, pp. 140–41.

Randolph. But "no one is volunteering for the job these days," Meany said. "We lost our last chairman because he got tired of being hit over the head."[36]

In his written reply to the censure report, Randolph maintained that neither the BSCP nor the NALC was "waging warfare" against Meany or the Federation, but rather "against race bias in the American Labor Movement, represented by the AFL-CIO, industry and government." Randolph then proceeded to answer the report point by point. Contrary to his previous position, Randolph now placed the failure of civil rights progress in the AFL-CIO "squarely at the door of George Meany" because neither "he, nor the Executive Council, ever placed the full moral weight of his or its powerful influence back of civil rights in the labor movement. Nor has President Meany ever involved himself seriously personally." Countering the charge that the BSCP was racist by pointing to its white lawyer, white accountant, and white economist, Randolph explained that there were no white porters because Pullman only hired blacks for the job. Furthermore, no BSCP members had ever complained of discrimination within the union.[37]

Randolph then quoted from the Report on Employment, issued by the Commission on Civil Rights on the same day that the censure report was released. The commission's findings, he argued, constituted a "complete refutation" of the AFL-CIO subcommittee report. The commission documented the extent of discrimination within organized labor and concluded, "Existing Federation law has had little impact on the discriminatory practices of labor organizations." Since the international unions' "voluntary" efforts to curb discrimination had been "largely ineffective," the Civil Rights Commission report called for federal legislation to ban racial discrimination in labor unions. Closing his response to the censure report, Randolph stated that "the tragic failure of the civil rights cause in the House of Labor" was a "symbol of the moral decay of the American Labor Movement," and that the lack of racial equality accounted for the loss of the "Messianic commitment" of the trade union movement.[38]

36. New York *Times*, October 13, 1961; "Unions and Discrimination," 140–41; "The Unhappy Mr. Randolph," *Reporter*, October 26, 1961, p. 18.

37. "Randolph Replies to AFL-CIO Report." See also *Jet* interview of A. Philip Randolph by Simeon Booker, November 7, 1961, in BSCP Papers, LC; New York *Times*, October 13, 1961.

38. Herbert Hill, "Racial Practices of Organized Labor," in Julius Jacobson (ed.), *The Negro and the American Labor Movement* (Garden City, N.Y., 1968), 298; "Randolph Replies to AFL-CIO Report."

Blacks were incensed by what they considered to be the executive council's mistreatment of Randolph. Roy Wilkins called the censure a "coverup" for "racial discrimination and segregation inside labor" and "an act of incredible stupidity" that "can only be regarded as a further indication of the moral bankruptcy of the A.F.L.-C.I.O. leadership." Martin Luther King labeled the report "shocking and deplorable." Whitney Young, head of the NUL, offered the services of his organization to find a way to eradicate "the pockets of racial discrimination in some unions." The *Black Worker*, as would be expected, denounced the censure motion as "a gross injustice."[39]

Blacks were also angered by the reaction of liberal white labor leaders. Cleveland Robinson of the NALC and secretary of New York District 65 Retail, Wholesale and Department Store Union was incredulous that the censure brought no objections from the "liberal" labor leaders and was met by a "wave of silence by white trade union leaders and many Negroes as well." Richard Parrish asked, "Where were all these liberals on the Council when the vote was taken?" David Dubinsky, James Carey, and Joe Curran, head of the National Maritime Union, all of whom considered themselves liberal and had previously supported Randolph, were present but did not oppose censure; Walter Reuther was not present.[40]

In November, 1961, a month after the censure of Randolph and a month before the biennial convention of the AFL-CIO in Florida, the Call for the Second Annual NALC Convention was issued. At the meeting, Randolph made a plea to retain the incumbent slate of national officers, all of whom were reelected. His keynote address, entitled "The Struggle for the Liberation of the Black Laboring Masses," traced the historic struggle of black workers for equal job rights. It touched on the failure of trade union organization drives, especially in the South; the indifference of AFL-CIO leadership to union race bias; and the recent Federation subcommittee report.[41]

By this time Randolph had come to agree with the conclusion of the Civil Rights Commission report: Only the federal government and not the labor federation could effectively fight racism in trade unions. Although he would continue to fight bias within the AFL-CIO, Randolph would not expect change within the Federation alone to alleviate the

39. Suggested Draft of Statement on AFL-CIO Executive Council for RW, n.d., in NAACP Papers, LC; New York *Times*, October 14, 1961; *Black Worker*, December, 1961, p. 2.
40. New York *Times*, November 13, 1961.
41. *Black Worker*, October, 1961, p. 3, November, 1961, p. 3.

situation. He would therefore again seek federal legislation making racist actions illegal in apprenticeship programs and providing for an overall FEPC.[42] Perhaps the climate of opinion in the country would be more conducive to such legislation in the 1960s, he reasoned, than it had been in the 1940s and 1950s.

Predictably, the NALC convention denounced the censure of Randolph. A motion was adopted to send a delegation in protest to the AFL-CIO convention in December "to let George Meany know that the Negro masses are behind Randolph." But, in an effort to heal the breach, just before the Federation convention Meany reversed his position on the NALC. He had previously ignored the council by refusing to send speakers to its meetings or have other dealings with it, but he now recommended a closer working relationship between the black group and the Federation. In an attempt to avoid an angry floor discussion at the convention, he gave assurance of his changed stance to a twenty-six-man delegation of the NALC. The group had presented Meany with a six-point program for adoption by the convention, the first point of which called for "the reconsideration and withdrawal of the attack" on Randolph. "Our concern is deep and grave over the growing gap between organized labor and the Negro community, a gap which has deepened and widened as a consequence of the A.F.L.-C.I.O. Executive Council's unjustified and unwarranted attack upon the integrity, sincerity and judgement of labor's foremost champion of civil rights," the statement read. In view of the findings of the Civil Rights Commission, it was "unconscionable" to let the charge against Randolph stand, the statement concluded. Later, at a luncheon with Meany and Webster, Randolph said that he was satisfied with the change in position toward the NALC; however, unless the censure was withdrawn, he would make an issue of it on the convention floor.[43] Meanwhile, the ousted International Brotherhood of Teamsters supported Randolph by adopting a resolution that called his censure a "great injustice."

Although Randolph and the Federation eventually put the controversy behind them, the course of reconciliation did not run smooth. Meany accused Randolph of reneging on his pledge not to speak critically of the executive council subcommittee that censured him. Randolph denied making any agreement on what he would say to the convention delegates,

42. New York *Times*, November 11, 1961.
43. *Ibid.*, November 13, December 6, 7, 1961.

and accused Meany of failing to keep his promise to send the censure report back to the executive council for reconsideration. Subsequently, Randolph agreed to have his remarks calling the censure report "dishonorable, disgraceful, petty and cheap" stricken from the record. In return, Meany agreed that the report would be "deposited" with the executive council, where both sides acknowledged it would die.[44] Ultimately, an executive board resolution praised Randolph for being a champion of both the labor movement and civil rights.

As a result of Randolph's pressure, labor's "most comprehensive" civil rights program was adopted by the 1961 AFL-CIO convention. The new civil rights resolution emphasized a voluntary approach by affiliates, set up a complicated procedure for processing complaints against offending unions, and, most important, empowered the Civil Rights Committee to initiate complaints of its own "on the basis of primafacie evidence that discrimination is being practiced." Randolph called it "the best resolution on civil rights that the AFL-CIO has yet adopted." He said that he favored stronger sanctions than those provided, but was determined to make the resolution work. The *Black Worker* editorialized, "We wish to congratulate the AFL-CIO upon the giant step forward on the civil rights front."[45] Meany appointed Secretary-Treasurer William F. Schnitzler as chairman of the new Standing Committee on Civil Rights and reappointed Milton Webster as one of the committee members.

Randolph, however, still believed that federal intervention was necessary and testified to that effect before a special House labor subcommittee. Federal legislation to assure equal opportunity in employment was especially needed, he argued, to help black workers "break through the institutionalized racial barriers to apprenticeship training courses." Exclusion from such programs trapped blacks in a "no-man's land" of unskilled workers, where "they constitute the hard core of joblessness . . . [T]hese workers remain unemployed during depressions, recessions, booms, inflation and deflation; during cyclical, seasonal, residual, technological, ethical and economic maladjustments of the economy." Whereas the overall unemployment rate was 7 percent, the unemployment rate for blacks approached 20 percent—a reflection of the basic truth that blacks were the last hired and the first fired. The number of skilled black workers was diminishing because blacks were losing ground, particularly in

44. *Ibid*, December 13, 1961, January 12, 1962.
45. *Ibid*, December 13, 1961; *Black Worker*, December, 1961, pp. 2, 4–5.

the South, in crafts and trades in which they traditionally had high representation. Even when race restrictions were removed from apprenticeship programs, nepotism and collusion between unions and employers operated to keep blacks out of jobs and promotion opportunities. Automation threatened to increase unemployment among blacks even further through mass elimination of jobs in which they were concentrated.[46]

The well-being of workers represented the common cause for which Meany and Randolph, who had known each other for many years, had spent their lives fighting. Paradoxically, the two were in agreement on the fundamental issue that embittered their relations—the place of blacks in organized labor. But Randolph believed that reliance on moral pressure to bring noncomplying unions into line was insufficient: Every international affiliate with local unions that practiced race discrimination should be suspended or expelled. Such a policy would affect all the big craft unions—a prospect that Meany was at first unwilling to accept.[47] Through Randolph's prodding, however, he gradually came to view the Federation as accountable for its affiliates' racial policies.

This commitment to racial equality remained, however, at the executive level; efforts to educate the rank and file were half-hearted at best. White laborers continued to resent their black fellows as competitors rather than see them as comrades-in-arms fighting a common battle. The "bureaucratized and elitist" union movement had to assume its share of responsibility for the racial savagery and ignorance exhibited by so many rank-and-file workers, observed one labor historian.[48] Equal treatment in plants and an equal chance at better jobs were still denied blacks in many parts of the country even after all Randolph's efforts. Thus despite a lifetime spent in working for black equality within the American trade union movement, Randolph was only slightly closer to his goal at the end of his life than at the beginning.

Concurrently with Randolph's campaign against bigotry in the AFL-CIO, the NAACP was carrying on its own struggle against discrimination in the Federation. In 1958 Herbert Hill, labor secretary of the NAACP, at-

46. *Black Worker*, January, 1962, p. 2.
47. "Racism in Labor," *America*, November 25, 1961, p. 276.
48. Jacobson (ed.), *Negro and American Labor Movement*, 21.

tacked the AFL-CIO for failing to erase the color line retained by its member unions. Hill faulted the organization for its lofty public posture and support for federal legislation while its affiliates maintained rigid exclusionary practices at the local level. Thereupon Hill submitted to Meany evidence and affidavits of antiblack actions in the ranks of the Federation. Following the presentation of Hill's documents, Wilkins wrote to Meany in December, saying that he was receiving increasing numbers of complaints from the NAACP membership regarding discriminatory practices by the Federation. Wilkins said that although the NAACP and the AFL-CIO had always cooperated, he owed it to his membership to address the charges.[49]

Hill then filed complaints against several AFL-CIO unions, charging them with excluding blacks by constitutional provision and tacit consent, discriminating against blacks on job referrals, maintaining separate lines of promotion that limited blacks to menial jobs, and maintaining segregated or auxiliary locals. The AFL-CIO was particularly displeased with Hill's public accusation against the International Ladies Garment Workers Union on charges of bias, as well as his attempts to get the National Labor Relations Board to decertify two unions. Meany threatened that the AFL-CIO would no longer cooperate with the NAACP unless Hill mended his ways.[50]

Randolph, Wilkins, Hill, and Meany met in March, 1959, to discuss what Meany called the "unfounded" complaints of the NAACP regarding the Federation's policy on civil rights. By the time the meeting ended, the AFL-CIO had assured the NAACP of "its continuing determination to strive for the elimination of discrimination in the American trade union movement as prescribed in the AFL-CIO Constitution." Both the Federation and the NAACP agreed to continue to cooperate "within and without the labor movement."[51]

---

49. See the following clippings in BSCP Papers, CD: "Bias in Labor's Ranks," New York *Times*, January 10, 1959; "Labor and Race," New York *Post*, January 7, 1959; "NAACP Attacks Bias in Unions," *Business Week*, January 10, 1959, pp. 78–80; New York *Herald Tribune*, January 5, 1959; *Christian Science Monitor*, January 10, 1959. See also Wilkins to Meany, December 19, 1958, in BSCP Papers, CD.

50. Myrna Bain, "Organized Labor and the Negro Worker," *National Review*, June 4, 1963, p. 455.

51. News Release from the AFL-CIO, March 20, 1959, Statement released by Meany and Wilkins, both in BSCP Papers, CD; *Black Worker*, April, 1959, p. 7.

Hill's charges were not so easily dismissed, however. They were based on the deteriorated position of black workers relative to that of whites, a situation for which Hill believed the unions were largely to blame. Unions discriminated against blacks by a variety of methods, according to Hill: by excluding them according to custom, or according to agreement between employers' associations and unions to hire white union members over blacks; by insisting on segregated working conditions for blacks; and by establishing auxiliary organizations for blacks that did not offer equal employment opportunities. No black attending high school, whether integrated or segregated, need learn the printer's trade, plumbing, bricklaying, or electrical work because he had no chance to join a major union. As a result, the average rate of unemployment among blacks in 1963 was almost twice that for whites. Although the South was accused of tokenism in school integration, "the fact remains that there are still more children attending integrated schools in the South today than parents working and belonging to integrated unions," noted one observer.[52]

Randolph endorsed the NAACP's detailed criticisms of the civil rights record of the AFL-CIO. Addressing the NAACP convention in June, 1961, Randolph said that the NALC considered the association's report "timely, necessary and valuable," its basic statements true and sound: The BSCP, he remarked, had "presented these facts to convention after convention of the American Federation of Labor for a quarter of a century."[53]

Testifying before the House Committee on Education and Labor later that month, Randolph spoke of the need for understanding among whites of the problem facing the black community: a crisis of unemployment almost two and a half times greater than that of the white community. Fair employment practices legislation was meaningless if blacks were denied the opportunity to secure industrial and technical training. Less than 1 percent of apprentices in the American construction industry were black. If in apprenticeship programs at all, blacks were trained in shoe repair, upholstery, and cooking for restaurants. Since craftsmen earned higher wages than unskilled workers, the dearth of trained black craftsmen deprived the Afro-American community as a whole by denying it a potential source of high income. These facts explained why Afro-Americans constituted a permanently depressed segment of American society, Randolph

52. Bain, "Organized Labor and Negro Worker," 455.

53. Hill, "Racial Practices of Organized Labor," in Jacobson (ed.), *Negro and American Labor Movement,* 290.

maintained.[54] Conditions for blacks in the labor movement had become so bad that the NAACP chapter in Connecticut refused to counsel blacks against strike breaking.

Preventing an open break between organized labor and the NAACP, his two most important allies, became Randolph's primary objective at the 1961 NALC convention. Toward this end, Randolph would not allow black and Puerto Rican members of the International Ladies Garment Workers Union to testify before the House Labor Committee in its investigation of Hill's charges. He tried to steer a middle course at the convention by praising Hill and trying not to affront Meany—a difficult task. In his keynote address to the convention, Randolph said, "It is not the function of the NALC to become the ally of any Congressional Committee of politicians to help train its guns of investigation through harassment and persecution against the ILGWU, the union of our fellow workers, brothers and sisters." Yet the resolution passed by the convention stated: "This Convention views any attack on the NAACP as ultimately attacks on all of us who support the NAACP's program." Caught in the controversy between his trade union allies and the seemingly antilabor stance being adopted by the NAACP, Randolph proposed that Wilkins and Dubinsky try to work out their differences. If, ultimately, they could not, he suggested that they turn the disagreement over to an arbitration panel composed of prominent citizens.[55]

A few days after the convention, Meany and other AFL-CIO leaders signed pledges sponsored by the President's Committee on Equal Employment Opportunity "to eliminate discrimination . . . and unfair practices wherever they exist." In the wake of his rapprochement with the NALC, Meany said: "Even a little discrimination in the labor movement is too much. It makes a mockery of our principles and must be wiped out."[56]

The split between the NAACP and organized labor also affected black-Jewish relations, despite the traditional financial and moral support given to Afro-American causes by Jews. Jewish unions maintained the Jewish Labor Committee, with field offices in major cities, to promote equali-

54. Excerpts from Randolph's Statement Before the House Committee on Education and Labor in New York City, June 16, 1961, rpr. in *Black Worker*, June, 1961, p. 3+.
55. Thomas Brooks, "The Negro's Place at Labor's Table," *Reporter*, December 6, 1962, pp. 38–39; New York *Times*, November 10, 1962.
56. Brooks, "Negro's Place at Labor's Table," 39.

tarian policies and perform advisory and fact-finding services for the AFL-CIO. When conflict arose between the NAACP and the AFL-CIO, the Jewish Labor Committee's representatives, not all of whom were Jewish, sided with the Federation. These differences were aired publicly in the mass media. Hill's allegations, which appeared in *Commentary* magazine in 1959, brought emphatic denials from the Jewish Labor Committee's representatives. Hill replied that Jews should stop apologizing for racists in the labor movement and join with black workers and the NAACP in directly attacking the broad pattern of racial discrimination. He maintained: "The civil rights department of the AFL-CIO is a public relations department. It's a hollow ritual and a cover-up. It's a complete fraud. Unions take the lily-white clauses out of their constitutions but go right on practicing job discrimination. The union leaders go right on collecting brotherhood medals and then turn around and tell me, 'Hill, don't rock the boat.'"[57]

In December, 1959, an article appeared in the Pittsburgh *Courier* stating that black and Jewish labor leaders were on the brink of outright warfare. The article gave several reasons for the split, among which were the failure of the AFL-CIO Civil Rights Committee to move against Jim Crow practices; the "reckless effort" by certain staff members of the Jewish Labor Committee to "assume the primary role" of leadership in the civil rights activity of labor; and the "paternalistic and missionary" attitude of Jewish labor leaders toward blacks. According to the writer of the article, Jews accused blacks of being blacks first and trade unionists second. For their part, blacks resented Zimmerman's leadership of the AFL-CIO Civil Rights Department since he was also chairman of the Jewish Labor Committee and vice-president of the garment workers' union—the union whose reluctance to give blacks official and staff positions originally instigated the controversy. Rumors circulated that Zimmerman had even wanted to bar Hill from meeting with Meany, Randolph, and Wilkins in March of that year. Randolph, the NUL, and the NAACP all denounced the *Courier* article.[58]

Emanuel (Maury) Muravchik, a longtime Jewish ally of Randolph's, was appalled at the *Courier* article, which he thought was designed to

57. Hill, quoted in Joseph Wershba, "Closeup: NAACP's Labor Secretary Herbert Hill," New York *Post*, December 14, 1959.

58. Harold L. Keith, "Will Negro, Jewish Labor Leaders War over Civil Rights?" Pittsburgh *Courier*, December 12, 1959.

"drive wedges between old co-workers and comrades in a common cause," and encouraged Randolph to repudiate it. Whether he would have done so without prompting from Muravchik is unclear, but Randolph did release a statement implying that the article sounded anti-Semitic, though the *Courier* itself was not. Even though differences of opinion might arise, as they had over Hill's statements, Randolph wanted to "emphatically affirm that there is no war over civil rights between Negro and Jewish labor leaders and in my opinion such a thing is utterly unthinkable." Still, Randolph tried to straddle the fence, saying that although some labor leaders condemned Hill's report, in his opinion it was "timely, factual and constructive." Randolph went on to observe that blacks and Jews had worked together in the Prayer Pilgrimage and youth marches, "but even if Jewish labor leaders were not active in opposition to racial bias, Negro labor leaders would be indulging in suicidal folly to foster or countenance the dangerous and poisonous doctrine of anti-semitism." Responding to a point in the *Courier* article, Randolph said that he had not recognized a paternalistic attitude among Jewish labor leaders. In any case, such a posture was "not peculiar to Jews" but was a "sickness of our American culture" and even more common in non–trade union circles.[59]

The conflict was exacerbated in 1962 when Hill testified before a House education and labor subcommittee investigating the extent of discrimination in the garment industry. Hill, himself a Jew, claimed that his position had been misinterpreted: The discrimination he had documented was the result not of a conscious racist ideology but of the changing racial complexion of a trade being entered by increasing numbers of black and Puerto Rican operators. Injustice resulted from efforts of the all-white union leadership to maintain control in the face of fear that this new constituency was a growing threat to its hegemony.[60]

When the NAACP came out in support of Hill, Zimmerman resigned from the board of trustees of the Legal Defense and Educational Fund. Thus, even though Meany had recognized the NALC, relations between organized labor and the black community worsened over conditions in the garment workers' union. Ironically, it had traditionally been the fore-

59. Emanuel Muravchik to Randolph, December 11, 1959, in BSCP Papers, LC; *Black Worker*, January, 1960, p. 4; Statement for Release, December 24, 1959, in BSCP Papers, LC.
60. Marshall, *Negro and Organized Labor*, 76.

most liberal trade union in the country with the best record on race relations. Randolph himself had held Dubinsky and his union up as models
that were "not only free from racial prejudice, but [willing to] join with
Negro organizations to fight racial discrimination." Certainly the garment workers' union had always supported Randolph's racial betterment
schemes, and in 1944 it had earned his commendation for having not
only "thousands of black members but also paid Negro officials."[61]

Early in 1963, however, a report financed jointly by the United States
government and New York City confirmed Hill's analysis of the status of
blacks in the International Ladies Garment Workers Union. Thereupon,
Randolph became head of a New York group, A Citizens Committee for
$1.50 Minimum Hourly Wage, which accused the union of vested inter-
est in perpetuating exploitation, low-wage pockets, and poverty in the
city. The group worked for an increase in the minimum wage and the extension of the minimum wage law to all workers. At a "Freedom from
Poverty" rally in Harlem in February, 1964, Randolph issued a call for a
march on Albany on March 10 to press the demand for a $1.50 hourly
wage in the state. "New York State is the economic capital of our so-
called 'affluent society.' Yet," Randolph maintained, "in our state hundreds of thousands of families live not in affluence, but in poverty and deprivation." Blacks and Puerto Ricans constituted "an increasingly larger
and disproportionate segment of a growing underclass," the evidence of
which could be seen in the ghettos. Randolph warned that minorities
would "no longer tolerate in silence the abdication of responsibility by
public officials."[62]

Together with Bayard Rustin, Randolph led the march of three thousand on Albany. There the demonstrators demanded equal civil rights
and social reform from the governor and state legislature. Anna Hedgeman, in what by now had come to be the standard criticism of Randolph's stewardship, noted: "We won the minimum wage for which we
were working but fell apart as an organization, largely because Mr. Ran-

61. Statement of Resignation from Board of Trustees of NAACP Legal Defense and Educational Fund by Charles S. Zimmerman, October 11, 1962, Harry Fleischman to Herbert
Hill, October 26, 1962, both in CORE Papers; *Black Worker*, December, 1944, p. 4.
62. Hill, "Racial Practices Organized Labor," in Jacobson (ed.), *Negro and American
Labor Movement*, 329; *Black Worker*, February, 1963, p. 2, February, 1964, pp. 1–2. The
joint report of the federal government and New York City was entitled "A Study of the
Consequence of Powerlessness and a Blueprint for Change."

dolph did not offer the continued leadership necessary to further success. We did not know whether this was an accident or merely a reflection of the complexity of his commitments."[63]

Despite the Albany march, there was noticeable improvement in the relationship between blacks and labor by the time of the 1963 AFL-CIO convention. Randolph was selected to lead the discussion of civil rights— the first time he had ever been given an official role in connection with civil rights at a Federation convention. Taking their cue from Meany, the delegates gave Randolph a standing ovation. And as the meeting progressed, Randolph and Meany stood together on "the strongest civil rights resolution ever put before an AFL-CIO convention."[64]

Meany had arrived at his changed point of view reluctantly, but at his own pace had begun to move against discrimination inside and outside of unions. During the summer, he had set up a special task force on civil rights in the AFL-CIO's executive council. The task force, which included Randolph, Walter Reuther, and William Schnitzler, accomplished a number of things in a few months, attacking "discrimination in all aspects of community life" through community drives and committees against discrimination in big cities.[65] Although a few still existed, segregated locals were disappearing through mergers.

At the convention, Randolph toned down his customary demands for direct sanctions against unions that practiced discrimination. He did, however, propose that Meany and Reuther visit places like Birmingham to view the situation of southern black activists first hand, that an AFL-CIO committee be appointed to meet periodically with leaders of the six national civil rights organizations, and that representative committees of black trade unionists and AFL-CIO officers be established to formulate techniques to combat discrimination at the union level. Although only one delegate moved to adopt Randolph's specific suggestions as an amendment, Meany pledged that the executive council would give them consideration. Randolph's unrelenting pressure through the years to rid the labor movement of discrimination seemed at last to have been re-

63. Peter M. Bergman, *A Chronological History of the Negro in America* (New York, 1969), 302–303; Hedgeman, *The Trumpet Sounds*, 168.
64. Thomas R. Brooks, "Better Day for Brother Randolph," *Reporter*, December 5, 1963, p. 23.
65. *Ibid.* C. J. Hafferty of the Building and Construction Trades Department also joined the task force.

234 A. Philip Randolph, Pioneer of the Civil Rights Movement

warded, and Meany now referred to him as "our own Phil Randolph."[66] Nevertheless, Meany and the others on the executive council refused to back Randolph's March on Washington in August, 1963.

Randolph brought to the NALC, his last attempt at organizing an all-black civil rights group, a lifetime of immersion in the race question and concern about both the economic and psychological consequences of racial prejudice. With only temporary setbacks, the white community had entered a period of unprecedented affluence, and expectations were rising in the black community. Operating within the labor movement, where Randolph had his strongest base of support, the NALC would seem to have had an excellent chance for success. Yet the council foundered, plagued by the contradiction of being a black group working on behalf of black interests at the same time that its leader was courting liberal whites to support black civil rights activities. Also, Randolph failed to get the backing of his old allies, liberal white labor leaders, for an NALC that seemed to exude black chauvinism.

Although they believed that blacks should have equal rights and a better chance for job opportunities, white liberals in the labor movement began to resist when they realized that capitulation to Randolph's demands would upset the economic status quo. Randolph was asking for more than jobs: He was demanding black representation in the power structure, where decisions were made. White liberals believed that Afro-Americans should be represented in the collective bargaining process; they were not willing, however, to voluntarily relinquish their own leadership positions to make room for blacks.

That so many of the liberals in the labor movement were Jewish proved to be another obstacle to the council's success. Despite his protestations, Randolph could never quite rid the NALC of the taint of anti-Semitism. Of necessity he had to support the NAACP, his only remaining ally, in its fight against the garment workers' union, yet this position alienated some of his staunchest backers, Jewish labor leaders Dubinsky and Zimmerman.[67]

66. *Ibid.*; Marshall, *Negro and Organized Labor*, 81.
67. See *Black Worker*, November, 1959, p. 2, for an example of the type of article that consistently appeared lauding Israel for its help to the new African nations.

Having cut himself off from white liberal backing, Randolph became more dependent than ever on the NAACP for financial support for his black labor group. As he had found so many times before, however, the interests of the association did not necessarily parallel his own. This proved to be the case when Randolph asked Wilkins to speak at the NALC's Workshop and Institute on Race Bias in 1961. Without other allies, Randolph was forced to ask Wilkins for a donation of $2,500. "Since our program and that of the NAACP are identical in purpose," Randolph wrote Wilkins, "I feel free to let you know that we have no money and need the financial and moral support of the NAACP." Although the NAACP considered the NALC "a necessary unit in the on-going campaign to eliminate racial discrimination from American life," Wilkins revealed that the association had unfortunately run a deficit in 1960 and, consequently, was curtailing contributions to "other organizations." Besides, Wilkins observed, "the NAACP is asked for a specific amount which happens to be very nearly the whole estimated cost of a two-day meeting." The association subsequently donated $200 toward the workshop, a sum that did not go far toward alleviating the deficit. The expenses of the workshop ran to nearly $21,000, and its organizers took in only about $11,000 in receipts.[68]

By the time of the second NALC convention in Chicago in November, 1961, the council was in deep financial trouble. The Chicago chapter of the NALC paid out more than $3,500 toward the cost of the convention, but asked to be reimbursed only $104 "in recognition of the financial condition of the National Office." The Chicago chapter also picked up most of the tab for the mass rally, though the proceeds went to the national office.[69] But even this was not enough; the NALC remained debt-ridden.

In addition to the initial conflict over admitting women to the executive council, other problems within the NALC came to light at its 1961 convention, although they were overshadowed at the time by the defense of Randolph from Meany's attack. The Randolph administration barely beat back an attempt to lower membership dues from four to two dollars. The move was initiated by a group of young Chicago and Detroit trade

68. Randolph to Roy Wilkins, January 11, 1961, Wilkins to Randolph, January 31, February 3, 1961, all in RP Papers.
69. Willoughby Abner to Richard C. Parrish, November 27, 1961, in BSCP Papers, LC.

unionists who thought that cheaper dues would help develop a more militant organization with a broader mass base. The militants believed that the NALC was too narrow in concept and direction, and they were not entirely wrong. Membership declined from 10,000 to 4,500 during the first two years of the organization's existence. Randolph concluded that AFL-CIO opposition was the primary factor in the council's failure to grow when other civil rights organizations were flourishing. In an effort to reverse the decline, he declared publicly: "We are going to maintain our alliance with organized labor. It would be folly to break this alliance." Randolph then turned his considerable conciliatory talents to wooing the Federation, and when Meany accepted an invitation to speak at the NALC's third annual convention in 1962, Randolph concluded that his presence was tantamount to official recognition and would overcome the problem of Federation opposition.[70] Randolph failed to realize that more than Meany's blessing was required to revive an NALC rent by internal bickering over divergent goals.

There were additional reasons for the decline in NALC membership, according to labor analyst Ray Marshall. Some observers believed that many black laborers refused to join because of the opposition of their white employers. Other black workers feared that a separate black labor federation would be welcomed by racists and confirm their lily-white policies. Communists were reported to be active in some affiliates, despite Randolph's efforts to minimize their influence. The NALC threat to expose as "Uncle Toms" those who disagreed with its methods and procedures was resented by still other unionists. Like most of Randolph's movements, the NALC had little support in the South, where almost half of the one and a half million black unionists lived. Some critics were concerned that the council followed black nationalist tactics, which threatened to produce racial splits within unions. Other observers and critics claimed that the NALC had neither the staff nor the program to launch a significant antidiscrimination effort.[71]

Yet in founding the NALC, Randolph had again identified a newly wakened segment of the black community—in this case trade unionists, who were part of the AFL-CIO largely because of Randolph's previous efforts. By the early 1960s, however, Randolph's ties to the Federation

70. Minutes of Emergency Meeting, NALC; Quote in Brooks, "Negro's Place at Labor's Table," 38–39.
71. Marshall, *Negro and Organized Labor*, 72–73.

circumscribed his militancy, and the activism of young unionists far out-stripped that of the elderly leader. Although critic Manning Marable's characterization of Randolph is too simplistic, there is some merit to his assertion that "Randolph consistently perceived the problem of union organizing from a 'top-down' rather than grassroots, mass-based ap-proach" and that "especially later in his career," Randolph "failed to trust the deep militancy of the black working class masses, relying instead upon tactical agreement with white presidents, corporate executives and labor bureaucrats."[72]

The NALC had undergone subtle change since its original conception. Randolph had envisioned it as a national clearinghouse through which problems common to black trade union members could be aired and clarified, as a vehicle for agitation, and as a symbol of the black worker's discontent. He wanted to strengthen the lines of communication between black trade unions across the country, as well as within specific commu-nities. In a sense, however, the NALC became an organization of leaders: Its core consisted of minor trade union officials and union staff members. They were capable, ambitious men, but to rise higher in the union hierar-chy they needed a power base, which was what they had hoped to obtain from the NALC. Initially the council was intended to act as a spokesman for Afro-American labor leaders within their own community and as a civil rights organization working with like-minded community groups. It quickly became a union caucus fighting for civil rights and jobs, how-ever.[73] The caucus function was partly stimulated by pressure within the black community for better job opportunities from the unions.

After the NAACP made its charges against trade union racism public, the NALC began to break the color barrier within the unions. The coun-cil's primary weapon was black community pressure. Blacks threatened to defeat union legislative goals and candidates unless they received a better break.[74]

The NALC could have done much to promote and protect black inter-ests within the labor movement and to mediate differences between the labor movement and the black community. It could have activated blacks within their organizations, served as a valuable source of information on union racial practices, gained black support for unions with equalitarian

72. Marable, *From the Grassroots*, 83, 81.
73. Brooks, *Toil and Trouble*, 255.
74. "Negro Pressure on Unions," 139+.

racial practices, served as a training ground for black leadership within the trade union movement, and brought constant moral and political pressure on the AFL-CIO to overcome discriminatory practices. But it did not make much progress on any of these fronts, partly because of the persistent racism, corruption, and bureaucracy in organized labor.[75] Also, Randolph was in his seventies by the time he organized the NALC and consequently not capable of the vigorous leadership the organization demanded if it was to be dynamically successful. Yet Randolph continued to rule the council in his customary authoritarian manner, maintaining tight control of the decision-making process. Furthermore, his ambivalence about the role of white liberals in the NALC made it difficult to sell the masses on the value of the organization and may help account for the NALC's never having had the impact it was expected to have.

Randolph was beginning to suffer from the conflict of interest caused by his allegiance to the AFL-CIO as the concerns of the Federation veered away from those of the black community—a conflict that would be exacerbated in the late 1960s by the issue of community control of schools.

The NAACP had declared open war on the AFL-CIO over the discriminatory policies of some of its member unions—an action Randolph was never willing to take. He always managed to keep friends in the Federation and maintain a mutually respectful relationship with George Meany, for in his mind, the importance of the coalition with labor transcended the faults of individual unions. Randolph had refused to break with the AFL in the 1930s to align himself with the CIO, whose ideology he shared; he was not about to break with the Federation in the 1960s when he had just succeeded in opening the coffers of organized labor to the black fight for civil rights. The AFL-CIO's changing position toward racial integration had significant, although not widely recognized, consequences for the civil rights struggle. The organization's lobbying efforts were instrumental in the passage of civil rights legislation. It backed the southern sit-in movement for access to public accommodations when few other groups were prepared to do so. And voter-registration drives in both the North and the South relied heavily on organized labor for their accomplishments.

The NALC was buffeted by these currents of the equality struggle outside the labor movement, and was also constantly pressured from the in-

75. Marshall, *Negro and Organized Labor,* 73.

side by young militants who wanted to break completely with the Federation and transform the NALC into a black separatist labor organization. Randolph viewed separation as merely a short-term tactic to gain eventual integration, but the young militants saw black nationalism as an end in itself. According to Thomas Brooks, "Much of the civil rights progress in the unions—and in the country—came about through the efforts of one man, A. Philip Randolph, and his union, the Brotherhood of Sleeping Car Porters."[76] Brooks's statement, though valid, does not reflect the complexity of Randolph's role, late in life, as a disciple of the old liberal left confronting the altered world of the black New Left. The dissension between the aging Randolph and the new breed of black militants foreshadowed the discord that would erupt within the civil rights movement itself later in the decade.

76. Brooks, *Toil and Trouble*, 250–51.

VII / The March on Washington

After the 1961 NALC convention, Randolph suggested a March on Washington, undoubtedly in part to quiet rebellious forces within the organization. In his November address to the convention, Randolph documented the slow progress, even the loss of ground, in civil rights achievements since the beginning of the "revolution." More blacks attended segregated schools in 1961 than in 1952; more were unemployed than in 1954. The median income of blacks had slipped from 57 to 54 percent of that of whites, and the black family was suffering under the strains of poverty and inequality. "Negroes are jobless all over the nation," Randolph said. "Young Negroes are discontented. They're in a state of unrest. As a matter of fact, they have dropped out of school, they're out of work, and they have run out of hope."[1]

The following March, Randolph presented his plan for a March on Washington with a decidedly economic thrust, and at a meeting of the national executive board of the NALC, action was taken to develop the Job Rights' March and Mobilization. Randolph sought the cooperation of the NAACP, the NUL, CORE, and the SCLC for the demonstration, which was originally scheduled for June 13 and 14. In conjunction with a mass lobbying campaign on Capitol Hill on the day preceding the march, he planned to request a conference with President Kennedy. He would select a group of black youth, out of the multitudes participating, to

1. Some NALC members had suggested a march to protest the firing of Theodore E. Brown by the AFL-CIO. See Minutes of the Emergency Meeting of the National Executive Board, Negro American Labor Council, May 6, 1961, and Negro Trade Unionists Move for Reinstatement of Theodore E. Brown, n.d., both in BSCP Papers, LC; Brooks, "Negro's Place at Labor's Table"; New York *Times,* November 10, 1962; Transcript of television broadcast "March on Washington . . . ," August 29, 1963, in BSCP Papers, LC.

lobby members of Congress to stress the plight of minority teenagers and the need for congressional action to bring relief. The specially chosen teenagers would dramatically illustrate what Randolph perceived to be the major problem plaguing blacks: inferior education at a time when technological innovation was reducing the number of unskilled jobs. By April, Randolph had decided to move his proposed march to a later date because Roy Wilkins, Whitney Young, and James Farmer, all of whom agreed to cooperate, "wanted to be in on the planning stages."[2]

Martin Luther King had also talked of calling a march on Washington to urge passage of a strong civil rights act by Congress. Concerned that two marches would dissipate the impact of each one, Anna Hedgeman urged Randolph to work with King toward combining the marches. Thereupon the month of the demonstration was changed again, from October to August, and Randolph's Job Rights' March and Mobilization became the March on Washington for Jobs and Freedom.[3]

Randolph's proposal came during a time of change in the civil rights movement. The plan Randolph had outlined for the March on Washington Movement in the early 1940s had been partially implemented in February, 1960, when black college students sat down at a segregated dime-store lunch counter in Greensboro, North Carolina, and refused to move until they were served. They had read CORE's pamphlet *Erasing the Color Line*, for which Randolph had written the introduction, and which documented the organization's sit-ins in the 1940s. The intellectual connections with the earlier nonviolent demonstrations were clear.[4] The students called in organizers from CORE to train them in nonviolent direct action. The sit-in movement soon spread across the South, and supporting groups were also formed in the North. In April the youths formed the Student Non-Violent Coordinating Committee (SNCC) under the guidance of King's SCLC. The youth organization had close ties with the SCLC at first, but was always an independent entity.

Shortly after the SNCC came into being, CORE organized "Freedom Ride, 1961" to test implementation of the Supreme Court ruling that ex-

2. Randolph to Whitney M. Young, Jr., March 26, 1963, in NUL Papers; Randolph to James Farmer, March 26, 1963, in CORE Papers; Meeting with Brother A. Philip Randolph, April 4, 1963, in NUL Papers.

3. Hedgeman, *The Trumpet Sounds*, 169–70.

4. James Farmer, Interview by Harri Baker, October, 1969, pp. 5–6, Oral History Collection, Lyndon Baines Johnson Library, Austin.

tended the ban on segregation in public transportation to terminal facilities. As a result of the publicity the action engendered, CORE became a major civil rights organization. In August, 1961, King announced plans to stage stand-ins where blacks were not permitted to register to vote. Sit-ins, wade-ins, and kneel-ins, he declared, would continue until segregation ended at lunch counters, pools, and churches. Randolph signaled his approval through an editorial in the *Black Worker* hailing King, Farmer, and Wilkins for refusing to agree to a "cooling off period" in the equal rights crusade.[5]

In the spring of 1963, black youths not participating in King's organized protest in Birmingham retaliated against police brutality. Untrained in, and uncommitted to, nonviolence, they ignited demonstrations and violence that spread throughout the country and provoked white counterviolence. Alarmed, Randolph wired Kennedy, urging "immediate federal action." He requested that the president send federal troops because the "reign of terror being waged against Negroes must end." As the civil rights protest changed from a primarily middle-class movement to one engaging the poor masses in the streets, and television cameras brought the ensuing carnage to the American dinner table, a new, militant young leadership emerged. Black students displeased with the existing black stewardship revolted against both the white and the black power structures.[6] The success of the student movement threatened existing leadership arrangements in the black community by sparking rivalry between organizations. Disagreements over strategy and tactics became intertwined with disputes between personalities and organizations. The four leading civil rights groups, the SCLC, the NAACP, CORE, and the SNCC, began "headline grabbing." Desiring prestige and financial contributions, each organization sought credit for the mounting demonstrations.

The established rights groups found themselves adversely affected by the changed circumstances. The student challenge to the existing black power structure ended the NAACP's hegemony over the civil rights issue, and made the association merely one of several groups contending for publicity and funds. Hard-pressed in the altered atmosphere, the NAACP

5. *Black Worker*, March, 1960, p. 1, August, 1961; Press Release, March 31, 1961, in CORE Papers; *Black Worker*, June, 1961, p. 3.

6. Telegram, Randolph to The President, March 27, 1963, in John F. Kennedy Papers, John F. Kennedy Library, Boston; Louis E. Lomax, *The Negro Revolt* (New York, 1962), 79.

finally decided to make direct action a major part of its strategy. But this decision, not an easy one for the association, had the effect of exacerbating tensions between the NAACP and the newer groups. Wilkins' complaint that more militant groups "furnish the noise" while the NAACP "pays the bills" caused one CORE member to charge him with doing violence to the movement with his "ill advised, untimely and uncalled for" statement. James Farmer, who left CORE to become program director of the NAACP between 1959 and 1961, stated that he tried to interpret the motivation, philosophy, and goals of the sit-ins for the staff, but because of the organization's emphasis on legal action, the NAACP "found it difficult to understand any tactic which involved violation even of the local law." For its part, the NUL, which continued to depend on the generosity and goodwill of white businessmen to provide jobs, training, and funds for its work, was never able to resolve the dilemma of projecting a more vigorous image to maintain credibility in the black community while maintaining its old patron-client relationship with its white benefactors. For a time, the collapse of the league seemed imminent.[7] The SNCC and the SCLC also drifted further apart as black students became disenchanted with both nonviolence and King's leadership.

Black youths began to listen to counsel such as that of Robert F. Williams from North Carolina, who was permanently expelled from the NAACP for advocating that blacks meet violence with violence and stop lynching with lynching. Although shocking to many conservatives in the NAACP, Williams' statements did not differ substantially from those of Randolph in 1919, when he urged those "confronted with lynching or mob violence to act upon the recognized and accepted law of self-defense." Randolph counseled *Messenger* readers, "Always regard your own life as more important than the life of the person about to take yours, and if a choice has to be made between the sacrifice of your life and the loss of the lyncher's life, choose to preserve your own and destroy that of the lynch-

---

7. Murray R. Kempton, "A. Philip Randolph: 'The Choice, Mr. Pres. . . . ,'" *New Republic*, July 6, 1963, p. 17; Lois E. Elie to Roy Wilkins, June 17, 1963, in CORE Papers; Hedgeman, *The Trumpet Sounds,* 70; James Farmer, interview by Harri Baker, October, 1969, p. 4, Oral History Collection, Lyndon Baines Johnson Library, Austin; Lester B. Granger to Stephen R. Currier, March 19, 1958, in NUL Papers; Medgar W. Evers to Gordon R. Carey, May 4, 1961, in CORE Papers. Despite their differences, the SNCC cooperated with CORE's freedom ride. See Edward B. King, Jr., to Gordon R. Carey, May 9, 1961, in CORE Papers.

ing mob."[8] The young Randolph who uttered those statements had not yet entered the mainstream.

Early in his administration, President Kennedy remained quiet on civil rights issues because of the same need to cater to the coalition of southern white Democrats and conservative Republicans that his predecessors had faced. But like Truman, Kennedy became appalled by the mounting violence and soon labeled civil rights a moral issue, whereupon he introduced a civil rights bill in 1963. The bill was an attempt by his administration to control what it feared was fast becoming an uncontrollable situation. The sponsors of the March on Washington chose August for their demonstration in the hope that it would coincide with the expected Senate filibuster of the proposed legislation.

Initially, the administration was not pleased at the prospect of thousands of blacks marching on Washington. Kennedy therefore invited Randolph and other civil rights leaders to a meeting at the White House on June 22, where they discussed the goals and program of the march and tactics to obtain passage of the new bill. The president, concerned about civil disruption and the likelihood of congressional backlash, expressed his reservations about demonstrations in the Capital during congressional debate. "The Negroes are already in the streets," Randolph noted, and added with undeniable logic, "If they are bound to be in the streets in any case is it not better that they be led by organizations dedicated to civil rights and disciplined by struggle rather than to leave them to other leaders who care neither about civil rights nor about non-violence?" Besides, Randolph concluded, "If the civil rights leadership were to call the Negroes off the streets, it is problematic whether they would come."[9]

Kennedy agreed that demonstrations brought results: They had pushed the executive branch and were forcing Congress to entertain legislation that would otherwise not have had a chance. But he was concerned that demonstrations during the legislative phase would prompt Congress to reject the civil rights bill. Randolph, however, argued, "These fires of discontent and unrest and aggressive action in the streets, highways and byways must be kept burning" because "Congress will not act on any

<hr>

8. Robert F. Williams, "USA: The Potential of a Minority Revolution," rpr. in Broderick and Meier (eds.), *Negro Protest Thought in the Twentieth Century,* 330; Editorial, "How to Stop Lynching," *Messenger* (August, 1919), 8–9.

9. Arthur M. Schlesinger, Jr., *A Thousand Days: John F. Kennedy in the White House* (Boston, 1965), 969–70.

meaningful civil rights legislation unless it is made to act by pressure." Randolph maintained that the March on Washington would supply that pressure by disturbing "the conscience of the oppressors." After the sponsorship of the march was widened to include white liberals, the president's attitude changed. Announcing that he supported the "peaceful assembly," Kennedy faulted those who expressed alarm over demonstrations but "never talk about the problem of redressing grievances."[10]

The original sponsors of the march were Randolph, president of the NALC; Wilkins, executive secretary of the NAACP; Whitney Young, executive director of the NUL; Martin Luther King, president of the SCLC; twenty-three-year old John Lewis, the new chairman of the SNCC; and James Farmer, head of CORE. When the month of the march was changed to August and emphasis placed on passage of the civil rights bill, Protestant, Catholic, and Jewish religious groups sought representation on the march committee. On July 2, two hundred civil rights leaders, delegates from sympathetic national organizations, and officials of the United Auto Workers assembled in New York for a daylong meeting about the march. The National Council of Churches was represented by Dr. Eugene Carson Blake, the American Jewish Congress by Rabbi Joachim Prinz, and the National Catholic Conference for Interracial Justice by Matthew Ahmann. Numerous individual religious groups were also present. To Randolph's chagrin, however, the AFL-CIO did not send a delegate, eighteen out of twenty members of the executive council having voted against participation.[11] This meeting marked the official broadening of the march sponsorship from the sextet of civil rights leaders known as the Big Six to the Big Ten interracial coalition of black rights groups, religious groups, and labor. Both Randolph and Walter Reuther of the United Auto Workers represented labor.

As director of the march, Randolph had authority to name his administrators and turned again to Rustin, whom he considered the best organizer in the country. Other leaders supporting the project opposed the selection of Rustin, fearing that segregationists would smear the march by denouncing him on the floor of Congress as a Communist, a draft dodger, and a sex pervert. Rustin was vulnerable to all these charges be-

10. *Ibid.; Black Worker,* June, 1963, p. 6; News Release, Democratic National Committee, July 18, 1963, in NUL Papers.

11. See pamphlets in ULP Records; John DeVito to Randolph, September 6, 1963, in BSCP Papers, LC. See also WMCA Radio Editorial, August 20–21, 1963, in NUL Papers.

cause of his youthful affiliation with the Young Communist League, his prison sentence for refusing to serve in World War II on grounds of pacifism, and his arrest and conviction on a morals charge in California ten years earlier. Both King and Randolph rushed to Rustin's defense, however, Randolph voicing "complete confidence" in Rustin's "character, integrity and extraordinary ability." The object in bringing up Rustin's past, Randolph asserted, was not concern about Rustin but the hope of "discredit[ing] the movement." In a rare display of humility, Wilkins, who was adamantly against Rustin, later admitted, "History has attached the name of Reverend King to the march, but I suspect it would be more accurate to call it Randolph's march—and Rustin's." [12]

Influenced by Randolph, the 1963 march was initially economic in emphasis. Reflecting a compromise with the desire of the supporting organizations to stress the civil rights bill, its focus changed to the double goals of jobs and freedom. The call stated: "In their historic non-violent revolt for freedom, the Negro people are demanding the right to decent jobs. . . . [T]here is no way for Negroes to win and hold jobs unless the problems of automation, a stagnant economy, and discrimination are solved; therefore, the Federal government must establish a massive works program to train and employ all Americans at decent wages and at meaningful and dignified labor." [13]

Accordingly, the march demands were divided into two categories. Those in the first category included the prompt passage by Congress of effective, meaningful civil rights legislation; immediate desegregation of the nation's schools; and an end to police brutality directed against citizens using their constitutional right of peaceful demonstration. The demands in the second category included a massive federal public works program to provide jobs for the unemployed, accompanied by federal legislation to promote an expanding economy; a federal fair employment practices act to bar discrimination by the government, private employers, and trade unions; broadening of the Federal Fair Labor Standards Act to cover areas of employment where blacks and other minorities still

12. Rustin, *Down the Line,* 109–10; New York *Times,* August 16, 1963; Edward P. Gottlieb to Randolph, October 23, 1963, in BSCP Papers, LC; Mayer, "Lone Wolf of Civil Rights," 78. The selection of Rustin brought similar criticism from blacks who feared his "bad background." See, for example, Frank T. Walker to James Farmer, August 21, 1963, in CORE Papers; Wilkins, *Standing Fast,* 292.

13. Call, in ULP Records.

worked at slave wages; and the establishment of a national minimum wage of not less than $2 per hour—double the $1-per-hour legal minimum at the time.[14]

Dissension developed as the liberal white religious groups backing the march demurred at the demand for a $2 minimum wage and some of the other economic planks. Consequently, the minimum wage demand was modified to state that $2 per hour, according to government surveys, was the minimum income needed to guarantee a decent standard of living. A postscript added to the eight-page organizational manual stated that support of the march did not necessarily denote endorsement of every demand listed. Although its backers insisted that using the discretionary formula was better than truncating the demands to elicit universal approval, the compromise left the march organizers open to criticism.[15]

The march was to be nonpartisan: Neither funds nor organized participation was accepted from political parties. As would be expected of a Randolph movement, there was undue concern over possible Communist subversion. The aid or participation "of totalitarian or subversive groups of all persuasions" was expressly rejected.[16] Rustin decided to limit the list of sponsoring organizations to make Communist infiltration less likely.

To carry out their first task, publicizing the march, Rustin and his small staff of black and white volunteers circulated pamphlets, handbills, letters, and copies of the organizational manual. Pamphlets featuring the slogan "the time is NOW" were sent to all sponsoring organizations, which distributed them throughout the country. Participating groups were advised to make it a "main task" to bring the unemployed to the march by raising funds for their transportation—preferably, one unemployed person for every three workers able to pay their own way. Sponsoring groups were asked to lobby for the declaration of August 28 as Freedom Day in their states. These organizations were also asked to urge employers to grant their workers the day off as a paid vacation, and to encourage ministers to set aside the Sunday before the march to pray for its success.[17]

14. From Organizing Manual No. 1, March on Washington for Jobs and Freedom, *ibid.*
15. Tom Kahn, "March's Radical Demands Point Way for Struggle," *New America,* September 24, 1963, p. 4; Organizing Manual No. 2, Final Plans for the March on Washington for Jobs and Freedom, in NUL Papers.
16. From Organizing Manual No. 1.
17. *Ibid.;* New York *Times,* August 21, 1963.

The logistics of an undertaking the size of the planned march were staggering, but Rustin had gained valuable experience from the earlier demonstrations. He emphasized decentralization: Each organization was to arrange for transportation and food for its members and see that its buses were furnished with first-aid supplies. To avoid road congestion, march organizers discouraged the use of personal cars; they asked groups to consider coming by train. All persons had to be under the leadership of locally appointed captains; each bus, train, and plane should have a captain, who would keep a register of the participants and be "responsible for [their] welfare and discipline." The cost of transportation and food was to be borne by each participant. The organizers suggested that each marcher bring peanut butter and jelly sandwiches, which would not spoil unrefrigerated. Marchers were advised not to bring children under the age of fourteen. First-aid tents would be set up to care for the elderly who suffered from the sweltering Washington weather, and entertainment was planned to amuse the crowd while it waited in the heat for the march to begin.[18]

As it became apparent that the idea of the march was gaining momentum and that huge crowds might converge on Washington, observers paid increasing attention to logistical details, asking where the marchers would be fed, how they would take care of personal hygiene, and how they would be transported to the appropriate places. Sympathetic congressmen in particular were concerned that the presentation of a poor image by blacks would hurt the chances for passage of civil rights legislation.[19] The manner in which these issues were addressed made the march, like Randolph's previous demonstrations, a tightly controlled event. Ushers from Washington churches were selected to seat the people. Police and marshalls were assigned to flank the platform reserved for invited guests, thereby creating an island between the platform and the seats. Additional chairs were to be disbursed throughout the grounds. Concession stands would serve hot and cold drinks, bag lunches, and candy bars. Doctors and nurses would be on hand, as well as ambulances, portable toilets, and drinking fountains.

18. Organizing Manual No. 1, Organizing Manual No. 2.
19. Congressman Charles G. Diggs, Jr., to Reverend Martin Luther King, June 27, 1963, in NUL Papers; Paul H. Douglas to Randolph, April 9, 1963, in NAACP Papers.

Only signs and standards prepared by the march organization were to be carried to prevent interlopers from injecting extraneous messages. The march committee supplied a list of approved slogans, all of which were to include the expressions "We Demand" and "NOW." The latter was the theme of the march. A review committee, chaired by Theodore Brown, would check signs as the marchers swung into line.[20]

"We have our own system of internal marshalling," the organizational manual said. "Some 2,000 trained men stand *ready* to assist you in maintaining order." The march committee's goal, which was surpassed, was to bring in one thousand marshals from New York alone. At instructional meetings, organizers told the marshals to wear white shirts and dark trousers and to create, by example, an atmosphere "of passive, peaceful, nonviolent behavior." Perhaps most important, the marshals were to help the marchers return to their vehicles after the march "as quickly as possible." The organizers emphasized that participants were to "depart from the city" at the conclusion of the program at the Lincoln Memorial: "This is a one day demonstration. The size and scope of this March make it imperative that all participants come and go out on the same day."[21]

Rustin worked closely with federal officials and civic and police authorities to ensure peaceful movement into the heart of the city. Police, National Guardsmen, and firemen, augmented by black volunteers, were detailed to patrol the critical area from the Washington Monument to the Lincoln Memorial. The Defense Department agreed to supply troops for military intervention "if found to be necessary," but the march committee did everything possible to avoid violence. "We are asking each person to be a marshal of himself," Rustin emphasized, "since anybody who turns to violence will be a traitor to our cause."[22]

Randolph's militant original plan called for a "two-day action program" beginning with "a mass descent on Congress and a carefully chosen delegation to the White House." Randolph wanted to so flood congressmen "with a staggered series of labor, church, civil rights delegations

20. List of proposed slogans in NUL Papers; March on Washington Committee Meeting, August 17, 1963, *ibid.*; Organizing Manual No. 1.

21. Organizing Manual No. 2; Marshall's Manual, in NUL Papers.

22. Walter D. Tobriner (interviewee), recorded interview by Charles T. Morrissey, July 6, 1964, p. 4, John F. Kennedy Library Oral History Program, Warren R. Young and William Lambert, "Marchers' Master Plan," *Life*, August 23, 1963, p. 70.

from their own states that they would be unable to conduct business on the floor of Congress for an entire day." The delegation to the White House would put before the president proposals for legislative and executive action. The next day a mass rally would be held with the twofold purpose of projecting the marchers' "Emancipation Program" to the nation and of reporting the response of the president and Congress to the action of the previous day. The importance of the mass rally was originally subordinated to that of the lobbying effort. But talk about "sit-ins in the galleries of the House and the Senate and that sort of thing" clearly upset the administration, and according to Kennedy's biographer, the president persuaded the civil rights leaders in their June 22 conference with him not to lay siege to Capitol Hill.[23]

The plan was then amended so that marchers would assemble by state at points throughout the city and meet with their congressional representatives. When the number of participants grew larger than originally anticipated, this plan too was abandoned, and rather than have separate state locations, all buses were to proceed directly to the Washington Monument. The revised organizing manual noted, "In keeping with this new—and more profound—concept of lobbying, our 100,000 marchers will not go to Capitol Hill nor to the White House" but would invite the congressmen "to come to us." Invitations signed by the ten cochairmen were mailed to legislators, "cordially" requesting them to attend to hear "demands from your constituents for jobs and freedom."[24] Seats for legislators would be reserved in a special section marked "Congress," and the names of those attending would be made public.

This procedure represented a departure from the precedent set by other marches on Washington, in which the demonstrators went to Capitol Hill to present their petitions. Although 150 congressmen did attend the rally, Senator Hubert Humphrey believed that "the opportunity for constructive support of civil rights legislation was reduced considerably" by the decision to eliminate lobbying by separate state delegations. Humphrey argued that every participant, not just a chosen few, needed a spe-

23. Preamble, n.d., in CORE Papers; Theodore Sorenson (interviewee), recorded interview by Carl Kaysen, May 3, 1964, p. 141, John F. Kennedy Oral History Program. This view is confirmed by Simeon Booker (interviewee), recorded interview by John F. Stewart, April 24, 1967, p. 37, John F. Kennedy Oral History Program; Schlesinger, *Thousand Days*, 972.

24. Organizing Manual No. 2; New York *Times*, August 26, 1963.

cific objective. "Marching from the Washington Monument to the Lincoln Memorial simply cannot substitute for a direct meeting between the respective state groups and their Congressional delegations. Both activities are needed if the March is to be worth the tremendous time and effort that is being expended." Humphrey, therefore, "strongly" recommended reinstating the plan for morning meetings with congressmen, but this was not done.[25]

Most observers believed that the decision to center the march program on the Lincoln Memorial rather than on the Capitol was crucial. Kennedy's aide Theodore Sorenson maintained that he did not know whether the civil rights leaders themselves or government officials were responsible for the change. The White House and the Justice Department may have played a role in the decision, he said.[26]

After the violence in Birmingham, the civil rights movement had become grist for the media mill. As the idea of the march gained momentum, the word went out that it would be "the most covered event . . . in the history of this country." By August 19, fifty-five countries had applied for press passes. The march committee, aware of the spotlight trained on the upcoming event, tried to circumvent problems that might arise—a feat made more difficult by individual organizational sensitivities. Noting that press reports on confusion and disorganization, as well as the difficulty of keeping track of all events, "can . . . contribute to critical reporting, no matter how effectively the march is organized," the march committee deemed it essential for the sponsoring organizations to coordinate an information program for the march and put it into effect as quickly as possible. This recommendation was, however, "in no sense" intended to diminish the role of the public relations staffs of the cooperating organizations.[27]

Some staff members of the NUL were eager to take advantage of the opportunities opened by the media exposure. Thomas Hanlon, for one, believed that "no one in the *sextet* except Randolph" was prepared to exploit the opportunity presented by white religious support for the

25. Germantown *Courier*, September 5, 1963, in ULP Records; Hubert L. Humphrey to Stephen Currier, August 12, 1963, in NUL Papers.

26. Sorenson, interview by Kaysen, 143.

27. Sterling Tucker to Executive Directors of Urban League Affiliates, August 19, 1963, Memo on Information Policy for the August 28 March on Washington, n.d., both in NUL Papers.

march, "to bring off a huge victory where only a small one was originally intended." According to Hanlon, Randolph was "surrounded" by associates reluctant to utilize these new openings. Hanlon also believed that the pope "'*ordered*,' not suggested" the "now massive Catholic presence" in the demonstration, but the American bishops were not sufficiently interested to follow through on the church's dictum.[28]

In Hanlon's opinion, the regular staffs of the sponsoring groups and the veteran small-scale march experts on Rustin's staff could not envision the unique opportunity presented by the massive television audience. To take advantage of the publicity, Hanlon suggested that the march committee take sign making out of Rustin's "sole" control and get graphics displays more appropriate to television. Hanlon thought that Rustin would probably "not give up his super-centralized control system unless he is actively coerced or seduced, no matter how clear it is that the system is over-burdened and unable to exploit new opportunities that he may well like to see exploited."[29]

The extensive media involvement played an important role in the shifting of priorities. Tom Kahn, a protégé of Rustin, noted that the march received unprecedented coverage, but that the ten demands were "conspicuously downplayed." These demands, he believed, were what gave the march its "radical character," and its uniqueness came from infusing the demand for "freedom now" with economic content—a recognition "that there can be no political or social freedom without economic security."[30] But the news media were only interested in the spectacular: they emphasized the pageantry and interracial nature of the march and downplayed its ideology.

Apprehension remained that the establishment might take over the parade part of the march, and more if possible. Hanlon realized that key parts of the "law and order crowd" wanted to keep "the white-centered status quo" and would use every possible means to do so. He thought that the march committee should be aware that such persons could, and probably did, advise the rest of the establishment to "join 'em and control 'em." Writing to Whitney Young, Hanlon urged adoption of his ideas even though some members of the Big Six and their followers might not like a "*broad* alliance" instead of the relatively "*narrow* civil rights plus

28. Memorandum, Thomas J. Hanlon to Whitney M. Young, Jr., August 13, 1963, *ibid.*
29. *Ibid.*
30. Kahn, "March's Radical Demands," 1.

labor" front. The pluralist approach implied by the massive religious activity would not sit well with the more radical followers of Farmer and Forman and was probably "beyond the capacity or desire" of most of the sponsors.[31] The divergence of goals, both among the sponsoring groups and between the sponsors and the media, thus pushed the march in unanticipated directions.

When the march was first discussed, Young suggested to Randolph that the effort would be strengthened by asking the National Council of Negro Women to join the group of cosponsors. Randolph failed to contact the council, and as a result, the heads of all the sponsoring organizations and all the proposed speakers for the march were male. Anna Hedgeman then voiced her dissatisfaction over the slighting of women. The program committee responded that "since it is imperative that the role of women in the struggle be made clear," Rosa Parks, Mrs. Medgar Evers, Daisy Bates, Gloria Richardson, and Diane Nash Bevell would, on Randolph's suggestion, be invited to participate in the program. But because of "the difficulty of finding a single woman to speak without causing serious problems vis-a-vis other women and women's groups" the Committee decided that the best way to "utilize these women" would be for the chairman to introduce them, describe their role in the freedom struggle, and trace their spiritual ancestry back to Sojourner Truth and Harriet Tubman. The women would then stand for applause. The chairman's statement "would be well worked out" to give "a clear picture of the vital role the women have played in the Freedom Movement."[32]

Perceiving this plan as patronizing, Hedgeman wrote Randolph, "In light of the role of Negro women in the struggle for freedom and especially in light of the extra burdens they have carried because of the castration of our Negro men in this culture, it is incredible that no woman should appear as a speaker." Hedgeman argued that the difficulty of selecting one woman to speak was not an acceptable excuse; after all, the choice of the Big Six sponsors was not approved by all other black male leaders, but that did not deter their selection. She asserted that if her original suggestion—that the heads of the Negro women's organizations be on the national committee with the six men—had been adopted, black women would have had a responsible group to discuss their proper repre-

31. Memorandum, Hanlon to Young.
32. Young to Randolph, April 2, 1963, Proposed Program—Lincoln Memorial, both in NUL Papers.

sentation on the program. "Since the 'big six' have not given women the equality of participation which they have earned through the years," a woman rather than Randolph should introduce the "heroines," she stated. Insisting that her suggestion be adopted, Hedgeman noted "[My] service to the 'March Idea' . . . has been of the quantity and quality which merits reasonable recognition of my proposal." When Randolph failed to answer her, Hedgeman sent copies of her letter to the other five black cosponsors. That female fund-raisers for the NALC raised $14,000 for the march helped Hedgeman win her point, and Mrs. Evers was chosen to introduce the other "heroines."[33]

As the program for the march evolved, there was a lessening of emphasis on the jobless, who were initially projected as a quarter of the marchers. The program at first included a two-minute-long "carefully prepared talk" by one black and by one white unemployed worker, but as the priorities gradually shifted to civil rights demands, concern for the jobless evaporated. No longer was it deemed necessary to raise funds to bring in those who could not afford to pay their own way, and the unemployed were quietly dropped from the final program.[34]

Nor were these the only changes. John Lewis and James Forman insisted that the march include demonstrations against the Justice Department. "There was no serious opposition to this idea but somewhere later in the negotiations the plan was dropped—unquestionably to satisfy the white liberal contingent," Forman complained later.[35]

The march took place on August 28, an ideal summer day. In all, 250,000 well-dressed marchers arrived in Washington in excellent order. There was no trouble. White Washington stayed home; fewer than half of the federal government and District employees went to their jobs. All liquor stores and bars were closed. One observer described the atmosphere as "a combinaton of church picnic and political rally." Official placards reading "We March for Integrated Schools Now," "We Demand an End to Bias Now," and "We March for Jobs for All Now" were given out at headquarters near the Washington Monument. Checking in, each marcher signed a pledge stating, "I affirm my complete personal commitment for

33. Hedgeman to Randolph, August 16, 1963, AAH to ———, August 20, 1963, Program, March on Washington, all *ibid.*; Hedgeman, *The Trumpet Sounds*, 178.

34. Proposed Program—Lincoln Memorial; Program, March on Washington, in NUL Papers.

35. Forman, *Making of Black Revolutionaries*, 331–32.

the struggle for jobs and freedom for all Americans," and promised to remain nonviolent and not "relax until victory is won." In an effort to extend the participants' commitment beyond the one day of the demonstration, organizers also asked them to pledge "to carry the message of the March to my friends and neighbors back home and to arouse them to an equal commitment and an equal effort."[36]

The occasion, the culmination of a twenty-two-year-old dream, was somewhat marred for Randolph by the death of his wife three months earlier. Nevertheless, he fulfilled his role as chairman, giving the opening remarks and presenting the speakers. In his speech Randolph emphasized that "this is not the climax to our struggle but a new beginning" and prophesied that "wave after wave" would come back to Washington "if immediate changes were not made in American life." Randolph described the marchers as "the advance guard of a massive moral revolution for jobs and freedom." Then he tied the civil rights demands to the economic demands: "Yes, we want all public accommodations open to all citizens, but those accommodations will mean little to those who cannot afford them. Yes, we want a Fair Employment Practices Act, but what good will it do if profits geared to automation destroy the jobs of millions of workers, black and white? We want integrated public schools, but that means we also want Federal aid to education." Randolph understood that the realization of these objectives would "require many changes in the nation's political and social philosophies and institutions." He believed, however, that "we must destroy the notion that Mrs. Murphy's property rights include the right to humiliate me because of the color of my skin. The sanctity of private property takes second place to the sanctity of a human personality."[37]

In his speech, Wilkins paid tribute to his former colleague at the NAACP, W. E. B. Du Bois, who had died in Africa the day before the march at the age of ninety-five. Du Bois had grown embittered about life for blacks in the United States and been increasingly drawn toward the

36. "The 'March'—Photo Report," *U.S. News and World Report*, September 9, 1963, p. 39; Bernard Boutin (interviewee), recorded interview by Dan H. Fenn, Jr., June 3, 1964, p. 31, John F. Kennedy Library Oral History Program; New York *Times*, August 29, 1963. Pledge found in NUL Papers.

37. New York *Times*, April 15, 1963; "'March' Leader Randolph Struggle Just Begun He Says," *U.S. News and World Report*, September 9, 1963, p. 24; Lerone Bennett, Jr., "Masses Were March Heroes," *Ebony* (November, 1963), 119; New York *Times*, August 29, 1963.

Soviet Union. In 1961 he had joined the Communist party, and later took up residence in Ghana, where he became a citizen in 1963. Still, the death of Du Bois meant the loss of the great black intellectual of the early part of the century. Although he had veered away from the mainstream, Du Bois had been an inspiration to many of the march leaders.[38] Randolph had begun his career as a radical by denouncing Du Bois's conservativism, but by the time of his death, Du Bois had become far more radical than Randolph.

Martin Luther King, the last speaker, stirred the tiring crowd with his now famous "I Have a Dream" speech. To close the ceremonies, Randolph led the throng in the march pledge, after which participants boarded their buses and trains and left Washington. The leaders then went to the White House, where they gave Kennedy a brief report on the march and discussed the civil rights legislation pending in Congress. After listening to the president's summation of the situation in the House and Senate, Randolph remarked that clearly it would take nothing less than a crusade to win approval of the bill. "Nobody can lead this crusade but you," he tried to convince the president.[39] Kennedy, however, was more interested in quelling demonstrations than in leading a democratic crusade.

Although most attention has been paid to the leaders, one sociologist analyzed the marchers and found that the black participants were predominantly northern urbanites distinguished by their high education and income, their membership in civil rights organizations, and their high rates of prior activism. Equal job opportunities and school desegregation constituted the two areas in which they set their highest priorities and expected the greatest gains. The black marchers were least optimistic about obtaining integrated housing and greater respect from the white majority. Although they were uniformly in favor of future demonstrations, they were polarized over the tactic of civil disobedience. The white marchers, in contrast, were slightly more militant than the black.[40]

The only public expressions of disapproval of the march came from George Lincoln Rockwell, leader of the American Nazi party, and some

38. Wilkins, *Standing Fast*, 293.

39. Papers of John F. Kennedy, President's Office Files, Presidential Recordings, Item No. 108.2, August 28, 1963, March on Washington, Civil Rights Legislation, John F. Kennedy Library.

40. Albert E. Gollin, "Dynamics of Participation in the March on Washington," *Public Opinion Quarterly*, XXVIII (Winter, 1964), 648.

of his followers who gathered across from the rally, and from Black Muslim leader Malcolm X. He held a nearly nonstop news conference in a hotel during the march, denouncing the demonstrators for "seeking favors" from the white man's Government."[41] Behind the scenes, however, as we shall see, discord reigned.

Predictably, the intermediary leadership of the march displayed continuity with that of Randolph's other movements. Rustin was deputy director, and Cleveland Robinson of the NALC was chairman of the administrative committee. Others on that committee were Anna Hedgeman, Reverend Thomas Kilgore, Jr., from the Prayer Pilgrimage, Gloster Current of the NAACP, and Guichard Parris of the NUL. The coordinators were L. Joseph Overton of the NALC and Norman Hill, who would subsequently become an executive at the A. Philip Randolph Institute. Theodore Brown was also on the march staff. Not part of the Randolph clique were the southern administrators—Aaron Henry of the NAACP; Floyd McKissick of the SNCC; and Wyatt Walker, Martin Luther King's assistant—as well as representatives of the white religious groups. Even continuity of leadership, however, could not overcome the internal dissension.

To promote harmony and minimize jealousy, instead of choosing a chairman from one of the sponsoring groups Rustin gave the head of each group the official title of cochairman. But the coalition that produced the March on Washington was unstable from the beginning. The organizations diverged in strategy and tactics and would soon come to disagree on goals as well. King's SCLC, the SNCC, and CORE utilized direct action techniques; the NAACP, although it was beginning to project a more activist image, still emphasized legal procedures to obtain legislative and judicial relief; and the NUL continued to rely on interracial cooperation. Randolph originally planned that his labor organization, the NALC, would direct the Jobs Rights' March and Mobilization, but the council was itself suffering from internal strife. To foster cooperation, Randolph agreed that in cities where the NALC had local councils and had thus appointed a chairman, "each of the sponsoring organizations could appoint a co-chairman." In cities where the NALC did not have a local affiliate, the other sponsoring organizations could appoint a chairman.[42]

From early in March, 1963, when Randolph requested Whitney Young's "cooperation" in signing the Call for the Job Rights' March,

41. New York *Times*, August 29, 1963.
42. Meeting with Brother A. Philip Randolph.

Young was hesitant and wanted "clarification." The NUL, he said, preferred a relationship "which would suggest co-sponsorship rather than cooperation. We have found through some rather bitter experience that unless we participate at the level of planning and policy making, and are therefore together on decisions reached, embarrassing and unfortunate misunderstandings can occur." Young was concerned at the amount of planning and decision making already done by the executive board of the NALC. Regardless of what the march was called, he pointed out, its real goal was immediate legislative action and congressional activity. Since the NUL, unlike the other organizations, was "a tax-exempt agency and as such precluded from overt lobbying," it should not participate, he noted. But the southern sit-ins had put pressure on the NUL to take a more activist position; Young, therefore, pledged support in order not to "detract from the vigorous and forceful new image" that the NUL was "making every effort to project and implement."[43]

When the NUL finally overcame its qualms about jeopardizing its tax-exempt status and decided to participate in the march, the national office sent a memorandum to its affiliates distinguishing between responsible, broadly representative public demonstrations and picketing aimed against a specific employer, labor union, or institution. Arguing that the March on Washington fell in the former category, Young stated that its failing to identify itself with equal opportunity would "seriously damage our image and influence for a considerable time to come."[44]

Although the NUL wanted to be a cosponsor to dominate decision making, Young never felt he had such power and was continually concerned about exactly who was making decisions in the "intervals between meetings." The other sponsors, too, never completely trusted Rustin. The NUL consequently suggested that additional meetings be scheduled "minus the R-R team." League officials also feared that after the march Martin Luther King would utilize the demonstration files to garner publicity for himself.[45]

43. Young to Randolph, April 2, 30, 1963, Randolph to Young, May 16, 1963, all in NUL Papers.
44. Policy Statement on Non-violent Direct Action Techniques, Nos. 1–62, January 11, 1962, Confidential, Proposed Policy Statement with Reference to National Urban League Participation in the March on Washington, July 17, 1963, both *ibid.;* Andrew G. Freeman to Urban League Friends and Members, August 13, 1963, in ULP Records.
45. Sextet Agenda Comments, n.d., in NUL Papers.

Despite Young's professed desire for full cooperation with the march, the interests of the NUL clashed with those of the march committee. The NUL had just put forth its own domestic Marshall Plan, a massive "crash" program to help blacks take advantage of the various "equal opportunity" laws and policies.[46] The NUL, therefore, was more interested in publicizing its own plan than in promoting the march.

In addition to the problems between the sponsoring groups and Rustin's staff, there were also difficulties between the sponsoring groups themselves. Neither the NAACP nor the NUL was comfortable with the more activist organizations, and the leaders of both groups cooperated with white liberals in editing John Lewis' speech to make it less militant. When Farmer, who had been jailed for civil rights demonstrations, elected to remain locked up rather than attend the march, Young wired him to reconsider, saying that the movement needed a "symbolic and physical manifestation of unity."[47] Young himself, however, was unwilling to give the march priority over the interests of the NUL.

But the primary source of discord was financing. In keeping with his beliefs and a desire to stifle militant dissent within the NALC, Randolph first envisioned the march as a black-run event. "The finances for the March will come from various Negro groups and any liberal or labor groups that may be sympathetic, but," Randolph insisted, "we will rely upon Negro forces as a main source of the money to finance the March and Mobilization." The original fund-raising methods showed little change from those of other marches. Buttons displaying a black and a white hand clasped together were sold for 25¢ each, with the request that all proceeds be sent to the national office. Local sponsoring organizations were also asked to contribute to the national office. The Urban League of Philadelphia taxed each member $5 to meet its obligation, but as late as the following October, it was still trying to collect the money.[48]

As the projected march grew in size, it became apparent that such trifling sums would not go far in defraying the costs of the undertaking. The draft budget came to $117,240. Originally, $25,000 was set aside to pay for the transportation and other expenses of the unemployed and of

46. Press Release, August 2, 1963, *ibid.*
47. Telegram, Young to James Farmer, August 21, 1963, *ibid.*
48. Randolph to Young, March 26, 1963, *ibid.*; Randolph to James Farmer, March 26, 1963, in CORE Papers; Evangeline C. Bonner to members, October 11, 1963, in ULP Records.

groups wishing to voice protest that could not afford to pay their own way. Criticizing the budget, one NUL staffer noted that the appropriation for the unemployed might "drop by virtue of our not getting that much money in." He added, "It seems to me that no one will know anyway, on TV at least, because people will all look pretty much alike on parade." The $16,000 tab for loudspeaker equipment at the Lincoln Memorial was picked up by the United Auto Workers and the International Ladies Garment Workers Union, prompting Randolph to remark, "Although labor did not endorse the March, labor certainly supported the March." Even with unions contributing nearly half the projected budget and sponsoring organizations supplying staff members and volunteers and promising several thousand dollars to get the office work started, some observers wondered where the economically pinched black community would get the rest of the money.[49]

The answer to that question centered on Stephen R. Currier, a friend of the Kennedy family, and reveals why critics denounced the march as a sellout to white liberals. Currier and his wife, the granddaughter of millionaire Andrew Mellon, established the Taconic Foundation in 1958 because they believed that, as the possessors of wealth and advantages, they had an obligation to those less privileged than themselves. Studies conducted by the Taconic Foundation showed the most serious problem to be that of the "deprived" Afro-American, and the Foundation was devoting more and more money to alleviating the condition of blacks. Between the time of its establishment and August, 1963, the Foundation had contributed more than one million dollars to organizations working for equal rights for blacks—$400,000 in the first eight months of 1963 alone.[50] Currier became convinced that competition for funds was the central cause of the discord becoming apparent among the civil rights groups, and concluded that they needed greater coordination in their fund-raising activity. He began working toward a United Fund program for the civil rights organizations based on the model of the effective United Jewish Appeal. The Taconic Foundation founded the Council of

49. Draft Budget with handwritten notations, in NUL Papers; Young and Lambert, "Marchers' Master Plan," 63–70; A. Philip Randolph, "Today's Civil Rights Revolution," Address before the Fifth Constitutional Convention of the Industrial Union Department, AFL-CIO, November 8, 1963, p. 13.

50. New York *Times*, August 4, 1963. Currier had pumped $100,000 into the NUL in 1959, enabling the organization to remain viable. See Lester B. Granger to Stephen Currier, March 19, 1958, in NUL Papers. See also Taconic Foundation File, *ibid.*

Federated Organizations (COFO) to coordinate the Voter Education Project, a voter-registration drive in Mississippi, in 1963.

Largely through Currier's efforts, seven organizations also formed the Council for United Civil Rights Leadership (CUCRL) and the Committee for Welfare, Education and Legal Defense to coordinate fund raising. In Currier's view, the purpose of the CUCRL was to increase control over racial demonstrations to ensure that they would remain nonviolent, as well as to solicit $1.5 million in emergency funds for each of the member organizations to enable them to add to their professional staffs. Currier arranged a breakfast at the Kennedy-owned Carlyle Hotel in New York on June 19, 1963, at which the leaders of the seven organizations explained their needs to ninety-six corporation heads and foundation leaders. The meeting produced nearly $800,000 for the council. Although the announced aim of the CUCRL was to provide a forum for discussion, the primary element keeping the group intact was the promise and receipt of money. As Currier represented the source of funds, he did the most to hold the group together.[51]

Currier was present at the June 22 meeting between the civil rights leaders and Kennedy. The march sponsors did not believe that affiliation with Currier represented control over their activities and insisted that this was "not truly a case of infiltrating the revolution with money." Rather, they reasoned, "If you are going to have a revolution it might as well be solvent, and imbued with American know-how." But Currier's role left them open to censure. As if in support of the critics' view, Wilkins responded to one questioner, "It seems obvious that prevention of mayhem is one idea involved here."[52]

Although the Taconic Foundation denied contributing one million dollars to the march, and a spokesman for the march said that no such gift had been received, historian Louis Lomax asserted that if one dug "deep enough," one would find "some Kennedy money." This contribution, he argued, "was to reinforce the fabric of existing Negro leadership and keep things in hand." Even as sympathetic an observer as Lerone Bennett thought the march "was colored by the move to contain and control the rebellion." There is no question that the injection of enormous sums of money acted to drain off any display of militance and lessen black control

51. Forman, *Making of Black Revolutionaries*, 365–67.
52. Reese Cleghorn, "The Angels Are White—Who Pays the Bills for Civil Rights?" *New Republic*, August 17, 1963, p. 14.

of the demonstration. When Hubert Humphrey made suggestions about changing the format of the rally, for example, he made them to Currier, not to one of the black organizers.[53]

Even the speeches at the Lincoln Memorial came under white censorship. Rustin had left the selection of topics to the individual speakers, recommending only that they adhere to a strict time allotment. Given what we now know about the march's financial backers, the existence of an implicit agreement not to indulge in antiadministration rhetoric seems likely. Forman said that the SNCC wanted the march "to be the forum from which we articulated to the nation a militancy not heard before from civil rights organizations," but the "SNCC's intent was running in direct conflict with the intent of the power structure and most of the March leaders." As Forman saw it, "A blowup was inevitable."[54]

The day before the march, when John Lewis' speech was released to the press, it became known that he planned to announce, "The next time we march, we won't march on Washington, but we will march through the South, through the heart of Dixie, the way Sherman did." Hearing this, Cardinal O'Boyle of the Washington diocese stated his refusal to appear on the same platform as Lewis unless the latter's speech was altered. O'Boyle and Eugene Carson Blake also objected to Lewis' saying that the SNCC could not support the Kennedy civil rights bill. A committee was appointed to revise Lewis' speech, but it remained the most militant of the day.[55]

Because of this white intervention, militants ridiculed the march. Claiming that it "turned into a victory celebration for the Kennedy administration and its supporters," Forman argued that behind the backs of the militants, the sponsors and the administration had devised ways the march "could be used to advance their own respective interests." The SNCC had hoped that Lewis' speech "would puncture the tranquility of the March and the efforts of the Kennedy administration to make this look like a popular uprising in favor of his Civil Rights Bill." But according to Forman, the image of the United States had suffered abroad from

53. Lomax, quoted in Philadelphia *Inquirer*, August 20, 1963; Lerone Bennett, Jr., *Confrontation: Black and White* (Chicago, 1965), 285; Hubert H. Humphrey to Stephen Currier, August 12, 1963, in NUL Papers.

54. Forman, *Making of Black Revolutionaries*, 334–35.

55. *Ibid.*; New York *Times*, August 29, 1963; Lewis, *King*, 223–24. The committee consisted of Randolph, King, Abernathy, Rustin, Courtland Cox, Eugene Carson Blake, Forman, a representative of the Catholic Interracial Committee on Justice, and Lewis.

the publicity given to pictures of protesters in Birmingham being attacked by police dogs; as a result, "the United States Government as a whole worked diligently to make the March appear as one where black and white could come together in the 'democratic' U.S.A. and peacefully protest." Forman asserted, "People all over the country thought they were marching for jobs and freedom when in actuality the sellout leadership of the March on Washington was playing patsy with the Kennedy administration as part of the whole liberal-labor politics of Rustin, Wilkins, Randolph, Reuther, King, the Catholic and Protestant hierarchy. If people had known they had come to Washington to aid the Kennedy administration, they would not have come in the numbers they did." Forman also argued that the march served "to stifle manifestations of serious dissent and to take the steam out of the black anger then rising in the South, eventually to explode in many parts of the North as well." The disadvantage of "fancy productions like the March" was that they "tended to 'psych off' local protest and make people feel they had accomplished something—changed something, somehow—when, in fact, nothing had been changed."[56]

Another critic, Calvin Hernton, said that after the debacle in Birmingham, ghetto and field blacks "got mad and started talking about storming the White House, tying up Congress and even lying down on the runways of airports." According to Hernton, "As soon as the whitefolks heard about this, they mapped out plans for 'shaping up' the march on Washington."[57]

In a series of speeches following the march, Malcolm X attacked the demonstration as a fraud. According to the Black Muslim leader, Kennedy felt threatened by the grass-roots nature of the march, and told Randolph and the other black leaders to bring it "to a halt." When the president saw that he could not stop it, "He joined it; he endorsed it; he welcomed it and became a part of it; and it was he who put the six Negro civil rights leaders at the head of it. *It was he who made them the Big Six*." Malcolm X described a scenario wherein Currier explained that public squabbling by civil rights groups trying to extract money from white liberals was destroying their leadership "image." Currier therefore

56. Forman, *Making of Black Revolutionaries*, 331–36.
57. Calvin C. Hernton, "Dynamite Growing Out of Their Skulls," in Le Roi Jones and Larry Neal (eds.), *Black Fire: An Anthology of Afro-American Writing* (New York, 1968), 93, 99–100.

suggested that they unite for fund raising. Thus, said Malcolm X, "It took the white man to bring those Negro leaders together and to unite them into one group." It was this "*shrewd maneuver*" that "*placed the white liberal*" and the "*Taconic Foundation in the position to exercise influence and control over the six civil rights leaders and, by working through them, to control the entire civil rights movement, including the March on Washington.*"[58]

The press skillfully projected the Big Six as the leaders, Malcolm X maintained, and when their image became inseparable from the march, they invited four white leaders to become part of the march "Godhead." This group of leaders supposedly okayed all the plans and thereby controlled the "direction and the mood" of the demonstration. Since the four white leaders represented the liberal factions that had put Kennedy in the White House, Malcolm X claimed, "The white liberals took over the March on Washington, weakened its impact, and changed its course; *by changing the participants and the contents, they were able to change the very nature of the march itself.*" He argued: "The whites didn't integrate it; they infiltrated it. It ceased to be a black march; it ceased to be militant; it ceased to be angry; it ceased to be impatient. In fact it ceased to be a march. It became a picnic, an outing with a festive, circus like atmosphere."

According to Malcolm X, the administration made certain that whites were added to defuse the violence and exercise complete control. "The government told the marchers what time to arrive in Washington, where to arrive and how to arrive." White liberals who joined the march led the marchers "away from the White House, the Senate, the Congress, Capitol Hill, and *away from victory.*" The administration "told the marchers what signs to carry, what songs to sing, what speeches to make, and then told the marchers to be sure to get out of town by sundown . . . *and all of them were out of town by sundown.*"

There was enough factual material in the militants' charges to give them credibility. At the conference with Kennedy before the march, Randolph himself had admitted its grass-roots inspiration and the desire of

58. Quotations from Malcolm X in this paragraph and the next two paragraphs come from Benjamin Goodman (ed.), *The End of White World Supremacy: Four Speeches by Malcolm X* (New York, 1971), 140–45, and Malcolm X, "A Message to the Grassroots," Address to the Northern Grassroots Leadership Conference, November 10, 1963, on Afro Records.

moderates to channel it in nonviolent directions. But although Currier was funneling money to the civil rights groups, it is unlikely that he gave the amount the militants claimed. Randolph had written Whitney Young earlier in August of the "immediate and pressing financial problem" the march committee faced as a result of expenses expected on the day of the march. Unanticipated numbers of marchers were obliging the committee to "undertake sharply increased expenses to meet the cost of guaranteeing the success and safety of so huge a gathering." Randolph, therefore, needed to know "what share of the total budget" the NUL was prepared to assume and how much could be supplied "immediately." If the march committee were indeed assured of as much financial aid from Currier as rumor had it, Randolph would not have been so concerned about expenses.[59]

Accepting money from the Taconic Foundation represented the logical extension of the policy of soliciting foundation aid for black civil rights causes employed by Randolph in his efforts to desegregate the armed services in the 1940s. Taking the funds did lead to considerable white control, but the march's black sponsors, particularly those under Randolph's influence, tried to guard against complete white domination. One NUL staffer noted, "Major parts of the March staff here and in Washington still *are* radically opposed to extensive white participation, whether in preparing the March or in the actual events of the day." Cleveland Robinson, for example, "believe[d] passionately that such large-scale participation is wrong," that blacks must do the basic job by themselves, and that they should strenuously resist extensive white aid. Another staffer admitted "hid[ing] fifty buses from white people because there are too many whites now." The white National Council of Churches announced its plan to send 40,000 marchers, but no serious effort was made to enlist New York's black ministers.[60]

As much as Rustin endeavored to maintain control of decision making, once the march sponsorship was enlarged to include the four major white groups, and the numbers involved grew to such enormous propor-

59. Randolph to Young, August 12, 1963, in NUL Papers. Perhaps Currier's infusion of money did not arrive until after August 12. For a final statement on funds, see Memorandum to Members of the Call Committee of the March on Washington from John Morsell, November 25, 1964, in CORE Papers.

60. Memorandum, Hanlon to Young, August 13, 1963, in NUL Papers, LC; Memorandum, Young to Executive Directors of Urban League Affiliates, August 12, 1963, in ULP Records.

tions, the event took on a life of its own and veered off in a direction different from that Randolph intended with his original proposal. The altered character of the march can be seen by comparing the 1963 demonstration with the aborted 1941 march. In both instances the impetus for the march came from an economically pressed black minority community within a prosperous dominant white community, and in both cases economic demands took precedence in Randolph's planning. That integration of the armed services had already been won by 1963 accounted for the primary difference in demands. In 1941 Randolph agreed to call off his march for an executive order securing the FEPC; in 1963 the economic situation had become so complex that no executive order alone could ameliorate it. Overt discrimination had become less fashionable but had been replaced by more sophisticated forms, such as altered job titles, which were more difficult to fight against. In 1963 the addition of white liberals and religious leaders, close cooperation with Martin Luther King and the interracial NUL, and the new element of massive media coverage all combined to downplay the emphasis on economic priorities.

When planning the early march, Randolph insisted that blacks fight for their own rights; he would not accept white financing or white control. The costs of such a march, however, had risen substantially by 1963. In 1941 the estimated budget called for volunteer stenographic help, $200 for an assistant director, $100 for publicity, $500 for supplies, $100 for a month's office rent, and $200 for loudspeaking equipment at the Lincoln Memorial.[61] The estimated budget in 1963 was $117,240, of which $8,465 was allotted for office salaries and $16,000 for loudspeaking equipment. It was impossible for an economically deprived black community to finance a demonstration of these dimensions without outside assistance.

In 1941 Randolph insisted that all the marchers be black, and it was the prospect of many thousands of blacks invading white Washington that so frightened the Roosevelt administration. By 1963 Washington had become the first large city in the nation with a majority-black population, so the fear of black invasion had lost its potency. Furthermore, the 1963 march was integrated. Although the show of unity presented by blacks and whites marching together was useful for public relations, the force of a solid mass of blacks taking over Washington to demand equal

61. Estimate for National Budget, n.d., in NAACP Papers, LC.

rights was lost. There were attempts at control in 1941, but they took place behind the scenes, and the proposed march retained a spontaneous, grass-roots flavor. The managerial quality and publicized tight control in 1963 forfeited any feeling of spontaneity. To have marchers demand restaurant service and hotel accommodations in segregated Washington seemed truly revolutionary in 1941. In contrast, the 1963 demonstration, which had the marchers in and out of the city before sundown, with food provided for them on the grounds of the Washington Monument, came across as a tame, almost meaningless affair.[62] Despite government fears, in 1941 the white world knew nothing of the threatened march; indeed, Randolph accused the white press of a conspiracy of silence. In 1963 the white-controlled media, especially television, subverted the direction of the march toward its own ends.

The practical effect of the 1963 march was debatable. One of its benefits was intangible: the feeling of power and pride it fostered in Afro-Americans. The sheer weight of numbers participating was impressive, and the fact that one marcher in ten was white demonstrated that courting white aid paid off in more than just financial support. As August Meier pointed out, the March on Washington "actively involved in civil rights, for the first time, a number of white moderates—a few even from the South—who heretofore displayed no interest." The primary civil rights aim of the march, to garner congressional support for the civil rights bill, was not so positively fulfilled. It is unlikely that the march changed any votes on the bill. Lerone Bennett argued, "As a morale booster, the March was a stunning success. But as an exercise in leadership, it was something less than scintillating." The lack of accomplishment resulted from the organizers' failure to sustain the participants' commitment beyond a one-day demonstration. Bennett called attention to this weakness: "The March was not coordinated with anything that preceded it or anything that followed it. It led nowhere and was not intended to lead anywhere. *It was not planned as an event within a coherent plan of action.* As a result, the March was a stimulating but detached and isolated episode."[63]

62. Some limited accommodations were provided in 1963 for those who could not leave the city the same day, but they had to be booked in advance. See ULP Records.

63. August Meier, "Negro Protest Movements and Organizations," *Journal of Negro Education*, XXXII (Fall, 1963), 449; "The 'March'—Gains and Losses," *U.S. News and World Report*, September 9, 1963, p. 34; Bennett, *Confrontation*, 285.

The march also failed to fuse a unified national civil rights movement, although, conceivably, a permanent congress of black organizations could have capitalized on the momentum and coordinated simultaneous demonstrations all over the country. Rustin, with Randolph's encouragement, did make an attempt to maintain the coalition of forces represented in the march. In September he endeavored to obtain an ongoing commitment from the march sponsors, arguing that abandoning their unity would disillusion and demoralize their followers, and pointing out, "There ha[s] been a specific promise that MOW would continue." Rustin saw the primary value of such a coordinating group as preventing "diversity from becoming disunity" and counteracting "tendencies toward splintering." He of course added the obligatory proviso that such a continuation would not mean "a new competing organization but a moral force that reaches across all organizations."[64]

Rustin believed that the Big Ten should work together with the Leadership Conference on Civil Rights, to which each of the ten groups belonged, rather than seek to develop its own programs. In his view, the mass action image of the Big Ten should be utilized to aid passage of legislation supported by the conference. Consequently, he presented the sponsors with a plan for demonstrations against the anticipated filibuster of the civil rights bill. Randolph and Rustin talked about the possibility of a thousand people a day engaging in an antifilibuster project, constituting a "People's Congress."[65]

But the march sponsors were unable to unite on this plan, in part because they were reluctant to "confer implied post-March status on the R-R team."[66] Their cooperation for the march had been motivated by their common desire not to be left out of the huge undertaking. But the unity they exhibited in the demonstration was chimeric: The march came at a time when the various groups were beginning to show deep divisions over goals and methods. There would be no permanent congress of black organizations, and there would be no unified civil rights program. Randolph found himself caught between the moderate factions, which were

64. Memorandum, Bayard Rustin to The Chairmen of the March on Washington, September 27, 1963, in NAACP Papers, LC; *Black Worker*, October, 1963, p. 3.

65. Memorandum, Rustin to Chairmen; *Black Worker*, October, 1963, p. 3. See also Meeting of Committee of Deputies to the Ten Chairmen, September 27, 1963, in NAACP Papers, LC; Richard Haley To Gordon Carey *et al.* September 10, 1963, in CORE Papers; Transcript of television broadcast, "March on Washington . . . Report by the Leaders."

66. Sextet Agenda Comments.

not interested in his economic stress, and the militant groups, which held that his proposals did not go far enough.

In one of the great ironies of American history, the march that never took place in 1941 had greater lasting impact than the march that actually took place in 1963. The threat of the earlier march resulted in the FEPC, which marked the formal recognition of the federal government that it bore some responsibility for protecting minority rights in employment. As a consequence, blacks and other minorities began to look first to the federal government for the protection of their rights. One has difficulty finding any such lasting advance resulting from the later march.

Randolph's proposed 1941 march foreshadowed the midcentury civil rights movement in its rhetoric, strategies, personnel, coalitions, and conflicts, even though there were significant differences between the two movements. The MOWM began as a middle-class black movement, but Randolph proceeded to widen its appeal to include the lower-class masses in the ghettos. When Randolph turned to the more complex ideology of civil disobedience, the lower classes began to drop out, and the movement disintegrated. The midcentury, interracial civil rights movement also began with a middle-class following. The difference, however, was that in the 1950s and 1960s none of the older civil rights leaders made a conscious attempt to actively engage the ghetto masses. Thus when young militants came to the fore with black-power slogans and stressed black nationalism and strategies of community organizing, they filled a vacuum.

Randolph's overriding goal of economic equality transcended class in the 1940s, even if his means of nonviolent civil disobedience required too much discipline and commitment of the masses. The more narrow middle-class goals of integrated schools and public accommodations in the late 1950s, however, meant little to those without sufficient funds to enjoy those accommodations or keep their children in school; such goals were not worth the intensive training and sacrifice civil disobedience required. When the lower classes finally became involved in the movement, in Birmingham in the spring of 1963, they did not turn the other cheek, but instead turned to violence—looting brought immediate gratification. Not until it became apparent that the Civil Rights Act of 1964 brought no basic reallocation of community resources and, therefore, no real change in ghetto conditions did Martin Luther King come to realize what Randolph had always known: Economic improvement must precede any improvement in social conditions.

Furthermore, the interracial character of the midcentury movement restricted the number of blacks in intermediary leadership positions and did not promote the type of self-reliance Randolph thought necessary for true black liberation. White patrons still placed restraints on the militancy of black recipient organizations as they had in the past. The advocates of black power in the late 1960s castigated the moderate civil rights leadership for continuing to defer to white patrons in the same terms Randolph had used earlier. In their despair, these militants turned to a black nationalism similar to that espoused by Marcus Garvey in the 1920s. They rejected the more moderate separatism advocated by Randolph in the March on Washington Movement—racial exclusivism employed as a short-term tactic to gain the ultimate goal of equality.

The civil rights movement of the 1950s and 1960s also differed in the participants' approach to their leader. In Randolph's movements, the local affiliates sought visits from "the Chief" to give legitimacy to their groups. This contrasted with Martin Luther King's experience, wherein the young militants resented his appearances in their cities as an intrusion and a publicity-grabbing stunt. The youths believed that they had done the day-to-day work locally, whereas King arrived on the scene later merely to gain glory.[67] His inadequacy both in building a strong national organization and in extending sufficient autonomy and legitimacy to local groups contributed to King's failure to build a strong national civil rights movement at midcentury.

Although many of the liberal allies who joined the 1963 march were committed to integration, neither Randolph nor his disciples totally embraced integration as a means to ultimate equality. Randolph always saw Afro-Americans as a distinct group and, therefore, as needing to maintain pressure to protect their own interests. This particular angle of vision set him apart from the other civil rights leaders, who advocated either integration or black nationalism. By the 1960s the aspirations of too many within the black community had diverged from Randolph's; he was no longer a mass leader.

In 1941 Randolph was viewed as a crusader for black rights against the entrenched racism of the Roosevelt administration. In 1963 and 1964, however, Randolph's actions in support of the Johnson administration undercut his previous efforts to build a new political coalition. Once

67. Vincent Harding, "So Much History, So Much Future: Martin Luther King, Jr., and the Second Coming of America," in Michael V. Namorato (ed.), *Have We Overcome? Race Relations Since Brown* (Jackson, Miss., 1979), 59–73.

Randolph decided to back a candidate of one of the major political parties, his attempt to build a political bloc of outsiders—blacks, Socialists, laborers, and farmers—lost whatever credibility it may have had, as well as bringing down upon him the wrath of the young militants.

Thus the once-radical Randolph began to appear conservative to the young black militants in the period following the march. The break between them became pronounced after the radicals repudiated integration and nonviolent direct action, and took up separatist ideas of self-defense and community control for improving the quality of ghetto life. Randolph and the militants became embroiled in a destructive battle over the issue of black power, which ultimately alienated the aging leader from much of the black community.

After Kennedy's assassination, Johnson's skillful leadership secured passage of the Civil Rights Act in July, 1964. Even though it did not grapple with the economic inequality responsible for trapping the black underclass in the urban ghettos, many of the items on the march agenda, most notably in the area of public accommodations, were obtained by this act. With its passage, however, the attention of black activists turned increasingly toward the North, where major riots were occurring. Civil rights leaders were afraid that the rioting would encourage a white backlash just when blacks were beginning to make progress, and indeed, a backlash seemed to be developing. Conservative Barry Goldwater became the presidential nominee of the Republican party in 1964. When the pro-segregationist governor of Alabama, George Wallace, withdrew from the race as the Dixiecrat candidate, white northern conservatives alarmed by black militancy adopted Goldwater as their candidate. Thereupon Johnson declared publicly that violence would only impede the progress of blacks; privately, he and his aides urged Randolph and other influential blacks to get word into the ghettos that every bottle thrown was a help to Goldwater. Moderate black leaders needed little persuading, both because of the backlash potential of the riots and the "evidence" the riots presented "that they themselves might be losing control of the civil rights movement."[68]

Wilkins invited the leaders of the major civil rights groups to a meeting to discuss tactics and strategy, expressing his certainty that they would

---

68. Eric F. Goldman, *The Tragedy of Lyndon Johnson* (New York, 1969), 174–75; Memorandum for the President from Hobart Taylor, Jr., May 25, 1964, in LBJ Papers.

not wish to do anything to enhance Goldwater's chances of election or to hurt the civil rights movement. What the press later termed a "summit meeting" convened on July 29, 1964, to proclaim a moratorium on demonstrations for the duration of the presidential campaign. Although Wilkins did not say the action was requested by the White House, according to James Farmer the implication was clear that it came at the president's behest. In an unprecedented statement, the leaders asserted that the Goldwater forces were injecting "racism" into the campaign. The Republican states' rights platform, they maintained, was a threat to the "whole climate of liberal democracy in the United States" and to "the implementation of the Civil Rights Act and to subsequent expansion of civil rights gains." In their overriding desire for Goldwater's defeat, the moratorium backers urged blacks not to antagonize whites into voting for him. Since the minority could not achieve its goals if the entrenched and powerful majority opposed them, the civil rights groups must try to "win friends" by halting "ego satisfying" demonstrations. Afro-American energies, both north and south, should instead be devoted to "political action," enforcement of the civil rights laws, and the registration and voting of the black masses. Although Wilkins told reporters that the moratorium "is a civil rights document, not a Johnson document," its purpose nevertheless was to ensure Johnson's election.[69]

Their responses to the moratorium shattered the façade of unity the civil rights organizations had tried to maintain before the public. Although still part of COFO, the SNCC had come to the New Left position that the power structure of American society was rotten; therefore, it did not want to work within the establishment. CORE, which was giving up its commitments to nonviolence and interracialism, agreed that Goldwater should be defeated, but not that demonstrations should end because of white retaliation, or that such a policy should be enunciated by a handful of leaders. Randolph, King, Rustin, Wilkins, and Young signed the moratorium; Lewis of the SNCC and Farmer of CORE refused. Thus Randolph agreed to call off civil rights demonstrations to aid Johnson despite the pledge he had made after the march to continue demonstrations.[70]

69. James Farmer, Interview by Paige Mulhollan, July 20, 1971, p. 2, Oral History Collection, Lyndon Baines Johnson Library, Austin; James Farmer, *Freedom—When?* (New York, 1965), 44; Goldman, *Tragedy of Lyndon Johnson*, 174–75; "Negro Leaders Ban Demonstrations," *Christian Century*, August 12, 1964, p. 1005.

70. Farmer, *Freedom—When?*, 44. See the quotation in James Restin's column, New York *Times*, August 30, 1963.

Randolph's broad base of support was diminished by this decision, as well as by his dealings with the Mississippi Freedom Democratic party. The Mississippi Summer Project had been set up to overcome disfranchisement and the lack of political experience and education among Mississippi's heavily rural, black population. Since even those few blacks who were registered to vote were excluded from the regular state Democratic party, members of the Mississippi Freedom Democratic party decided to select a truly democratic delegation to represent them at the 1964 Democratic convention in Atlantic City. On the eve of the convention, Randolph and Richard Parrish, in their capacity as officers of the NALC, hailed the Mississippi Freedom Democratic party and pledged the council to full-fledged support of the group in the showdown at Atlantic City. Yet when the Johnson forces offered the compromise of two seats for "delegates at large," Randolph's protégé Rustin urged the Mississippi Freedom Democratic party to accept it. Believing the return was too small to justify the suffering endured by blacks not only in the Freedom Summer but for hundreds of years in Mississippi, the party leaders defied Rustin and refused the offer. Party members resented Rustin's counsel to "sell out."[71] After the rejection of the compromise, Randolph and Rustin aligned themselves with the moderate civil rights organizations.

When the Democratic convention ended, Randolph pledged that the porters would back Johnson for president on the grounds that he was largely responsible for the civil rights legislation of 1957 and 1960, as well as for the Civil Rights Act of 1964, which Randolph called "a Magna Carta of civil rights for people of color in America." Not only had Johnson appointed blacks to high policy-making positions in government, but he was the first president in American history to promote a bill to initiate a "War on Poverty," which would "reach and touch proportionately a higher number of Negroes than any other group of our population" because more Afro-Americans suffered from poverty than any other group. Randolph considered the election of 1964 a "crisis election" because Goldwater, in addition to being backed by the John Birch Society, the Ku Klux Klan, and the White Citizens Councils, supported right-to-work

71. *Black Worker*, October, 1964, p. 2; Forman, *Making of Black Revolutionaries*, 388; Paul Jacobs and Saul Landau, *The New Radicals* (New York, 1966), 311; Lewis, *King*, 253; Jennifer McDowell and Milton Loventhal, *Black Politics: A Study and Annotated Bibliography of the Mississippi Freedom Democratic Party* (San Jose, 1971), 14; Farmer, *Freedom—When?*, 44.

laws and had voted against the Civil Rights Act. "For the present," Randolph stated, "Negroes have left the streets and are now returning to the polls where they hope to bury Goldwaterism in the limbo of political oblivion from which it is hoped he would never emerge." This stance represented a complete reversal of position by the old Socialist. Randolph had never before committed himself to a presidential candidate of one of the major parties. The gesture earned him Johnson's lasting gratitude, as well as an invitation to join the president on the reviewing stand for the inaugural parade.[72]

Rustin asserted that Johnson's landslide victory amounted to "a vindication" of the moratorium on demonstrations. Nevertheless, by the time the election was over, liberal white sources of financial aid and manpower for the civil rights groups had dried up.[73] For the first time since the Montgomery bus boycott, almost ten years earlier, the steadily increasing momentum of the movement toward equality slowed. After the election, the Vietnam War replaced civil rights as the important political issue in American life.

In an effort to maintain the supremacy of the civil rights issue, Randolph called together black leaders representing church, labor, fraternal, and civil rights organizations to discuss the direction the civil rights movement should take for the coming year. Having never given up hope of coordinating black leadership, he called a two-day State of the Race Conference in New York City at the end of January, 1965, similar to the one in 1956.[74] Randolph used the occasion to urge "a transition from the politics of confrontation . . . in the streets to the politics of confrontation of ideas at the conference table," a transformation he saw as the "hope for the future."[75] Although they stressed political action, the leaders who attended the conference indicated that peaceful demonstrations would continue where they were needed.

Reflecting Randolph's concerns, the conference devoted much time to economic issues. Despite gains, the black community still faced "dispro-

72. *Black Worker*, October, 1964, p. 1+; Lyndon B. Johnson to Randolph, September 13, November 19, 1964, Day Letter, Jack Valenti to Randolph, January 15, 1965, all in LBJ Papers.

73. Rustin, *Down the Line*, 120.

74. He had tried even earlier. See Randolph to Wilkins, April 7, 1964, in NAACP Papers, LC.

75. Statement to Press, January 31, 1965, in RP Papers; *Black Worker*, March, 1965, p. 2; A. Philip Randolph, Foreword to Bennett, *Confrontation*, vii–x.

portionate unemployment, low wages, inadequate and segregated education, police brutality, the miseries of slum living and continued stubborn resistance to the right to vote." Even if racial barriers were abolished, Randolph noted, it would be impossible for the black work force to catch up with the white. "Automation may mean that Negro workers as young as thirty years of age may never work again, especially those without skills, training and education." Black civil rights organizations must therefore lead the war on poverty, Randolph argued, to make certain that human values were not lost in the technological revolution. To this end, blacks should take the lead in building "a coalition of conscience," a class-based alliance of black and white poor, "or history will again pass us by."[76] Like its predecessor, however, the 1965 State of the Race Conference did not effect any lasting coordination of black leadership.

Meanwhile, events were beginning to strip the civil rights leaders of their control. Malcolm X was killed in Harlem near the end of February, just as he appeared to be groping toward a new philosophy that did not preclude working with sympathetic whites. Frustration produced by the growing disparity between the status of poor blacks and their rising expectations contributed to an outbreak of ghetto riots in the summer of 1965. The riots, which did not reflect the mainstream of the civil rights movement, were not against white people per se; rather, they were aimed at a symbolic destruction of "whitey" through the destruction of white property.[77]

The CUCRL was raising less and less money while trying to push more of its conservative positions on the movement. SNCC leaders had begun to question the value of King's type of quick, scattered demonstrations, advocating instead permanently based efforts within communities to educate, register, and organize southern blacks, as in the Mississippi Summer Project. About this time, James Meredith, who had integrated the University of Mississippi, decided to march from Memphis to Jackson, Mississippi, in June of 1966 to inspire blacks to register and vote. When Meredith was shot, all the civil rights organizations descended on Memphis to exploit the opportunity for publicity by continuing the Meredith March. But during the march Stokely Carmichael, a leader of the SNCC

76. Statement to Press; *Black Worker*, March, 1965, p. 2; Randolph, Foreword to Bennett, *Confrontation*, iii–x.

77. Alex Haley (ed.), *The Autobiography of Malcolm X* (New York, 1965); *Black Worker*, June, 1976, p. 7, March, 1965, p. 2.

who had chosen not to participate in the March on Washington because he thought it more fruitful to remain in Mississippi and register black voters, advocated the use of black power. The slogan caught on, was taken up by the black press, and destroyed what was left of the appearance of unity among the civil rights organizations.

After the Meredith March, Martin Luther King ran a full-page advertisement in the New York *Times* condemning the black-power slogan. A few months later, Randolph, Rustin, Wilkins, and Young issued a statement, "Crisis and Commitment," which denounced black power in even more forceful terms than those used by King.[78] The established leaders blamed the power rhetoric for negating the moral appeal of the civil rights movement. Emphasis on power, coupled with ghetto riots and the growing importance of Vietnam as an issue of concern to white liberals, spelled doom for the nonviolent civil rights movement.

White activists, pushed out of the militant groups, also began to drop out of the moderate organizations. Seeing the unity of the march dissipating in the debate over strategy and tactics, Randolph deplored the new developments: "Black power has overtones of black racism," he said, "and black racism is just as indefensible as white racism." The disadvantage of black power was that it tended toward confrontation and violence "instead of mutual cooperation for social progress." Black-power advocates shared with their white New Left contemporaries the lack of a well-formulated ideology and a disdain for history. What was needed was a pragmatic plan to grapple with basic problems, but "black power is neither a program nor a philosophy," claimed Randolph. Rather, "It is, like white supremacy, merely a slogan."[79]

Randolph thought that black-power advocates were operating on an unsound, anachronistic assumption when they sought power through voluntary segregation. Black nationalists implicitly supported the view of conservative whites that Afro-Americans could solve their problems in isolation from the rest of society, but the ghettos did not have the resources to abolish poverty and slum housing and to upgrade education.

---

78. Forman, *Making of Black Revolutionaries*, 370; Rayford W. Logan and Michael R. Winston, *The Negro in the United States* (New York, 1970), II, 77.

79. UPI Release, September 4, 1967, in clipping files, Johnson Publications, Chicago; A. Philip Randolph, *The Negro Freedom Movement* (Lincoln, Pa., 1967), 12; *Black Worker*, March, 1966, pp. 4–5; *Congressional Record*, House, "A Tribute to A. Philip Randolph," April 29, 1969, H3192.

In Randolph's view, "These resources must come primarily from the federal government, which means that the fate of the Negro is unavoidably tied to the political life of this nation." Separatism and black nationalism, therefore, were not the answer. Power resulted from organization, which, in turn, had to be built. Blacks had great potential power by virtue of their unorganized, though organizable, numbers. But Randolph feared that the cry "black power" would inevitably provoke the countercry "white power," and he argued, "There needs to be a moratorium on inflammatory racist propaganda against white people merely because they are white." [80]

Randolph said, "I love the young black militants," but he thought that, because of their lack of historical knowledge, they failed to realize that every violent revolution was followed by a period of extreme reaction and oppression, which negated the gains. Thus violence was self-defeating, and riots only hurt the cause: "Riots cannot win civil rights but they can lose them." The ultimate responsibility for the riots, Randolph maintained, lay not with black demagogues but with white America, since racial and social injustices precipitated violence. Unemployment was the primary cause; jobless black teenagers, who often expressed their frustration, alienation, and hopelessness through rioting, had the highest unemployment rate of any group in the country, ranging as high as 40 to 50 percent in some cities. It was crucial that the government and black leaders find a way to provide these young people with jobs. America had "never seriously attempted" to meet the problem of economic discrimination against Afro-Americans, noted Randolph. "America has sown the winds of racial hate and oppression and it is now reaping the whirlwinds." [81]

Recognizing, but seeming to excuse, the growing gulf between the black middle class and the masses, Randolph maintained that it was the function of the masses to supply the manpower for demonstrations, whereas the "qualified and specialized talent" required to solve complex problems like de facto school and housing segregation had to come from the leadership. Randolph was afraid that the deepening hatred between black and white poor could halt the civil rights "revolution," and that a white backlash would put an end to liberalism in government. Despite

80. *Black Worker*, March, 1966, pp. 4–5; Rustin, *Down the Line*, 227.
81. Garland, "A. Philip Randolph," 31, 38; *Black Worker*, March, 1966, pp. 4–6; *Congressional Record*, House, "A Tribute to A. Philip Randolph"; *Black Worker*, June, 1967, p. 7, September, 1967, pp. 1–2.

the elderly leader's lifelong record of fighting on behalf of blacks, such statements turned the young militants against Randolph. His antipathy toward black power brought denunciation even from longtime allies in CORE.[82]

Although Randolph believed that demonstrations probably would be necessary indefinitely because "demonstrations in the streets are to the Civil Rights Revolution what strikes and pickets have been to the revolution of the workers," he nevertheless favored a temporary moratorium for an evaluation of the strategy and tactics of the movement. When broadcasters invited civil rights leaders to discuss the problems of the movement on television in the summer of 1966, Randolph wired Wilkins to "sincerely implore" him and the others to decline, fearing "that a televised debate prior to constructive deliberation among ourselves can only further stimulate confusion and disunity, weakening the integrity and overall aims of our movement." Wilkins, however, viewed the telecast "as another opportunity to restate the NAACP platform" and was unwilling to decline the invitation.[83] Black rights organizations had become more fiercely competitive than ever as the war in the Far East drained away financial support.

Randolph also found himself in disagreement with Martin Luther King—whom he had once called "the moral leader of the nation"—over the issue of the Vietnam War. Randolph wired the president to express support for his policies in Southeast Asia, whereas King began to voice dissent against American involvement in the war. King's attempt to assume leadership in both the civil rights and antiwar movements at the same time was, Randolph believed, "tactically unsound."[84] Remembering how World War II had ultimately submerged the fight for black equality, Randolph dreaded another diversion of energy from the black rights struggle. He regretted that the current war had practically "pushed the Civil Rights Revolution off the center of the stage of contemporary American history," and that peace marches had taken the place of freedom marches for white liberals and students. Afro-American interests, fur-

82. *Black Worker*, March, 1965, p. 2, March, 1966, pp. 4–6; Don Smith to Randolph, May 12, 1967, in BSCP Papers, LC.

83. *Black Worker*, March, 1966, pp. 4–6; Telegram, Randolph to Wilkins, August 8, 1966, Wilkins to Randolph, August 8, 1966, both in NAACP Papers, LC.

84. Lyndon B. Johnson to Randolph, April 15, 1965, in LBJ Papers; Coretta King, *My Life with Martin Luther King, Jr.*, 241; Randolph, *Negro Freedom Movement*, 14.

thermore, did not appear to be served by antiwar activity: Since Randolph's success in forcing integration of the armed services, the military had provided a way out of the ghetto for many young blacks.

Eroded by a complex combination of factors, the civil rights movement faced a crisis in the late 1960s. Moreover, the organizations that had engaged in direct mass action beginning in the early days of the protest movement began to show evidence of decline by 1967, and the older betterment groups ignored Randolph's emphasis on economics. Realizing that the lot of ghetto blacks had not been improved by the civil rights advances of the previous decade, young black leaders became convinced that greater militancy was the only way to gain their objective: The number of black organizations openly advocating violence began to proliferate in 1967; by early 1970, the Black Panthers, for one, had established chapters in more than thirty cities.

Disapproving of the violence being advocated, Randolph nevertheless appreciated the fact that the actions of the militants and nationalists made the country aware "that here is a grave injustice that is being done to a great people." The violent methods of the militants had further value: "The black man has been recreated as a new individual, a new social force." Still, two major problems remained unsolved: the "pace of progress is too slow," and what progress had been made had "not touched these great masses in the slums." Randolph urged, "We must begin to reach these unreached."[85] Yet without cooperation, neither Randolph nor the militants were able to substantially improve the plight of the ghetto masses.

In a sense, the 1963 March on Washington marked both the high point of the civil rights movement and the beginning of its unraveling. In the new alignment of civil rights groups that emerged after the Meredith March in 1966, Randolph, Rustin, and King took a position halfway between the alienated militants of the SNCC and CORE on the one hand, and the interracialists of the NUL and many older members of the NAACP on the other. Randolph and Rustin believed that the administration had a commitment to civil rights, but thought that powerful outside pressure was needed to push it further. To them it was apparent that the primary focus of civil rights activity would now be the large urban ghettos, rather

85. Randolph, quoted in Garland, "A. Philip Randolph," 31–32; UPI Release, September 4, 1967.

than the South. Recognizing Johnson's sensitivity to black demands, Randolph and Rustin nevertheless believed that urban slum dwellers would have to overturn the Democratic machines and that blacks would have to elect their own representatives. The two persisted in their belief that black interests would be best advanced by a coalition of blacks, liberals, church, and labor that was not part of the Democratic political establishment and that, therefore, could press for more comprehensive political action for all poor Americans. Such a coalition demanded compromises, but Randolph and Rustin were not adverse to compromise, so long as the ultimate goal of complete equality remained intact.

VIII / The Legacy of Randolph

*A democracy which does not provide health, bread and free-
dom for its people will not long endure.*
                                    —*A. Philip Randolph, 1949*

After spending almost a half century fighting for race equality, Randolph
decided to found an institution that would carry on his ideas and methods when he was no longer able to direct events personally. He presided
over the founding of the A. Philip Randolph Institute in 1964, by which
time the existing civil rights organizations had become hopelessly divided; at this time, too, the white community was about to become preoccupied with the Vietnam War and use it as an excuse to justify ignoring
the plight of blacks. The NALC did not turn out to be the vehicle that
Randolph had hoped it would become, and the institute came to replace
the NALC as the cornerstone of his equalitarian activity within the labor
movement.[1] The institute provided the synthesis of civil rights activity
with the interests of labor that was Randolph's unique contribution. Yet,
paradoxically, it contributed to the black community's altered perception
of the octogenarian.

In part Randolph settled on the institute to give Bayard Rustin, who by
this time had become a kind of alter ego for the aged leader, "some sort of
organizational base" of his own. After the March on Washington, A. J.
Muste and Norman Thomas convinced Randolph that without a platform Rustin would not get a hearing, so Randolph decided, "We have to
invent something for Bayard." Rustin was consequently appointed executive director of the institute, a position in which he could devote himself
to the development and promotion of programs to cure the basic economic and social ills of the United States. Norman Hill of CORE and the
March on Washington became associate director. The interracial board

1. Randolph resigned as head of the NALC in May, 1966, and Cleveland Robinson
became the new president. The name was subsequently changed to the National Afro-
American Labor Council.

of directors was composed of individuals representing all ranges of the civil rights coalition. Roy Wilkins, Vernon E. Jordan, John Lewis, and Dorothy Height were among those on the national advisory committee.[2]

Writing in the *AFL-CIO News*, Randolph set forth the primary objective of his new institute as strengthening the ties between the labor movement, civil rights groups, and other progressive organizations. Randolph and Rustin still believed that, with all its faults, an alliance with labor nevertheless held the greatest advantages for blacks. Although white workers feared that blacks were trying to steal their jobs and that blacks moving into a white neighborhood diminished property values, the labor movement continued to be the largest single force in the country pushing for progressive social legislation. Only a coalition of blacks and labor would stand a chance of getting programs enacted that would benefit workers of all races. Afro-Americans might hold the balance of power, but to be effective a swing vote depended on other votes: "In that sense it can never be independent, but must opt for one candidate or the other, even if by default." Although Randolph had been unsuccessful in uniting the various civil rights organizations, the institute could set an example for the others by its affiliation with the labor movement. As Rustin pointed out: "Political alliances are not based on love. They are based on mutual interest."[3]

To many observers, the passage of the Civil Rights Act of 1964 and the Voting Rights Act of 1965 seemed to mark the end of the legislative phase of the civil rights movement. Randolph, however, saw that the largest problem—implementation—remained. Blacks faced the challenge of transforming "the Civil Rights Revolution into a Social Revolution." Randolph realized that achievement of social change necessitated the development of new tactics and strategies because actual alteration of the status quo met with even greater resistance than the passing of laws.[4] Randolph and the institute began work on these new techniques for achieving social justice.

2. Interview with Bernice Wilds, June 12–23, 1978; Randolph, quoted in Mayer, "Lone Wolf of Civil Rights," 78. Thomas R. Brooks called Rustin "A Strategist Without a Movement," in *New York Times Magazine*, February 16, 1969, p. 24+; *AFL-CIO News*, March 20, 1965.

3. *AFL-CIO News*, March 20, 1965; Rustin, *Down the Line*, 120, 119; Bayard Rustin, *The Alienated: The Young Rebels Today . . . and Why They're Different*, Pamphlet, [1967], 8.

4. Randolph, "Negro Freedom Movement," 11; Randolph, quoted in Garland, "A. Philip Randolph," 36.

Thus the institute's programs blended the interests of Randolph and Rustin. It represented their view that civil rights in isolation would not bring economic equality—the movement alone could not furnish blacks with jobs, better housing, and educational opportunities. Reiterating their old stand, the pair argued that blacks must work through a broad coalition including labor, liberal, religious, and progressive business groups. The institute was designed to provide the framework to strengthen this coalition. Its projected program included research and education in the fields of social and economic problems, development of understanding and cooperation between labor and the black community on common problems, and guidance on joint community action. Since Randolph never gave up the idea of coordinating black leadership, the institute also planned to encourage "mass action by the civil rights organizations at the national level" to mobilize the total resources of the movement against the obstacles to racial equality.[5]

The institute realized some gains in labor organization. Black trade unionists were becoming increasingly involved in political action, and according to Thomas Brooks, the Randolph Institute reached more black unionists than any other single national organization. The institute assisted the Memphis sanitation workers in 1968 when they went on strike for the right to unionize and bargain collectively for higher wages, and it supported Cesar Chavez and his United Farm Workers' organizing committee in the grape fields of California.[6] Both the Memphis sanitation workers and the grape pickers subsequently won recognition, although the former attained union status only after the assassination of Martin Luther King, who had gone to Memphis to promote their cause.

Another goal of the institute was "to increase the political power of the poor through voter education and registration." The institute planned nonpartisan voter-registration campaigns among blacks in key cities and counties across the country and distributed more than one million pieces of literature urging blacks to vote in the 1968 presidential election. This was a concerted effort, in conjunction with local trade unions and the NAACP, to counteract the New Left admonition to boycott the election. The position of the institute was that abstaining from voting constituted, not radicalism, but submission to white power by default.[7] The institute

5. *AFL-CIO News*, March 20, 1965.
6. Brooks, *Toil and Trouble*, 326, 318–19.
7. Program, "Eightieth Birthday Dinner in Honor of A. Philip Randolph," 1969, at A. Philip Randolph Institute; Rustin, *Down the Line*, 242.

considered its stand vindicated when 85 to 90 percent of registered blacks voted, although even this percentage was not sufficient to defeat Richard Nixon.

The Randolph Institute also helped organize support for the delegation of the Mississippi Freedom Democratic party that challenged the regular state delegation at the 1968 Democratic convention in Chicago. Calling themselves the Loyal Democrats of Mississippi, the delegates this time were successful in their quest to be seated at the convention. But by 1968 both the cause of civil rights and the Democratic party were losing influence.

To help bring out an unusually large number of blacks in the off-year elections of 1970, the institute stepped up its efforts at voter registration, and some 300,000 new voters were enrolled. As a result, blacks made greater gains than in any election since Reconstruction, boosting their numbers in office by 22 percent.[8] The politicization of the black masses may be the most significant accomplishment of the Randolph Institute, since increasing the number of black voters and black officeholders offers the greatest hope for major social change in the United States.

A tax-exempt arm of the institute, the A. Philip Randolph Educational Fund, was established in 1965. Its purpose was "to provide a forum in which concerned individuals could debate the means of giving programmatic content to the ideals of justice and equality." Its main activities were the publication of literature analyzing "issues of basic concern to the civil rights movement"; the organization of conferences to bring together minority leaders and representatives of other groups; and the sponsorship of the Joint Apprenticeship Training Program to place black and Puerto Rican youths in the building trades. Through the apprenticeship program, Randolph saw steps taken toward accomplishing "the biggest task confronting the Negro today . . . the transformation of a body of unskilled workers into highly skilled craftsmen and technicians."[9]

The Educational Fund was divided into three departments: Economic Development, which supervised the Joint Apprenticeship Training Program and sponsored conferences on economic problems for civil rights activists, trade unionists, and community leaders; Housing, which worked on strategies to end racially segregated housing patterns, and on guide-

8. "Vote Mobilization for the 70's," Ebony (July, 1971), 84; Pamphlet, The A. Philip Randolph Institute, n.d.
9. Program, "Eightieth Birthday Dinner"; Randolph, "If I Were Young Today," 82.

lines for the reconstruction and integration of urban residential areas; and Educational Affairs, which was concerned with monitoring black-studies programs to ensure their integration and high academic standards, as well as developing programs for quality integrated education and endeavoring to build alliances between parents and teachers. In 1969, the Educational Fund set about establishing a Department for Youth Affairs, "the goals of which would be to imbue alienated and potentially-violent black youths with a faith in nonviolence as a means to social change, and to counter any separatist tendencies which exist among them." [10]

The Educational Fund realized its greatest success with the Joint Apprenticeship Training Program. In 1963 and 1964 changes in federal and state legislation, resulting largely from legal suits brought by the NAACP, had provided for selection of apprentices in the building-trades unions on the basis of merit. The new laws eliminated "father-son" clauses and "sponsorship" requirements, opening the way for the admission of non-white apprentices. The Joint Apprenticeship Training Program was the first and most successful effort to enroll blacks in the building-trades unions. Its major strength lay in its direct tie between training on the job at a good rate of pay and admission to the union upon attaining journeyman's status. [11] But the program reached only minute numbers, and the majority of blacks, whose hopes had been raised by the civil rights acts, were looking for quicker, more certain forms of gratification.

When President Johnson announced his billion-dollar antipoverty program in 1965—a year after he awarded Randolph the Presidential Medal of Freedom—he named Randolph to the national advisory council representing the public in the operation of the new program. In response to white violence against participants in the Selma-Montgomery march in 1965, Johnson proclaimed, "We Shall Overcome." The president's apparent determination to attack the problems of the poverty-stricken ghettos, however, gave way to embitterment; after a year of antipoverty measures, rather than seeing any tangible results, he was confronted with intensified ghetto rioting; embarrassed by the television coverage given the Watts uprising, which exposed the failure of American democracy to the world; and subjected to the condemnation of his Vietnam policy by King, the most prominent civil rights leader. In late August, Johnson utilized the

10. Program, "Eightieth Birthday Dinner."
11. Nathan Glazer and Daniel Patrick Moynihan, *Beyond the Melting Pot* (Cambridge, Mass., 1970), xiix; Brooks, *Toil and Trouble*, 260.

White House conference on equal employment opportunity to speak out against urban violence.[12]

Johnson had proposed that a White House conference on civil rights, with the theme "To Fulfill These Rights," be held in June, 1966. Planning sessions began a full year ahead, and Randolph agreed to serve as honorary chairman of the conference. In his opening remarks to one of the planning sessions, in November, 1965, Randolph called for a Freedom Budget of one hundred billion dollars. This was his first public announcement of the program he projected as the cornerstone of the institute's activity. He pledged to have economists and sociologists work out the specifics in time to be used by the president's staff in their preparation for the forthcoming conference. Randolph admitted that blacks in Watts were better off in 1965 than their counterparts fifty years earlier, and were also better off than most Americans during the Depression thirty years earlier, but, he argued, "the unemployment and poverty of those earlier times was merely a tragedy, because we had neither the economic resources nor the know-how to deal with them." In contrast, "Today, because we have both the resources and know-how, the millions of unemployed and the far more than thirty million living in poverty take on also the aspects of a national crime."[13]

In the course of the year of preparation, the White House began to exercise increasingly tighter control to make certain that the Conference on Civil Rights did not become a forum for antiadministration rhetoric. As early as spring, 1966, *Freedomways* magazine charged that Johnson's Great Society was not a serious effort to end poverty and condemned the upcoming conference as a sham, "an exercise in tokenism," part of an administration strategy to end street demonstrations while holding on to the black vote. Johnson was advocating "economy" at the expense of public health and welfare programs. As long as Congress voted to give

12. Telegrams, Randolph to The President, January 24, June 8, 1964, Lee C. White to Randolph, June 17, 1965, all in LBJ Papers; *Black Worker*, October, 1964, p. 1; C. W. Thomas, "Three Negroes Receive 1964 Presidential Freedom Medal," *Negro History Bulletin*, XXVIII (December, 1964), 58–59; *Black Worker*, March, 1965, p. 1.

13. For The President from Lee White, August 10, 1965, Lee White to Randolph, September 10, 1965, Lyndon Johnson to Randolph, November 25, 1965, Randolph to The President, December 3, 22, 1965, Clifford L. Alexander, Jr., to Randolph, January 18, June 28, 1966, "To Fulfill These Rights," June 1–2, 1966, To Governor Farris Bryant from Clifford L. Alexander, Jr., August 23, 1966, all in LBJ Papers; *Black Worker*, December, 1965, pp. 4–5+.

$50 billion a year to the military, "the 'Great Society' can never be anything more than mere phrasemongering; empty gestures toward a dream deferred," the editor maintained.[14]

By the time the conference was held in June, Johnson was distressed by King's position against the Vietnam War, and black leaders were disturbed by what they saw as a lessening of the president's commitment to civil rights. According to James Farmer, the conference was a failure because of the administration's attempt to structure it; it became merely a kind of cosmetic operation to give the appearance of doing something. The militants dissociated themselves from the conference, but the more moderate organizations did not want to cut off access to the resources of the dominant community. Randolph promised delivery of his Freedom Budget while deploring the "obvious lack of interest" in black problems on the part of the federal government. When Rustin first submitted a copy of the Freedom Budget to the administration in November, 1966, it was ignored. On December 6, when Rustin testified before a Senate subcommittee in favor of the Freedom Budget, he accused Johnson of breaking his word to the civil rights leaders by cutting back on the war on poverty. By this time, the weakening of the president's commitment was one of the few points on which Randolph and Rustin and the New Left could agree.[15]

The Freedom Budget for All Americans was Randolph's most grandiose conception. A solution to the economic problems of Afro-Americans formulated by the Randolph Institute, the Freedom Budget represented the efforts of a formidable group of public figures and economic scholars and was endorsed by leaders in business, labor, religious, and civil rights circles. It was based on the thesis that the only way to abolish poverty was to create full employment. Randolph's proposal was an effort to provide semiskilled and unskilled jobs. Afro-Americans would benefit proportionately more than others from the plan, not because they were black, but because they suffered more from the rising unemployment accompanying new technology and automation.[16]

14. Editorial, "The White House Conference and the 'Great Society,'" *Freedomways*, VI (Spring, 1966), 101–102.

15. James Farmer, Interview by Paige Mulhollan, 16–19; Bayard Rustin to Dear Friend, November 1, 1966, Bayard Rustin to Dear Mr. President, July 31, 1967, both in LBJ Papers; Randolph, quoted in Garland, "A. Philip Randolph," 42; "Bayard Rustin," in Charles Moritz (ed.), *Current Biography Yearbook, 1967* (New York, 1968), 362.

16. Address by A. Philip Randolph, October 26, 1966, in NAACP Papers, LC; *Black Worker*, September, 1967, p. 1, December, 1965, pp. 4–5+.

The Freedom Budget followed the precedent set by the Full Employment Bill of 1946, which had been emasculated by Congress. The budget's authors tried to convince the American people that it was economically feasible for the federal government to accept the responsibility for full employment, and that it was the duty of the government to take care of its people when they were unable to take care of themselves. Thus the Freedom Budget was a sort of crash domestic Marshall Plan. Randolph asserted, "In this, the richest and most productive society ever known to man, the scourge of poverty can and must be abolished—not in some distant future, not in this generation, but within the next ten years!" He argued: "The tragedy is that the workings of our economy so often pit the white poor and the black poor against each other at the bottom of society. The tragedy is that groups only one generation removed from poverty themselves, haunted by the memory of scarcity and fearful of slipping back, step on the fingers of those struggling up the ladder. And the tragedy is that not only the poor but all Americans are the victims of our failure as a nation to distribute democratically the fruits of our abundance." Randolph sincerely believed that "a democracy which does not provide health, bread and freedom for its people will not long endure." [17]

The Freedom Budget called for a national expenditure of $18.5 billion a year over a ten-year period. The eighty-four-page proposal was designed to attack and eradicate in one decade all the major causes of poverty in the United States. The budget sought to fulfill seven basic objectives: the restoration of full employment as rapidly as possible and the maintenance of it thereafter; the assurance of adequate incomes for those employed; the guarantee of a minimum level of income to all those who could not or should not be gainfully employed; the wiping out of slum ghettos and the provision of decent housing for every American family; the provision of modern medical services as well as educational opportunity up to the limits of an individual's abilities and ambitions, at an affordable cost; the overcoming of other manifestations of neglect in the public sector, by purifying the air and water and bringing American transportation systems and natural resource development into line with the needs of a growing population and an expanding economy; and the

17. Bayard Rustin, "'Black Power' and Coalition Politics," *Commentary* (September, 1966), 39–40; A. Philip Randolph, Introduction to *A "Freedom Budget" for All Americans: A Summary* (A. Philip Randolph Institute, January, 1967); *Black Worker*, May, 1949, p. 8.

uniting of sustained full employment with sustained full production and high economic growth.[18]

The budget set a time schedule for the accomplishment of its goals. Since Americans can not enjoy "what we do not produce," all goals had to be supported by the output of the United States economy—output that should grow from year to year under policies designed to assure continued maximum employment, production, and purchasing power. Total national production should rise over the ten-year period, resulting in an "economic growth dividend" on which the Freedom Budget could draw to fulfill its objectives. The Freedom Budget thus had both moral and materialistic purposes.[19]

That "every individual would receive a basic income, not in the form of welfare, but as part of the national economic budget," was one of the recommended measures. Although every attempt would be made to provide people with jobs, even if they were not working they would be assured of an income. The economic logic behind this, Randolph argued, was that income would be used to purchase goods and services. As they were purchased, more goods and services would have to be produced, and therefore employment would be increased. "This leads to a more stable economy, for a truly stable economy can only exist when every individual is involved as a consumer." The question was not whether we had the means, since before 1975 the United States would have a one-trillion-dollar economy, but, rather, whether we had the will. "Ten years from now will two-fifths of our nation still live in poverty and deprivation? This is, above all, a moral question. And upon the answer hangs not only the fate of the Negro—weighted down by centuries of exploitation, degradation and malice—but the fate of the nation."[20]

In part, the Freedom Budget was Randolph's answer to the self-help programs advocated by black nationalists. Unless they mobilized people as "power units capable of effecting social change," such programs could deteriorate into mere self-improvement efforts. In a period when small businesses were faltering, when advanced technology was creating massive unemployment, and when blacks had little chance of obtaining vast amounts of risk capital, to give the ghettos over to black-power propo-

18. Randolph, Introduction to *A "Freedom Budget" for All Americans*.

19. Press Release, Randolph Institute, n.d., in clipping files of Johnson Publications, Chicago.

20. Randolph, quoted in Garland, "A. Philip Randolph," 42.

nents would only aid the reactionaries, who "have no objection to letting Negroes run their own slum tenements, dilapidated schools, and tax-starved communities." Rather than let whites off the hook, the federal government should commit itself to the massive new programs set forth in the Freedom Budget, which, Rustin claimed, was more advanced than other antipoverty and full-employment proposals. Based on the assumption that an expenditure of 6 percent of the national budget would suffice to realize the specified goals, the Freedom Budget not only set priorities and timetables but also indicated how the necessary money could be made available. The economists who drew up the budget estimated that if its provisions were enacted, the federal government would receive $8 to $10 billion a year during the decade without raising the tax rates existing in October, 1966. That amount would exceed the cost of the federal outlays called for by the program.[21]

In 1947 the United States had invested 3 percent of its gross national product in the Marshall Plan. Randolph and Rustin argued that it would be intolerable if the United States's plan for domestic social reform was "less audacious and less far-reaching than our international programs of a generation ago."[22] Although the Freedom Budget represented the logical culmination of Randolph's belief that economics was the key to restructuring society, it was introduced at an inauspicious time and never received serious attention. The budget required a total reordering of national priorities when government concern and expenditures were being ever more deeply invested in the Vietnam War.

Neither Congress nor the administration was interested in the wholesale social changes the Freedom Budget would have entailed. To work the way its authors envisioned, the budget required that huge sums be pumped into the economy quickly; its innovation lay, not in its ideas, but in the projected scale of implementation. But Johnson had never considered a restructuring of American society; rather, his antipoverty measures were planned on the minimum scale his advisers thought necessary to defuse black protest. When Randolph and other civil rights leaders attacked the administration for budget cuts in the war on poverty, Johnson told an aide to call "and tell them to cut this stuff out."[23]

21. Rustin, *Down the Line*, 185; Rustin, "The Lessons of the Long Hot Summer," 42.
22. Rustin, "'Black Power' and Coalition Politics," 40.
23. See note from LBJ/mf to Joe Califano, March 3, 1968, on Memorandum, Mr. President from Marvin, February 27, 1968, in LBJ Papers.

Johnson's program failed largely because of the publicity buildup it was given. Buoyed by rising expectations, ghetto residents became ever more frustrated when there was no visible change in their daily lives. Randolph complained that propaganda promoting the war on poverty as a "failure" was merely "an excuse for cutting down or abolishing its funds. . . . The Fault with the War on Poverty is not the idea or its administration but inadequate financing." [24]

Unlike his earlier initiatives, the Randolph Institute met with relatively few problems in its association with the NAACP. The NUL, however, was concerned about the institute's Freedom Budget, which differed from its own domestic Marshall Plan, put forward three years earlier, primarily in its call for the expenditure of more money. [25]

Financing for the institute caused the conflict between Randolph's affiliation with organized labor and his fealty to the black community to surface again. The original $25,000 grant to set up the institute came from the Industrial Union Department of the AFL-CIO. The institute's total income from May, 1965, to August, 1966, was $62,000, of which only $1,000 came from individual contributions; the rest was provided by the AFL-CIO and individual unions. In 1970 international unions and the Committee on Political Education (COPE) contributed $200,000 to the institute for its voter-education program. [26] This high level of union financial support demonstrated Randolph's success in forging a coalition with organized labor, but it also indicated that the institute would be unlikely to take a position at variance with the interests of the labor movement. Randolph appeared to compromise his independence even more when he became embroiled in a bitter strike over the issue of community control of the public schools in 1968.

Not only did the younger black militants eject whites from their organizations and opt for separation, but they also began to argue that even school integration was irrelevant to the needs of the ghetto masses. Their assertions that Afro-Americans should not give up their cultural identity and must lead their own movements became most pronounced at the time Randolph had overcome most of his earlier reservations and become even

24. *Black Worker*, March, 1967, p. 1.
25. *Time*, August 11, 1967, p. 14.
26. A. Philip Randolph Institute Statement of Income and Expenses, in NAACP Papers, LC; *Annual Report of the A. Philip Randolph Institute* (September, 1969–December, 1970), 3.

more deeply committed to the black, white liberal, church, and organized labor alliance. Insistence on nonviolence and interracial alliances, active support of the Johnson administration, the "sell-out" of the Mississippi Freedom Democratic party, and support for the 1964 moratorium on demonstrations all contributed to growing alienation between Randolph and Rustin on the one hand and younger, more activist blacks on the other. Randolph never fully appreciated the power of cultural nationalism, but had the young truly listened to him, they would have heard him advocate a separate black identity and black control of black movements. By the 1960s, however, Randolph had come to believe that the economic differential between whites and blacks prohibited Afro-Americans from doing it alone; blacks needed white allies more than ever.

It seems ironic that Randolph met with the greatest opposition as a result of the coalition with organized labor that he had devoted so much effort to melding. He was sharply criticized when his loyalty to trade union principles came into conflict with what younger leaders perceived to be the greater good of the black community. The controversy was foreshadowed when Randolph refused to let blacks and Puerto Ricans testify against discrimination in the International Ladies Garment Workers Union in the early 1960s. The conflict intensified in 1968 when Randolph and Rustin backed the United Federation of Teachers against the black community in their strike over decentralization and community control of schools in New York City. The supporters of community control argued that, for true decentralization of schools, the local governing board must have independent power to transfer teachers out of the district and to hire teachers other than those on the union's "eligible" list. Some partisans even advocated total elimination of the white middle-class teacher from ghetto schools. The quarrel was exacerbated when the Ocean Hill–Brownsville experimental school declared it should have the right to change current practices and contract terms, and transferred nineteen teachers to other schools. Thereupon a power struggle with racial overtones ensued between the Ocean Hill–Brownsville community and the teachers' union.[27]

Randolph and Rustin supported the United Federation of Teachers when the union insisted that the issue behind the strike was not de-

27. Martin Mayer, The Teachers' Strike: New York, 1968 (New York, 1969), 17–18; Philip Taft, United They Teach: The Story of the United Federation of Teachers (Los Angeles, 1974), 153–218.

centralization but "due process": Every worker should have the right to job security and a guarantee against being transferred or fired at the whim of the employer; every worker should be judged on merit, not on color or creed. Although consistent with trade union principles, these views seemed racist and exclusionary to most blacks, especially since the proportion of blacks and Puerto Ricans among the city's teachers in 1968 was less than 10 percent, and their numbers in administrative positions were infinitesimal.

The Ocean Hill–Brownsville governing board refused to take the transferred teachers back, and when the teachers tried to reenter the schools, they were subjected to intimidation and harrassment. The situation was unique because in this case the opponent of the union was not a powerful corporation but a coalition of poor blacks and Puerto Ricans seeking control over the educational systems in their community. The union's insistence that changes could be made only in the prescribed manner was interpreted as an attempt to scuttle community control. But the union argued that if one community school district could violate its contract, there would be no basis for preventing other districts from following suit, and union job security would be lost.[28] Randolph supported the union as the protector of the principles of job security, seniority, and collective bargaining. To local blacks, however, he appeared to be siding with the "racist" union leadership against the interests of the Afro-American community. His reputation suffered even more when, shortly after the 1968 teachers' strike, the Randolph Institute moved into the building owned by the United Federation of Teachers, presumably at reduced rental.

Before the strike, the elder statesman Randolph had already earned the wrath of black militants for committing the Randolph Institute to support for the Jews and their state of Israel.[29] This position was diametrically opposed to that of the black radicals, who saw Afro-American interests as aligned with those of the darker peoples of the Third World; it was, however, completely consistent with Randolph's lifelong position on the Jews. He had always felt an affinity with Jews because they, too, had been discriminated against yet endeavored to keep their cultural heritage. Because of their history, Randolph thought they understood the black struggle to maintain ethnic integrity while at the same time making a so-

28. Mayer, *The Teachers' Strike;* Taft, *United They Teach.*
29. Pamphlet, *The A. Philip Randolph Institute.*

cial accommodation to the established power structure. He also never forgot Jewish financial support of his early Socialist groups.

Randolph believed that Jews had been great benefactors of the black race, and many of his closest white colleagues were Jewish. Since blacks themselves suffered from race hatred, they should not hate others, he maintained. The faults that were attributed to Jews, in his opinion, were actually the result of capitalism. Because Jews were shopkeepers, real estate agents, pawnbrokers, and rent collectors in the ghettos, blacks identified them with exploitation and cheating. But, Randolph argued, "It is bad and dangerous logic for Negroes to condemn the Jewish people because of the action of one or more Jews. Just as it is silly and foolish for white people to condemn Negroes as a whole because one drunken Negro may be found on the highways." In Randolph's mind, "The crucial fight against Jim-Crowism is definitely and inevitably tied up with the fight against anti-Semitism and fascism." When Jews fought for an independent state in 1948, Randolph had expressed his hope that their "Saga of Group Action" would fire the ambition of black America to struggle for first-class citizenship.[30]

The Randolph Institute tried to preserve its coalition with liberal Jewish groups even as it maintained its alliance with the labor movement. Rustin spoke to the Anti-Defamation League of B'nai B'rith in May, 1968, making a plea for Jewish understanding of the conditions that were producing the growing anti-Semitism among blacks. Rustin explained that most ghetto blacks saw only four kinds of white people—the policeman, the businessman, the teacher, and the welfare worker—and in many cities three of the four were predominantly Jewish. When the frustrated attacked, they lashed out first at those they knew. In addition, Randolph, Rustin, and the liberal community, to which the Jews had made "greater contributions than anyone else," had become the target of black criticism when the programs they put forward proved insufficient to better the lot of the poorest blacks. Thus, not only Jews, but black leaders as well, were under attack by the extreme left in the black community. Despite the problems, Rustin and the institute requested "the understanding, the cooperation and the aid of Jews."[31]

The charge of anti-Semitism was linked with the 1968 teachers' strike

30. *Black Worker*, August, 1938, December, 1948, p. 1+; St. Louis Scrapbook, in BSCP Papers, CD; *Black Worker*, March, 1949, p. 8.

31. Bayard Rustin, "The Anatomy of Frustration," Address before 55th National Convention Meeting of the Anti-Defamation League of B'nai B'rith, May 6, 1968, New York.

when the number of teachers ordered out of the Ocean Hill–Brownsville district was reduced from nineteen to ten, every one of whom was Jewish—as were a majority of the teachers in the New York City system. Some of the Ocean Hill activists began distributing anti-Semitic literature, which was seized by the United Federation of Teachers, duplicated, and given mass circulation to earn sympathy for the union's position. The strike thus developed religious as well as racial overtones, and Randolph and Rustin appeared not only to be taking a stand against community control but also to be favoring the welfare of Jews over that of blacks. Their stance further alienated Randolph and Rustin from the black militants.

The teachers' strike was one of Randolph's last public involvements. Illness sent him to the Mayo Clinic in April, 1968, and that summer he retired as president of the BSCP and vice-president of the AFL-CIO executive council. Johnson lauded him, stating, "Where monumental civil rights legislation was rising and injustices were falling—there stood Phil Randolph." In a personal letter to Randolph, the president said that he and Mrs. Johnson were "grateful for your long support and treasure your friendship." [32] The railroad industry's decline paralleled Randolph's, and his beloved union was soon absorbed into the Brotherhood of Railway and Airline Clerks.

A. Philip Randolph died May 16, 1979, on the eve of the twenty-fifth anniversary of the Supreme Court decision outlawing segregation in the public schools. By the time of his death, the prestige of St. Philip of the Pullman Porters had so diminished that the head of the NAACP had cause to comment, "It's so sad because there are so many young people today for whom that name means very little." Yet within a dozen years of his death, Randolph would be looked upon as one of the legendary black leaders. In 1989 his likeness would appear on the United States postage stamp for Black Heritage Month, and in its Centennial Edition, the *Wall Street Journal* would place him in its "Gallery of the Greatest"—the "People Who Made a Difference" in shaping the way Americans did business over the past one hundred years. [33]

32. Lyndon B. Johnson to Randolph, April 5, 1968, Nightletter, Johnson to Randolph, May 23, 1968, both in LBJ Papers.
33. Benjamin L. Hooks, quoted in New York *Times*, May 18, 1979; *Wall Street Journal*, Centennial Edition, 1989, p. B20.

Randolph's ideas had not modified appreciably, nor had his rhetoric changed substantially through the years, but the historical circumstances within which he operated had altered greatly. In the new climate of opinion that emerged, the class coalition of underdogs that Randolph endeavored to put together caused black observers to perceive his loyalties as divided and favoring the interests of organized labor over those of the Afro-American community. Although Randolph tried to keep a balance between maintenance of a separate black identity and accommodation to the establishment, his critics claimed that the former was sacrificed for the latter.

Yet Randolph remains a pivotal figure in Afro-American history. His career, spanning the first two-thirds of the twentieth century, demonstrated that blacks were not merely acted upon in an oppressive society; to a large extent they determined their own destiny. An understanding of Randolph's strategies, the coalitions he attempted to forge, and the constraints that circumscribed his endeavors helps one comprehend both the problems and the achievements of blacks in recent American history.

The emergence of Randolph as a black civil rights leader coincided with the decline of patron-clientage relationships in black political life and the institutionalization of efforts by blacks to have the federal government redress their grievances. In these altered circumstances, black organization heads had to formulate policies that met the interests of assorted black groups, they had to cope with much opposition from other black and interracial organizations, and they had to mobilize a great many resources, like prestige and money, to shape decision and action. Randolph was not the only black spokesman to face these challenges; his ascendancy marks the appearance of a new type of black leadership attuned to a whole range of interest groups. In his various campaigns, Randolph managed to anticipate segments of the black community that were just beginning to find their voice. He went beyond the legal action of the NAACP by claiming a whole range of new rights for blacks, the most significant of which was the right to bargain collectively on behalf of Afro-American group interests.

Randolph was able to make novel demands because he realized that historical circumstances had created a new black world. As a result of the "Great Migration," blacks in the northern urban areas had become a significant political force. More so than his contemporaries, Randolph understood that the large black ghettos in northern industrial cities provided blacks with the means to employ pressure politics. Because they required massive numbers, all Randolph's civil rights movements were calculated to take advantage of the huge concentrations of blacks in these areas. Despite some lip service and voter-registration efforts in the South from 1944 on, his organizations did not seriously attempt to reach rural southern blacks.

Under the New Deal, the federal government assumed responsibility for coping with poverty and labor troubles, and created a wide range of agencies to handle these problems. Although it was expensive for minority interest groups to obtain arbitration from these agencies, the results were more predictable than gains dependent on the whims of wealthy white employers or patrons. Capitalizing on this situation, Randolph's strategies resulted in a reorientation of the relationship between Afro-Americans and the federal government. In addition to government recognition that it bore some responsibility for preventing discrimination in employment, Randolph also forced the federal government to desegregate its own facilities. As a result, from the most segregated institution in the nation, the military became the most successfully integrated, and the primary means of social mobility for ghetto blacks. The army's rigid 10 percent quota of blacks before 1948 gave way to a 22-percent rate of blacks among enlisted men by 1975.[34]

The New Deal era that saw Randolph's emergence on the national civil rights scene also saw the rise of industrial unionism; indeed, Roosevelt's labor policies were crucial to Randolph's achieving recognition of the BSCP from the Pullman Company. With "big labor" came public acceptance and government underwriting of collective bargaining. Randolph was the first black man to build a successful labor union. The problems inherent in labor organization were compounded in his case by the difficulty of trying to organize an oppressed minority. Having succeeded with the union, Randolph proceeded to work for greater equality for Afro-Americans in all walks of life. He was then faced with the problem of finding a new ideology to legitimize his unprecedented claims. This proved an obstacle. Applying economic determinism to the race question, Randolph preached an atheistic rationalism to the black masses accustomed to religious emotionalism. Analyzing his career late in life, he said, "The

---

34. Manning Marable, "Blacks and the Draft: A History of Racism," in Marable, *Black Praxis*, IX (Dayton, Ohio, 1980).

level of intelligence of the people might not have been ready for this kind of an effort."[35] Furthermore, Randolph's advocacy of a black-white class alliance contradicted the everyday experience of most blacks, who encountered the greatest racial prejudice from working-class whites.

Randolph provided a solution for one segment of Afro-American society—the Pullman porters. A very small group of black workers who held a monopoly over their occupation, when prohibited from joining a white union, resolved the problem by forming a black union—following the old separate-but-equal philosophy, except that the BSCP eventually obtained true equality with other unions in the AFL. The BSCP, then, substantiated Randolph's belief that racial exclusivism was a viable short-term tactic as it gave blacks self-confidence and experience in leadership and decision making. A racially segregated union worked for the porters. Since it was difficult to find another occupation over which blacks held a monopoly, however, the all-black union did not provide an answer for the majority of black laborers.

Because they had steady jobs, porters were considered to have middle-class status in black society. But the porters were a new middle class—cosmopolitan, accustomed to working with whites, schooled in the trade union methods of collective bargaining, and thus ready to challenge the status quo to demand new rights. The old black bourgeoisie had had prestige but little power. In contrast, members of the BSCP did not hesitate to complain even to the president of the United States when his trains used nonunion porters. BSCP members also had a news network that extended to black communities throughout the country. Rural southern blacks learned of racial developments from copies of northern black journals that the porters threw off the trains as they sped by.[36] The porters thereby helped increase the potential constituency for a mass movement. Through the medium of the *Black Worker,* Randolph reinforced the porters' middle-class values and encouraged them to fight for equality. The BSCP thus enabled Randolph to shape a new class of intermediary leadership for his civil rights groups.

Since the porters' union provided the membership base for Randolph's civil rights efforts, those efforts all began as essentially middle-class move-

35. Randolph, "Reminiscences," 281.
36. Ashley L. Totten to Col. H. McIntyre, August 14, 1936, McIntyre to Edward F. McGrady, August 18, 1936, McGrady to McIntyre, August 28, 1936, all in FDR Papers; E. D. Nixon, interviewed in Terkel, *Hard Times,* 118.

ments with the porters providing most of the secondary leaders. Randolph's organization of strong national groups had the reciprocal effect of extending autonomy to local groups. Although on the national level Randolph controlled decision making, he gave provincial leaders sufficient leeway in judgment on local matters to keep them content. Randolph's style had great appeal for the upwardly mobile class of blacks exemplified by the porters. Ironically, given his stated goals, only briefly did it command as much allegiance from the masses.

The black minority could not succeed on its own, so Randolph had to search for allies. Continuously frustrated in his efforts to coordinate Afro-American leadership to make the most effective use of black political pressure, Randolph found that even his coalition with his most important ally, organized labor, proved to have inherent difficulties. By the late 1950s he began to see Afro-Americans reap the benefits of their partnership with labor as some segments of organized labor financially backed the civil rights movement. Although there was only limited labor support for the March on Washington in 1963, the Randolph Institute received the wholehearted backing of the AFL-CIO. Paradoxically, the very success of the coalition in the form of financial aid necessitated compromises that contributed to Randolph's declining image in the black community.

Randolph's civil rights career was characterized by both success and failure. His most obvious victory, brought about by his threat to march on Washington, was Executive Order No. 8802, which created the FEPC. Critics have concluded that Randolph's failure to win desegregation of the armed services on his first try, and the ineffectiveness of the strategy of mass civil disobedience after the fall of 1942, as well as the collapse of the civil disobedience strategy after winning desegregation of the military in 1948, should be classified as defeats. Indeed, Richard Dalfiume has argued that the original march threat itself was a failure because it achieved only one of its twin goals, the executive order. Dalfiume, however, missed the crucial point: Randolph's success lay in "forcing" any concessions at all rather than begging for them as blacks had in the past. Moreover, Randolph extracted the concessions without actually mounting a demonstration. Even Dalfiume admits that "no one was sure" the march "would occur."[37]

37. Dalfiume, *Desegregation of the U.S. Armed Forces,* 117–20; Richard M. Dalfiume, "The 'Forgotten Years' of the Negro Revolution," in Bernard Sternsher (ed.), *The Negro in Depression and War: Prelude to Revolution, 1930–1945* (Chicago, 1969), 306.

Randolph's real achievement was that, as a low-status, black minority-group leader whose following largely lacked the resources of education, financial security, and influence in the dominant white community, he nevertheless devised a technique enabling blacks to make demands on the established decision makers. Randolph was undoubtedly the most creative black leader of the time; realizing that changed conditions called for novel strategies if blacks were to gain more political power and economic equality, he endeavored to supply those strategies so that the black community might benefit from the expanding wartime economy. Prior to his march threat, the white power structure had been unwilling to reallocate the resources of the larger community to help Afro-Americans. After Randolph's rise to prominence, freedom from oppression would no longer be sufficient; from then on, blacks would demand their proportionate share of the nation's economic wealth. Never again would the Afro-American minority be content to beg for favors from white patrons. "Rather we die standing on our feet fighting for our rights than to exist upon our knees begging for life," Randolph proclaimed.[38]

Unlike the old-style black spokesmen, Randolph did not consider placing a few token blacks in high political office a goal worth striving for. "Of course, I want to see Negroes go to Congress and become senators etc.," he said, "but this is not going to solve the Negro problem any more than it has solved the problems of the Jews or Irish. The Negro people need organization from the bottom up." Rather than high visibility for a few, Randolph demanded that blacks as a group be treated as an ethnic minority entitled to the same concessions received by white ethnic minorities in American society, and that their group demands be taken into account in the allocation of community resources: "We don't want to have just one conference with the President; we want our rights for systematic contact with the President in the form of conferences on vital issues effecting [sic] the Negro people definitely recognized."[39]

It is a tribute to Randolph's integrity that the personal fidelity he commanded withstood organizational competition. Not only did Randolph maintain a longstanding working partnership with his fellow officers in the BSCP, but he also maintained lasting relationships with many whites in the labor and Socialist movements—William Green and George Meany

38. Randolph, quoted in Sancton, "Something's Happened to the Negro," 177.
39. Randolph to A. J. Johnson, March 7, 1944, Randolph to J. Finley Wilson, September 1, 1942, both in APR Files.

in the AFL, and Socialist-leaning union leaders such as David Dubinsky and Walter Reuther. Differences between organizations were never allowed to sever personal ties, so that Randolph was able to continue his affiliation with George Houser and James Farmer of FOR even though their organizations would temporarily break. Morris Milgram of the WDL remained one of Randolph's closest white allies, and Walter White of the NAACP was like a brother, despite the ideological differences between the two and White's concern over Randolph's various competing groups.

Randolph returned as well as inspired the loyalty of his colleagues. He defended Milton Webster when many of his associates condemned Webster as being crude and a boor, and he defended Rustin when Rustin was subjected to attack, even though Rustin had earlier ill-treated him.

Still, Randolph's deficiencies as a leader cannot be denied. While he could successfully marshall participation in dramatic demonstrations, he was never able to solve the conundrum of turning short-term activism into a long-term commitment to the civil rights cause. He never fully comprehended the importance of cultural nationalism. The concept of expressing resistance through art forms eluded him, as did the possibility that the church could play a positive role in fomenting rebellion. He was not an administrator and consequently met with frustration in trying to institutionalize his various movements. Because he was involved in so many different reform efforts, he was unable to give any of them the attention they deserved, yet he ran authoritarian rather than democratic associations and was reluctant to share national decision-making power. His organizations suffered from the demands on his time and his disinclination for detail. It might be argued that the lack of a symbiotic relationship similar to that he enjoyed with Milton Webster in the BSCP hampered Randolph's civil rights activity. He eventually came to enjoy such a partnership with Bayard Rustin, but by the time it was cemented, Randolph was an old man and had given up the idea of founding his own mass rights organization.

Although he established mutually rewarding working relationships with men, Randolph was unable to do the same with women. He could run his civil rights organizations on shoestring budgets in part because he enjoyed the faithful support of women, but he never treated them as equals. In the 1920s Lucille Randolph's beauty-shop earnings supported her husband's endeavors, yet in later life she accused Randolph of ignoring her when she needed him. Randolph appointed Pauline Meyers and Anna Hedgeman as executive secretaries because they would work for less money than men, yet he never gave serious consideration to their advice, and when the movements could no longer afford their meager salaries, he summarily dismissed them. Moreover, Randolph did not understand the resentment engendered by his treatment of women. When he was invited to address the Press Club prior to the 1963 march, women reporters complained because they were not allowed in the Club and had to sit in the balcony. When Randolph asked, "What's wrong with the balcony?" the women replied, "What's wrong with the back of the bus?" Randolph proceeded to speak at the Press Club anyway.[40]

Coming out of the Social Democratic tradition, Randolph inherited the virulent anticommunism common among Social Democrats, many of whom saw the Party as part of an international conspiracy. In the 1920s and 1930s not many whites, even those who considered themselves liberal, thought much about the race question. Of those few who did concern themselves with greater opportunities for blacks, most belonged to the Communist party and/or the CIO. Holding a monopoly on education, skills, and funds, the Communist and CIO patrons of Randolph's first venture into the civil rights field, the NNC, began to assume an ever-greater role until they finally co-opted the organization in 1940. This experience and the belief that blacks must run their own liberation movement prompted Randolph to experiment with keeping his subsequent March on Washington Movement all black.

Randolph began extolling the virtues of black consciousness shortly before 1920. This stance was not unique to him. Harold Cruse traces the modern ideological split in the black community back to the quarrel between Booker T. Washington and W. E. B. Du Bois at the turn of the century. Washington gave primacy to black economic development over civil rights agitation, whereas at that time Du Bois was devoted to such mainstays of "noneconomic liberalism" as the right to vote, civic equality, and the education of youth according to their ability. Marcus Garvey would subsequently take up Washington's economic position and wed it to his Back-to-Africa program, thereby continuing the quarrel with Du Bois.[41]

40. See correspondence of Lucille Randolph in BSCP Papers, LC; Interview with Pauli Murray, October 15, 1984.
41. Cruse, *Plural but Equal*, 76.

But Du Bois, especially as he grew older, gravitated toward the nationalist position.

Randolph, Washington, Garvey, and Du Bois all promoted race consciousness in their own way. But Randolph's labor orientation gave him a unique angle of vision among the black leaders. The thrust of his rhetoric, while militant, differed from the pragmatic economics of Washington, the separatism of Garvey, and the elitism of Du Bois. Only Randolph provided a fusion of the economic and civil rights perspectives. Although not a thoroughgoing nationalist, Randolph believed that blacks should finance and run their own organizations. Yet, also a pragmatist, Randolph found it difficult to eliminate sympathetic white allies. He was always torn between an interracial, laboring-class alliance and a black race alliance.

But Randolph never equivocated on the primacy of economics. He always believed that income parity was the important issue: Once blacks had economic equality, social equality would follow. Randolph's goal of raising black living standards required a reordering of national priorities, however, and on this score he met with steadfast resistance from the dominant community. As a result of the civil rights movement, liberal whites came to believe that blacks should have access to public accommodations as a matter of simple justice, but they were not willing to change the distribution of income to allow Afro-Americans a greater percentage of the national wealth. Nor were whites willing to step out of their places in the decision-making power structure to make room for blacks. Even Randolph's victories, therefore, were circumscribed.

Throughout his career, Randolph endeavored to cement a coalition of the underdogs in American society—blacks, labor, and Socialist radicals. Yet many of his actions unwittingly undercut the achievement of his goal. His support for the Socialist party lessened his political clout with a Democratic president, just as his NALC's demand for economic parity and positions in the union power structure provoked resistance from former Socialist allies within the labor movement. By the end of his life, Randolph's proposed class alliance of out-groups drew fire from militant young blacks bent on separatism and opposed to any affiliation with Jews. Had he been successful in forging a lasting union of these fringe groups, Randolph's advocacy of a third political party based on ideology would not have seemed so illogical. Yet there remains the striking paradox of this elegant man with middle-class values and Shakespearean accent attempting to unite the outcasts in American society.

Randolph's espousal of nonviolent, direct mass action had enormous consequences for the future of the black community in America. The idea did not originate with Randolph; it built on earlier forms of black protest beginning with the streetcar boycotts at the turn of the century and borrowed liberally from the Don't-Buy-Where-You-Can't-Work campaigns and Communist-backed rent strikes in the 1930s, as well as from Gandhi and the sit-down strikes of the CIO.[42] Not only Randolph, but FOR and CORE were practicing direct action in the early 1940s. But Randolph was the only proponent of the technique to envision it on a coordinated, nationwide basis. In opposition to restrictive patrons, and in the face of unrelenting white prejudice and a severe shortage of resources, he thus gave new shape to the means of collective action. Out of this development emerged a distinctive kind of leadership of mass organizations of which Randolph was a pioneer.

Although triumphant for short periods, Randolph never sustained a mass following for an extended period of time. Yet his ideas and strategies prevailed in the long run because they met the needs of the black community. The constraints imposed on his efforts by the lack of skills and assets within that community seemed almost insurmountable; it is difficult to mobilize the hungry and the unemployed for action. Despite such overwhelming odds, Randolph rallied the poor masses and used their political power, not to extract favors for a few, but to pressure for rights Afro-Americans as a group had not previously possessed.

Randolph's most enduring legacy was the influence of his civil rights movements and his ideology and tactics on the younger generation. The program of action outlined for the MOWM in 1943, for example, contained many goals and methods employed in the civil rights movement of the late 1950s and 1960s: a nonpartisan political bloc, mass voter registration, institutes for training in nonviolent, goodwill direct action, and the employment of different techniques in the South from those used in the North in recognition that discrimination "must be approached in terms of the conditions of the racial climate of the community."[43] These strategies remained with Randolph's youthful followers in a dormant state until the environment became conducive; they were reemployed by

42. See Meier and Rudwick, *Along the Color Line,* Chap. 12, on the streetcar boycotts.
43. St. Louis Scrapbook, BSCP Papers, CD; Randolph, "March on Washington Movement Presents Program for the Negro," 150.

his disciples as the modern civil rights movement emerged. The downfall of that movement came about because the leaders failed to incorporate Randolph's economic thrust. Frustration was inevitable once it became obvious that the confirmation of legal rights did not materially change the situation of the poor locked in urban ghettos.

One indication of the persistence of Randolph's ideas is the refurbishing of his image by a new generation of Afro-American scholars. Theodore Cross laments the fact that without the "catalytic force" of Randolph and King, "there is no viable body of institutionalized black power in this country capable of putting significant nonviolent black consensus pressure into action. . . . Using the threat force of collective action *without actually fighting* or taking overt action has always been a potent weapon of those who are otherwise powerless." Manning Marable, while admitting that Randolph's "contribution to the ongoing struggle for black self-determination was unique and profoundly important," criticizes him for the contradictions that plagued his career. Noting that Randolph preferred compromise to confrontation, approached unionization from the top down rather than from the bottom up, and was unduly hostile to black nationalists, Marable concludes, "In the next stage of history, black working people and activists must transcend Randolph's contradictions" in order to "carry out the legacy of Randolph, that he was unable to achieve for himself and his own generation." [44] What Marable fails to acknowledge is that Randolph's unique contribution of the synthesis of economics with civil rights goals was never given a fair trial. Had Randolph's call for fusion of economic with civic equality goals been heeded, we would not today be lamenting the unfinished revolution.

44. Cross, *The Black Power Imperative*, 29; Marable, *From the Grassroots*, 59–85.

Bibliography

Primary Sources

Manuscript Collections

Barnett, Claude A. Papers. Chicago Historical Society.

Brotherhood of Sleeping Car Porters. Papers. Library of Congress, Washington, D.C.

Brotherhood of Sleeping Car Porters, Chicago Division. Papers. Chicago Historical Society.

Congress on Racial Equality Papers. State Historical Society of Wisconsin, Madison.

Eisenhower, Dwight David. Papers. Dwight David Eisenhower Library, Abilene, Kans.

Johnson, Lyndon Baines. Papers. Lyndon Baines Johnson Library, Austin.

Kennedy, John F. Papers. President's Office Files, Presidential Recordings. John F. Kennedy Library, Boston.

King, Martin Luther, Jr. Papers. Mugar Memorial Library, Boston University.

McGrath, J. Howard. Papers. Harry S. Truman Library, Independence, Mo.

McLaurin, B. F. Papers. Schomburg Collection, New York Public Library.

Morrow, E. Frederic. Papers. Mugar Memorial Library, Boston University.

National Association for the Advancement of Colored People. Papers. Library of Congress, Washington, D.C.

National Negro Congress. Papers. Schomburg Collection, New York Public Library.

National Urban League. Papers. Library of Congress, Washington, D.C.

Office of the Secretary-Treasurer of the CIO. Files. Archives of Labor History and Urban Affairs, Wayne State University, Detroit.

Parrish, Richard. Papers. Schomburg Collection, New York Public Library.

Randolph, A. Philip. Personal Files. A. Philip Randolph Institute, New York City.

(*Note:* While this book was in press, many sources in the Randolph Files were being moved to the Library of Congress.)

Roosevelt, Eleanor. Papers. Franklin D. Roosevelt Library, Hyde Park, New York.

Roosevelt, Franklin D. Papers. Franklin D. Roosevelt Library, Hyde Park, New York.

Truman, Harry S. Papers. Harry S. Truman Library, Independence, Mo.

Urban League of Philadelphia. Records. Urban Archives Center, Temple University, Philadelphia.

Government Documents

Code of Federal Regulations. Title 3—The President, 1938–43 Compilation. Washington, D.C., 1968.

Code of Federal Regulations. Title 3—The President, 1943–48 Compilation. Washington, D.C., 1948.

Congressional Record, 80th Cong. 2nd Sess., Vol. 94, Pt. 4, pp. 4312–18.

Congressional Record, House. "A Tribute to A. Philip Randolph." April 29, 1969, H3190–H3204.

Hearings, Committee on Armed Services. Senate. 80th Cong., 2nd Sess. "Universal Military Training." 1948.

New York State Department of Labor. "Memo: A. Philip Randolph." *Industrial Bulletin.* XXXIX (January–February, 1960), p. 2+.

State of New York. *Report of the Joint Legislative Committee Investigating Seditious Activities.* 1920.

U.S. Department of Justice. Investigation Activities, *Senate Documents,* 66th Cong., 1st Sess., No. 153, Exhibit No. 10, *Radicalism and Sedition Among the Negroes as Reflected in Their Publications.* 1919.

U.S. President's Commission on Civil Rights. *To Secure These Rights.* 1947.

Public Documents

American Federation of Labor. *Report of Proceedings.* 1932–1954.

Official Proceedings of the National Negro Congress. Chicago, February 14–16, 1936.

Official Proceedings of the Second National Negro Congress. Philadelphia, October 15–17, 1937.

Proceedings of the AFL-CIO Constitutional Conventions. 1955–1959.

Newspapers and Periodicals

Black Worker, 1929–1968.

Chicago *Defender,* 1936–1959.

Messenger, 1917–1928.

Pittsburgh *Courier,* 1941–1959.

Oral Interviews

Kemp, Maida Springer, October 18, 1972.
Murray, Pauli, October 15, 1984.
Randolph, A. Philip, September 4, 1973, September 9, 1976.
Shackelford, Leroy, Jr., November 9, 1972.
Wilds, Bernice, June 12–23, 1978.

Recorded Interviews

Oral History Transcripts. Dwight David Eisenhower Library, Abilene, Kansas.
    Morrow, E. Frederic, by Dr. Thomas Soapes, February 23, 1977.
Oral History Collection. Lyndon Baines Johnson Library, Austin.
    Farmer, James, by Harri Baker. Tape I. October, 1969.
    Farmer, James, by Paige Mulhollan. Tape II. July 20, 1971.
    Wilkins, Roy, by Thomas H. Baker, April 1, 1969.
Oral History Program. John F. Kennedy Library, Boston.
    Booker, Simeon, by John F. Stewart, April 24, 1967.
    Boutin, Bernard, by Dan H. Fenn, Jr., June 3, 1964.
    Sorensen, Theodore, by Carl Kaysen, May 3, 1964.
    Tobriner, Walter D., by Charles T. Morrissey, July 6, 1964.
    Wilkins, Roy, by Berl Bernhardt, August 13, 1964.
Oral History Research Office. Columbia University, New York. "The Reminiscences of A. Philip Randolph." Transcript of interview by Wendell Wray, 1972.

Books, Bulletins, and Pamphlets

Bulletin of the Brotherhood of Sleeping Car Porters. Chicago, November, 1925.
Davis, John P., ed. *Let Us Build a National Negro Congress.* Washington, D.C., 1935.
Dubinsky, David, and A. H. Raskin. *David Dubinsky: A Life with Labor.* New York, 1977.
Hedgeman, Anna Arnold. *The Gift of Chaos: Decades of American Discontent.* New York, 1977.
———. *The Trumpet Sounds: A Memoir of Negro Leadership.* New York, 1964.
Randolph, A. Philip. *The Negro Freedom Movement.* American Studies Institute pamphlet. Lincoln University, Pa., 1967.
———. *Victory's Victims?—The Negro's Future.* Socialist party pamphlet. New York, n.d.
———. *The World Crisis and the Negro People Today.* Pamphlet. N.d.
Ross, Malcolm. *All Manner of Men.* New York, 1948.

Rustin, Bayard. *The Alienated: The Young Rebels Today . . . and Why They're Different.* AFL-CIO pamphlet. 1967.

———. *Down the Line.* Chicago, 1971.

Schuyler, George S. *Black and Conservative.* New Rochelle, 1966.

Tarry, Ellen. *The Third Door: The Autobiography of an American Negro Woman.* New York, 1955.

Truman, Harry S. *Years of Trial and Hope.* Garden City, 1956. Vol. II of Truman, *Memoirs.*

White, Walter. *A Man Called White.* New York, 1948.

Wilkins, Roy, with Tom Mathews. *Standing Fast: The Autobiography of Roy Wilkins.* New York, 1982.

Articles, Essays, and Addresses

Bain, Myrna. "Organized Labor and the Negro Worker." *National Review,* June 4, 1963, p. 455.

Beecher, John. "8802 Blues." *New Republic,* February 22, 1943, pp. 248–50.

Birnie, William A. H. "Black Brain Trust." *American Magazine* (January, 1943) 36–37+.

"Black Brotherhood." *Time,* September 20, 1937, pp. 10–11.

Brooks, Thomas R. "Better Day for Brother Randolph." *Reporter,* December 5, 1963, p. 23.

———. "The Negro's Place at Labor's Table." *Reporter,* December 6, 1962, pp. 38–39.

Brown, Earl. "American Negroes and the War." *Harper's Magazine* (April, 1942), 545–52.

Buckler, Helen. "The CORE Way." *Survey Graphic* (February, 1946), 50+.

Cleghorn, Reese. "The Angels Are White—Who Pays the Bills for Civil Rights?" *New Republic,* August 17, 1963, pp. 12–14.

"Crisis in the Making: U.S. Negroes Tussle with Issue of Resisting a Draft Law Because of Racial Discrimination." *Newsweek,* June 7, 1948, pp. 28–29.

"Democracy Demands Justice: Case of Odell Waller." *Christian Century,* June 3, 1942, pp. 717–18.

Ellison, Ralph. "A Congress Jim Crow Didn't Attend." *New Masses,* May 14, 1940, pp. 5–8.

"Face the Music." *Time,* April 12, 1948, p. 21.

"FEPC Vs. the Railroads." *Time,* December 27, 1943, pp. 18–19.

"A Few Lights Burn." *Commonweal,* April 3, 1942, p. 581+.

Frazier, E. Franklin. "The American Negro's New Leaders." *Current History Magazine of the New York Times* (April, 1928), 56–59.

Gibson, Roland A. "The 'New Negro' Takes Another Step." *World Tomorrow* (February, 1927), 81–82.

Good, Paul. "Beyond the Bridge." *Reporter*, April 8, 1965, pp. 23–26.

Granger, Lester B. "The National Negro Congress: An Interpretation." *Opportunity* (May, 1936), 151–53.

———. "The National Negro Congress—Its Future." *Opportunity* (June, 1940), 164–66.

Green, William. "Negro Wage Earners." *American Federationist* (October, 1925), 878–79.

———. "Yellow-Dog Contracts." *American Federationist* (June, 1930), 662–65.

Harris, Abram L. "The Negro Problem as Viewed by Negro Leaders." *Current History Magazine of the New York Times* (June, 1923), 410–18.

High, Stanley. "Black Omens." *Saturday Evening Post*, June 4, 1938, pp. 14–15.

"Ideas for a New Party." *Antioch Review*, VI (Fall, 1946), 449–72.

Johnson, Charles S. "The Rise of the Negro Magazine." *Journal of Negro History* XIII (January, 1928), 7–21.

Kahn, Tom. "March's Radical Demands Point Way for Struggle." *New America*, September 24, 1963, pp. 1–4.

Lewis, Theophilus. "Plays and a Point of View." *Interracial Review* (July, 1942), 111–12.

"The March." *Nation*, September 14, 1963, p. 121.

"The 'March'—Gains and Losses." *U.S. News and World Report*, September 9, 1963, pp. 33–35.

"'March' Leader Randolph Struggle Just Begun He Says." *U.S. News and World Report*, September 9, 1963, p. 24.

"March on Washington." *America*, August 10, 1963, p. 131.

"The 'March'—Photo Report." *U.S. News and World Report*, September 9, 1963, pp. 39–44.

Martin, Ralph G. "FEPC Rally." *New Republic*, March 18, 1946, p. 380.

Miller, Loren. "Freedom Now—but What Then?" *Nation*, June 29, 1963, pp. 539–42.

"Negroes and Pullmans." *Commonweal*, May 9, 1941, pp. 51–52.

"Negroes and Unions." *Nation*, November 7, 1942, pp. 464–65.

"Negroes Are People: Pullman Decision." *New Republic*, May 5, 1941, p. 616.

"Negro Leaders Ban Demonstrations." *Christian Century*, August 12, 1964, p. 1005.

"Negro Leadership in America." *World's Work* (March, 1921), pp. 435–36.

"Negro Pressure on Unions." *Business Week*, April 30, 1960, p. 139+.

"Now a New Worry for Kennedy: The White Vote in '64." *U.S. News and World Report*, September 9, 1963, pp. 36–39.

"On the March." *Newsweek*, September 2, 1963, pp. 17–20.

Ottley, Roi. "Negro Morale." *New Republic*, November 10, 1941, pp. 613–15.

"Phil Randolph Joins PR Council." *National Municipal Review* (November, 1943), 560.

"Porters' Powwow." *Newsweek*, September 30, 1940, p. 42.

"President's Order Against Race Discrimination." *Monthly Labor Review* (August, 1941), 398.

"Racism in Labor." *America*, November 25, 1961, p. 276.

Randolph, A. Philip. "The Case of the Pullman Porter." *American Federationist* (November, 1926), 1334–39.

———. "The Civil Rights Revolution and Labor." Address to NAACP Convention, July 15, 1959.

———. "Conciliation and Arbitration." In *Proceedings of the National Conference of Social Work.* New York, 1939.

———. "The Crisis of Negro Railroad Workers." *American Federationist* (August, 1939), 807–21.

———. "Don't the Railroads Want to Stay in Business?" *American Federationist* (July, 1958), 18–20.

———. "The Economic Crisis of the Negro." *Opportunity* (May, 1931), 145–59.

———. "The Fight for Civil Rights." *New Leader*, November 13, 1948, p. 5.

———. "Filibuster of the People." *New York Times Magazine*, September 29, 1963, pp. 92–93.

———. Foreword to *Confrontation: Black and White*, by Lerone Bennett, Jr. Chicago, 1965.

———. Foreword to *Erasing the Color Line*, by George M. Houser. New York, 1945.

———. "Government Sets Pattern of Jim Crow." *Interracial Review* (July, 1942), 101–103.

———. "If I Were Young Today." *Ebony* (July, 1963), 82.

———. "I Saw Ghana Born." *American Federationist* (May, 1957), 10–11.

———. "Keynote Address to the Policy Conference of the March on Washington Movement." In *Negro Protest Thought in the Twentieth Century*, edited by Francis L. Broderick and August Meier. Indianapolis, 1965.

———. "Labor and the Negro." In *American Labor and the Nation*, edited by Spencer Miller, Jr. Chicago, 1933.

———. "Labor's Stake in an Emerging New Africa." *American Federationist* (October, 1957), 20–21+.

———. "March on Washington Movement Presents Program for the Negro." In *What the Negro Wants*, edited by Rayford W. Logan. Chapel Hill, 1944.

———. "The 'March'—What Negroes Expected . . . What They Want Next." *U.S. News and World Report*, September 9, 1963, pp. 82–85.

———. "The Menace of Communism." *American Federationist* (March, 1949), 19.

———. "National Negro Labor Conference." *American Federationist* (September, 1930), 1054–57.

———. "The Negro and Economic Radicalism." *Opportunity* (February, 1926), 62–64.

———. "The Negro in American Democracy." *Social Action,* January 15, 1943, pp. 23–39.

———. "Negro Labor and the Church." In *Labor Speaks for Itself on Religion,* edited by Jerome Davis. New York, 1929.

———. "Negro Labor Leader, Now 80, Concerned over 'Separatism.'" *Philadelphia Bulletin,* May 20, 1969.

———. "One Union's Story." *American Federationist* (November, 1953), 20–23.

———. "An Open Letter to Mr. J. P. Morgan." *American Federationist* (July, 1933), 704–10.

———. "Porters Fight Injunction." *American Federationist* (June, 1931), 681–92.

———. "Porters Fight Paternalism." *American Federationist* (June, 1930), 666–73.

———. "Pullman Porters Vote for Organization They Want." *American Federationist* (July, 1935), 727–29.

———. "Pullman Porters Win." *Opportunity* (October, 1937), 299–300+.

———. "A Reply to My Critics." Chicago *Defender,* June 12–July 17, 1943.

———. "The Trade Union Movement and the Negro." *Journal of Negro Education,* V (January, 1936), 54–58.

———. "United Nations and Labor." *American Federationist* (November, 1955), 21.

———. "Why a National Negro Congress?" In *Let Us Build a National Negro Congress,* edited by John P. Davis. Washington, D.C., 1935.

———. "Why a Trade Union?" *American Federationist* (December, 1930), 1470–82.

———. "Why I Would Not Stand for Re-election in the National Negro Congress." *American Federationist* (July, 1940), 24–25.

———. "Why Should We March?" *Survey Graphic* (November, 1942), 488–89.

"Randolph Urges Negroes to Repudiate 'Work' Law." *AFL-CIO News,* February 22, 1964, p. 11.

"Randolph Urges Negroes to Try Non-Violence." *Fellowship,* IX (February, 1943), 35.

"Randolph Withdraws from Anti-Jimcrow League." *Fellowship,* XIV (October, 1948), 34.

Rauschenbush, Winifred. "Green Light for the FEPC." *Survey Graphic* (December, 1943), 498–501+.

"Reply to 8802 Blues." *New Republic,* March 15, 1943, pp. 351–52.

"Resentment over Negro Policy Coming to Head." *Christian Century*, February 17, 1943, p. 189.

Reynolds, Grant. "A Triumph for Civil Disobedience." *Nation*, August 28, 1948, pp. 228–29.

Rustin, Bayard. "The Anatomy of Frustration." Address Before the 55th National Convention of the Anti-Defamation League of B'nai B'rith, New York, May 6, 1968.

———. "'Black Power' and Coalition Politics." *Commentary* (September, 1966), 35–40.

———. "From Protest to Politics." *Commentary* (February, 1965), 25–31.

———. "The Labor-Negro Coalition—A New Beginning." *AFL-CIO American Federationist* (May, 1968).

———. "The Lessons of the Long Hot Summer." *Commentary* (October, 1967), 39–45.

———. "The Myths of the Black Revolt." *Ebony* (August, 1969), 96–104.

———. "The Negro and Non-Violence." *Fellowship*, VIII (October, 1942), 166–67.

Rustin, Bayard, and Tom Kahn. "Civil Rights." *Commentary* (June, 1965), 43–46.

Ryan, Eleanor. "Toward a National Negro Congress." *New Masses*, June 4, 1935, pp. 14–15.

Sancton, Thomas. "Big Brass and Jim Crow." *Nation*, October 2, 1947, pp. 365–66.

———. "Something's Happened to the Negro." *New Republic*, February 8, 1943, pp. 175–79.

"The Supreme Court and Racialism." *Nation*, December 30, 1944, p. 788.

Thomas, C. W. "Three Negroes Receive 1964 Presidential Freedom Medal." *Negro History Bulletin*, XXVIII (December, 1964), 58–59.

Thrulelsen, Richard. "Men at Work: Pullman Porter." *Saturday Evening Post*, May 21, 1949, p. 38+.

"To A. Philip Randolph." *America*, May 3, 1969, pp. 521–22.

"Top Negro's Plea for Nonviolence." *U.S. News and World Report*, May 19, 1969, p. 22.

"Toward Negro Unity." *Nation*, March 11, 1936, p. 302.

"The Unhappy Mr. Randolph." *Reporter*, October 26, 1961, p. 18.

"Unions and Discrimination." *Commonweal*, November 3, 1961, pp. 140–41.

Wechsler, James A. "Phil Randolph and Adam Powell." New York *Post*, December 28, 1966, p. 40.

Weybright, Victor. "Pullman Porters on Parade." *Survey Graphic*, XXIV (November, 1935), pp. 540–44+.

"What the Marchers Really Want." *New York Times Magazine,* August 25, 1963, pp. 7–9+.

"Who's in the News." *Scholastic,* March 25, 1946, p. 17.

Young, Warren R., and William Lambert. "Marchers' Master Plan." *Life,* August 23, 1963, pp. 63–70.

Material at the A. Philip Randolph Institute

A. Philip Randolph at 80: Tributes and Recollections. Pamphlet. 1969.

The A. Philip Randolph Institute. Pamphlet. N.d.

Annual Report of the A. Philip Randolph Educational Fund. September, 1969–December, 1970.

Annual Report of the A. Philip Randolph Institute. September, 1969–December, 1970.

Browne, Robert S., and Bayard Rustin. "Separatism or Integration—Which Way for America?" Dialogue before the National Jewish Community Relations Advisory Council, June 30–July 3, 1968.

"Eightieth Birthday Dinner in Honor of A. Philip Randolph." Program. 1969.

A "Freedom Budget" for All Americans: A Summary. January, 1967.

Negro Pioneers in the Chicago Labor Movement. N.d.

Rustin, Bayard. *Conflict or Coalition? The Civil Rights Struggle and the Trade Union Movement Today.* 1969.

———. *Three Essays.* 1969.

Secondary Sources

Books

Adams, Julius J. *The Challenge: A Study in Negro Leadership.* New York, 1949.

Aiken, Michael, and Paul E. Mott, eds. *The Structure of Community Power.* New York, 1970.

Anderson, Jervis. *A. Philip Randolph: A Biographical Portrait.* New York, 1973.

Bardolph, Richard. *The Negro Vanguard.* New York, 1959.

Bennett, Lerone, Jr. *Confrontation: Black and White.* Chicago, 1965.

———. *What Manner of Man: A Biography of Martin Luther King, Jr.* Chicago, 1968.

Bergman, Peter M. *A Chronological History of the Negro in America.* New York, 1969.

Berman, William C. *The Politics of Civil Rights in the Truman Administration.* Columbus, Ohio, 1970.

Bernstein, Irving. *The Lean Years: A History of the American Worker, 1920–1933.* Boston, 1970.

———. *Turbulent Years: A History of the American Worker, 1933–1941.* Boston, 1960.

Bonjean, Charles M., Terry N. Clark, and Robert L. Lineberry, eds. *Community Politics: A Behavioral Approach.* New York, 1971.

Bontemps, Arna. *One Hundred Years of Negro Freedom.* New York, 1961.

Brazeal, Brailsford Reese. *The Brotherhood of Sleeping Car Porters: Its Origin and Development.* New York, 1946.

Broderick, Francis L., and August Meier, eds. *Negro Protest Thought in the Twentieth Century.* Indianapolis, 1965.

Brooks, Thomas R. *Toil and Trouble: A History of American Labor.* New York, 1971.

———. *Walls Come Tumbling Down: A History of the Civil Rights Movement, 1940–1970.* Englewood Cliffs, N.J., 1974.

Bunche, Ralph J. *The Political Status of the Negro in the Age of FDR.* Chicago, 1975.

Burk, Robert Fredrick. *The Eisenhower Administration and Black Civil Rights.* Knoxville, 1984.

Burns, James MacGregor. *Roosevelt: The Soldier of Freedom.* New York, 1970.

Cayton, Horace R., and George S. Mitchell. *Black Workers and the New Unions.* Chapel Hill, 1939.

Chatfield, Charles. *For Peace and Justice: Pacifism in America, 1914–1941.* Knoxville, 1971.

Cronon, Edmund David. *Black Moses.* Madison, Wis., 1962.

Cross, Theodore. *The Black Power Imperative: Racial Inequality and the Politics of Nonviolence.* New York, 1984.

Cruse, Harold. *The Crisis of the Negro Intellectual.* New York, 1967.

———. *Plural but Equal: A Critical Study of Blacks and Minorities and America's Plural Society.* New York, 1987.

Dahl, Robert A. *Who Governs? Democracy and Power in an American City.* New Haven, 1961.

Dalfiume, Richard M. *Desegregation of the U.S. Armed Forces.* Columbia, Mo., 1969.

DeCaux, Len. *Labor Radical: From the Wobblies to CIO: A Personal History.* Boston, 1970.

Derber, Milton, and Edwin Young. *Labor and the New Deal.* Madison, Wis., 1957.

Drake, St. Clair, and Horace R. Cayton. *Black Metropolis.* New York, 1945.

Draper, Theodore. *American Communism and Soviet Russia.* New York, 1960.

Dubofsky, Melvin, ed. *American Labor Since the New Deal.* Chicago, 1971.

Dubofsky, Melvin, and Warren Van Tine. *John L. Lewis: A Biography.* New York, 1977.

Eckman, Fern Marja. *The Furious Passage of James Baldwin.* New York, 1966.

Embree, Edwin R. *Thirteen Against the Odds.* 1944; rpr. Port Washington, N.Y., 1968.

Erikson, Erik. *Gandhi's Truth: On the Origins of Militant Nonviolence.* New York, 1969.

Farmer, James. *Freedom—When?* New York, 1965.

Foner, Philip S. *American Socialism and Black Americans: From the Age of Jackson to World War II.* Westport, Conn., 1977.

———. *Organized Labor and the Black Worker, 1619–1973.* New York, 1974.

Forman, James. *The Making of Black Revolutionaries.* New York, 1972.

Foster, William Z. *The Negro People in American History.* New York, 1954.

Franklin, Charles Lionel. *The Negro Labor Unionist of New York.* New York, 1936.

Franklin, John Hope. *From Slavery to Freedom: A History of Negro Americans.* 4th ed. New York, 1974.

Frazier, E. Franklin. *The Negro in the United States.* New York, 1957.

Freidel, Frank. *F.D.R. and the South.* Baton Rouge, 1965.

Friedlander, Peter. *The Emergence of a UAW Local, 1936–1939: A Study in Class and Culture.* Pittsburgh, 1975.

Galenson, Walter. *The CIO Challenge to the AFL.* Cambridge, Mass., 1960.

Garfinkel, Herbert. *When Negroes March.* Glencoe, Ill., 1959.

Glazer, Nathan, and Daniel Patrick Moynihan. *Beyond the Melting Pot.* Cambridge, Mass., 1970.

Golden, Harry. *Mr. Kennedy and the Negroes.* Cleveland, 1964.

Goldman, Eric F. *The Tragedy of Lyndon Johnson.* New York, 1969.

Goldston, Robert. *The Negro Revolution.* New York, 1968.

Goodman, Benjamin, ed. *The End of White World Supremacy: Four Speeches by Malcolm X.* New York, 1971.

Gouldner, Alvin W., ed. *Studies in Leadership: Leadership and Democratic Action.* New York, 1950.

Haley, Alex, ed. *The Autobiography of Malcolm X.* New York, 1965.

Hamby, Alonzo L. *Beyond the New Deal: Harry S. Truman and American Liberalism.* New York, 1973.

Harris, William H. *Keeping the Faith: A. Philip Randolph, Milton P. Webster, and the Brotherhood of Sleeping Car Porters, 1925–37.* Urbana, Ill., 1977.

Hentoff, Nat. *Peace Agitator: The Story of A. J. Muste.* New York, 1963.

Higham, John, ed. *Ethnic Leadership in America.* Baltimore, 1978.

Hill, Robert A., ed. *The Marcus Garvey and Universal Negro Improvement Association Papers.* 5 vols. Berkeley, 1983.

Howe, Irving, and Lewis Coser. *The American Communist Party: A Critical History.* 1962; rpr. New York, 1974.

Hughes, Langston. *The Big Sea*. New York, 1940.
Hunter, Floyd. *Community Power Structure: A Study of Decision Makers*. Chapel Hill, 1953.
Jacobs, Paul, and Saul Landau. *The New Radicals*. New York, 1966.
Jacobson, Julius, ed. *The Negro and the American Labor Movement*. Garden City, 1968.
Jacques-Garvey, Amy. *Philosophy and Opinions of Marcus Garvey*. New York, 1968.
Johnson, James Weldon. *Black Manhattan*. 1930; rpr. New York, 1968.
Kempton, Murray. *Part of Our Time*. New York, 1955.
Kesselman, Louis. *The Social Politics of FEPC: A Study in Reform Pressure Movements*. Chapel Hill, 1948.
King, Coretta Scott. *My Life with Martin Luther King, Jr.* New York, 1969.
King, Martin Luther, Jr. *Stride Toward Freedom*. New York, 1958.
Kirby, John B. *Black Americans in the Roosevelt Era: Liberalism and Race*. Knoxville, 1980.
Kornweibel, Theodore, Jr. *No Crystal Stair: Black Life and the Messenger, 1917–1928*. Westport, Conn., 1975.
Lash, Joseph P. *Eleanor and Franklin*. New York, 1973.
Leuchtenburg, William E. *A Troubled Feast: American Society Since 1945*. Boston, 1973.
Lewis, Anthony, and the New York *Times*. *Portrait of a Decade*. New York, 1964.
Lewis, David L. *King: A Critical Biography*. New York, 1970.
Litt, Edgar. *Beyond Pluralism: Ethnic Politics in America*. Glenview, Ill., 1970.
Locke, Alain, ed. *The New Negro*. New York, 1925.
Logan, Rayford W. *The Negro in the United States*. Vol. 1 of 2 vols. New York, 1970.
Logan, Rayford, W., and Michael R. Winston. *The Negro in the United States*, Vol. II of 2 vols. New York, 1970.
Lomax, Louis E. *The Negro Revolt*. New York, 1962.
———. *To Kill a Black Man*. Los Angeles, 1968.
McCoy, Donald R., and Richard T. Ruetten. *Quest and Response: Minority Rights and the Truman Administration*. Lawrence, Kans., 1973.
McDougall, Curtis D. *The Decision and the Organization*. New York, 1965. Vol. 2 of McDougall, *Gideon's Army*. 2 vols.
McDowell, Jennifer, and Milton Loventhal. *Black Politics: A Study and Annotated Bibliography of the Mississippi Freedom Democratic Party*. San Jose, 1971.
McKay, Claude. *Harlem: Negro Metropolis*. New York, 1940.
Marable, Manning. *Black American Politics: From the Washington Marches to Jesse Jackson*. London, 1985.

———. *Black Praxis*, IX. Dayton, Ohio, 1980.

———. *From the Grassroots: Essays Toward Afro-American Liberation*. Boston, 1980.

———. *Race, Reform and Rebellion: The Second Reconstruction in Black America, 1945–1982*. Jackson, Miss., 1984.

Marshall, Ray. *The Negro and Organized Labor*. New York, 1965.

Mayer, Martin. *The Teachers' Strike: New York, 1968*. New York, 1969.

Meier, August, and Elliott Rudwick. *Along the Color Line: Explorations in the Black Experience*. Urbana, 1976.

———. *Black Detroit and the Rise of the UAW*. New York, 1979.

———. *CORE: A Study in the Civil Rights Movement, 1942–1968*. New York, 1973.

———. *From Plantation to Ghetto*. 3rd ed.; New York, 1976.

Minton, Bruce, and John Stuart. *Men Who Lead Labor*. New York, 1937.

Moon, Henry Lee. *Balance of Power: The Negro Vote*. Garden City, N.Y., 1949.

Morgan, Ruth P. *The President and Civil Rights: Policy-Making by Executive Order*. New York, 1970.

Morris, Aldon D. *The Origins of the Civil Rights Movement: Black Communities Organizing for Change*. New York, 1984.

Morrow, E. Frederic. *Black Man in the White House*. New York, 1963.

Moses, Wilson Jeremiah. *The Golden Age of Black Nationalism, 1850–1925*. Hamden, Conn., 1978.

Myrdal, Gunnar. *An American Dilemma*. New York, 1944.

Naison, Mark. *Communists in Harlem During the Depression*. Urbana, 1983.

Nichols, Lee. *Breakthrough on the Color Front*. New York, 1954.

Northrup, Herbert R. *Organized Labor and the Negro*. New York, 1944.

Osofsky, Gilbert. *Harlem, The Making of a Ghetto: Negro New York, 1890–1930*. New York, 1968.

Ottley, Roi. *New World A-Coming*. New York, 1943.

Ottley, Roi, and William J. Weatherby, eds. *The Negro in New York*. New York, 1967.

Parris, Guichard, and Lester Brooks. *Blacks in the City: A History of the National Urban League*. Boston, 1971.

Peck, James. *Freedom Ride*. New York, 1962.

Polsby, Nelson W. *Community Power and Political Theory*. New Haven, 1963.

Preis, Art. *Labor's Giant Step: Twenty Years of the CIO*. New York, 1964.

Rayback, Joseph G. *A History of American Labor*. New York, 1966.

Record, Wilson. *The Negro and the Communist Party*. Chapel Hill, 1951.

———. *Race and Radicalism*. Ithaca, N.Y., 1964.

Redding, Saunders. *The Lonesome Road*. Garden City, N.Y., 1958.

Richardson, Ben. *Great American Negroes*. New York, 1945.

Ross, Joyce. *J. E. Spingarn and the Rise of the NAACP, 1911–1939.* New York, 1972.

Ruchames, Louis. *Race, Jobs, and Politics: The Story of FEPC.* New York, 1953.

Saunders, Doris E., ed. *The Day They Marched.* Chicago, 1963.

Schlesinger, Arthur M., Jr. *A Thousand Days: John F. Kennedy in the White House.* Boston, 1965.

Schmidt, Karl M. *Henry A. Wallace: Quixotic Crusade 1948.* Syracuse, 1960.

Shannon, David A. *The Socialist Party of America: A History.* New York, 1955.

Shapiro, Yonathan. *Leadership of the American Zionist Organization, 1897–1930.* Urbana, 1971.

Sitkoff, Harvard. *A New Deal for Blacks: The Emergence of Civil Rights as a National Issue: The Depression Decade.* New York, 1978.

———. *The Struggle for Black Equality, 1954–1980.* New York, 1981.

Spear, Allan H. *Black Chicago: The Making of a Negro Ghetto, 1890–1920.* Chicago, 1969.

Spero, Sterling D., and Abram L. Harris. *The Black Worker.* 1931; rpr. New York, 1968.

Stein, Judith. *The World of Marcus Garvey: Race and Class in Modern Society.* Baton Rouge, 1986.

Stillman, Richard J., II. *Integration of the Negro in the U.S. Armed Forces.* New York, 1968.

Taft, Philip. *United They Teach: The Story of the United Federation of Teachers.* Los Angeles, 1974.

Terkel, Studs. *Hard Times.* New York, 1970.

Thompson, Daniel C. *The Negro Leadership Class.* Englewood Cliffs, N.J., 1953.

———. *Sociology of the Black Experience.* Westport, Conn., 1974.

Turner, Robert E. *Memories of a Retired Pullman Porter.* New York, 1954.

Velie, Lester. *Labor U.S.A.* New York, 1959.

Vincent, Theodore G. *Black Power and the Garvey Movement.* Berkeley, n.d.

Walsh, J. Raymond. *C.I.O.: Industrial Unionism in Action.* New York, 1937.

Weber, Max. *Economy and Society: An Outline of Interpretive Sociology.* Vol. 3 of 3 vols. New York, 1968.

Weinstein, James. *The Decline of Socialism in America, 1912–1925.* New York, 1969.

Weiss, Nancy J. *Farewell to the Party of Lincoln: Black Politics in the Age of FDR.* Princeton, 1983.

———. *The National Urban League, 1910–1940.* New York, 1974.

Willner, Ann Ruth. *Charismatic Political Leadership: A Theory.* Princeton, 1968.

Wilson, James Q. *Negro Politics: The Search for Leadership.* New York, 1960.

Wittner, Lawrence S. *Rebels Against War: The American Peace Movement, 1941–1960.* New York, 1969.

Wolters, Raymond. *Negroes and the Great Depression: The Problem of Economic Recovery.* Westport, Conn., 1970.

Zangrando, Robert L. *The NAACP Crusade Against Lynching, 1909–1950.* Philadelphia, 1980.

Articles and Essays

"A. Philip Randolph." *American Labor,* I. (August, 1968), 46–54.

Alexander, Will W. "Pioneers in the Struggle Against Segregation." *Survey Graphic* (January, 1947), 91–96.

Barber, Bernard. "Participation and Mass Apathy in Associations." In *Studies in Leadership: Leadership and Democratic Action,* edited by Alvin W. Gouldner. New York, 1950.

Berman, William C. "Civil Rights and Civil Liberties." In *The Truman Period as a Research Field,* edited by Richard S. Kirkendall. Columbia, Mo., 1967.

Bernstein, Barton J. "The Ambiguous Legacy: The Truman Administration and Civil Rights." In *Politics and Policies of the Truman Administration,* edited by Barton J. Bernstein. Chicago, 1970.

Brody, David. "The Expansion of the American Labor Movement: Institutional Sources of Stimulus and Restraint." In *Institutions in Modern America: Innovation in Structure and Process,* edited by Stephen E. Ambrose. Baltimore, 1967.

Brooks, Thomas R. "A Strategist Without a Movement." *New York Times Magazine,* February 16, 1969, p. 24+.

Bunche, Ralph J. "A Critical Anaylsis of the Tactics and Programs of Minority Groups." *Journal of Negro Education,* IV (July, 1935), 308–20.

————. "The Programs of Organizations Devoted to the Improvement of the Status of the American Negro." *Journal of Negro Education,* VIII (July, 1939), 539–47.

Dalfiume, Richard M. "The 'Forgotten Years' of the Negro Revolution." In *The Negro in Depression and War: Prelude to Revolution, 1930–1945,* edited by Bernard Sternsher. Chicago, 1969.

DeReid, Ira. "Negro Movements and Messiahs, 1900–1949." *Phylon,* No. 4 (1949), 362–69.

Dufty, William. "A Post Portrait: A. Philip Randolph." New York *Post,* December 28, 1959–January 3, 1960.

Finkle, Lee. "Conservative Aims of Militant Rhetoric: Black Protest During World War II." *Journal of American History,* LX (December, 1973), 692–713.

Garland, Phyl. "A. Philip Randolph: Labor's Grand Old Man." *Ebony* (May, 1969), 31–34+.

Gollin, Albert E. "Dynamics of Participation in the March on Washington." *Public Opinion Quarterly,* XXVIII (Winter, 1964), 648.

Gordon, Eugene. "The Negro Press." *American Mercury* (June, 1926), 207–15.

Harding, Vincent. "So Much History, So Much Future: Martin Luther King, Jr., and the Second Coming of America." In *Have We Overcome? Race Relations Since Brown,* edited by Michael V. Namorato. Jackson, Miss., 1979.

Hernton, Calvin C. "Dynamite Growing Out of Their Skulls." In *Black Fire: An Anthology of Afro-American Writing,* edited by Le Roi Jones and Larry Neal. New York, 1968.

Jones, Lester M. "The Editorial Policy of Negro Newspapers of 1917–18 as Compared with That of 1941–2." *Journal of Negro History,* XXIX (January, 1944), 24–31.

Kempton, Murray. "A. Philip Randolph: 'The Choice, Mr. Pres. . . .'" *New Republic,* July 6, 1963, pp. 15–17.

Kilson, Martin. "Political Change in the Negro Ghetto, 1900–1940s." In Vol. II of *Key Issues in the Afro-American Experience,* edited by Nathan I. Huggins, Martin Kilson, and Daniel M. Fox. 2 vols. New York, 1971.

McWilliams, Carey. "What We Did About Racial Minorities." In *While You Were Gone: A Report on Wartime Life in the United States,* edited by Jack Goodman. New York, 1946.

Mandelbaum, David G. "The Study of Life History: Gandhi." *Current Anthropology,* XIV (June, 1973), 177–206.

"Marching On." *Nation,* April 21, 1969, p. 485.

Marx, Gary T., and Michael Useem. "Majority Involvement in Minority Movements: Civil Rights, Abolition, Untouchability." *Journal of Social Issues,* XXVII, No. 1 (1971), 81–104.

Maslow, Will. "FEPC—A Case History in Parliamentary Maneuver." *University of Chicago Law Review* (June, 1946), 407–44.

Mayer, Martin. "The Lone Wolf of Civil Rights." *Saturday Evening Post,* July 11, 1964, pp. 76–78.

Mayfield, Julian. "Challenge to Negro Leadership: The Case of Robert Williams." *Commentary* (April, 1961), 297–305.

Meier, August. "Negro Protest Movements and Organizations." *Journal of Negro Education,* XXXII (Fall, 1963), 437–50.

———. "The 'Revolution' Against the NAACP: A Critical Appraisal of Louis Lomax's *The Negro Revolt." Journal of Negro Education,* XXXII (Spring, 1963), 146–52.

Moore, Richard B. "Africa Conscious Harlem." *Freedomways,* III (Summer, 1963), 315–34.

Morrison, Allan. "A. Philip Randolph: Dean of Negro Leaders." *Ebony* (November, 1958), 103–14.

Mott, Paul E. "Power, Authority and Influence." In *The Structure of Community Power,* edited by Michael Aiken and Paul E. Mott. New York, 1970.

"The Negro and the American Labor Movement." *Labor History* (Summer, 1969), 323–46.

Parenti, Michael. "Power and Pluralism: A View from the Bottom." *Journal of Politics*, XXXII (August, 1970), 501–30.

Polsby, Nelson W. "How to Study Community Power: The Pluralist Alternative." *Journal of Politics*, XXII (August, 1960), 474–84.

Pratt, Henry J. "Politics, Status and the Organization of Minority Group Interests: The Case of the New York Protestants." *Polity* (Winter, 1970), 222–46.

Ransom, Leon A. "Education and the Law." *Journal of Negro Education*, XII (Spring, 1943), 250–53.

Reddick, L. D. "The Negro Policy of the American Army Since World War II." *Journal of Negro History*, XXXVIII (April, 1953), 194–215.

Sitkoff, Harvard. "Harry Truman and the Election of 1948: The Coming of Age of Civil Rights in American Politics." *Journal of Southern History*, XXXVII (November, 1971), 597–616.

———. "Racial Militancy and Interracial Violence in the Second World War." *Journal of American History*, LVIII (December, 1971), 661–81.

Stevenson, Janet. "Rosa Parks Wouldn't Budge." *American Heritage* (February, 1972), p. 57+.

Thompson, Daniel C. "Civil Rights Leadership (An Opinion Study)." *Journal of Negro Education*, XXXII (Fall, 1963), 426–36.

Tucker, Robert C. "The Theory of Charismatic Leadership." In *Philosophers and Kings: Studies in Leadership*, edited by Dankwart A. Rustow. New York, 1970.

Velie, Lester. "The Porter Who Carried Hope to His Race." *Readers Digest* (May, 1959), 121–25.

Weiss, Nancy J. "From Black Separatism to Interracial Cooperation." In *Twentieth-Century America: Recent Interpretations*, edited by Barton J. Bernstein and Allen J. Matusow. New York, 1972.

"The White House Conference and the 'Great Society.'" *Freedomways*, VI (Spring, 1966), 101–102.

Wiebe, Robert H. "White Attitudes and Black Rights from Brown to Bakke." In *Have We Overcome? Race Relations Since Brown*, edited by Michael V. Namorato. Jackson, Miss., 1979.

Wittner, Lawrence. "The National Negro Congress: A Reassessment." *American Quarterly*, XXII (Fall, 1970), 883–901.

Zangrando, Robert L. "From Civil Rights to Black Liberation: The Unsettled 1960's." *Current History* (November, 1969), 281–86+.

Dissertations

Kellogg, Peter John. "Northern Liberals and Black America: A History of White Attitudes, 1936–1952." Northwestern University, 1971.

Lawrence, Charles Radford. "Negro Organizations in Crisis: Depression, New Deal, World War II." Columbia University, 1953.

Smith, Donald High. "Martin Luther King, Jr.: Rhetorician of Revolt." University of Wisconsin, 1964.

Index

Service and Training: founding of,
136–37; Commission of Inquiry hearings, 161–62, 164, 165; funding of,
163–64; disbanding of, 166; mentioned,
133, 137, 140, 140*n*18, 142*n*23, 146,
149, 151, 161, 162, 163, 165. *See also*
League for Non-Violent Civil Disobe-
dience Against Military Segregation;
Military desegregation
Committee for Welfare, Education and
Legal Defense, 261
Committee on Equal Employment Opportunity, 229
Committee on Industrial Organization
(CIO): founding of, 27; and NNC, 39;
Non-Partisan League, 124; merger of,
with AFL, 206–208; Civil Rights Committee, 208; mentioned, 28, 58, 126,
135, 172, 208, 238, 302, 304
Communism, 131, 208
Communist front. *See* United Front
Communist party: 18, 24, 34–39, 256, 302
Communists, 20, 23, 26, 30, 35, 39, 48, 56,
58, 117, 123, 127, 128, 144, 157, 158,
163, 169, 176, 182, 188, 196, 197, 206,
212, 215, 217, 236, 245, 247, 302, 304
Congress on Racial Equality (CORE):
founding of, 61, 62; and MOWM, 63,
149; and military desegregation, 149,
150, 169; and Journey of Reconciliation,
149, 150, 153, 169; and March on
Washington (1963), 240, 245, 257; and
Freedom Ride (1961), 241; and post-
march (1963) activity, 272, 278, 279;
mentioned, 198, 241, 242, 243, 243*n*7,
281, 304
Cookman Institute. *See* Bethune-Cookman
College
Council for United Civil Rights Leadership
(CUCRL), 261, 275
Council of Federated Organizations
(COFO), 260–61, 272
Council to Abolish Segregation in the
Armed Forces, 159

Cross, Theodore, 305
Crosswaith, Frank, 198
Crusade for Citizenship, 186
Cruse, Harold, 18, 189, 302
Curran, Joe, 223
Current, Gloster, 191, 257
Currier, Stephen R., 260–62, 260*n*50,
263, 265, 265*n*59

Dahlberg, Rev. Edwin T., 191
Dalfiume, Richard, 85, 299
Davis, John P., 32, 36, 37, 38, 42, 124
Dawson, William, 122
Debs, Eugene, 11
Dellums, C. L., 30, 32, 36, 79
Democratic party: and Democratic Na-
tional Committee, 137; 1964 conven-
tion, 273; 1968 convention, 284; Loyal
Democrats of Mississippi, 284; men-
tioned, 90, 105, 119, 122, 124, 125,
128, 129, 130, 138, 142, 146, 173, 199,
200, 201, 202, 303
Department of Justice, 18
Depression, 30, 32, 33–34, 36, 45, 46
Detroit race riot (1943), 87
Dewey, John, 126
Dickerson, Earl, 121
Direct action. *See* Civil disobedience
Dixiecrats, 106, 128, 129, 146, 271
Dodson, Thurman, 100
Domingo, W. A., 17
"Don't-Buy-Where-You-Can't-Work," 35,
304
Dubinsky, David, 110, 126, 163, 208, 223,
229, 232, 234, 301
Du Bois, W. E. B., 9, 33, 178, 255–56,
302, 303

Ebony, 189, 207
Economic determinism, 10, 297
Economic radicalism, 21
Eisenhower, Dwight D., 108, 139, 175–
85, 194, 195, 196, 198, 199